Cricket and National Identity in the Postcolonial Age

Following on

Edited by Stephen Wagg

LONDON AND NEW YORK

First published 2005
by Routledge
2 Park Square, Milton Park, Abingdon, Oxon, OX14 4RN

Simultaneously published in the USA and Canada
by Routledge
270 Madison Ave, New York NY 10016

Routledge is an imprint of the Taylor & Francis Group

Transferred to Digital Printing 2008

© 2005 editorial matter and selection, Stephen Wagg;
individual chapters, the contributors.

Typeset in Goudy by
Keystroke, Jacaranda Lodge, Wolverhampton

All rights reserved. No part of this book may be reprinted or
reproduced or utilised in any form or by any electronic,
mechanical, or other means, now known or hereafter invented,
including photocopying and recording, or in any information
storage or retrieval system, without permission in writing from
the publishers.

British Library Cataloguing in Publication Data
A catalogue record for this book is available from the British Library

Library of Congress Cataloging in Publication Data
Stephen Wagg.
     p. cm.
  Includes bibliographical references and index.
  ISBN 0–415–36348–9 (hardback) — ISBN 0–203–01460–X (ebook)
  1. Cricket—Social aspects—Commonwealth countries. 2. Cricket—Political aspects—
Commonwealth countries. 3. Nationalism and sports—Commonwealth countries.
I. Wagg, Stephen.

  GV927.5.S63C75 2005
  796.358—dc22

2004030312

ISBN10: 0–415–36348–9 (hbk)
ISBN10: 0–415–48489–8 (pbk)

ISBN13: 978–0–415–36348–8 (hbk)
ISBN13: 978–0–415–48489–3 (pbk)

For Phil Crane, Mick Paget, Dave Makins and his
Pearl Harbour, Horace and Baz Suffolk

and for the memory of Steve Wilkinson

Cricket is not an English game any more. It has been subject to the influences of, to name but a few, Islam, Indian politics, Partition, Tamil separatism, Marxist writing, Rastafarianism, the New Zealand Prime Minister, the Bishop of Liverpool, Bob Marley, King Dyall, Benazir Bhutto, aboriginal and Maori rights . . . the question of trade embargo, the question of diplomatic relations, the pleasure of drugs, the morality of liars, the morality of money, but also the matter of the importance or otherwise of the rights of mankind to freedom in the face of the forces of oppression. Cricket is not a simple game. It just started off that way.

Simon Barnes, *The Times* (London), 12 April 1990, p. 42

Contents

List of contributors	xi
List of abbreviations	xv
Introduction: Following on STEPHEN WAGG	1

PART I
Cricket and the former dominions

7

1 **Unity, difference and the 'national game': cricket and Australian national identity**
BRETT HUTCHINS

9

2 **Kiwi or English?: cricket on the margins of New Zealand national identity**
GREG RYAN

28

3 **'No one in Dolly's class at present?': cricket and national identity in post-apartheid South Africa**
JON GEMMELL AND JAMES HAMILL

48

PART II
Cricket in the New Commonwealth

75

4 **Play together, live apart: religion, politics and markets in Indian cricket since 1947**
SHARDA UGRA

77

5 **History without a past: memory and forgetting in Indian cricket**
SATADRU SEN

94

x *Contents*

6 Cricket in 'a nation imperfectly imagined': identity and tradition
   in postcolonial Pakistan   110
   CHRIS VALIOTIS

7 Sri Lanka: the power of cricket and the power in cricket   132
   MICHAEL ROBERTS

8 One eye on the ball, one eye on the world: cricket, West Indian
   nationalism and the spirit of C. L. R. James   159
   TIM HECTOR; COMPILED AND WITH EDITORIAL COMMENTARY BY
   STEPHEN WAGG

PART III
Cricket in the Old Country   179

9 Calypso kings, dark destroyers: England–West Indies Test
   cricket and the English press, 1950–1984   181
   STEPHEN WAGG

10 'A carnival of cricket?': the Cricket World Cup, 'race' and
   the politics of carnival   204
   TIM CRABBE AND STEPHEN WAGG

11 Sheffield Caribbean: the story of a Yorkshire cricket club   223
   CHRIS SEARLE

12 Clean bowl racism?: inner-city London and the politics of
   cricket development   233
   NICK MILLER

13 The ambush clause: globalisation, corporate power and the
   governance of world cricket   251
   MIKE MARQUSEE

   Index   266

Contributors

Tim Crabbe is Reader in Social and Cultural Studies in Sport at Sheffield Hallam University in the United Kingdom. His research interests relate to notions of 'race' and identity, crime and deviance, community and social exclusion in the context of sport, leisure and popular culture. He is co-author of *New Perspectives on Sport and 'Deviance': Consumption, Performativity and Social Control* (Routledge, 2004) and *The Changing Face of Football: Racism, Identity and Multiculture in the English Game* (Berg, 2001).

Jon Gemmell teaches Sociology and History at Kennet School, Thatcham, near Reading in the United Kingdom. He is the author of *The Politics of South African Cricket* (Routledge, 2004).

James Hamill lectures in Politics at the University of Leicester in the United Kingdom. His research focuses upon South Africa's post-1990 transition, an area on which he has published for *International Relations*, *The World Today*, *Diplomacy and Statecraft* and *The Commonwealth Journal of International Affairs*.

Leonard 'Tim' Hector was a lecturer, writer, administrator and political activist on the Caribbean island of Antigua. He died in 2002.

Brett Hutchins teaches in the School of English, Communications and Performance Studies at Monash University in Australia. He is the author of *Don Bradman: Challenging the Myth* (Cambridge University Press, 2003) and has published several articles and chapters on the social and cultural dimensions of sport in Australia. His current research interests are in social theory and the media.

Mike Marqusee is an American writer and political activist who has lived in London since the 1970s. His books include *Anyone but England* (Verso, 1994), *War minus the Shooting* (Heinemann, 1996), *Redemption Song: Muhammad Ali and the Spirit of the Sixties* (Verso, 1999) and, most recently, *Chimes of Freedom: The Politics of Bob Dylan's Art* (New Press, 2003).

Nick Miller is the Partnership Development Manager for the School Sport Coordinator Programme, based at Southfields Community College in

xii *List of contributors*

Wandsworth, south-west London in the United Kingdom. Having spent ten years as a Sports Development Officer working in the inner London areas of Westminster and Camden, he is now part of the British government's initiative aimed at improving physical education and sport in schools. Nick has been involved in developing grass-roots cricket in London for the Middlesex and Surrey boards and is himself a keen cricketer.

Michael Roberts is a Sri Lankan Australian whose secondary and university education was in Sri Lanka, where he graduated in History at the University of Ceylon at Peradeniya before going to Oxford on a Rhodes Scholarship. He taught at the University of Peradeniya from 1966 to 1976. He has been teaching in the Department of Anthropology at the University of Adelaide since 1977. He is now retired and serves as Adjunct Associate Professor. His special interests are in cultural anthropology and historical sociology, and he has published many articles and books on Sri Lanka.

Greg Ryan is a Senior Lecturer in history at Lincoln University, New Zealand. His most recent book is *The Making of New Zealand Cricket 1832–1914* (Routledge, 2004). As well as undertaking ongoing research into twentieth-century New Zealand cricket, he has also published a number of articles on Australasian rugby and edited *Tackling Rugby Myths: Rugby and New Zealand Society 1854–2004* (Otago University Press, 2005).

Chris Searle has taught in east London, Grenada, Mozambique, Sheffield, Goldsmiths College of the University of London, and Canada. He has also been a community worker and political activist. He is the author of a number of books, including *The Forsaken Lover: White Words and Black People* (Routledge), which won the Martin Luther King Award in 1972, and *Pitch of Life* (Parrs Wood Press, 2001).

Satadru Sen teaches Indian history at Washington University in St Louis. He is the author of *Migrant Races: Empire, Identity and K. S. Ranjitsinhji* (Manchester University Press, 2004) and *Disciplining Punishment: Colonialism and Convict Society in the Andaman Islands* (Oxford University Press, 2000). He also co-edited (with James Mills) *Confronting the Body: The Politics of Physicality in Colonial and Postcolonial South India* (Anthem Press, 2004).

Sharda Ugra is a sports writer for *India Today* magazine and lives in Delhi. She grew up in Bombay, the home of Indian cricket, and graduated in History from St Xavier's College there. She has reported on cricket now for 15 years, starting out with *Mid-Day*, a city evening paper, before moving on to *The Hindu* and its sister publication *The Sportstar* magazine. She is co-author, with Ian McDonald, of *Anyone for Cricket? Equal Opportunities and Changing Cricket Cultures in Essex and East London*, a 1998 report on the participation of ethnic minorities in grass-roots cricket in the region.

Chris Valiotis is a PhD candidate in the School of History at the University of New South Wales in Sydney, Australia. He works on issues of identity and

List of contributors xiii

diaspora. His current research deals with the construction of a Pakistani cricket nationalism and transnationalism by numerous competing groups within Pakistan and England.

Stephen Wagg teaches at Roehampton University in London. He has written widely on the politics of sport, comedy and childhood, and is writing a book on the politics of English cricket since 1945.

Abbreviations

ACB	Australian Cricket Board
ACC	Antigua Cricket Club
ANC	African National Congress
ANZUS	Australia, New Zealand and the United States
ATSIC	Aboriginal and Torres Strait Islander Commission
BBC	British Broadcasting Corporation
BCCI	Board of Control for Cricket in India
BCCP	Board of Control for Cricket in Pakistan
BCCSL	Board of Control for Cricket in Sri Lanka
BCL	Barbados Cricket League
BJP	Bharatiya Janata Party
CBC	Ceylon Broadcasting Corporation
CBI	Central Bureau of Investigation (in India)
CCA	Ceylon Cricket Association
CCC	Colombo Cricket Club
CENTO	Central Treaty Organisation
COGOC	Concerned Group of Cricketers
COSATU	Confederation of South African Trade Unions
CRR	Ceylon Rifle Regiment
ECB	England and Wales Cricket Board
EEC	European Economic Community
FDI	foreign direct investment
FIFA	*Fédération Internationale de Football Association*
FtF	*Fan the Flame* (website of the late Tim Hector)
GCC	Global Cricket Corporation; Georgetown Cricket Club
GDP	gross domestic product
GEAR	Growth, Employment and Redistribution strategy (in South Africa)
HR46	Hit Racism for Six
ICC	International Cricket Council
IMF	International Monetary Fund
JVP	*Janatā Vimukti Peramuna*
lbw	leg before wicket
LTTE	Liberation Tigers of Tamil Eelam

xvi *List of abbreviations*

MCB	Middlesex Cricket Board
MCC	Marylebone Cricket Club
MDC	Movement for Democratic Change (Zimbabwe)
MKV	Maharaj Kumar of Vizianagram
NCC	Nondescripts Cricket Club
NESB	non-English-speaking backgrounds
NRI	non-resident Indian
NUS	National University of Singapore
NWFP	North-West Frontier Province
NZC	New Zealand Cricket Inc.
NZCC	New Zealand Cricket Council
NZRFU	New Zealand Rugby Football Union
ODI	one-day international
PCB	Pakistan Cricket Board
PPP	People's Progressive Party (Jamaica)
RAF	Royal Air Force
RDP	*Reconstruction and Development Programme* (in South Africa)
SACB	South African Cricket Board
SACOS	South African Council on Sport
SACP	South African Communist Party
SACU	South African Cricket Union
SADACCA	Sheffield and District Caribbean Association
SEATO	South-East Asia Treaty Organisation
SLFP	Sri Lanka Freedom Party
SNCS	Stoke Newington Cricket School
SSC	Sinhalese Sports Club
TCCB	Test and County Cricket Board (in England)
UCB	United Cricket Board of South Africa
UNP	United National Party (Ceylon/Sri Lanka)
WAPDA	Water and Power Development Authority (of Pakistan)
WICB	West Indies Cricket Board
WSC	World Series Cricket

Introduction
Following on

Stephen Wagg

In September 2004, the day after I began to write this introduction, the 51-year-old Old Etonian Simon Mann was sentenced by a court in Zimbabwe to seven years in jail for trying to buy arms with which to overthrow the government of oil-rich Equatorial Guinea (Carroll and Meldrum 2004). A photograph on the front of the London *Guardian* (11 September 2004) showed Mann offering a fairly unambiguous 'V' sign to waiting cameramen. Mann, it turned out, was heir to the Watney Mann brewing fortune and the son of George Mann, once an amateur cricketer for Middlesex, who'd captained England on tour to South Africa in the winter of 1948–9. The image of the bedraggled, khaki-clad Mann brandishing his defiant two fingers was evocative. Mann was a link with a past, which – drawing on an axiom of postcolonial study – survives into the present. Quite by accident, he called up an apparently vanished world in which British merchant adventurers took large parts of the world as their own, beating back the people who lived there with often murderous force. And while Equatorial Guinea may itself be typical of the kleptocratic regimes that have plundered the postcolonial state in Africa, he was also a reminder that governments of the former colonial territories still have to deal routinely with the depredations of the Western powers and their agents. Indeed, these depredations are recognised in the widespread use of the term 'neocolonialism' and in challenges to the appropriateness of the term 'post-colonial' itself: Robert Young, for example, prefers 'tricontinental' – referring to Latin America, Africa and Asia (2001: 4–5). Finally, Mann's lineage, widely remarked on in the British press, drew attention to the historic link between the British Empire, the English upper middle classes and the game of cricket. Many colonial subjects were taught to play this game, often as part of a frequently invoked 'civilising mission'. Cricket is quintessentially the imperial game (Sandiford and Stoddart 1998). It remains an identifiable element in the national cultures of many ex-British territories and it is the nature of the part played by cricket in the forging by these various countries of a new, independent national identity that is the subject and purpose of this book.

2 *Stephen Wagg*

Cricket and the postcolonial

This book is clearly an attempted contribution to the literature on postcolonial culture. In this context it explores the relationship between national identity and an important and, originally, imported cultural activity in countries that were once variously territories within the British Empire. That empire, as is widely acknowledged, once comprised one-fifth of the world's land mass and one-quarter of its population. The process of dismantling this and other European empires began after the Second World War, and the period between then (1945) and the present is, generally speaking, the chosen time span of the chapters that follow. So, the book deals with the postcolonial in the following specific sense: it covers the postcolonial period and thus the time during which political self-government was established and, in tandem with this, an independent national identity was sought.

There is, of course, a prodigious and ever-growing literature on the post-colonial. Much of it is in the realm of theory and takes the form, as so often in the social sciences and humanities, of academics writing essentially about what other academics write about the postcolonial. Those leafing through this (substantial) section of the postcolonial canon may occasionally be tempted to endorse what the Canadian singer Leonard Cohen told a music journalist in 1988: 'As you get older, you get less willing to buy the latest version of reality' (de Lisle 2004: 4). In one intermittently tortuous essay, the influential writer Stuart Hall once accused another (equally influential) contributor to the postcolonial debate of 'a desire to out-theorise everyone else' (1996: 249) – a charge which, in this field of textual wrangling and rising opacity of language, almost anyone could justifiably level at almost anyone else. This part of the postcolonial argument seems to be confined almost wholly to academics.

Much of the debate over the postcolonial is contoured by postmodernism and there are therefore frequent invocations of the death of 'grand narratives', the evasiveness of meaning and, importantly, of the crucial need for formerly colonial subjects to speak for themselves. The noted rhetorical question of the Bengal-born, American-based academic Gayatri Spivak – 'Can the subaltern speak?' – has greatly informed argument on this latter issue. Rather in the manner of Jean Baudrillard's enigmatic claim that the Gulf War of 1991 'never happened', Spivak's remark has launched a thousand conference papers, not to mention a new discrete field of academic enquiry known as subaltern studies. As Leela Gandhi observed, 'it is postcolonial studies which has responded with the greatest enthusiasm to Spivak's "Can the subaltern speak?" Utterly unanswerable, half serious and half parodic, this question circulates around the self-conscious scene of postcolonial texts, conferences and conversations' (1998: 2). For good or ill, however, this book has avoided taking up 'utterly unanswerable' questions. 'Subalterns' or not, a number of its writers are nationals of the countries of which they have written. Others are not. All of them share, however, the assumption widely held in postcolonial studies that in all the ex-colonies and dominions the imperial past strongly informs the present: independence day was not – and could

Introduction 3

not be – some cultural 'year zero' (ibid.: 6). Indeed, the continued presence and importance of cricket in these societies attests to that. The cricket cultures of the world are the product both of imported imperial practices and of the indigenous response to them. As the Caribbean Marxist C. L. R. James observed, 'The British tradition soaked deep into me was that when you entered the sporting arena you left behind the sordid compromises of everyday existence. Yet for us to do that we would have had to divest ourselves of our skins' ([1963] 2000: 66).

It is ironic, then, that postcolonial writing and debates have thrown up almost no reference to sport. Huge recent introductory texts such as those by Young (2001), Ashcroft *et al.* (1995) and Williams and Chrisman (1993) carry no mention of sport, although these books are 400, 500 and 500 pages long respectively and, as John Bale and Mike Cronin recently observed, sport is 'one of the most globalized and commonly shared forms of human activity' (2003: 2). This is plainly because postcolonial debates are concerned almost wholly with literature and hardly at all with physical activities such as sport. Thus, for example, discussion of postcolonial India may concentrate on novels such Salman Rushdie's *Midnight's Children* (whose title is a direct reference to the granting of Indian independence), even though, as chapters in this book make clear, cricket has had a far greater purchase on the popular imagination of Indian society than Rushdie or any other writer. Similarly, it is difficult to think that any Australian novelist or poet could be accorded a state funeral on the scale of the one staged for the ex-Test cricketer Sir Donald Bradman in 2001.

Among the few academics to recognise, and to try to remedy, the lack of interest hitherto in the relationship between sport and the postcolonial are John Bale and Mike Cronin, whose edited collection *Sport and Postcolonialism* appeared in 2003. In their introduction they prescribe three avenues of inquiry for researchers: the 'when' questions – that is, '[c]hronologically, what should we consider as postcolonial in relation to sport?'; the 'what' questions, dealing with the different forms that sport has taken in postcolonial culture; and the 'how' questions, which relate to method. This method will, among other things, entail 'emphasizing aspects of colonial relations between the colonizer and the colonized; providing alternative readings of conventional colonial wisdoms and dominant meanings . . . [and] displaying awareness of resistance to colonization in texts written during and after the generally accepted period of colonialism' (Bale and Cronin 2003: 3–7). This book, it is hoped, complies at least in part with these recommendations. It is a book primarily about history, politics and culture, and looks variously at the place of cricket in those ex-British territories that are today the game's principal international exponents. In this regard it is hoped that the book will add to the small but growing literature on cricket, politics and nationhood. Pre-eminent in this literature is C. L. R. James's often autobiographical polemic on Caribbean cricket, *Beyond a Boundary* ([1963] 2000), coupled with Hilary Beckles's exhaustive two-volume political history of cricket in the West Indies (1999a, b); there is Mike Marqusee's delightful dissection of English cricket in its relation to class, race and empire (1994, 1998) and, more recently, Jon Gemmell's excellent analysis of the politics of South

4   *Stephen Wagg*

African cricket (2004). (Mike and Jon are both contributors to this volume.) There is also, as mentioned earlier, the important collection of essays assembled by Keith Sandiford and Brian Stoddart in 1998 which examine cricket as an imperial phenomenon (Sandiford and Stoddart 1998). But a broad examination of cricket's postcolonial progress has so far not been written. It is as well, however, to note right at the beginning that this progress has been influenced at least as much by factors of globalisation as by postcolonial factors – that is, factors, be they political, economic, cultural . . ., that derive specifically from colonial heritage. It is a commonplace, for example, that Australian society is no longer run, as in the 1950s, by an Anglophile elite that since the Second World War, it has drawn many of its immigrants from southern Europe or the Pacific Rim; and that it enjoys a particularly vibrant national identity-through-sport. Likewise, recent developments in Caribbean cricket seem to have been more affected by neo-liberal policies urged by the World Bank and the International Monetary Fund and by the spread of 'American' consumer culture than it has by colonial residues. Similarly, the liberalising of the Indian economy in the 1990s has greatly affected cricket culture there. And so on.

Central to each chapter, then, are questions of national identity. The chapters are arranged as follows. The book is in three parts. The first deals with the societies that constituted the 'white' dominions within the British Empire. These were essentially settler colonies, governed by European settlers and their descendants, indigenous ethnic groups having been repressed and disenfranchised. These territories have enjoyed effective independence since the beginning of the twentieth century. In this part of the book, **Brett Hutchins** traces the origins of cricket in Australia in the nineteenth century and explores the relationship between cricket, politics and national identity in post-Second World War Australia. Much of his analysis is organised around the life and death of Sir Donald Bradman, leading Australian cricketer between the 1920s and the 1940s and frequently claimed to be Australia's one national hero. **Greg Ryan** then examines the fitful progress of New Zealand cricket in the second half of the twentieth century and probes, in particular, the efforts of the New Zealand cricket fraternity to maintain a significant place in the national consciousness in the face of formidable competition from the All Blacks rugby team and the exploits of the mountaineer Sir Edmund Hillary. Finally in Part I, **Jon Gemmell** and **James Hamill** look at the politics of South African cricket after apartheid, concentrating in particular on efforts to bring about a team that faithfully reflects the 'racial' composition of contemporary South African society. It might be argued, with some justification, that the 'postcolonial' period in South Africa should refer only to the years since 1994, when the constitution was rewritten and free elections held.

The second part of the book covers the cricket-playing countries of what is usually termed the 'New Commonwealth', inhabited principally by people of brown or black skin and granted independence during the post-Second World War period. Here there are five chapters. First, **Sharda Ugra** discusses the politics of Indian cricket, documenting its progress from colonial pastime to the national popular cultural obsession that it is today. She analyses Indian cricket in relation both to the sectarian strife that has characterised Indian society since the partition of India in 1948, and was heightened by the rise in the 1990s of the Bharatiya Janata (Hindu Nationalist) Party (BJP) and to the adoption of neo-liberal economics – again, enthusiastically promoted by the BJP. **Satadru Sen** also contributes an elegant chapter on Indian cricket culture, which examines the changing place of memory in this culture and talks insightfully about cricket and the 'new' postmodern India, brought about by liberalising economic reforms, the growth of televised and one-day cricket, and increased use in India of the Internet. The next chapter, by **Chris Valiotis**, discusses the politics of Pakistani cricket, addressing the paradox of how the Pakistan team's successes have been achieved in spite of a series of scandals and controversies in the country's domestic cricket. This is followed by a detailed political history of cricket in Sri Lanka by **Michael Roberts**. Part II closes with an essay on the political journey of West Indian cricket compiled from the writings of **Leonard 'Tim' Hector**. Tim Hector died not long after he agreed to write for the book, so I have compiled the chapter for him posthumously, drawing on the writings he had published on the Internet. In these writings Tim was particularly acute about the ravages of neo-liberal economic policies on the Caribbean and the consequences for cricket there.

The final part of the book looks at cricket in relation to post-imperial England. Here, first, I examine the fluctuating descriptions of Caribbean cricketers in the British sports press between the 1950s and the 1980s. During this time, of course, West Indian migrants moved from being (comparatively) welcome settlers with dual citizenship to being a purportedly menacing presence, bringing crime and rioting to British streets. The British Nationality Act of 1981 effectively pulled up the legislative drawbridge on those Caribbean people seeking a new life in the United Kingdom. This, to a significant degree, is reflected in the reporting of Test matches between England and the West Indies during the period. Next, **Tim Crabbe** and I discuss the contradictions in the invocation of carnival that accompanied the staging of the World Cup by the England and Wales Cricket Board in 1999. **Chris Searle** then provides an account of the struggles of Sheffield Caribbean Cricket Club, founded in the 1950s and making its way in conditions perhaps surprisingly adverse for a city said by the British press in the 1980s to be the capital of 'the People's Republic of South Yorkshire'. The following chapter, by **Nick Miller**, is based on his experience as a sport development officer in London and examines the progress of initiatives to combat racism and widen participation in cricket in the metropolitan area. Finally, **Mike Marqusee** discusses the contemporary governance of cricket in relation to globalisation, arguing that control of cricket in the era of globalisation has drifted away from Lord's towards entrepreneurs on the South Asian subcontinent and other powerful interests such as Rupert Murdoch's News Corporation. Greater efforts will be made, he anticipates, to 'break' cricket in the United States.

This book, as I have indicated, is global in its reach and its authors are scattered far and wide. I should like to thank Tim Chandler, Paul Dimeo, Jon Gemmell, Gideon Haigh, Malcolm Maclean, Mike Marqusee, Jim Mills, Satadru Sen,

6 *Stephen Wagg*

Rob Steen and Sharda Ugra for help in bringing them together. Jon Gemmell, James Hamill and Alan Bairner were also kind enough to read and comment on drafts of some sections of the book.

References

Ashcroft, Bill, Griffiths, Gareth and Tiffin, Helen (eds) (1995) *The Post-Colonial Studies Reader*, London: Routledge.

Bale, John and Cronin, Mike (eds) (2003) *Sport and Postcolonialism*, Oxford: Berg.

Beckles, Hilary McD. (1999a) *The Development of West Indies Cricket*, vol. 1, *The Age of Nationalism*, London: Pluto Press; Kingston, Jamaica: University of the West Indies Press.

Beckles, Hilary McD. (1999b) *The Development of West Indies Cricket*, vol. 2, *The Age of Globalization*, London: Pluto Press; Kingston, Jamaica: University of the West Indies Press.

Carroll, Rory and Meldrum, Andrew (2004) 'Coup plot leader gets seven years', *Guardian* (London), 11 September.

de Lisle, Tim (2004) 'Who held a gun to Leonard Cohen's head?', *Guardian* (London), 17 September.

Gandhi, Leela (1998) *Postcolonial Theory: A Critical Introduction*, Edinburgh: Edinburgh University Press.

Gemmell, Jon (2004) *The Politics of South African Cricket*, London: Routledge.

Hall, Stuart (1996) 'When was "the postcolonial"? Thinking at the limit', in Iain Chambers and Lidia Curti (eds) *The Post-Colonial Question: Common Skies, Divided Horizons*, London: Routledge, pp. 242–60.

James C. L. R. ([1963] 2000) *Beyond a Boundary*, London: Serpent's Tail.

Marqusee, Mike (1994) *Anyone but England: Cricket and the National Malaise*, London: Verso.

Marqusee, Mike (1998) *Anyone but England: Cricket, Race and Class*, London: Two Heads.

Sandiford, Keith and Stoddart, Brian (1998) *The Imperial Game: Cricket, Culture and Society*, Manchester: Manchester University Press.

Williams, Patrick and Chrisman, Laura (eds) (1993) *Colonial Discourse and Post-colonial Theory*, Hemel Hempstead, UK: Harvester Wheatsheaf.

Young, Robert J. C. (2001) *Postcolonialism: An Historical Introduction*, Oxford: Basil Blackwell.

Part I

Cricket and the former dominions

1 Unity, difference and the 'national game'

Cricket and Australian national identity[1]

Brett Hutchins

The political character of cricket and nation is conflicted. At different times the game has demonstrated the capacity for both liberation and repression; bound up, for example, in both the cause of West Indian self-government and the enforced racial segregation of the South African apartheid regime (James [1963] 1986; Booth 1998). It is a sport that unifies and divides, leads and follows, is ahead of its time, of its time and behind the times. As Hall (1985) reminds us, however, unity does emerge from the cacophony of representations and stories that create the world we live in. Dominant or preferred readings do develop in relation to specific frameworks of history and culture. In the case of Australian cricket, the picture that comes into view is one of social conservatism, of a sport that shows a limited desire to shake the vestiges of a past that is intimately connected to the British Empire. It is a proudly traditional sport that emerged from an imperial age and appears reluctant to transcend the social and cultural boundary markers that defined this bygone era.

The political character that I describe has not precluded the game from pioneering new sporting forms and practices. McKay and Miller (1991) pointed out over a decade ago that cricket, in the guise of the one-day revolution of the 1970s, was at the centre of a far-reaching commodification process that fundamentally altered the economic practices and institutional structures of Australian sport. It was a revolution that sat comfortably alongside the ascendancy of neo-liberalism in official political forums, the decline of the welfare state, and the spread of individualist ideologies and technologies. It is in the social arena that cricket has shown itself to be at best inattentive, or at worst stubbornly resistant, to the ebb and flow of change. The political impacts of Aboriginal self-determination, multiculturalism and second-wave feminism have not passed the game by completely, but other sports such as the various Australian football codes, athletics and basketball have coped better with the challenges posed by them. This is a curious situation, as it is cricket that has been most successfully modelled as the 'national game'. Geographically, cricket has achieved a national spread; it is played in centres across the length and breadth of the country. In social and cultural terms, however, it has fallen short of welcoming and including all those groups and communities that constitute the nation.

The aim of this chapter is to provide a critical commentary on cricket's relationship to politics in Australia. Those who officially represent the game continue to believe that sport and politics should remain separate, a stance defended as recently as the 2003 World Cup (an issue that is discussed later). As Harms (2002–3) pinpoints, this is another example of the 'establishment' ruse that conservative politics is life – the 'natural' state of order – while critical or radical politics is 'politics' and to be resisted. Political power lies in the intersection between official institutional contexts and the 'everyday', the 'popular'; to pretend otherwise is to ignore both historical experience and the demands of political citizenship. Therefore, both formal and informal political matters are examined, from government involvement in the game through to the people who watch and play.

In completing this chapter I owe a debt to historians such as Cashman (1984, 1994, 1995, 1998), Haigh (1993, 1997, 1998, 2001) and Mandle (1973, 1976, 1977, 1982), whose research makes my job easier. I bring to the party my own work on Australian national mythologies and the champion cricketer Sir Donald Bradman (1908–2001) (Hutchins 2002). 'The Don' is an inescapable figure when examining cricket and/or nation given his dominance of the Australian game and the cottage industry that has been built around his memory. He is used here to coordinate my examination. The beginning of each section, under the headings of 'History and nation', 'England, Australia and politics' and 'Gender, race and ethnicity', supplies a snapshot of media reaction to his death. Of concern are the nationalist narratives that featured in the coverage, with these connecting to the issues then examined. This is followed by a discussion of the relevant issues that moves across and between decades and eras, designed to provide a compelling case about the political character of a sport that emerged from empire and has not moved far outside this framework in the contemporary age.

A short note is required on Don Bradman for those not intimately familiar with his story. Australia's greatest cricketer, he passed away in his Adelaide home on 25 February 2001, aged 92. He has been described as Australia's one national hero, is referred to simply as 'the Don' by many, and was once described by the current prime minister, John Howard, as 'the greatest living Australian'. Biographers and commentators have alluded to Einstein, Mozart, Keats and Shakespeare in measuring his skill. Bradman's first-class playing career spanned the years 1927 to 1949. He continuously broke batting records, finishing with the unsurpassed and totemic Test average of 99.94 runs per innings. He captained the national side, never losing a series. In retirement he received a knighthood and a Companion of the Order of Australia, and served as chairman of the Australian Cricket Board (ACB). *International Who's Who* named him as one of only two Australians among the top 100 people who did the most to shape the twentieth century.[2] He is also one of the few sportspeople in the world to have a museum, the Bradman Museum in Bowral, New South Wales, dedicated to his memory. In sum, he is an icon of Australian sport and culture.

History and nation

The linking of representations to ideals of nation and national identity is deeply embedded within contemporary ways of thinking. News stories reporting Bradman's death asserted that he was Australia's greatest-ever sportsman, the world's greatest cricketer, Australia's most notable hero and the greatest Australian of the twentieth century. The vital feature of these hyperbolic reports was the implication that he was somehow a hero for all Australians and that these outpourings had the consent of the entire nation. This manufactured unity featured in claims that he was a hero, genius and the embodiment of the ideal Australian. The then governor-general, William Deane, told us that Bradman 'was a man who embodied the best of the Australian spirit – a love of life, a love of sport and the ability to bring out the enthusiasm in all who knew him' (*Sir Donald George Bradman Memorial Service* 2001). Readers, listeners and viewers were assured that Bradman's death would not diminish his legend and that his stature as a national hero had moved from unquestioned in life to untouchable in death.

The national unity that was assumed in these responses highlights a dominant narrative of Australian history. Submerged or smothered under the imputed unity and uniformity are difference and diversity. A genuinely national embrace and romance with cricket appears to have been long taken for granted by many of those who play, write and comment on the game. A by-product of this attitude is a reluctance or failure to acknowledge those groups and individuals historically excluded from the field of play. For example, at the turn of the twentieth century, cricket reflected the policy of racial exclusivity that was at the heart of the constitution agreed upon by the states and that confirmed Federation in 1901. It was a white man's sport played in an outpost of empire. Nonetheless, as Mandle (1976) details, alongside the motifs of the bush, goldfields and city, cricket played an important role in the formation of an Australian national identity for those lucky enough to be recognised as legitimate members of the nation.

Cricket came to be seen as the national game during the nineteenth century. Football in its many variations, swimming, rowing, tennis and athletics were vehicles for national pride, but cricket most clearly announced the imperial bond and offered the first chance for a nascent Australian nation to match itself against the mother country. Australian teams started recording victories against English XIs from the mid-1870s. These victories were accompanied by erosion in deference towards English touring sides. As Sissons and Stoddart (1984: 41) report, Plum Warner, the leader of the 1903–4 English tour of Australia, believed the behaviour of Australian spectators to be loutish and ill-mannered. After enduring a boisterous Ballarat crowd, he made the suggestion that some vocal young males be caned in order to discourage them from growing into 'barrackers', the scourge of touring sides then and now. On the field, success against English sides hints at the young nation's growing confidence. At the end of 1899, England had won 26 Test matches to Australia's 20 (11 Test series to Australia's 6). However, from 1901 to 1926, Australia registered 27 victories to England's 16 (7 series wins to England's 5).

12 Brett Hutchins

A unique feature of cricket in Australia is that it achieved the appearance of unifying the nation prior to Federation. National teams were officially competing from 1877.[3] In taming the 'tyranny of distance', plotted by Blainey (1966) as a defining feature of Australian history, cricket was a popular activity played in both city and country areas and in all states. This was unusual when compared to the nation's football codes, in which loyalties were fractured from state to state and remain so to this day. As the travails surrounding the consummation of Federation demonstrate, getting the states to agree on uniform arrangements over the distances encompassed by the great southern land was a major feat.

In conjunction with cricket's almost spiritual connection with empire during the nineteenth century, its appeal may be understood through its easily understood spectacle and the unspoken message that accompanied the playing of the game every summer across the country – in spite of the distances separating communities, 'we' have something in common. This is an idea that fits well with Anderson's concept of the 'imagined community'. Anderson (1991) describes the 'natural' feeling of solidarity that accompanies routine activities such as reading the daily newspaper, or in this instance playing a game with a bat and ball. The meaning and significance of such mundane acts are increased exponentially by thousands of other people, far away, whom you may never meet, having the same interests and doing the same thing. The act of play becomes both physical reality and collective cultural expression. During the nineteenth century, Australia was a place where the need for 'togetherness' and the subsequent search for shared experience between white communities proved especially fervid. A small population – about 3 million by the late 1880s – was dispersed across an enormous island continent, with communities isolated from one another by limited communications and transport infrastructure. News from afar was slow, infrequent and often stale upon arrival, with this situation only gradually improving after the introduction of the telegraph in the 1870s (Blainey 1966: 225). Further historical research on the spread of the game in Australia and its regional variations is needed in order to understand the divisions and nuances that comprised the 'togetherness' perpetuated by cricket.

The point has already been made that the historically dominant skin colour in Australia is white. The gendered character of the nation is masculine – in part, a consequence of an imbalance that saw men outnumber women for the first 125 years of British settlement (Blainey 1966: 170).[4] The sporting field proved fertile ground for the cultivation of the 'Australian type', a mythical figure defined by a masculine, Anglo-Celtic and intensely nationalistic character (Turner 1993). The origins of the type are thought to lie in the 1890s, a period during which, according to Palmer (1966), a distinctive Australian tradition and impulse developed. The 'type' was measured in the military theatre of the Sudan and the Boer War, appraised at Oxford and Cambridge, and, significantly, put to test in cricket and sculling (White 1981). Ward's ([1958] 1989) famous thesis about the forging of the national character by the 'Australian legend', the tough, taciturn, independent, itinerant male rural worker who preferred the social company of his mates to that of women and his wife, helped to disseminate and popularise the

Australian national identity   13

image of the 'typical' Aussie bloke. This is an effigy that features prominently in contemporary Australian television drama and beer and truck advertisements, and has resonance when observing the steely-eyed demeanour of Australian Test captain Steve Waugh, and the rugged assuredness of former master batsman David Boon. A difficulty with celebrating this image, besides the inferior status awarded to men who fail to live up to the ideal, is the inevitable subordinate role of women and women's cricket, an issue that is taken up in an upcoming section.

In continuing the theme of difference that lies submerged within narratives of national unity, a brief examination of participation and spectatorship statistics in Australia is worthwhile. These reveal the historical legacy of what has been discussed. Many of those who make up the nation do not necessarily play or watch the 'national game'. In 1996–7, according to a national survey conducted by Sweeney Sports Research Consultants (1997), cricket ranked only 17th in terms of sporting participation, well behind swimming, tennis, golf and cycling.[5] Of those who stated that they played cricket, males outnumbered women by a ratio of 5:1. Cricket was most popular as television viewing, with 54 per cent of respondents saying they watched games. Matches televised are mostly international fixtures, with contests between state sides being comparatively unpopular both on television and with paying spectators. Interestingly, a much closer male–female breakdown of 5:4 was reported in television viewing, suggesting that while the game is popular with both men and women as a media spectacle, the culture of participation is not as inclusive. Nonetheless, this leaves over 40 per cent of the survey respondents neither watching nor playing the summer sport. Even conceding the contestability of survey statistics, this leaves the national game looking more like a sectional pursuit, albeit one that is reasonably popular on television.

The question is, where does the compulsion to claim cricket as a source of national unity come from? The answer arguably lies in a desire for national mythologies that offer steadfast ontological security: the 'psychological state that is equivalent to feeling "at home" with oneself and the world', or the nation as it may be (Cassell 1993: 14; Giddens 1984: 50). Like other settler societies, Anglo-Australia lacks such stories, especially when compared to many European countries with comparatively lengthy histories, dense mythologies and 'the stories, the tunes, the images and the names of heroic ancestors' that award their national identities the appearance of naturalness and authenticity (Turner 1994; Bauman 2000: 81). Similarly, the Aboriginal community have 'the dreaming' and a complex range of rituals to explain their presence and spirituality. White Australia has limited material with which to fashion a history that naturalises the nation as 'home'. The eighteenth and nineteenth centuries offer up an array of colourful explorers, motley convicts, rebellious prospectors and recalcitrant bushrangers, but precious little that clearly announces an Australian identity to the world. The Anzac experience of the First World War, read as a story of sacrifice and courage, has gone closest to achieving the status of a foundation myth. Spoilsports have rightly questioned the celebration of the landing at Anzac Cove in 1915, given that it involved the death of at least 7,000 Australian soldiers

14   *Brett Hutchins*

and that celebrating it runs the risk of glossing over the ugly realities of warfare (Buchanan and James 1998–9). In the canon of Anglo-Australian stories it is the indomitable Bradman in the 1930s and cricket – the 'national game' before the nation even existed – that come most readily to mind after the Anzacs. Cricket consistently announced Australia as an independent and successful country to the world, or at least the Empire. Australia needs cricket and the figures of Victor Trumper, Bradman, Keith Miller, Dennis Lillee, Alan Border and Steve Waugh to create the vision of a glorious history and a unified and triumphant nation. The problem with this situation is twofold: the era of empire is long past, and whatever symbolic unity the game and its heroes can muster can only ever be partial and contested. The following section shifts the analysis of cultural unity and difference on to the issue of British–Australian relations, as well as the official level of politics and the use of cricket by politicians.

England, Australia and politics

In the past decade, Bradman's death was one of the few events about which both sides of Federal Parliament openly concurred. Then opposition and Labor Party leader Kim Beazley recognised Bradman as 'an icon, exemplar, hero'. However, it was the prime minister and Liberal Party leader, John Howard, who took the lead in political mourning. Howard's association with Bradman was demonstrated by his visit to the cricketer's home less than a fortnight before his death and by his attendance at the Don's private funeral. A number of national newspapers carried a dedication to Bradman penned by Howard. Visibly moved upon hearing of Bradman's death, the prime minister spoke at length about his abiding affection for the 'great man': 'In many ways he was the most remarkable figure that Australia has produced in the last hundred years. He had an impact on our country that is difficult to properly calculate' (*Lateline* 2001). Other statements made by Howard stressed that 'no individual has so inspired successive generations of Australians across such a breadth of age, geography and circumstance' and that Bradman was 'the quintessential Australian hero who was as gracious as he was valiant'. As with media reaction generally, Howard's comments assume that Bradman was a hero for all Australians, irrespective of gender, politics, race, class, cultural heritage or interests. A small group of commentators contested this assumption, explaining that many people were simply unmoved by Bradman's passing. It was said that his death would finally allow a diverse and self-confident Australian nation to cast off the musty uniform of empire once and for all. This claim, however, over-simplifies matters.

In analysing the relationship between Australia and England, Horne (1968) discusses an uneasy tension that exists between cultural independence and dependence. On the one hand, there is admiration for those who represent a defiant and independent Australian character; the self-styled underdog who 'knocks' authority figures and loves to lambast a 'whingeing Pom'. On the other hand, the Union Jack has pride of place on the national flag, and the Queen of England is on the country's coinage. With the 'no change' vote actively supported by the prime minister, a majority of the public decided at the 1999 Republic referendum that Queen Elizabeth was an appropriate head of state. Cricket is implicated in this independence–dependence dynamic, with the bodyline series of 1932–3 between Australia and England having been discussed at length:

> England's body-line tactics in 1932–33 struck so deeply at the core of Australia. Devised and implemented to stop Bradman from making his match-winning centuries, it was a negative philosophy born of defeatism. . . . Its employment by the patrician Jardine was interpreted as a symbol of Britain's determination to keep Australia under her dominion.
>
> (Wright 1998: xiii)

The story is repeatedly told that the bodyline series gave rise to an independent and assertive Australian identity. Yet the statement unfolded through cricket, a game originating from and inextricably bound to British culture. When faced with the tactics of the English captain, Douglas Jardine, no one in the settler society challenged cricket itself. Although not strictly the same situation, in Ireland the decision of the Gaelic Athletic Association to ban cricket among its members in the 1880s is an instance where such a challenge was launched. In other words, Australia, like many other Commonwealth countries, accepted the legitimacy of the British game and many of the cultural values that travelled with it.

Of the Australian prime ministers, it is the longest-serving, Sir Robert Gordon Menzies (1939–41, 1949–66), who best personifies an Australian identity that is almost elementally aligned with British culture. Considered a founder of the Liberal Party and its most revered hero (Henderson 1998), he was a man who believed that Australia was a loyal and willing member of the British Empire and that the nation's political and cultural arrangements should uniformly adhere to those of England. He openly admired the Queen, declared himself 'British to the bootstraps' (Clark 1993: 487), and felt that the connection between Britain and Australia was so strong that in early 1941 he entertained serious thoughts about attempting to claim England's prime ministership from the clutches of Winston Churchill (Day 2001). Presiding over a period of unparalleled economic stability, Menzies stood for anti-communism, the monarchy, free enterprise and individualism. His electoral popularity was built on appeal to and elevation of the middle classes, those he called 'the forgotten people' in his famous 1943 address and subsequent weekly radio talks (Brett 1992).

Menzies' favourite recreation was watching and following cricket. The Australian cricket community throughout the 1950s and 1960s epitomised 'the Liberal ethos of free enterprise and moral decency' (Haigh 1997: 259), with this ethos probably contributing to the friendship that existed between the prime minister and Bradman. Menzies thought cricket a potent tool in the communication and spread of English cultural ideals, encapsulated in maxims such as 'playing a straight bat' and 'it's just not cricket'. He wrote on the game, including a regularly quoted article in the 1963 *Wisden Cricketers' Almanack*, in which he stated, 'Great Britain and Australia are of the same blood and allegiance and history and

16 Brett Hutchins

instinctive mental processes' (Cashman 1998: 47). He composed verse of uneven quality, addressed Test dinners, served as a trustee of the Melbourne Cricket Club, and was founder of the annual Prime Minister's XI match. Notably, Sir Robert resolutely proclaimed that sport and politics should be kept separate. In contradiction of this position, he used cricket for political ends. First, he believed the game was 'a unifying factor' for the Australian population and publicly displayed his admiration for it (Martin 1993: 222). Second, and more explicitly, he deployed cricket as a diplomatic tool in relations between Commonwealth nations. Haigh (1997: 69–71) describes a prime example of this strategy in 1953. After an entreaty from Jamaica's governor, Sir Hugh Foot, at a Commonwealth economic conference, Menzies personally wrote to the Board of Control (later to become the ACB) expressing support for a proposed Australian tour of the West Indies in 1955. The tour would celebrate the three hundredth anniversary of British settlement and was declared by Menzies to be 'a very sound move' in terms of British–Commonwealth relations. Despite the Board's demonstrated reluctance to accept touring invitations outside the Ashes cycle, the trip went ahead.

An appreciation of cricket is not limited to the conservative side of Australian politics. Men and women of the Labor Party – Evatt, Hawke, Kernot, Ray and Faulkner – have expressed a love of the game. However, it is the Liberals, especially Menzies and the current prime minister, John Howard, whose beliefs and values have coincided most felicitously with the politics and history of cricket, the sport of empire. Both Menzies and Howard have paraded their veneration of men dressed in creams or coloured pyjamas openly, and sometimes brazenly. Statements uttered by John Howard over the past few years underline this point:

> I really have regarded being captain of the Australian cricket team as the absolute pinnacle of sporting achievement, and really the pinnacle of human achievement almost, in Australia.
>
> (Winkler 1997)

> Nothing will shake my love of cricket, nothing.
>
> (Voices of the Week 2000)

> Even now, in another century, in a world scarcely recognisable to that in which he played, the name Bradman resonates with meaning – talent, determination, commitment, fair play, honour.
>
> (Howard 2001)

These are outlandish statements that imbue cricket and its heroes with an almost religious aura that is difficult to live up to, and this is to say nothing of the challenge of convincing many Australian people that any sport or activity could possess such qualities. Furthermore, Howard has openly publicised his friendship with the former national cricket captain Mark Taylor, paralleling that of Menzies and Bradman.

Australian national identity 17

Not coincidentally, Howard nominates Menzies as one of his heroes and a political inspiration, is openly pro-monarchy, and espouses the worth of anti-collectivism, free enterprise, and 'family values'. A proud and politically dominant social conservative, Howard is nostalgic about the Menzies years during which he grew up: 'I think of the Menzies period as a golden age in terms of people. Australia had a sense of family, social stability and optimism during that period' (Henderson 1998: 13). Howard's affection for men's cricket is inextricably linked to his idealisation of the Menzies era and the propagation of an Australian brand of social conservatism that has its historical basis in the era of empire. Howard's love of cricket is about more than simply gaining political capital among the electorate. Consider the ideological sub-text the next time Howard offers his views on the national side's selection, speaks on the Channel Nine or ABC radio cricket coverage, publicly wishes the national men's team well before a game, sends messages of support and congratulations to the players, expresses disappointment at a cricket scandal, comments on the legality of a bowler's action, or reflects on a player's contribution to the sport on the eve of their retirement. The meaning of Howard's cricket romance runs deeper than the publicity associated with these actions. The personal, social and political dimensions of his devotion to cricket are indivisible and extend to the reinvigoration of a social conservative political tradition.[6] This tradition is underpinned by middle-class values and dovetails nicely with a white, pro-imperial Australian past that is both protective and proud of its British origins. In other words, cricket is part of a popular political and cultural package, ensuring that the balance between dependence on, and independence from, British culture does not swing too far away from the former.

Cricket has been politically and popularly constructed as part of 'mainstream' Australian culture (Dale 2000). It is a superficially convincing image, given the long history of cricket being represented as the national game and the open and emotive support this perception has received from national leaders. Such representations demonstrate the irreducibility of national identity to politics. The propagation of a mainstream Australian identity sets up an 'us' and 'them' opposition that excludes marginalised political and/or cultural identities, forms and practices that exist in relation to it, such as those stressing cultural or racial diversity (Hage 1998; Stratton 1998). In promoting an Anglocentric mainstream national character, the current minister for employment and workplace relations, Tony Abbott, asked in 1990:

> The issue is the sort of Australia we want our children and grandchildren to inherit. Will it be a relatively cohesive society that studies Shakespeare, follows cricket and honours the Anzacs; or will it be a pastiche of cultures with only a geographic home in common?
>
> (Jamrozik *et al.* 1995: 200)

Cricket is an integral plank of a 'common culture' featuring distinctively British overtones. Abbott expressed regret at this statement only recently and conceded

18 *Brett Hutchins*

that Australian society has effectively absorbed and adapted to cultural change. The problem is that cricket has not achieved a similar proficiency. As will be shown, its culture and players remain largely homogeneous, consisting mainly of Anglo males.

Continuing cultural uniformity presents a problem for cricket, with two main issues standing out. First, homogeneity in sport is increasingly difficult to sustain and justify as, proportionally, Australia has more migrants than any other nation in the world except Israel (Bessant and Watts 2002: 230). Finding common reference points among myriad cultural differences is necessarily a process of collective negotiation and exchange. Cricket gives the appearance of being unwilling to enter, or uninterested in, such a process. Second, given the game's history, cricket's reputation as the national sport relies on the continuing maintenance of a seamless link between an Australian identity and an English-derived cultural activity. In other words, the case must be ceaselessly propagated that the essence of the Australian nation is firmly, exclusively and timelessly allied to British culture. Yet as White (1981) convincingly argues, national identity has no essence and is an ongoing project. Australian culture is a series of historically competing identities, alternatively dominant and marginal, that are the products of social change, cultural exchange, geographical context and political power. I am not claiming that these identities are somehow unreal, or are imaginative fictions; only that the social and cultural character of the nation does and will change. Cricket's readiness to accommodate cultural shifts and developments remains in question. In supporting this line of reasoning, issues of gender, race and ethnicity are now examined.

Gender, race and ethnicity

A feature of the reception to Bradman's death was the similarity of those people who responded. At the risk of sounding disrespectful, it was predominantly white males mourning a dead white male. Voices heard on television and radio and in the newspapers belonged to current and past male cricketers and sportsmen, politicians, journalists and commentators. Only seven of the seemingly endless newspaper articles I examined were by women. This is to be expected, given the male dominance of both sport and media institutions, although it did run counter to the statements of those who claimed the nation was in mourning and spoke on behalf of all Australians in honouring the Don. In *The Australian* newspaper, Deborah Jones (2001) dared to state that Bradman's death left her and many other women unmoved, for which she was roundly, although not totally, condemned in articles and in the letters pages. ABC media commentator Stuart Littlemore described the coverage of Bradman's death as 'unremittingly blokey' (*Littlemore* 2001). As for Aboriginal Australians, and those from non-English-speaking backgrounds (NESB) – routinely described as belonging to 'ethnic communities' – their silence after Bradman's passing was telling. Either the event was not thought worthy of comment, or no one bothered to ask representatives for a reaction, a small but telling indication of the history and culture of the game in Australia. In the end, Bradman, a deeply conservative man, saw his way clear to recognise the realities of the past and present. He left a request that half of those invited to his memorial service in Adelaide be female, and prompted the founding of a special 'Bradman Memorial Fund' that aims to foster cricket among disadvantaged groups, including indigenous communities.

The history of women's cricket in Australia is one of success and inattention. The first recorded game was at the Sydney Cricket Ground in 1886 before 1,000 spectators, with the start of international competition coming against the English in 1934–5 (Cashman and Weaver 1991). Australia has been affiliated to the International Women's Cricket Council since 1958 and is ranked number one in the world. In the World Cup, staged for the first time in 1973, Australia has won four out of seven tournaments. In 1998 the current national captain, Belinda Clark, was recognised as the cricketer of the year by *Wisden Australia*, beating the likes of Glenn McGrath, the Waugh brothers and Shane Warne. Despite all this, Cashman (1994: 67–9) describes women as having to endure constant media and public apathy towards, or prejudice against, their participation. There have been signs of improvement lately, with access provided to major grounds and slowly improving newspaper coverage. Sadly, probably the most attention the game has ever received was the result of a 1994 media scandal when an Australian player, Denise Annetts, made poorly founded and damaging accusations of biased selection policies involving lesbianism (Burroughs *et al.* 1995; Jefferson Lenskyj 1995). Such a situation is not helped by the Prime Minister, a self-confessed 'cricket tragic', only belatedly holding an official reception for the women's team after their 1997 World Cup victory. Suffice to say that there was no such reluctance in 1999 when the men's side won their World Cup.

For those living under the umbrella of nation, relations of power are not limited to gender. Race is another key dynamic in Australian society and history, with prevalent patterns of race relations firmly rooted in the soil of Empire. Williams (2001) makes the determination at the outset of his book *Cricket and Race* that the British Empire was built upon the assumption of white supremacy, and Australian cricket bears this legacy. Up to 1987 there had been just eight Aboriginal first-class cricketers from a pool of about 3,000 players (Whimpress 1999: 22). Only one man, Jason Gillespie, and one woman, Faith Thomas, have ever gained national selection, which is a poor record compared to indigenous sportspeople's success in rugby league, Australian Rules football and boxing (Tatz 1995). Whimpress (1999) and Colman and Edwards (2002) demonstrate that the past treatment of outstanding Aboriginal cricketers, such as Queensland fast bowler Eddie Gilbert, is cause for regret.[7] Small of stature with a slinging action, Gilbert bowled with startling pace off a short run, notably claiming Bradman for a duck in a 1931 State match. It was the fastest stint of bowling the Don ever witnessed. During the 1930s and the age of the White Australia Policy,[8] Gilbert had to endure being called for throwing by suspect umpiring, teammates refusing to speak to him, as well as a demonstrated reluctance to share taxis and rooms with him (Whimpress 1999: 228–46). It has been suggested that on another occasion he had to suffer the indignity of Bradman refusing to play in a social tour

20 *Brett Hutchins*

match at Gympie if the paceman was a member of the opposing side. Gilbert was conveniently withdrawn from the match due to a 'shoulder injury', and Bradman's possible motives are unknown (Colman and Edwards 2002: 112–13).

The ACB has conceded the lack of indigenous interest, involvement and progress in the sport. It is obvious, for instance, that few Aborigines are found in cricket crowds at major grounds. Ross Turner, of the ACB, admits, 'It's a game of whites. . . . Cricket whites, white picket fences, green greens. It all represents a historically white anglo [sic] point of view' (Dossier 2001). This recent realisation prompted the ACB to create an Aboriginal Cricket Working Party in 2001 that aims to develop the game in indigenous communities. Initiatives associated with this programme include an annual national indigenous cricket competition, which is proving popular and successful. Also, John Howard has lately come to the party in a symbolic, if not practical, act of reconciliation. With a nod to the example of Menzies, he initiated an annual Prime Minister's XI match against an Aboriginal and Torres Strait Islander Commission (ATSIC) XI in 2001. However, there are question marks over both the longevity of the fixture beyond Howard's prime ministership and the medium- to long-term future of ATSIC, especially if the current government maintains power.

The experience of Australians from NESBs in cricket is more likely to be one of ethnocentrism than of outright discrimination (McKay *et al.* 2000: 290). While the names of players of European and, very occasionally, Asian heritage appear in player lists, by and large cricketing culture has proved unattractive to 'new Australians'. The case of the Australian fast bowler Len Pascoe, who played for the national team between 1977 and 1982, is occasionally used to represent the experience of 'new Australians' in the game. He was a first-generation Australian from a Yugoslavian family whose surname was Durtanovich. He changed this name to Pascoe in order to avoid ethnic abuse on the field, a move that was not altogether successful when bowling to the Chappell brothers (Cashman 1995: 168). The Pascoe story is an interesting historical example of why the culture of cricket has not been widely regarded as welcoming to Australians from NESBs. Contributing to this situation is the homogeneous, mythical and overwhelmingly white image that accompanies cricket when it is promoted and discussed as the 'cornerstone sport in Australian culture' (Derriman 2000). As Roebuck reminds us, the stain of imperialism and Anglo dominance remains:

> Cricket is still struggling to reach beyond its confines . . . still the game is mainly Anglo-Saxon. For a long time this has been the game's main limitation. Apart from a few dubiously treated Aboriginals in decades past, and some sons from families of European origin, cricket has been unable to convince new communities that it is a game worth playing.
>
> (Roebuck 1999; see also Stoddart 1998: 153)

Cricket is emblematic of a wider national pattern. Participation rates in sport for people born overseas are significantly lower than Australian-born individuals, particularly if they are female (McKay *et al.* 2000: 290). One of the few exceptions

Australian national identity 21

to this pattern is soccer, with many clubs maintaining traditional cultural affiliations connected to the post-Second World War immigration boom.

While cricket might be popularly considered the national game, the above summary illustrates that a nation is defined as much by its differences as its similarities. To claim that cricket defines and unifies Australian society imposes a cultural order onto the population that is not necessarily present, and privileges a dominant white identity that is intimately connected to the former British Empire. This is undoubtedly part of its appeal to people such as the prime minister, who only three years ago maintained, 'Most Australians still regard our relationship with Britain as the most important' (Henderson 2000). It is a declaration more nostalgic than substantive, given Australia's inevitable cultural and economic engagement with South-East Asia and the importance of the United States in the development and implementation of national defence strategies. Australia's past might come neatly wrapped in the Union Jack, but to contain its present and future is a more unwieldy proposition.

As I was writing this chapter, the 2003 World Cup was unfolding in Southern Africa. The depressing events in Zimbabwe demanded that a postscript be added to this section. Race and the relationship between sport and politics were again brought to the fore, recalling a long history of political actions by athletes at the Olympics, in football, boxing and athletics. Discussion and debate over whether the Australian team should play in Zimbabwe, a country ruled by the dictatorial and brutal regime of Robert Mugabe, was a poignant reminder of disputes over the worth and effect of sporting boycotts during the apartheid years in South Africa.[9]

Attitudes towards South African sport during the decades of apartheid were marred by disengagement, disagreement and protest (Booth 1998; Nauright 1997). Menzies argued for the strict separation of sport and politics, derided anti-apartheid protestors and defended South Africa's right to national sovereignty (Menzies 1970: 276–85). Even in the context of the time, his opinions appear misplaced. He claimed that apartheid was 'a rude word' that simply meant 'separate development' and defended the former president, Dr Vorster, claiming he was no racist. The cancelled 1971–2 Springbok cricket tour of Australia was a disappointment to Menzies and signalled a bloodletting in Australia's disassociation from the Republic. The Board, chaired by Sir Donald Bradman, made it deliberately clear that the tour's cancellation had been for security reasons and was in no way politically motivated. Social justice and the lamentable living conditions of the majority of the South African population were not the business of the cricket community. This attitude was confirmed by Bradman's 1974 visit to the Republic and meeting with President Vorster, in which discussion was solely devoted to resolving the cricket situation (Page 1983: 356).

The 2003 World Cup stand-off revealed that the case made by the ACB, which had the full backing of the International Cricket Council (ICC), was the same as in 1971–2 but produced a different result. Administrators held fast to the position that the decision of the Australian team to play in Zimbabwe was based purely on player security. As during the apartheid era, there was no concession that playing there might lend legitimacy to an unjust, anti-democratic and violent regime that was systematically starving its people and eliminating its political opponents. Irrespective of whether Australia should have played or not, the apparent indifference to this suffering was puzzling, and the deliberate short-sightedness of the administrators' case was clear after Zimbabwe's first match, when their leading batsman, Andy Flower, and leading bowler, Henry Olonga, wore black armbands protesting against the 'death of democracy' and human rights abuses in their country. To the chagrin of the Zimbabwe Cricket Union, their brave action was widely reported around the world.

The argument of Australian cricket administrators on the issue of South Africa in 1971–2 and Zimbabwe in 2003 is instructive, highlighting an unavoidable tension that exists between their sporting roles and the political meanings attached to their actions. They maintained that participation or non-participation was a sporting and security decision. For example, speaking in support of playing in Bulawayo, the Australian one-day captain, Ricky Ponting, stated on separate occasions:

> We're not going to Zimbabwe to support any political regime or go against any political regime. . . . We're 14 cricketers going to Zimbabwe to hopefully bring back some World Cup points. That's about where it sits with us at the moment.
>
> (Brown 2003a)

> We're not ignoring or condoning what is happening in that country but as far as we're concerned we're a team of cricketers, we're going there to hopefully play well and get some World Cup points on the board. . . . [Australia's position will change] only if safety and security gets a lot worse.
>
> (Brown 2003b)

The problem for the captain, the ACB and the ICC is that it is impossible to limit their comments and actions to cricket and its administration. In both statements Ponting's initial qualifier gives away the fact that his comments are made with political considerations in mind. Attempting to disguise as apolitical what were inescapably political issues and practices is a clumsy sleight of hand that failed to fool many journalists, editors, callers to talkback radio and those who wrote letters to newspapers on the issue. Recalling many of the protests against apartheid, the actions of Flower and Olonga further underline this argument. A well-known slogan of anti-apartheid protest was 'no normal sport in an abnormal society'. Those who control and play cricket in Australia and elsewhere would do well to note that there is no apolitical sport in a world where politics is central to social life and human consciousness.

Conclusion

Elsewhere I have argued that it is both unnecessary and unfair to set up one cricketer, Don Bradman, as the ideal embodiment of the Australian nation (Hutchins 2002). No individual can adequately symbolise the innumerable meanings, values, ideas and beliefs that create the colour and texture of an ever-changing national culture. The same may be said of cricket. Claims that it is the 'national game' create an unreasonable expectation that the sport offers an all-embracing inclusiveness, both culturally and politically. The sport's emergence from the British Empire and its continuing masculine, white Anglo complexion ensures that for all those included, others are excluded or feel unwelcome. Cricket cannot avoid the fact that a body politic is sustained as much by difference and negotiation as by unity and consensus. Past attempts at setting the game up as a fundamental component in a 'mainstream' Australian culture reinforce my point. To express faith in such an entity condemns those on the 'outside' to make their way alone, unaided in the tributaries. It is time to move on from such ideas, to try to find unity among difference, and to develop a more measured appreciation of the game, its political character and social function. The problem is that, on balance, Australian cricket remains tied to images of the past, not visions of the future.

As stated at the outset, Australian cricket has had difficulties transcending the social and cultural boundary markers of empire. This is an argument supported by examination of English–Australian relations, national mythologies, politics and politicians, and issues of race, gender and ethnicity. Measures such as the ACB's Working Party for indigenous cricket hint at a growing critical understanding of the game's past and cultural character, although this is an uncommon measure. Faced with the obedience to the past exhibited by those who represent and follow the game, the issue is whether a desire exists to change cricket. Those in control of the sport appear comfortable with the notion of the 'national game', which offers them cultural legitimacy and dominance, and makes matters of social justice and politics irritants that detract from the sporting spectacle.

The prevailing cultural and political winds in Australia are blowing in cricket's favour. It is a sport that offers the certainty of the past in the face of global uncertainty, anxiety and violence. In this environment, perhaps those who run and play the game cannot imagine failing to honour its male-dominated imperial past and the moral rectitude that accompanies image of both cricket and empire. As if to stamp a seal of approval, the prime minister, a man who has proved popular with the electorate over the past seven years, incorporates cricket into a vision of the nation that embraces its British heritage and bows before the traditions of yesteryear. Cricket is not merely a reflection of the national political culture; it actively contributes to and structures it. Success on the field is matched by consistent television ratings and widespread media coverage, at least for the men. The impetus to change must seem slight. Problems lie ahead, however, if the winds of political opinion change direction.

Future generations may slowly begin to find the sameness on the cricket field unappealing. It is a game played mainly by white, Anglo-Celtic males and falls

24   Brett Hutchins

well short of representing the cultural diversity of the population. Constantly staring at the past in the rear-vision mirror may also become a liability. The sport's main icon, Bradman, is a cricketer from the age of the White Australia Policy, and the quality international touring sides who reach Australia's shores rarely come from outside the boundaries of an Empire that collapsed long ago. Tradition can quickly become unfashionable in our contemporary consumer society. The prime minister's effusive support of the game may also prove a problem in the future, as he openly politicises a sport that tries in vain to distance itself from politics. The worth and enjoyment of playing and watching cricket is not in question, only the game's readiness and flexibility to move with the rhythms of social, cultural and political change. Cricket will never appeal to all those groups who make up the Australian community, but it can aspire to represent a broader cross section of the population by creating a more inclusive environment. Substantial moves in this direction would ensure that rather than relying on the well-worn garments of the past staying in fashion, cricket would be able to adapt effectively to change in the future and possibly even lead the way forward.

Acknowledgements

Thank you to Keith Jenkins, Jim McKay and Janine Mikosza for their comments and help on drafts of this chapter.

Notes

1   Parts of this chapter contain arguments that first appeared in my book *Don Bradman: Challenging the Myth*, published by Cambridge University Press in 2002.
2   The other former Australian was Rupert Murdoch. Bradman was one of just three sportspeople selected, alongside boxer Muhammad Ali and football's Pele.
3   This ignores the first Australian team that toured England in 1867–8, consisting of Aboriginal players. Administrators stubbornly refuse to recognise this side as an official Test team (see Mulvaney and Harcourt 1988).
4   Blainey shows that in 1831, men outnumbered women by more than 3 to 1. By 1850 there were 143 males for every 100 females, although the disparity was more marked among the adult population. By 1900 there were 110 males for every 100 females. It was not until 1916 that a balance was achieved, and this was due to the fact that many men were abroad fighting in the First World War.
5   Similar results were also reported in a 1997 Australian Bureau of Statistics report (see McKay *et al.* 2000).
6   For a more substantial account of this argument, see Hutchins (2002: 108–28).
7   Gilbert claimed 87 wickets at 28.98 in 23 first-class matches between 1930 and 1936 (Colman and Edwards 2002: 264).
8   Regarded as a key plank in the Federation of the Australian States in 1901, the White Australia Policy was a deliberately restrictive and discriminatory government policy designed to maintain racial unity in Australia, or a 'white Australia'. The policy was initiated in 1901 and was not formally abandoned until the election of the Whitlam government in 1972.
9   A tragic irony is that Robert Mugabe is on record as stating in 1984, 'Cricket civilises people and creates good gentlemen. I want everyone to play cricket in Zimbabwe. I want ours to be a nation of gentlemen' (Fitzsimons 2003). In the history of cricket's

Australian national identity   25

association with dictatorial politics, this statement was recently rivalled by the 2001 decision of the ICC to admit Taliban-ruled Afghanistan as its 74th member (Miller *et al.* forthcoming).

References

Anderson, B. (1991) *Imagined Communities: Reflections on the Origin and Spread of Nationalism*, London: Verso.

Bauman, Z. (2000) 'On writing: on writing sociology', *Theory, Culture and Society*, 17 (1): 79–90.

Bessant, J. and Watts, R. (2002) *Sociology Australia*, Crows Nest, NSW: Allen & Unwin.

Blainey, G. (1966) *The Tyranny of Distance: How Distance Shaped Australia's History*, Melbourne: Sun Books.

Booth, D. (1998) *The Race Game: Sport and Politics in South Africa*, London: Frank Cass.

Brett, J. (1992) *Robert Menzies' Forgotten People*, Sydney: Macmillan.

Brown, A. (2003a) 'Runs, not politics, a focus in Zimbabwe', *The Age*, 24 February, Sport, p. 8.

Brown, A. (2003b) 'Zimbabwe pair make brave stand', *Sydney Morning Herald*, 11 February.

Buchanan, R. and James, J. (1998–9) 'Lest we forget', *Arena*, 38: 25–30.

Burroughs, A., Seebohm, L. and Ashburn, L. (1995) '"A leso story": a case study of Australian women's cricket and its media experience', *Sporting Traditions*, 12 (1): 27–46.

Cashman, R. (1984) *"Ave a Go, Yer Mug!": Australian Cricket Crowds from Larrikin to Ocker*, Sydney: Collins.

Cashman, R. (1994) 'Cricket', in W. Vamplew and B. Stoddart (eds) *Sport in Australia: A Social History*, Cambridge: Cambridge University Press.

Cashman, R. (1995) *Paradise of Sport: The Rise of Organised Sport in Australia*, Melbourne: Oxford University Press.

Cashman, R. (1998) 'Australia', in B. Stoddart and K. A. P. Sandiford (eds) *The Imperial Game: Cricket, Culture and Society*, Manchester: Manchester University Press.

Cashman, R. and Weaver, A. (1991) *Wicket Women: Cricket and Women in Australia*, Sydney: New South Wales Press.

Cassell, P. (1993) 'Introduction', in P. Cassell (ed.) *The Giddens Reader*, Stanford, Calif.: Stanford University Press.

Clark, M. (1993) *Manning Clark's History of Australia*, Melbourne: Melbourne University Press.

Colman, M. and Edwards, K. (2002) *Eddie Gilbert: The True Story of an Aboriginal Cricketing Legend*, Sydney: ABC Books.

Dale, L. (2000) 'Mainstreaming Australia', in R. Nile (ed.) *The Australian Legend and Its Discontents*, St Lucia: University of Queensland Press.

Day, D. (2001) *Menzies and Churchill at War*, East Roseville, NSW: Simon & Schuster.

Derriman, P. (2000) 'Cornerstone of sport, cricket's averages just keep getting batter', *Sydney Morning Herald*, 10 March, p. 40.

Dossier: Inside Cricket (2001) 'The white man's game', *The Australian*, 2 April, p. 11.

Fitzsimons, P. (2003) 'The Fitz files', *Sydney Morning Herald*, 1 March.

Giddens, A. (1984) *The Constitution of Society*, Cambridge: Polity Press.

Hage, G. (1998) *White Nation: Fantasies of White Supremacy in a Multicultural Society*, Annandale, NSW: Pluto.

26 Brett Hutchins

Haigh, G. (1993) *The Cricket War: The Inside Story of Kerry Packer's World Series Cricket*, Melbourne: Text Publishing.

Haigh, G. (1997) *The Summer Game: Australia in Test Cricket 1949–71*, Melbourne: Text Publishing.

Haigh, G. (1998) 'Bradman at ninety', *Wisden Cricket Monthly*, September, pp. 36–39.

Haigh, G. (2001) *The Big Ship: Warwick Armstrong and the Making of Modern Cricket*, Melbourne: Text Publishing.

Hall, S. (1985) 'Signification, representation, ideology: Althusser and the post-structuralist debates', *Critical Studies in Mass Communication*, 2 (2): 91–114.

Harms, J. (2002–3) 'Don Bradman: challenging the myth' [book review], *The Yorker*, 35 (Summer): 11.

Henderson, G. (1998) *Menzies' Child: The Liberal Party of Australia*, Sydney: HarperCollins.

Henderson, G. (2000) 'The alliance we can't do without', *Sydney Morning Herald*, 25 July, p. 15.

Horne, D. (1968) *The Lucky Country: Australia in the Sixties*, 2nd edn, Sydney: Angus & Robertson.

Howard, J. (2001) 'Transcript of the Prime Minister the Hon John Howard MP Sir Donald Bradman Oration, Melbourne', 17 August 2000, Prime Minister of Australia News Room at http://www.pm.gov.au/news/speeches/2000/speech406.htm (accessed 13 February 2001).

Hutchins, B. (2002) *Don Bradman: Challenging the Myth*, Melbourne: Cambridge University Press.

James, C. L. R. ([1963] 1986) *Beyond a Boundary*, Melbourne: Stanley Paul.

Jamrozik, A., Boland, C. and Urquhart, R. (1995) *Social Change and Cultural Transformation in Australia*, Melbourne: Cambridge University Press.

Jefferson Lenskyj, H. (1995) 'Sport and the threat to gender boundaries', *Sporting Traditions*, 12 (1): 47–60.

Jones, D. (2001) 'Women's rites a different ball game', *The Australian*, 28 February, p. 4.

Lateline (2001) ABC Television, 26 February.

Littlemore (2001) ABC Television, 5 March.

McKay, J. and Miller, T. (1991) 'From old boys to men and women of the corporation: the Americanization and commodification of Australian sport', *Sociology of Sport Journal*, 8 (1): 86–94.

McKay, J., Hughson, J., Lawrence, G. and Rowe, D. (2000) 'Sport and Australian society', in J. M. Najman and J. S. Western (eds) *A Sociology of Australian Society*, South Yarra, Vic.: Macmillan, pp. 275–300.

Mandle, W. F. (1973) 'Games people played: cricket and football in England and Victoria in the late nineteenth century', *Historical Studies*, 15 (60): 511–35.

Mandle, W. F. (1976) 'Cricket and Australian nationalism in the nineteenth century', in T. D. Jaques and G. R. Pavia (eds) *Sport in Australia: Selected Readings in Physical Activity*, Sydney: McGraw-Hill.

Mandle, W. F. (1977) *Going It Alone: Australia's National Identity in the Twentieth Century*, Ringwood, Vic.: Allen Lane.

Mandle, W. F. (1982) 'Sports history', in W. F. Mandle and G. Osborne (eds) *New History: Studying Australia Today*, Sydney: Allen & Unwin.

Martin, A. W. (1993) *Robert Menzies: A Life*. vol. 1, *1894–1943*, Melbourne: Melbourne University Press.

Menzies, R. G. (1970) *The Measure of the Years*, London: Cassell.

Miller, T., Rowe, D., McKay, J. and Lawrence, G. (forthcoming) 'Globalization, the over-production of US sports, and the new international division of cultural labor', *International Review for the Sociology of Sport*, 4: 427–40.

Mulvaney, D. J. and Harcourt, R. (1988) *Cricket Walkabout: The Australian Aboriginal Cricketers on Tour 1867–68*, South Melbourne, Vic.: Macmillan.

Nauright, J. (1997) *Sport, Cultures and Identities in South Africa*, London: Leicester University Press.

Page, M. (1983) *Bradman: The Illustrated Biography*, Melbourne: Macmillan.

Palmer, V. (1966) *The Legend of the Nineties*, Melbourne: Melbourne University Press.

Roebuck, P. (1999) 'Time to strive for 100 percent and to add a little bit more colour', *Sydney Morning Herald*, 15 November, p. 31.

Sir Donald George Bradman Memorial Service (2001) ABC Television, 25 March.

Sissons, R. and Stoddart, B. (1984) *Cricket and Empire: The 1932–33 Bodyline Tour of Australia*, Sydney: Allen & Unwin.

Stoddart, B. (1998) 'At the end of the day's play: reflections on cricket, culture and meaning', in B. Stoddart and K. A. P. Sandiford (eds) *The Imperial Game: Cricket, Culture and Society*, Manchester: Manchester University Press.

Stratton, J. (1998) *Race Daze: Australia in Identity Crisis*, Annandale, NSW: Pluto Press.

Sweeney Sports Research Consultants (1997) *1996/97 Australians and Sport*, Melbourne: Brian Sweeney.

Tatz, C. (1995) *Obstacle Race: Aborigines in Sport*, Sydney: University of New South Wales Press.

Turner, G. (1993) *National Fictions: Literature, Film and the Construction of Australian Narrative*, St Leonards, NSW: Allen & Unwin.

Turner, G. (1994) *Making It National: Nationalism and Australian Popular Culture*, St Leonards, NSW: Allen & Unwin.

Voices of the Week (2000) *Sydney Morning Herald*, 4 November, p. 46.

Ward, R. ([1958] 1989) *The Australian Legend*, Melbourne: Oxford University Press.

Whimpress, B. (1999) *Passport to Nowhere: Aborigines in Australian Cricket 1850–1939*, Sydney: Walla Walla.

White, R. (1981) *Inventing Australia: Images and Identity 1688–1980*, Sydney: Angus & Robertson.

Williams, J. (2001) *Cricket and Race*, Oxford: Berg.

Winkler, M. (1997) 'Brylcreemed heroes', *The Age*, 15 November, p. 6.

Wright, G. (1998) 'Introduction', in G. Wright (ed.) *Wisden on Bradman*, South Yarra, Vic.: Hardie Grant Books.

2 Kiwi or English?

Cricket on the margins of New Zealand national identity[1]

Greg Ryan

Indications of the status of New Zealand cricket were no more apparent than in 1956. On 13 March, against the West Indies at Eden Park, Auckland, and at their 45th attempt, the New Zealand cricket team finally won a Test match. While this was recognised as a considerable achievement, reactions from the press were hardly euphoric and followers of the game were reminded that New Zealand had been heavily defeated in the first three Tests of the series. As one editor observed, 'We have snatched a victory from them in a final Test when the keen edge of their endeavour was possibly a little dulled.' Another stressed that 'One swallow does not make a summer, and one Test match victory in 30 years does not make New Zealand a top-class cricket country.' Less than six months later, on 1 September, also at Eden Park, the All Blacks defeated the Springboks in a test series for the first time in perhaps the most intensely contested and supported rugby encounters ever witnessed. Their prize was the unofficial world rugby 'crown', and the outcome cemented the status of the game as one of the cornerstones of a popular New Zealand conception of national identity (McLean 1956; Andrewes 1998).

Other events of the 1950s also dwarfed the status of a first cricket Test victory. Edmund Hillary's completion, with Tenzing Norgay, of the first ascent of Mt Everest in 1953 was quickly mythologised as very much a New Zealand contribution to perhaps the last great imperial achievement (Hansen 2000; Booth 1993). At the end of the decade, Peter Snell embarked on an athletics career that yielded six world records and three Olympic gold medals in 1960 and 1964. He would eventually surpass such national 'icons' as the 1905 All Blacks and George Nepia to be recognised as New Zealand's sportsman of the twentieth century (Palenski 2000).[2]

This chapter is inevitably about such contrasting fortunes. As with the period prior to the Second World War, the local and international profile of New Zealand cricket since 1945, and its consequent impact on national identity, has remained to a considerable extent in the shadow of other achievements and especially, in sporting terms, the continued dominance of the All Blacks on the international stage. As rugby strengthened its place at the core of a set of interlocking myths about the distinctive egalitarian and pragmatic (masculine) qualities of New Zealand society, cricket epitomised a lingering strand of cultural

Britishness and dependence. By virtue of very limited international success from which to derive confidence, cricket remained until the late 1970s bound to a conservative preoccupation with the best amateur virtues of the English game. This position was reinforced by a combination of demographic, economic and climatic impediments and a largely dysfunctional cricketing relationship with New Zealand's dominant Australian neighbour.

As British cultural and economic influences decreased in significance during the 1970s, cricket, and the one-day version especially, certainly had a role to play in New Zealand's resurgent relationship with Australia. Consistent international success during the early 1980s and at the 1992 World Cup also boosted the profile of the game and prompted its administrators to fully address the requirements of professional international sport and the demands of sponsorship and marketing. Yet progress for cricket was only relative. As much as the game moved forward, rugby moved faster – and especially so once it became openly professional in 1995. The decidedly negative public reaction to industrial action by New Zealand cricketers at the end of 2002 was a clear indication of the secondary cultural importance of the game to New Zealand.

As New Zealand cricket embarked on the post-war period, it remained shackled to the same combination of amateurism and Anglophilia that had characterised its nineteenth-century development. Yet in doing so it merely reflected broader cultural trends. Colonial New Zealand eschewed its diversity of settler origins and experiences in favour of a mythology of itself as being settled and shaped by the best type of carefully selected, loyal British 'stock' – or 'better Britons'. Critical to this process was an over-emphasis on Edward Gibbon Wakefield's systematic colonisation schemes of the 1840s wherein the careful selection of migrants and close attention to the regulating of class relationships had supposedly produced an ordered and unified pre-industrial society.[3] Implicit was a distinct separation from the supposed convict taint of neighbouring Australia. Despite a multitude of trans-Tasman interactions and certain elements of an 'Australasian' identity prior to 1914, New Zealand exhibited a tone of moral superiority and resisted all overtures to federate as part of the Commonwealth of Australia in 1901 (Belich 2001: 46–52, 76–87).

Notwithstanding perceptions of an emergent national identity, and especially those derived from achievements on rugby field and battlefield, New Zealand's links to Britain were strengthened during the twentieth century. The consolidation of a collective 'Australian' identity after Federation and a stronger sense of cultural separation from Britain accentuated the divergence from New Zealand and produced an environment in which formal trans-Tasman interactions were both limited and frequently characterised by mutual disregard (Belich 2001; see also Ross 1978). At the same time, New Zealand forged a substantial economic relationship with distant Britain rather than closer Australia. Britain provided at least 60 per cent of imports prior to 1914 and took 85.2 per cent of New Zealand exports by 1935 (Grey 1994: 345). Thus, by preference and necessity, New Zealand remained firmly committed to preserving its British connection until at least the late 1960s (Belich 2001: 46–52, 440–3).

30 Greg Ryan

This cultural climate led the middle-class elite who dominated early New Zealand cricket to an almost obsessive preoccupation with replicating the manners and mores of the English game. While cricketing contacts with Australia were both frequent and relatively inexpensive until the late 1920s, the preference of administrators and spectators alike was for contact with England. The New Zealand Cricket Council (NZCC) made constant overtures to Lord's and to its Australian counterpart in an effort to entice visits from English teams after they had toured Australia (see Ryan 2003, esp. chs 7–10). As a microcosm of the broader pattern of trans-Tasman relations, the desire for English teams was reinforced from the 1930s by the increasing reluctance of Australian authorities to assist New Zealand cricket. Its very low standard had little to offer at a time when Australian international commitments were moving to embrace other emergent cricketing powers such as South Africa and the West Indies. While 19 Australian teams visited New Zealand between 1878 and 1928, there were no more until an ill-conceived Test match in March 1946. With first-class cricket hardly recovered from the abeyance of the war years, and a number of its best players still overseas on active service, New Zealand scored 42 and 54 to lose by an innings within two days. Thereafter, New Zealand was accommodated within the increasingly crowded Australian itinerary only in so far as it provided a useful opponent against which to trial emerging players. Five Australian 'B' teams visited New Zealand between 1949 and 1969. From their first visit in 1898–9, New Zealand teams played only 29 first-class games in Australia until 1973–4, when the two countries finally began regular Test match competition.[4]

The perceived 'English' character of New Zealand cricket also endured because the game never produced a pattern of success necessary to sustain expressions of assertive colonialism and later emergent nationalism such as those characteristic of New Zealand rugby or cricket in Australia and the West Indies. The few victories by New Zealand provincial and representative teams prior to the Second World War were against very weak opposition (Payne and Smith 2002: 395–9, 414–18, 471–8; Neely et al. 1985: 35–58).[5] After waiting 26 years for its initial Test victory in 1956, New Zealand did not win again until 1962 in South Africa and not at home until 1968. It did not win a series until 1969–70 and had won only 53 of 301 Test matches to the end of the 2002–3 season.

When compared to its international rivals, New Zealand cricket has faced a set of impediments to both the scale and the standard of the game. First, although the population increased from 1.72 million in 1945 to 3.87 million in 2001, it is still significantly smaller than that of any other major cricket-playing country – including the combined nations of the West Indies (*World Guide 2001/2002* 2001 *passim*). Certainly a developed country such as New Zealand is better able to draw potential players to the game, but this advantage is mitigated by the wider variety of recreational and sporting opportunities offered in such countries.

It follows that the pool of potential players, paying spectators and sponsors from which to derive revenue is also smaller than in other cricketing countries. The average population of the five New Zealand cities in which international cricket is regularly staged is one-sixth of that of their Australian counterparts (*World*

New Zealand national identity 31

Guide 2001/2002 2001: 82, 94). Yet the NZCC has faced many of the same, and sometimes greater, running costs for the game in terms of such necessities as travel, accommodation and ground preparation. Accordingly, its finances were precarious throughout the twentieth century, with irregular profits from some international tours, and especially those to and from England, being rapidly absorbed by losses on other tours and the basic running costs of the domestic game.[6] In this environment there was no scope for retaining professional players and little compensation to amateurs for basic expenses, let alone lost earnings.

Given these parameters, the NZCC was reluctant to make demands on its players. Although the addition of Central Districts in 1950–1 and Northern Districts in 1956–7 increased the number of first-class teams to six, the fixture list did not extend beyond five matches a season for each province until 1975–6. Moreover, the staging of this first-class programme around the Christmas holiday period to minimise the need for work leave, and the timing of most visits from touring teams in late February or early March after a series in Australia, meant that players were frequently expected to make the transition to Test cricket without adequate preparation. For good reason, New Zealand teams were often given the sobriquet 'Saturday afternoon cricketers' (e.g. Cartman 1980: 26–7).

Nor was New Zealand cricket assisted by climatic conditions. As with Andrew Hignell's examination of English cricket, there is equally a case to make that wet or cold weather contributed to the financial vulnerability of the New Zealand game as playing hours were lost and spectators less inclined to brave the conditions. Various surveys suggesting a correlation between lower batting averages and lower bowling averages on wet or damp wickets and outfields are also applicable. While batsmen thrived and bowlers frequently toiled on hard wickets in Australian heat, New Zealand batsmen were simply not accustomed to making large scores, and bowlers required a narrower range of skills to exploit inferior surfaces (Hignell 2002: 113–70; Ryan 2003: ch. 7). These limitations were to be repeatedly exposed by international opposition.

The years immediately after the Second World War certainly offered contradictory messages to New Zealand cricket followers. As already mentioned, in March 1946 a strong Australian team visited and dismissed its ill-prepared New Zealand counterpart for 42 and 54 in what was retrospectively recognised as the first Test match between the two countries.[7] While some suggested that New Zealand should not have the temerity to tackle Australia and should restrict itself to second-string MCC sides and Australian state teams, at least one editor felt that

> If that is to be the reaction, then let us give up cricket altogether. The occasion is not one for despair, rather it is one in which hope should rise Phoenix-like from the ashes. . . . Was defeat final? Was Dunkirk final?[8]

The New Zealand team to England in 1949 more than met this challenge as they lost only one first-class match and drew all four of the three-day Test matches. More importantly, they gained a reputation for playing 'bright' cricket in the best

32   Greg Ryan

amateur spirit. 'New Zealand cricket', observed the editors of the *New Zealand Cricket Almanack* at the end of the tour, 'may be said to have reached maturity, and our aim must be to so continue to develop our players that the position now won can be fully held' (Carman and Macdonald 1949: 7).

Yet the 1949 tour was an aberration, to be followed by the most calamitous decade in the history of the New Zealand game. New Zealand lost 21 of its 32 Test matches during the 1950s and provided perhaps the most consistently inept batting performances seen in international cricket. Nine of its 53 completed innings failed to reach 100 and another 24 failed to reach 200. The nadir was obviously a completed innings of 26 against England at Eden Park in March 1955. But five scores under 100 from nine completed innings during the 1958 series in England were little better. The 1960s produced a marked improvement among batsmen, but only six wins and 18 losses from 45 Test matches.

Responses to such consistent failure reveal the paradox of the amateur game in New Zealand. Inevitably there were calls for more international cricket – especially against Australia – and greater commitment from players. As the *New Zealand Herald* observed after the 1955 debacle,

> So long as our players get an opportunity to play in a big match only at long intervals, so long will they be liable to psychological failures at key moments. Vigorous promoting of contests with other countries would give our cricketers the experience they lack.[9]

But most recognised that as long as New Zealand lacked the financial resources to sustain professional cricketers and an expanded international programme, the chances of success were limited. As the *Evening Post* put it after another bad performance against England in 1963,

> One stark fact emerges from the current tour – weekend cricketers are no match for seasoned players. And our team need make no apology for this. It only stands to reason that men having played as a team in cricket-hardened Australia for some time now, and who consistently pack more cricket into one season than the average New Zealander does into three, must be more than a match for a team drawn together for a quick tryout before taking their place against Test odds on Eden Park.[10]

It was accepted that amateurism was a product of necessity.

But there is a stronger sense in which many administrators and followers of New Zealand cricket were amateur by inclination and seemingly quite happy to place ideals above success. Typical was the decidedly unambitious response to repeated suggestions that New Zealand should capitalise on the success of the 1949 tour by including a team in the Australian Sheffield Shield competition.

> Would New Zealand be wise to endeavour to lift cricket from its present standing as a popular and respected form of recreation by making it, so far as the leading players are concerned, a part-time profession? We think that

there would be a strong body of public opinion against such a proposal. . . . Nor is there real reason to believe that New Zealand, by straining its resources to the utmost, could establish itself on a par with England and Australia, the admitted champions of the cricket field. . . . The accomplishments of a team are measured against its background, in New Zealand's case that of a game still regarded as a pastime.[11]

In 1953 the *New Zealand Listener* embarked on a lengthy critique of certain media and public reactions to failure in a home series against South Africa. The particular target was excessive scrutiny and an overly 'scientific' analysis of the game:

Cricket is a game good to play and watch; but it is only a game, and the quickest way to kill it is to turn it into a contest weighed down by international prestige and rivalry. . . . Yet it is idle to ask for yesterday. New Zealand is in international cricket, for better or worse, and we can argue in vain that players would do better if they were given less attention. When cricket is a little more than a game, it is not a science, but an art; and art should never be separated from joyfulness. A hard fought match is a joy to play in, and a joy to watch if it can be understood that the chances and wilful risks are all in the tussle. Afterwards, however, it should be like the sunlight fading from the grass, or the bouquet of a remembered wine. The paradox in our present situation is that we are crying out for a return to carefree cricket, and at the same time are insisting on conditions – the big game, the statistics, the publicity and the inquest – which make it impossible.[12]

The following year, the same journal outlined its preferred circumstances for any New Zealand success:

Some day, perhaps, a New Zealand team will win fame in the cricketing countries. It is a success devoutly to be looked for – but only if it can be gained without any loss of that easy friendliness and sportsmanship, on and off the field, which help us to remember that cricket is still a game even when it is played by international sides.[13]

In similar context, the comprehensive failures of the 1958 tour were deflected into a positive light by the *Evening Post*:

Though it may not have added to New Zealand's reputation on the cricket field, it has fully maintained the Dominion's name for good sportsmanship and good fellowship – and that, as it is repeated at public function after public function, is the essence of cricket. Perhaps it is the most important point on which to have succeeded.[14]

In 1962, inspired by the refreshing cricket played by a touring Fijian team and with an eye to the growing politicisation of sporting contacts with South Africa,

34   Greg Ryan

the editors of the *New Zealand Cricket Almanack* presented an unequivocal manifesto:

> Cricket is a game to be played first of all for the pleasure of participant and spectator, and heaven forbid that we should so organise our sport that the same seriousness and intensity that dominate our politics should drive from our game its natural enjoyment. . . . Let us, then, of New Zealand so play our games that we will be remembered for the style of our play and the pleasure we gave rather than merely because of securing a certain number of victories. It is possible to be more honoured in defeat than victory.
>
> (Carman and Macdonald 1963: 7–8)

As late as 1973, when the New Zealand team came closer than any of its predecessors to achieving an elusive first victory over England, the *Almanack* was still convinced that 'When all is said and done, our cricket will be far better known by its quality than by the mere tally of wins or losses' (Carman 1973: 39).

Such sentiments were not merely the domain of conservative elements within the press. The NZCC also pursued an agenda in which progress and success were often secondary considerations. This is most apparent in the 'inclusive' itineraries they designed for touring teams wherein the objective was to give opportunities to as many players as possible rather than the best players. Despite repeated complaints from touring teams dating back to at least 1903 (Warner 1903: 140; Carman and Macdonald 1950: 7; 1957: 7), the Council persisted until the 1960s with a plethora of non-first-class fixtures against regional teams. Only 50.7 per cent of games on the full tours by Australia B in 1950, 1957 and 1960, the West Indies in 1956 and the MCC in 1960–1 were first class.

The Council was also extremely cautious, and sometimes reactionary, in responding to the crucial changes occurring in world cricket from the late 1960s – and particularly the introduction of one-day cricket and its attendant commercialisation of the game. In August 1969, when it was suggested that a domestic one-day competition could generate as much public interest in New Zealand cricket as had the Gillette Cup and Sunday League in England, the NZCC quite rightly pointed out that any new competition would impose greater economic strain on a body that already ran its domestic affairs at a consistent loss. But a further suggestion that money could be saved by scheduling one-day games on the Sunday of existing first-class games was met with a concern that injury to players in the 'lesser' game could detract from their performance in the 'more important' one. Further, as the five-match first-class programme already made 'considerable' physical demands on players, it was important to maintain a rest day during these fixtures.[15] On religious grounds, others objected to the expansion of Sunday play. Indeed, this issue sat uncomfortably with the NZCC from the mid-1960s onwards and its gradual introduction for first-class and one-day cricket curtailed the representative careers of several leading players with strong religious convictions (Carman 1968: 7).[16]

New Zealand national identity 35

The NZCC's decision to embrace one-day cricket in 1971–2 was motivated not by a desire to modernise local cricket, but by a more pragmatic determination to prepare New Zealand teams for the Australian inter-state V&G Knockout tournament, to which they had been invited from 1969–70. The domestic one-day competition, generally scheduled before the first-class season, gained little momentum or public interest until the knockout format was replaced by a round-robin in 1980–1 (Payne and Smith 1984: 119). Similarly, although New Zealand was the first country to schedule one-day internationals for touring teams on a regular basis during the early 1970s, two of the first five were in Dunedin and one in Wellington – the two international venues with the lowest spectator capacity. A fixture was not played at the largest venue, Eden Park, until February 1976. Thereafter, and despite New Zealand reaching the semi-finals of the 1975 and 1979 World Cups, only one other one-day international was played in New Zealand during the next six years.[17] If one-day cricket had originally been conceived as a means of addressing declining attendances and fragile finances in the English game, these objectives were apparently not uppermost in the minds of the even more vulnerable NZCC.

The emergence of Glenn Turner as New Zealand's first fully professional international cricketer also posed problems for the Council. Having established himself in county cricket during the late 1960s, Turner was forthright in his determination to be treated as a full-time professional player and to ensure that other New Zealanders were adequately compensated while playing for their country.[18] However, his approach was frequently viewed as fractious and mercenary. In 1977 the NZCC chairman, Walter Hadlee, a former New Zealand captain and father of Richard Hadlee, insisted that New Zealand did not have the population to sustain professional cricketers, and players should play purely for the 'fun' of the game. Predictably, the editor of the *Cricket Almanack* added, 'It will be a sad day when players perform for financial gain rather than for the sake of sport itself and for the honour of representing one's country or province' (Carman 1977: 7).[19] Turner responded that those who made such statements generally did so from the comfort of expensive cars en route to expensive homes and did not appreciate that an expanding international programme was placing severe financial strain on players.[20] Amid further acrimonious exchanges over money, and a brief suspension by the NZCC in June 1978, the most successful batsman produced by New Zealand generally absented himself from the national team after 1977.[21]

When set against such popularly acclaimed achievements as the conquest of Mt Everest by Edmund Hillary, world-renowned athletic performances by Peter Snell and others during the early 1960s, and the triumph of the All Blacks over the Springboks in 1956 and their dominance of international rugby for much of the remainder of the twentieth century, the lack of cricketing success and seeming lack of ambition on the part of many of its administrators and supporters left the game with nothing to contribute to the strengthening rhetoric of a New Zealand national identity during the post-war years. More to the point, and as I have argued elsewhere for the period prior to 1914, reactions to New Zealand cricket

36 Greg Ryan

during the 1950s in particular highlight the banality and shallowness of much of that rhetoric and the limitations of the subsequent interpretation of it (Ryan 2003: ch. 10). On the one hand, the exploits of Hillary, Snell and the All Blacks were repeatedly attributed to the supposedly dominant characteristics of the New Zealand setting. Geographical and cultural isolation, a small population, and limited funds and facilities are supposed to have imbued the New Zealand male with a unique determination and ability to overcome obstacles with 'Kiwi ingenuity'. It was also supposed to be no coincidence that many of the most successful national 'icons' apparently hailed not from urban privilege but from the egalitarian world of the 'ordinary' New Zealander in a small town or rural setting. In turn, these interpretations of success and the myths they embody have been seized upon by later scholars as a vital part of New Zealand's emergent 'national identity' (see, for example, Phillips 1984; 1987: 108–22; Sinclair 1986: 143–55; Fougere 1989). Yet the contemporary rhetoric and the subsequent chronicling of it ignore the fact that this same setting produced a cricket team incapable of overcoming these same obstacles. Moreover, the prevailing cricket culture was tied to a set of conservative 'Old World' values that were supposedly anathema to much that shaped success in New Zealand. The obvious polarity between these two positions calls for a recasting of the standard scholarship of New Zealand identity that is well beyond the scope of this chapter.[22]

It was coincidental, but highly advantageous in terms of enhancing its profile, that cricket began to enjoy greater international success at a time when New Zealand was embarking on something of a cultural realignment, distancing itself from Britain and Britishness. Following a series victory over Australia B in 1967 and home Test match victories against India in 1968 and the West Indies in 1969, New Zealand drew a series in India and won its first series in Pakistan in 1969–70. A drawn series in the West Indies in 1972 was followed by strong performances during the 1973 tour of England, a first victory over Australia in 1974, semi-final appearances at the 1975 and 1979 World Cups and, finally, a first victory over England at Wellington in February 1978. Following the lead of Glenn Turner, an increasing number of players secured English county and league contracts. With Richard Hadlee in particular developing as a world-class player, New Zealand could finally boast a team with professional commitment and experience. In turn, and especially in the post-Packer era, the domestic first-class programme was expanded and sponsorship was secured as administrators found the confidence to replace their conservative attitude to professionalism with a relatively progressive approach that better prepared New Zealand for international cricket (Hadlee 1993: 202–5).[23]

In terms of results and attitude the early 1980s are the true halcyon period for New Zealand cricketers. They did not lose a Test series on home soil from 1980 to 1992, completed first series victories in Australia in 1985 and England in 1986, and managed a ratio of Test match wins exceeded only by the West Indies during the 1980s (Devlin 1987).[24] But the most enduring feature of this period was the role of cricket in a markedly changed relationship with Australia.

New Zealand national identity 37

The fall of Singapore to the Japanese in 1942 and the subsequent reliance on the United States to win the war in the Pacific signalled to New Zealand that the traditional reliance on Britain could not be taken for granted. From 1951 the Cold War ANZUS alliance between Australia, New Zealand and the United States, paralleled with Britain's gradual withdrawal from empire and shift towards Europe, ensured a pronounced change to New Zealand's international perspective. By necessity and inclination, New Zealand gradually came to identify itself as a Pacific nation with distinctive regional interests. For many, although not the politicians, who had anticipated it for more than a decade, this change was also reinforced by Britain's entry to the EEC on 1 January 1973 and the consequent erosion of New Zealand's long-established preferential economic relationship. At the same time, the expansion of global media, communications and international travel after the Second World War also reduced New Zealand's traditional cultural insularity as British influences were joined by American and Australian elements. From the mid-1960s, when it became apparent that better economic conditions in Australia were not a temporary phenomenon, the number of New Zealanders visiting and settling in Australia increased dramatically. By 2001 there were 435,000 New Zealanders permanently resident in Australia, and 1.5 million people criss-cross the Tasman each year. Consequently, recent decades have witnessed a much greater awareness of Australian mores, events and personalities, and Australia became culturally, economically and politically important to New Zealand in a way that had not been apparent since the 'Australasian' connection prior to 1914 (Belich 2001: 440–3; Sinclair 1987; Grimes *et al.* 2002). Certainly the relationship is a lopsided one in that the disparity in size and population between the two countries, among other factors, dictates that New Zealand is rather more preoccupied with Australia than vice versa. But in New Zealand minds at least, the greater interaction has contributed to a heightened trans-Tasman rivalry in which sporting encounters became the most visible manifestation – and none more than the 'underarm' incident on 1 February 1981.

The World Series of 1980–1 was of considerable importance to the profile of New Zealand cricket because it represented the first exposure for players and television viewers alike to the Packer-driven intensity of one-day international cricket with floodlights, white balls and coloured clothing. When New Zealand required six runs off the last ball to win the third final of the series at the Melbourne Cricket Ground, the Australian captain, Greg Chappell, ordered his brother to bowl the last delivery underarm. Although New Zealand lost the game, it claimed a significant moral victory. Responding to Chappell's apparent cowardice, the New Zealand Prime Minister, Robert Muldoon, said, 'I thought it was most appropriate the Australian team was dressed in yellow.'[25] The underarm incident 'confirmed' many long-held opinions about the Australian character, and 'underarm' quickly became a New Zealand byword for things devious or unethical. For its part, Australia was rather less consumed by New Zealand feelings, and its cricketers placed much greater emphasis on enduring rivalries with England and the powerful West Indies.

38   Greg Ryan

When Chappell's team visited New Zealand in February 1982, an unprecedented 43,000 people turned out for the first one-day international at Eden Park. If some traditionalists were unnerved by the 'boisterous' antics of many new followers of New Zealand cricket, and especially those who were intoxicated by much more than the play,[26] none could deny that there was a refreshing change from the timidity and deference of earlier decades. Nor could they argue when the new fascination for one-day cricket translated into a dramatic increase in playing numbers. While registered competitive adult players increased by only 22.5 per cent in the three years after 1981, those engaged in ostensibly 'social' cricket, such as mid-week competitions between business teams, increased by 211 per cent. Perhaps more importantly, the total number of registered schoolboys jumped by 184 per cent between 1981 and 1985, and many other children were introduced to the game through coaching programmes and modified forms of the game such as Kiwi Cricket, which used a softer ball and ensured full participation by all players. There was also a marked increase in the numbers of women and girls following and playing the game.[27]

Cricket also benefited greatly from blows to the credibility of rugby caused by the 1981 Springbok tour of New Zealand. The tour, conducted despite the ongoing sports boycott of South Africa, produced large and violent protests. Although rugby retained a strong core of support, to judge by the large television audiences and sold-out grounds during the tour, many others dissociated themselves from the game, and New Zealand was subjected to considerable scrutiny within the international community – not least in terms of threats to its participation in events such as the 1982 Commonwealth Games (see Templeton 1998, esp. pp. 178–203; Richards 1999). At the same time, an entirely unheralded New Zealand team was advancing to its only appearance at the soccer World Cup, and many of those disillusioned with rugby found a new outlet for their winter sporting passions (Keane 1999). While cricket did not gain custom from these changes, it shared with soccer a brief period of positive results and public enthusiasm relatively unimpeded by the dominance of rugby.

But popular enthusiasm and a high profile for cricket was relatively short-lived, and the game was ultimately unable to capitalise on the advantages it enjoyed during the early 1980s. Although New Zealand continued to prosper in Test matches at home and overseas during the late 1980s, the retirement of Richard Hadlee in 1990 signalled a sharp decline in confidence and results. During the first half of the 1990s New Zealand won only four and lost 18 of 37 Test matches. Moreover, one-day cricket, so crucial in attracting new support at the start of the 1980s, was no longer a novelty and New Zealand's performances were decidedly erratic. It failed to reach the semi-finals of the 1983 and 1987 World Cups and after 1985–6 the relationship with Australia was seldom rewarding – producing only six one-day international victories from 28 attempts during the next decade. As the young enthusiasts of 1982 moved on to the more time-consuming demands of higher education and employment, those who followed found rather less to captivate them. Indeed, the playing numbers of 1984–5 had decreased by as much as a third by 1991.[28]

New Zealand national identity 39

Amid these declining fortunes, the 1992 World Cup was an aberration – but one that was to have significant consequences for the direction of New Zealand cricket. Although New Zealand co-hosted the tournament with Australia, its recent performances, and especially a series of comprehensive failures against England, suggested little prospect of success.[29] Yet the innovative captaincy and brilliant batting of Martin Crowe and spectacular hitting by the opening batsman Mark Greatbatch contributed to New Zealand winning seven games in succession before succumbing to Pakistan in a semi-final. As the tournament progressed, one detected the same mix of confidence and exhilaration that had greeted the one-day game a decade earlier. In turn, playing numbers in all junior grades increased during the following two seasons.[30]

As popular 'euphoria' echoed throughout the 1992 World Cup, those who administered New Zealand cricket were, not surprisingly, determined to harness and cultivate the feeling. Their primary method was an emphasis on various forms of one-day cricket at the expense of the longer form of the game. For the 1992–3 season the NZCC officially sanctioned Action Cricket – a 20 overs per innings format that allowed for two games on the same day. The following season it introduced a second round to the domestic one-day competition and began to significantly reduce the amount of domestic first-class cricket. From 1991–2 to 1995–6 the one-day programme doubled while first-class cricket was reduced by a third (Payne and Smith 1995: 9–10). In 1995–6 the one-day game was condensed still further with Cricket Max – a three-hour package in which each team has two 10-over innings and an opportunity to double the value of runs by hitting the ball straight into a 'Max Zone'.[31] That Cricket Max was largely designed and marketed by Martin Crowe, the architect of the 1992 World Cup success and more recently director of cricket for Sky Television, is no coincidence (Crowe 1995: 241–8).

The 1990s also saw New Zealand Cricket Inc. (NZC), the successor to the NZCC, greatly expand its marketing, 'branding' and merchandising activities. Going to the cricket was presented as a complete 'entertainment package' replete with music between overs and a wide range of souvenirs to satisfy young consumers. The national team, supported by extensive sponsorship and television advertising, was recast firstly as the 'Young Guns' – despite being on average older than most of their predecessors – and latterly as the 'Black Caps'. Provincial teams were also adorned with such sobriquets as 'Knights', 'Firebirds' and 'Wizards'.

Cricket followers were largely unimpressed by such strategies – perceiving many of them as an attempt to artificially inflate the credentials of the national team and disguise its continued inconsistency and failure to perform at crucial moments.[32] Despite propaganda to the contrary, Cricket Max largely failed to generate public interest and did not expand to club, business league and junior competitions in the manner envisaged by its promoters. As an increasing amount of Australian cricket appeared on New Zealand pay television, there was a growing awareness that the success of and support for cricket across the Tasman was a product of attitude and ability in the two established forms of the game – rather than to the artificiality of team names and 'slogathons' such as Cricket Max.[33]

40 *Greg Ryan*

By the late 1990s, attendances at one-day international series in New Zealand had dwindled to less than one-third of those during the early 1980s, and those for domestic competitions spiralled downwards to the point where NZC abandoned gate charges for first-class cricket.[34] Eventually, moves were made against the unproductive preoccupation with the one-day game as Cricket Max became a pre-season event with little fanfare and the balance between one-day and first-class domestic cricket was significantly redressed with the introduction of a second full round of inter-provincial fixtures. Efforts were also made to secure development tours by academy and 'A' teams to and from New Zealand (Payne and Smith 2002: 129, 172).[35]

The substantial increase in televised international cricket during the 1990s was also a mixed blessing for NZC. It is probable that the relative quality of cricket on offer is more attractive to some than watching domestic competitions or the exertion of playing. Nor is there an imperative to attend international matches, which, because of their frequency, now lack the air of anticipation and importance that once accompanied short and irregular visits from touring teams. In a sense, cricket has become a victim of its own promotion. Alternatively, it has been suggested that the shift of most New Zealand cricket coverage to pay television in 1998 has reduced access to the game among those, especially in lower socio-economic groups, who are unable or unwilling to subscribe and can least afford to attend games.[36]

But in fairness to the efforts of NZC, the ability of New Zealand to produce successful cricket teams on a regular basis remains bound to certain of the impediments that have been present throughout its history – and several new ones. While the potential pool of players has obviously increased in accordance with growth in the New Zealand population as a whole, a number of recent surveys indicate that fewer people are able or willing to play cricket and that the standard of the game at all levels below international declined markedly during the 1990s. By way of explanation, several of the arguments of Robert D. Putnam with respect to the decline of community in the United States (2000, esp. pp. 184–284) are equally applicable to New Zealand. First, economic reforms and liberalisation of employment practices since the 1980s have produced an increasingly casualised workforce wherein many are obliged to work on Saturday or Sunday and take a weekly holiday at another time (Canterbury Cricket Association 1997: B2). This, combined with increases in both single-parent and two-career families, has greatly undermined the traditional notion of the 'week-end' as a time that can easily be devoted to team sport. Second, more disposable income and elements of cultural globalisation have exposed New Zealand to a much wider range of individual and team sports that erode the numbers playing the traditionally dominant sports such as cricket and rugby. At the same time, there is evidence to suggest that participation and club membership among all sports have declined sharply in favour of sedentary leisure activities such as computer games, films, live music, theatre and television watching (Hillary Commission 1996). Although long-term analysis of New Zealand trends has not yet been conducted, it is also likely, as Putnam argues, that generational change

New Zealand national identity 41

has a role to play. As those whom he terms the 'civic generation', whose more cooperative social habits were shaped by the mid-twentieth-century experience of war and depression, were gradually replaced by generations of less involved individuals without the same overarching imperative to cooperate, there was an attendant decline in such things as team and club membership (Putnam 2000: 247–76). Certainly all these factors are equally apparent in other developed cricket-playing countries such as Australia and England, but they are accentuated by New Zealand's small population and economy.

Without systematic inquiry, it is also uncertain how far cricket has adapted to significant changes in the composition and location of the New Zealand population – especially in terms of its appeal to burgeoning Maori and Pacific Island communities in the largest cities. Although historical accounts greatly exaggerate the Maori embrace of rugby, it is nevertheless substantial when compared to that for cricket. For much of the twentieth century the largely urban base and relative expense of cricket placed it out of reach of a predominantly rural and economically vulnerable Maori population (Ryan 2003: ch. 4). Yet rapid Maori urbanisation and relative economic improvement from the 1950s, at the same time as significant migration by various Pacific peoples to New Zealand, has yet to be consistently reflected in the upper echelons of New Zealand cricket. The explanations and speculations for this are varied, complex and well beyond the scope of this chapter. Suffice it to say that whereas the two rugby codes and netball have experienced something of a 'Polynesianisation' in terms of dominant players (Hyde 1993), cricket can boast no more than a handful of Polynesians at first-class or international level.[37] Although NZC and its affiliated associations have certainly lent their support to various initiatives for Maori and Pacific island cricket tournaments and for kilikiti, the Pacific derivation of the game (Payne and Smith 2001: 142–4), cricket remains disproportionately the domain of European New Zealanders.

The greatest impediment to the popularity and profile of cricket has been the rehabilitation of rugby since the mid-1980s. Certainly the game was slow to digest the lessons of 1981 and the threat that continued sporting contact with South Africa posed to the broader interests of New Zealand sport. Despite renewed public protests, an All Black tour of South Africa in 1985 was only stopped by a high court injunction. But a rebel 'Cavaliers' team did tour in 1986 – meeting with minimal disciplinary action from the rugby authorities upon its return (Templeton 1998: 269–90).[38] However, in 1987, as the cricket 'boom' was beginning to subside, New Zealand and Australia hosted the inaugural Rugby World Cup, in which the All Blacks triumphed with a style of open, entertaining rugby not generally associated with their uncompromising quest for rugby supremacy. They would remain unbeaten until 1990 and fully consolidate the position of rugby as New Zealand's 'national game' in terms of the size and passion of its following (Hyde 1995).

After enduring elements of an internal crisis during the early 1990s as rugby struggled to reconcile its supposedly amateur status with increased commercial-isation, nascent professionalism and a more direct threat from professional rugby

42   Greg Ryan

league, the rugby authorities finally embraced open professionalism in 1995. With seemingly limitless funding from the News Corporation empire of Rupert Murdoch, rugby was able to expand its national, regional and international competitions and establish an attendant media and public profile that simply dwarfed the comparatively limited domestic and international cricket programme. Moreover, the expanding rugby fixture list began to encroach on both ends of the cricket season, to the extent that cricket has struggled to secure preferred venues and acceptable playing surfaces – to say nothing of an adequate share of discretionary consumer income.[39]

Perhaps the most crucial aspect of this transformation of rugby has been the commodification of the All Blacks. Individual players and the team as a whole are central to a media and marketing campaign in which rugby followers are conditioned to expect success. Selective nostalgia has made much of the historical success of All Black teams and the obligation to the past borne by those who wear the All Black jersey. This was no more apparent than in the saturation coverage accorded the team and all aspects of its preparation prior to the 1999 Rugby World Cup. Despite very erratic form during 1998–9, the All Blacks were expected to win and there was a sense in which all 'right-thinking' New Zealanders were supposed to offer them unconditional support in their endeavour (Hope 2002). There is an obvious contrast here with the somewhat muted coverage and lack of expectation surrounding the departure of the New Zealand cricket team to cricket's own World Cup earlier in the same year. While rugby has maintained a consistently strong public following irrespective of the quality of performance, support for cricket is decidedly fickle in that its teams have to succeed in order to briefly acquire the status that All Black teams enjoy almost as of right.

Running parallel to the forces of commercialisation, there has been a shift in the conception of New Zealand identity. In broad terms, New Zealand's economic and cultural disengagement from its preoccupation with Britain by the 1970s greatly reduced the relevance of comparison and measurement, whether expressed as deference or a more assertive nationalism, against the standards of an external British or Commonwealth reference point. Moreover, the consolidation of a distinctly independent identity during the 1980s – not least in the form of a radical anti-nuclear policy that precipitated the suspension of the ANZUS alliance in 1985 (Belich 2001: 426–9; James 1986) – has perhaps produced an environment in which, without as pressing a need to prove anything to the wider world, confidence is accentuated and success becomes a legitimate and normal expectation that is almost taken for granted.

This is not to suggest that international sport has become less important to expressions of national prestige. The best efforts of those who manufacture 'hype' ensure that awareness of the connection remains strong. But the most intense expressions of the relationship are revealed not in the sort of celebrations of success and conferring of mythic status that accompanied the 1905 and 1924 All Blacks or the exploits of Sir Edmund Hillary, but through invective against failure. Failures produce an exaggerated negative reaction precisely because they represent a departure from what is expected. The defeat of the All Blacks by

France in the semi-finals of the 1999 Rugby World Cup produced far greater comment and analysis from rugby administrators and the public than their victory in 1987. Rugby followers, aided by the same media that had inflated their expectations in the first place, saw the World Cup loss as confirming an erosion of those masculine character traits and rural values that are supposedly at the core of a strong New Zealand society. As one journalist bitterly observed,

> It is sad to relate that the All Blacks have become soft, living the life of luxury week after week in posh hotels away from the real world, and becoming part of a money-making entity that seemed almost to lose sight of the team's objective – to win the World Cup. They were pampered like gods and movie stars. They became the Spice Boys.
>
> (Ryan forthcoming)

The social and sporting transformation of the past decade has inevitably altered the nexus between cricket and conceptions of national identity. Because New Zealand cricket does not possess a legacy of international achievement to match that of the All Blacks and has enjoyed only brief moments of elevation to the same heights of public expectation, reactions to its fluctuating performances during the 1990s were not as pronounced. Few would respond to the failings of New Zealand cricket teams with the sort of apoplexy widely apparent after the 1999 Rugby World Cup. But perhaps the consequence of the sense of confidence among cricket followers that derived from strong performances during the early 1980s and at the 1992 World Cup is the same double-edged sword that hangs over rugby: a certain expectation of success that has resulted in an excessively negative reaction if success does not materialise. The past decade has exhibited the same vulture-like tendency to dwell on the frailties and failings of New Zealand cricket rather than celebrating its achievements. The most intense coverage of and public interest in New Zealand cricket during the 1990s has focused not on the semi-final appearance at the 1999 World Cup, the first Test series win in England during the same year or the ICC Knockout Trophy victory in 2001, but on controversies and internal politicking – and none more than the events of the calamitous NZCC centennial season of 1994–5 in which a string of heavy defeats was compounded by acrimony between players and officials and a series of off-field indiscretions and controversies culminating in the sacking of the national coach and the suspension of three players for smoking marijuana on tour (Payne and Smith 1995: 7–8).[40]

Notwithstanding the erratic performances of New Zealand rugby teams at all levels since 1998, and a certain degree of disillusion with the impact of professional rugby, it remains the case that cricket suffers in comparison against the profile of rugby. The polarity between the two sports was most evident in reactions to a strike by New Zealand first-class cricketers amid their efforts to form a players' association in 2002. Galvanised by the substantial incomes of their rugby counterparts, the players sought a 60 per cent increase in overall remuneration and the full funding of their association by New Zealand Cricket Inc. After six

44 Greg Ryan

weeks of negotiation they secured a settlement slightly in excess of 20 per cent and no funding for the association.[41] More importantly, they entirely failed to generate public sympathy for their claims. Some critics argued that the inflated salaries of professional rugby players were no basis for negotiation. Others pointed to the sharp decline in support for domestic cricket during the 1990s and its considerable annual losses. This, coupled with the erratic performances of the New Zealand team, did not stand comparison with the demands and expectations confronting professional rugby players.[42] As one columnist lamented at the height of the strike,

> Even cricket stalwarts must now question the future of what was once our national summer game. Gone are the days when rugby and cricket shared the 12 months of the sporting year. Today rugby occupies pride of place, attracting fans for nine or ten months of the year, while crowd-strapped cricket competes against so many other summer attractions. With the prospect of many top players out of action for industrial reasons, it might be argued that this season at least we no longer have a national summer sport.[43]

It is doubtful whether the resolution of the strike will alter this perception in many minds.

The prospects for New Zealand cricket are difficult to predict. Consistently strong performances from the national team will undoubtedly boost credibility and sustain public interest. But there is also a sense in which the destiny of the game is beyond its own control, in that any cricketing achievement is more likely than ever to be subsumed by a more intense media and public focus on comparable successes in rugby. Even if the All Blacks fail, rugby can fall back on a much stronger financial base, a more comprehensive infrastructure and a range of domestic competitions that attract considerable public support irrespective of the performance of the national team. Yet there is solace for New Zealand cricket in the knowledge that at various times during the past half-century it has been able to surmount internal and external obstacles to become genuinely competitive at international level and secure a share of popular adulation at home.

Notes

1 *New Zealand Herald*, 14 March 1956, p. 10; *The Press*, 14 March 1956, p. 12.
2 See also the *Evening Post*, 18 February 2000, p. 6.
3 For differing perspectives on Wakefield, see E. Olssen (1997) and Martin (1997).
4 For a general discussion of this relationship, see Ryan (1996: 382–7).
5 Unless otherwise stated, all statistics concerning the playing record of New Zealand teams are derived from these sources.
6 See, for example, *New Zealand Cricket Council Annual Report 1959–60; 1961–62; 1962–63*.
7 The match was retrospectively granted Test status at a meeting of the Imperial Cricket Conference in 1948 (Harte 1993: 412).
8 *Evening Post*, 1 April 1946, pp. 5–6.
9 *New Zealand Herald*, 29 March 1955, p. 10.

New Zealand national identity   45

10 *Evening Post*, 5 March 1963, p. 14.
11 *Evening Post*, 17 August 1949, p. 6. See also 23 February 1960, p. 12.
12 *New Zealand Listener*, 2 April 1953, p. 4.
13 *New Zealand Listener*, 26 February 1954, p. 4.
14 *Evening Post*, 27 August 1958, p. 20.
15 *New Zealand Listener*, 7 September 1970, pp. 56–7.
16 See also *New Zealand Cricketer*, September 1973, p. 39.
17 *Dominion Sunday Times*, 18 February 1992, p. 26.
18 *The Cricket Player*, July 1978, p. 2; September 1978, pp. 2, 14–15.
19 See also *New Zealand Listener*, 12 February 1977, p. 20.
20 *New Zealand Listener*, 12 February 1977, p. 20. See also *The Cricket Player*, January 1975, p. 1.
21 *The Cricket Player*, July 1978, pp. 2–4; September 1978, pp. 2, 12–17.
22 For a corrective as it relates specifically to rugby, see Ryan (2001).
23 See also *The Cricket Player*, September 1980, p. 1; December 1982, p. 1. W. Hadlee, *The Innings of a Lifetime*, Auckland, David Bateman, 1993, pp. 202–5.
24 See also *New Zealand Cricket Council Annual Report 1989–90*.
25 *The Press*, 3 February 1981, p. 34.
26 *The Press*, 15 February 1982, p. 1; 16 February 1982, p. 34.
27 *New Zealand Listener*, 6 April 1983, p. 14; *New Zealand Cricket Council Annual Report 1984–85*.
28 *New Zealand Cricket Council Annual Report 1988–89*, p. 11; *1990–91*, p. 12.
29 For example, *Benson & Hedges World Cup: Official Souvenir Magazine and Program*, Sydney: PBL Marketing, 1991, pp. 8–9.
30 *New Zealand Cricket Council Annual Report 1992–93*; *1993–94*.
31 *Dominion Sunday Times*, 3 March 1996, p. 2; *Sunday Star Times*, 20 October 1996, p. 11.
32 For example, *The Press*, 15 May 1997, p. 27; 30 January 1998, p. 21; *Sunday Star Times*, 1 February 1998, p. 7; *Evening Standard*, 16 April 1998, p. 7; 13 November 1998, p. 24.
33 For example, *The Dominion*, 17 January 1998, p. 57; 24 August 2001, p. 23; *Sunday Star Times*, 9 April 2000, p. 2; *Evening Post*, 25 May 2001, p. 29.
34 *Sunday Star Times*, 21 February 1999, p. B2.
35 For example, see also *Evening Post*, 24 February 1999, p. 36; *Waikato Times*, 6 May 1999, p. 8; *The Press*, 12 February 2001, p. 25.
36 *Timaru Herald*, 10 March 1998, p. 4; 24 January 2000, p. 4; *Daily News*, 11 March 1998, p. 3; *The Press*, 15 April 1998, p. 29.
37 Since 1990 the New Zealand players of Maori ancestry have been Adam Parore, Heath Davis and Daryl Tuffey. Murphy Su'a, a Samoan, also played Test cricket.
38 The NZRFU suspended the players for two Test matches.
39 For example, *The Dominion*, 1 September 1999, p. 43; *New Zealand Herald*, 2 October 1999, p. 19.
40 See also *Evening Post*, 5 September 1995, p. 5.
41 For example, *New Zealand Herald*, 8 October 2002, p. 13; *Dominion Post*, 11 October 2002, p. 12; *Sunday Star Times*, 10 November 2002, p. 1; 17 November 2002, p. 7.
42 For example, the *Nelson Mail*, 24 October 2002, p. 26; *The Press*, 24 October 2002, p. 8; *Waikato Times*, 7 November 2002, p. 13; *Dominion Post*, 7 November 2002, p. 6.
43 *The Press*, 6 November 2002, p. 14.

References

Andrewes, F. (1998) 'Demonstrable virility: images of masculinity in the 1956 Springbok rugby tour of New Zealand', *International Journal of the History of Sport*, 15 (2): 119–36.

46 Greg Ryan

Belich, J. (2001) *Paradise Reforged: A History of the New Zealanders from the 1880s to the Year 2000*, Auckland: Allen Lane.

Booth, P. (1993) *Edmund Hillary: Life of a Legend*, Auckland: Hodder Moa Beckett.

Canterbury Cricket Association (1997) *The Report of the Taskforce on Club Cricket*, Christchurch: CCA.

Carman, A. H. (ed.) (1968) *Cricket Almanack of New Zealand 1968*, Wellington: Sporting Publications.

Carman, A. H. (ed.) (1973) *Cricket Almanack of New Zealand 1973*, Wellington: Sporting Publications.

Carman, A. H. (ed.) (1977) *1977 Shell Cricket Almanack of New Zealand*, Wellington: Sporting Publications.

Carman, A. H. (ed.) (1980) *1980 Shell Cricket Almanack of New Zealand*, Wellington: Sporting Publications.

Carman, A. H. and Macdonald, N. S. (eds) (1949) *Cricket Almanack of New Zealand 1949*, Wellington: Sporting Publications.

Carman, A. H. and Macdonald, N. S. (eds) (1950) *Cricket Almanack of New Zealand 1950*, Wellington: Sporting Publications.

Carman, A. H. and Macdonald, N. S. (eds) (1957) *Cricket Almanack of New Zealand 1957*, Wellington: Sporting Publications.

Carman, A. H. and Macdonald, N. S. (eds) (1963) *Cricket Almanack of New Zealand 1963*, Wellington: Sporting Publications.

Crowe, M. (1995) *Out on a Limb*, Auckland: Reed Publishing.

Devlin, P. (1987) *Victorious '80s: A Celebration of New Zealand Cricket 1980–87*, Auckland: Moa Publications.

Fougere, G. (1989) 'Sport, culture and identity: the case of rugby football', in D. Novitz and B. Willmott (eds) *Culture and Identity in New Zealand*, Wellington: GP Books.

Grey, A. H. (1994) *Aotearoa and New Zealand: A Historical Geography*, Christchurch: Canterbury University Press.

Grimes, A., Weavers, L. and Sullivan, G. (eds) (2002) *States of Mind: Australia and New Zealand 1901–2001*, Wellington: Institute of Policy Studies.

Hadlee, W. (1993) *The Innings of a Lifetime*, Auckland: David Bateman.

Hansen, P. (2000) 'Confetti of empire: the conquest of Everest in Nepal, India, Britain and New Zealand', *Comparative Studies in Society and History*, 42 (2): 307–32.

Harte, C. (1993) *A History of Australian Cricket*, London: André Deutsch.

Hignell, A. (2002) *Rain Stops Play: Cricketing Climates*, London: Frank Cass.

Hillary Commission (1996) *Survey on Sport and Physical Activity in New Zealand*, Wellington: Hillary Commission.

Hope, W. (2002) 'Whose All Blacks?', *Media, Culture and Society*, 24: 235–53.

Hyde, T. (1993) 'White men can't jump: the growing Polynesian influence in New Zealand sport', *Metro* (September).

Hyde, T. (1995) 'What's up with rugby?', *Metro* (December).

James, C. (1986) *The Quiet Revolution: Turbulence and Transition in Contemporary New Zealand*, Wellington: Allen & Unwin.

Keane, W. F. (1999) '"Ex-pats" and "poofters" rebuild the nation: 1982, Kiwi culture and the All Whites on the road to Spain', in B. Patterson (ed.) *Sport, Society and Culture in New Zealand*, Wellington: Stout Research Centre.

McLean, T. P. (1956) *Battle for the Rugby Crown*, Wellington: Sporting Publications.

Martin, G. (1997) 'Wakefield's past and futures', in The Friends of the Turnbull Library, *Edward Gibbon Wakefield and the Colonial Dream: A Reconsideration*, Wellington.

New Zealand national identity 47

Neely, D. O., King, R. P. and Payne, F. K. (1985) *Men in White: The History of New Zealand International Cricket 1894–1985*, Auckland: Moa Publications.

Olssen, E. (1997) 'Mr Wakefield and New Zealand as an experiment in post-Enlightenment experimental practice', *New Zealand Journal of History*, 31 (2): 197–218.

Palenski, R. (2000) *Champions: New Zealand Sports Greats of the Twentieth Century*, Auckland: Moa Beckett.

Payne, F. and Smith, I. (eds) (1984) *The 1984 Shell Cricket Almanack of New Zealand*, Wellington: Sporting Publications.

Payne, F. and Smith, I. (eds) (1995) *The 1995 Shell Cricket Almanack of New Zealand*, Wellington: Sporting Publications.

Payne, F. and Smith, I. (eds) (2001) *2001 New Zealand Cricket Almanack*, Auckland: Hodder Moa Beckett.

Payne, F. and Smith, I. (eds) (2002) *2002 New Zealand Cricket Almanack*, Auckland: Hodder Moa Beckett.

Phillips, J. O. C. (1984) 'Rugby, war and the mythology of the New Zealand male', *New Zealand Journal of History*, 18 (2): 83–103.

Phillips, J. O. C. (1987) *A Man's Country*, Auckland: Penguin.

Putnam, R. D. (2000) *Bowling Alone: The Collapse and Revival of American Community*, New York: Simon & Schuster.

Richards, T. (1999) *Dancing on Our Bones: New Zealand, South Africa, Rugby and Racism*, Wellington: Bridget Williams Books.

Ross, A. (1978) 'Australia and New Zealand relations: historical perspectives', in R. H. C. Hayburn (ed.) *Foreign Policy School, 1978*, Dunedin: Department of University Extension.

Ryan, G. (1996) 'New Zealand', in R. Cashman, W. Franks, J. Maxwell, B. Stoddart, A. Weaver and R. Webster (eds) *The Oxford Companion to Australian Cricket*, Melbourne: Oxford University Press.

Ryan, G. (2001) 'Rural myth and urban actuality: the anatomy of All Black and New Zealand rugby 1884–1938', *New Zealand Journal of History*, 35 (1) (April): 45–69.

Ryan, G. (2003) *The Making of New Zealand Cricket 1832–1914*, London: Frank Cass.

Ryan, G. (forthcoming) 'The end of an aura: All Black rugby and rural nostalgia since 1995'.

Sinclair, K. (1986) *A Destiny Apart*, Auckland: Allen & Unwin.

Sinclair, K. (ed.) (1987) *Tasman Relations: New Zealand and Australia, 1788–1988*, Auckland: Auckland University Press.

Templeton, M. (1998) *Human Rights and Sporting Contacts: New Zealand Attitudes to Race Relations in South Africa 1921–94*, Auckland: Auckland University Press.

Warner, P. F. (1903) *Cricket across the Seas*, London: Longmans.

World Guide 2001/2002, The (2001) Oxford: New Internationalist Publications.

3 'No one in Dolly's class at present?'

Cricket and national identity in post-apartheid South Africa

Jon Gemmell and James Hamill

In 1976 when Dr Ali Bacher, the emerging head of white South African cricket, was asked about the chances of South Africa fielding a multiracial Test team and of the emergence of black players such as Basil D'Oliveira, he announced:

> [T]o be honest, a Test team picked on merit now would be all white, but in two or three years it may be a different story. We don't have anyone in Dolly's class at present, but there are many promising Indian and coloured players and a few outstanding blacks.
>
> (Marsden 1977)

The development programmes launched during the height of the most turbulent of periods in South Africa were meant to unearth such talent. They were also seen as a means of integrating all sections of apartheid society. At the time of Nelson Mandela's release from prison in 1990, Bacher enthusiastically proclaimed that 'If we had a South African Under-15 or Under-17 team, there is no question it would be composed of players from all the population groups' (quoted in Cook 1993: 150–1).

This chapter looks at the progress made towards non-racial cricket in South Africa in the period since the end of white minority rule. Such an examination, it will be argued, is only possible if accompanied by a consideration of the economic and political forces that have shaped the 'new South Africa'. The chapter will therefore explore a number of themes:

- the role of the government in encouraging sport;
- the role of sport in the formation of national identity;
- the relationship between class and playing cricket;
- racial attitudes among South African cricketers;
- the success or otherwise of the development programmes in delivering cricketers from the disadvantaged communities onto the first-class stage.

Ultimately the chapter seeks to evaluate whether the old slogan 'no normal cricket in an abnormal society'[1] can yet be laid to rest, considering the massive inequalities that still define the country.

Colonialism

> [T]he features of classic colonialism are the hallmark of the relations that obtain between the black majority and white minority.
>
> (Statement of the Lisbon Conference of the ANC)[2]

To understand the special role that cultural phenomena have been afforded in post-apartheid South Africa, it is necessary to appreciate that attitudes to the old regime were akin to those of coloniser and colonised. As with other countries being studied in this book, colonialism has been a leading and formidable presence in shaping the history of South Africa. Although South Africa enjoyed, along with Australia and New Zealand, dominion status and greater freedoms within the overall structure of British imperialism, a colonial presence remained and was exploited by the Afrikaner nationalist movement in order to forge a political opposition to the status quo. The election victory of the National Party in May 1948 would lead to a transformation process that not only formally relegated black South Africans to an inferior status, but also undid a number of elements within society associated with the hegemony of the English-speakers. If we consider, then, 1910 (the year of self-government) and 1948 as defining moments in the historiography of colonialism in South Africa, those of us interested in cricket would add 1961, the year South Africa became a republic. Membership of the Imperial Cricket Council (the world's governing body) was dependent upon allegiance to the British Crown. The whole controversy about relations with South African cricket begins not with the subsequent 'D'Oliveira affair' (of 1968) but with this nationalist strike against English hegemony.

The purpose of this exercise, however, is a study not of the history of colonialism, but rather of its enduring effects on contemporary cricket. For that purpose, this chapter focuses primarily on the period following the ending of white rule. We are concerned with the development of cricket since the formation of the United Cricket Board of South Africa (UCB) in 1991. There is, of course, a theoretical motive for adopting such a standpoint. In South Africa the liberation movement was naturally engaged in the question of the nature of the future post-apartheid state.[3] In order to maintain a coalition that included an emerging black petit bourgeoisie and middle strata, the liberation movement flinched from a rigid socialist orthodoxy, although its rhetoric and sloganising certainly drew upon the vocabulary of socialism. Instead, the South African Communist Party (SACP), the formal ally of the African National Congress (ANC), formulated a strategy known as 'internal colonialism'. This theoretical approach perceived the white apartheid regime as colonisers and so allowed for an alliance of the workers' movement with the forces of nationalism. 'Colonialism is not monolithic', declared the Statement of the ANC's Lisbon Conference in 1977. Africa has experienced 'differing forms of colonial domination', which have shared one central characteristic: 'the denial of the African people of their rights of national self-determination'.[4] In the SACP's two-stage theory, national liberation would precede socialism, but it would be an important step down the path to that

50 Jon Gemmell and James Hamill

ultimate goal. The economic pillars of the 1955 Freedom Charter, the movement's principal pre-1990 philosophical statement – which contained a specific reference to nationalisation as well as vaguer formulations such as 'the people shall share in the country's wealth' and 'the land shall be shared among those who work it' – remained impossible to separate from the 'aspects of national liberation struggle'.[5]

This study is one of cricket in South Africa following the demise of white rule. There were no meaningful steps towards socialism in that period. As a critic of the 'two-stage' theory pointed out, fighting racial oppression challenges 'capitalism in its present form' but 'does not guarantee its fundamental transformation'.[6] Cricket has developed in a country whose economic structure has remained largely intact. This reaffirms that a nationalist ideology has always tended to lean more towards the political rather than the economic and, militant rhetoric apart, ultimately the liberation struggle appears to have been conducted against the precise form that capitalism assumed in South Africa, namely a racialised and discriminatory model, rather than against capitalism *per se*. It is within such a setting that the development of cricket in the post-apartheid era is examined.

Reconciliation and national identity

> [T]he most significant and important [day] in the history of South African cricket
> (Ali Bacher on the formation of the UCB, quoted in Bishop 1991: 12)

The new democratic South Africa faces the same problem as other states in the global community, namely, that of finding common factors around which it can unify its disparate inhabitants. The diverse South African population combines any number of different ideological, ethnic, linguistic and racial interests. This 'rainbow nation' emerged from a sustained period of turmoil unprecedented in the contemporary world, with the possible exception of the ongoing conflict in Israel/Palestine. It immediately confronted a period during which two mighty and suspicious powers, the economic and the political, based on racial foundations, struggled to assert themselves as key shapers of the social fabric.

A politically diverse population, including hard-line Afrikaners, Zulu ethnic nationalists, liberal whites, coloured communities, descendants of South Asian immigrants, and both urban and traditional Africans, would prove difficult to unite around political notions such as 'national liberation' and 'democracy'. Democracy was something of a double-edged sword in this respect; the downside was that in a racially divided society it threatened to entrench the dominance of the majority's favoured party, namely the ANC. On a more positive note, a democratic system that would allow *all* political formations some space and scope to develop and a democratic infrastructure embracing a separation of powers, a Bill of Rights, a free press, an independent judiciary and a vibrant civil society would help temper that one-party dominance. Predictably, the first free elections, in 1994 and 1999, saw the electorate divide along racial lines, indicating that ideological differences will take generations to mould into any form of national

National identity in South Africa 51

identity free of racial and ethnic undertones. Symbols such as the flag and the national anthem have proved to be areas that, in the immediate post-1994 period at least, have ignited passions, and so while claiming to be symbolic and representative of the new South Africa, they could not initially claim to be *truly* national. Sport, however, was something that could potentially draw people from all sectors of society together. Cricket was in an advantageous position to assist in this process. It had a traditionally strong following in the English-speaking, coloured and Indian populations; was becoming more popular within the Afrikaner community (four of the 1992 World Cup squad – Wessels, Cronje, Bosch and Donald – had Afrikaans as their first language); and had always attracted players of African descent. No other major sport could claim such a reservoir of potential from which to build a future nationally representative team.

Cricket was the first sport to benefit from the relaxation of sanctions against South Africa. This was attributable to the timing of the 1992 World Cup following President F. W. de Klerk's historic political initiative of February 1990, the subsequent release of Nelson Mandela and other ANC activists from prison, and the beginning of negotiations for a new post-apartheid constitutional dispensation. Sport offered the political elite an opportunity to fashion a national identity representative of all people. President de Klerk even exploited South African participation in the cricket World Cup by holding a white referendum in March 1992, while the competition was still taking place, in which he sought the approval of the white electorate for his power-sharing strategy, threatening to 'bring the boys back home' if he was unsuccessful. (In fact, he secured a resounding 68 per cent 'Yes' vote, a figure probably swollen by the cricket factor.) The ANC leadership, with the power to offer South Africans an entry ticket to the World Cup, used sport to anchor its reconciliation process.

In December 1990 the black South African Cricket Board (SACB) and the white South African Cricket Union agreed, at a meeting chaired by the ANC's Steve Tshwete, to merge as the United Cricket Board of South Africa.[7] Their initial statement of intent included a number of points that established the political role that cricket would play in the redevelopment of the nation. Point A set the UCB the task of endeavouring 'to achieve peace and harmony in cricket in our country'. The new body hoped to 'formulate strategies to redress urgently imbalances in regard to separate educational systems, sponsorships and facilities'. The most ambitious and directly political statement, however, was its aspiration to 'contribute, through cricket, to the creation of a just society in South Africa where everybody democratically has a common say and a common destiny'.[8] This document subordinated the task of creating a great national side to a more important role: the reconstruction of the nation, built upon the notion of equality of opportunity. Geoff Dakin, the UCB's first president, described the establishment of a unified cricket board as 'a catalyst for all other sporting codes to bring about a new South Africa' (Day 1991: 10). This optimistic theme would continue as an integral part of cricketing culture in the new South Africa. At the 1994 annual meeting, for example, UCB president Krish Mackerdhuj's address stated that cricket would play a leading role in 'the social uplift of communities'

52   Jon Gemmell and James Hamill

(Owen-Smith 1994: 56).[9] At the 2003 World Cup, hosted by South Africa, the prevailing theme was one of black empowerment.[10]

It is clear, then, that South African cricket would remain fully engaged in and shaped by the political process. This actually worked to the advantage of those who had previously decried the relationship between sport and politics. Raymond White, chairman of the Transvaal Cricket Board (a man who had previously held the ANC to be a terrorist organisation and who believed the SACP wanted to create another 'Lebanon' in South Africa), accepted that without ANC support South Africa's readmission to the ICC would be 'inconceivable' (White 1991: 3). The case for readmission was supported by a letter to all foreign ministers of the ICC full member countries from the then head of the ANC's International Affairs Department – Thabo Mbeki.

Considering the UCB's statement of intent, and its association with the political process, just how could cricket assist in 'the creation of a just society in South Africa'? Initially it was seen as a vehicle to assist in the reconciliation process. White South Africans were encouraged to embrace democratic and 'normal' civilian life in return for the maintenance of their living standards (and their disproportionate economic power, at least in the short to medium term) and the lifting of their ostracism within the international community. In the long term the ANC sought to consolidate its regime around a notion of national identity. In this way, then, a just society would be one that became legitimised in the eyes of its disparate parts. As Lincoln Allison has noted, 'sport has a complex and important interaction with nationality and the phenomenon of nationalism' (1993: 4–5). It allows for the symbols, icons and anthems to be displayed and performed. Conversely, it provides an arena within which these national symbols can be challenged and reformed. So, while the whites secured their return to international cricket, they did so under a cricket authority represented not by the Springbok, but by South Africa's flower, the Protea, and with two national anthems: *Die Stem* and *Nkosi Sikeleli' Afrika* (although the latter gradually began to supplant the former as the 'true' national anthem).

Was this merely the triumph of image over substance? A just society and the fostering of a national identity will require more than supposedly unifying symbols such as anthems and flags. A just society is one that allows each South African to reach his or her potential in every field of endeavour, including sport. This requires not only political changes but economic changes too, especially in the area of poverty relief. So, was a process of national reconciliation unachievable without fundamental socio-economic transformation, as Thabo Mbeki would subsequently argue? Probably. Hassan Howa, the veteran campaigner against sport in an 'abnormal society', complained that the drive towards amalgamation was premature and 'happening with indecent haste and disregard for the realities of South African life' (Owen-Smith 1992: 53). He protested that the first ever Indian visit in 1992–3 was 'dishonest', as the South African team 'represented only those players who enjoyed the great benefits of racial discrimination. It was not a South African team but a white South African team' (quoted in Desai *et al.* 2002: 20). Rushdi Magiet, the first black convener of the South African selection

National identity in South Africa 53

committee, conceded that 'a lot of our community did not agree with unification' (Owen-Smith 1999: 46). To Nelson Mandela, however, integrated sport assisted the country's broader political momentum. Late into the whole sports boycott issue, the ANC enjoyed the luxury of being able to dismiss long-held positions:

> We have extremists who say there can be no normal sport in a racial society. But it seems to me that sport is sport, and quite different from politics. If sportsmen here take steps to remove the colour bar, then we must take that into account.
>
> (Nelson Mandela, quoted in Ahmed 1991: 9)

Respect for the moratorium on international cricket, agreed by both parties in the unity talks, was now sacrificed in order to satisfy the 'changing conditions and requirements of the wider liberation struggle' (Desai *et al.* 2002: 364–7).[11] Although Nelson Mandela's tendency to develop policy 'on the hoof', and to indulge in diplomatic freelancing without fully testing opinion in the ANC as a whole, became a standard feature of post-1990 South African politics, on this occasion the ANC, including Steve Tshwete, its chief spokesperson on sporting issues and subsequently Sports Minister in the 1994–9 government, backed the new approach. That said, it might be asked if this position was really so different from that advocated by the so-called bridge-builders of the 1980s who urged the international community to ignore politics and allow South Africa back into the fold – much to the dismay of the ANC, then tied to a position Mandela now characterised as 'extremist'?

Ten years on and the reconciliation process still generates a fierce controversy. Just how far have black players advanced during this decade? Many have been provided with opportunities that were legally denied them in the past. But is this enough? Has the reconciliation process proved beneficial only to those who might have prospered under the old regime? It has certainly been seen in such a way. A leading article in the South African *Independent* complained that 'all the "reconciliation", "forgiveness", "understanding", "compromise", and the "rainbow-nation" stuff has come from black cricketers and administrators' (Independent 1998). This raises a number of questions: is there peace and harmony in South African cricket? How have the imbalances been redressed, and, more importantly, how far has the ANC gone in delivering the 'just society'?

Targets

> South Africa has been a broken society. We need to do our little bit in cricket to bring stability back to South African life. The whole of our cricket and country is in a fragile state.
>
> (Percy Sonn[12])

> Both the rugby and cricket national teams remain lily-white, despite their much publicised development programmes in previously disadvantaged communities.

54 Jon Gemmell and James Hamill

> Those who had been picked and had proved themselves were constantly forced to warm the substitutes' bench and carry drinks to the other players.
>
> (Lulu Xingwana[13])

A national identity is usually defined in terms of common origin, ethnicity or cultural ties (Miscevic 2001). South Africa, though, has been forged out of a number of distinct ethnic and racial identities, reinforced through an apartheid system rooted in the notion of separateness. This creates obvious difficulties and problems for the promoters of nationhood. For the nationalist, the claims of the nation usually supersede those of other contenders for authority and loyalty. But is such an allegiance possible in a society that has been legally stratified according to ethnic and racial origin? In a country as starkly divided as South Africa, though, perhaps the idea of 'nation' is one of the few areas that can unite people with a sense of common interest (this is certainly an area in which sport can become involved, as witnessed famously at the 1995 Rugby World Cup, where Mandela wore the Springbok shirt at the cultural capital of the Afrikaner). This liberal interpretation of the merits of nationalism ignores, of course, the questions of power and justice. However, the nation has proved to be an apparatus around which the ANC could attempt to reconcile and then transform South Africa. Its project, therefore, has been to overturn a social consciousness that was based on division, and attempt to define a common identity as the basis for the creation of a non-racial sense of nationhood.

Under apartheid, the South African Cricket Board (SACB) argued that black cricketers would not be able to compete on an equal footing with their white counterparts because of the vast social and economic differences. Whites attended the best schools, took the higher-paid jobs, enjoyed superior accommodation and played sports on the best grounds. These inequalities were enshrined in law. South Africa was a starkly divided society, with social provision determined by the gruesome racial hierarchies of apartheid. This was the form assumed by colonialism in South Africa. Following relaxation of some of the 'petty apartheid' regulations in the 1970s and 1980s, mixed cricket could at last be permitted. However, how could individuals who had been categorised as inferior and denied access to the privileges of the 'white club' compete on an equal footing with white cricketers? Such an argument formed the crux of the position 'no normal sport in an abnormal society'.

National identity is supposedly characterised by a sense of cultural homogeneity. It is not possible in a society where status and inequality are primarily determined by skin colour. The reconstruction of post-apartheid society, then, called for measures that would bestow a sense of empowerment on the disadvantaged communities. Positive discrimination or affirmative action would not be an end in itself but the chosen instrument for the creation of a fairer and more equal non-racial social structure. The need for such a policy was explicitly recognised in the Constitution of the Republic of South Africa Act, 1996, in the Bill of Rights, which states, 'Equality includes the full and equal enjoyment of all rights and freedoms. To promote the achievement of equality, legislative and other measures designed to protect or advance persons, or categories of persons, disadvantaged by unfair discrimination may be taken.'[14]

Elsewhere in the constitution there are a number of references to 'redressing the imbalances of the past to achieve broad representation' – for example, in local government, the judiciary, public service, and so on.[15] There is a clear constitutional recognition, therefore, that the discrimination of the past was based on race, gender and the skewed allocation of resources and that it needs to be redressed. Ideological discourse therefore recognises diversity while attempting to account for suppressed histories. This recognition of difference (as opposed to its celebration and enforcement in the apartheid era) forms part of the process of reconciliation, and thus is the starting point for the development of a sense of national identity (captured in the ANC's phrase 'unity in diversity'), for affirmative action is a mechanism through which the government hopes to normalise society, and by doing so to begin the process of merging its various parts. That commitment to affirmative action was taken forward with the passage of the 1998 Employment Equity Act, which compels companies employing over 50 people to take measures to ensure that previously disadvantaged groups – blacks, women and the disabled – are adequately represented in the workforce. The ultimate objective of the legislation is to encourage companies, on pain of financial penalty, to bring their workforce – from shopfloor to boardroom – into line with the demographic composition of the population as a whole.[16]

How would the affirmative action initiatives affect cricket? The ANC's 1994 *Reconstruction and Development Programme* (RDP) stated that sport was 'an integral part of reconstructing and developing a healthier society'. This could not be left entirely in the hands of the sporting bodies, though; the government also had a role to play.[17] The UCB was charged with encouraging the disadvantaged communities to take up the sport. Shaun Pollock, the former captain of the national team, commented that 'we have to create a new culture in which the youngsters [in the townships] want to be associated with cricket' (Agnew 1998: 30). The fact that Pollock had made such a comment in 1998 indicated that progress at the top level had been slow. The development programmes were introducing players of colour to cricket of a higher standard, but it would take more than the few years Ali Bacher had predicted before the national side would be representative of the nation as a whole. If political forces were exploiting sport, they were failing.

In December 1997 Thabo Mbeki became ANC president as Mandela, still the state president, began his carefully choreographed withdrawal from the political stage. Mbeki, as ANC president, as an increasingly assertive deputy president of the country, and as state president from June 1999 has effectively discarded the harmonious mood music of inter-racial reconciliation with which Mandela was so closely associated in the period 1994–7. Instead, he has chosen to emphasise the need for a thoroughgoing project of socio-economic 'transformation' – the latter being the key buzzword of the Mbeki era – as the only route to political and social stability, to *true* reconciliation, and to a genuinely non-racial society. Mbeki's politics gave much greater attention to the question of race and of

56 Jon Gemmell and James Hamill

continuing racial inequality, and whites have been encouraged (often in quite apocalyptic language) to embrace the transformation project 'consciously and voluntarily' or else risk widespread social upheaval. Mbeki's message to whites has been consistently stark: 'too little change is a threat' and 'non-racialism means that inequities based on race must be removed' (Southscan 1997). In November 1997, one month before assuming the presidency of the ANC, he put it in characteristically blunt terms for *The Economist*:

> The white population I don't think has quite understood the importance of this challenge . . . if you were speaking of national reconciliation based on the maintenance of the status quo, because you did not want to move at a pace that frightens the whites, it means that you wouldn't carry out the task of transformation. You would not produce reconciliation on that basis. It might look so to the people who benefited from apartheid – everybody's forgiven us, nobody's after nationalising our swimming pools. It isn't, because you have the anger that would be boiling among the black people. So you've got to transform the society.
>
> (The Economist 1997)

This more impatient and abrasive racial discourse has inevitably proved controversial. Many whites have come to view Mbeki as something of a racial sabre-rattler when compared to his more emollient predecessor, a leader who seeks to scapegoat minorities for the ANC government's own failings. For his part, Mbeki considers his approach to be an honest attempt to reacquaint white South Africans with the grotesque divisions of South African society which the 'rainbow nation' rhetoric may have obscured but had certainly not removed. He also felt that whites needed to be disabused of the notion that merely by acquiescing in the political formalities of transition they had more than met their obligations to the new South Africa. Whatever Mbeki's precise motivation, these periodic interventions have undoubtedly contributed to a renewed racial polarisation of South African political debate.[18]

Cricket became embroiled in this process through the visit of the West Indies side in 1998. The West Indian team were held in special affection by the cricket-minded among the African population. They had shown that the African athlete was every bit as capable as his white counterpart. Moreover, the West Indies had discarded the shackles of colonialism and, by adopting an overtly political stance, had conquered the cricket world.[19] In the townships, role models came in the form of Brian Lara and Curtley Ambrose rather than Shaun Pollock and Hansie Cronje. The tactless selection of an all-white XI for the first Test led to obvious criticisms about the racial imbalance of the national side. The UCB responded with a Transformation Charter that confirmed its commitment to the government's strategy of redressing the imbalances of the past through the principles of positive discrimination. Targets would be set for both national and provincial sides. Wherever possible, South Africa would not be represented by an all-white XI again. Significantly, considering subsequent events, when the

National identity in South Africa 57

outcome of a series was decided, remaining games would provide opportunities to promote players of colour into the national team (The Cricketer 1999).

These measures were supplemented by a UCB initiative that sought to transform cricket by seeking racial parity in all features of the sport by 2002. General targets were in place for school, tertiary education and provincial cricket. The wider game was also considered, with guidelines concerning the appointment of more people of colour as ground staff, umpires, managers, scorers, coaches and administrators.[20] The UCB was even considering a scheme to enable the training of aspirant black cricket journalists. Bacher said that 'in three years' time, if [transformation] happens, then we tear up the [development] document. Our aim is to find parity and then let the future be dictated by natural forces' (Cricinfo 1999). Resistance came from the national captain, the coach and the UCB president, Ray White, who warned that cricket in South Africa was 'fracturing along racial lines' and that the UCB had become 'little more than an organ of the ANC'.[21] In all probability, the measures were adopted by a reluctant Cricket Board to prevent the government, in an election year, from acting first. Despite its assigned role in the process of reconciliation, the UCB and ANC have remained uneasy bedfellows.

The controversy accompanying targets reached boiling point at the turn of 2002 when the UCB president, Percy Sonn, intervened in the third Test against Australia, and demanded that the selectors pick the coloured Justin Ontong rather than the selected player Jacques Rudolph. The South Africans were two-nil down in a series of three, so the moment was opportune to select a player for the future (a criterion both fulfilled). The No. 6 'all-rounder' Lance Klusener was being dropped. According to Sonn, Ontong was selected to cover the late middle-order/all-rounder's position; Rudolph was cover for the top three. Sonn said that including Rudolph, whether as a No. 6 or to allow someone else to drop down the order, 'amounted to exclusion of a person of colour who has the right to be given the opportunity'. He added, 'If there is an opportunity for a person of colour to represent his country then we must make sure that he does get that opportunity. I regarded that as not having been complied with'.[22] Sonn followed up by expressing a desire for the South African side to be more representative of the country at large, and said that it was time to increase the number of players of colour selected to two. There was a sense of disbelief from the media, both in South Africa and overseas. The former captain Clive Rice was among those who criticised the position of the UCB president. The reconciliatory and transformative role that cricket had been allocated seemed forgotten. All that mattered was the principle that selection should come from the best available, regardless of the social and economic circumstances that determine who gets selected and who is 'the best available'. This debate reflected the time-honoured intellectual and political struggle between two competing concepts of equality: the classically liberal notion of equality of opportunity, anchored in equality of treatment before the law, and the more radical attempt to address the socio-economic inequalities that are held to make a genuine equality of opportunity impossible.

58 Jon Gemmell and James Hamill

Economic inequalities

> The distribution of income and wealth in South Africa may be the most unequal in the world.
>
> (*Poverty and Inequality in South Africa*[23])

At the heart of the philosophical opposition to multiracial cricket under apartheid was the belief that everyday normal activities, such as sport, could not be such amid the abnormalities of the wider racial economic and political structure. A policy statement by South African Council on Sport (SACOS) in 1980 pointed out that 'there is an inter-dependence between a society and its sporting system. Sport is a by-product of society. It reflects the spiritual wealth of a society. Or it reflects its political decay'.[24] Poverty was racially defined. It was expressed through the education system, the labour market and poor housing. Each of these affected the development of cricket among South Africa's disadvantaged populations. Even though the white cricketing authorities eventually made approaches to the black communities, there could be no parity of contest. How could schoolchildren compete if the one side had been coached by ex-first-class players and the other could not even afford textbooks, let alone cricket bats?

The roots of these abnormalities were economic. With just 5 per cent of the population (white) owning 88 per cent of the wealth and an African unemployment rate that approached 50 per cent, apartheid South Africa was one of the most unequal states on the global stage (Murray 1994: 28). Class came to take on a form that was distinctly racial. An individual's identity would be first determined by his or her racial grouping, and under the bantustan or 'grand apartheid' policy of H. F. Verwoerd's premiership (1958–66) a further layer of ethnic division was added with the creation of distinct territorial units in which each ethnic group would be encouraged to exercise 'self-government' up to and including full 'independence'. This 'multinational policy'[25] ensured that no sense of national identity was nurtured, no actual sense of being South African. Indeed, the apartheid government envisaged South Africa developing as a loose confederation of sovereign states in which, for the black population, a narrow ethnic nationalism would be prioritised over the broader pan-tribal nationalism championed by organisations such as the ANC. This actually created problems for the apartheid regime, for, beyond those obvious accomplices in the creation of the bantustan system such as the Matanzimas, Sebes and Mpephus, it lacked reliable allies within the black communities. Requiring support for constitutional change and socio-economic reforms that might prolong the longevity of white minority control, the regime set about the task of manufacturing and co-opting an African middle class to serve as a buffer against revolutionary change. The expansion of this middle class in the 1980s resulted in a 40 per cent increase in income within the wealthiest fifth of African households. This was not redistribution from the wealthier white sector to the less prosperous African community, however, but intra-distribution within the African population itself.

National identity in South Africa 59

To allow for such a pattern, the poorest two-fifths of African households experienced a real income decline of 40 per cent during the same period (Booth 1998: 208).

Today it is argued that because the political apparatus of apartheid has been dismantled, South African sports teams can be chosen on ability alone. It is a proposition, of course, that assumes that South Africa is finally a 'meritocracy'. It is not. For most whites the new South Africa is, economically at least, little different from the old one – the very point that has informed Mbeki's more overtly racial style of politics and his commitment to 'transformation', as discussed in the previous section. They have kept their maids, houses and cooks and continue to enjoy a good standard of living. They send their children to the best schools. The only difference today is that they now live in a democracy. Politically, everyone has the vote and enjoys legal equality. This formal equality, though, fails to take account of *opportunity*, which is still largely determined by social (and of course racial) circumstance, even if Mbeki rather oversimplifies the situation, and gives inadequate attention to the emergence of a more affluent section of the black community, when claiming that South Africa is 'two nations – one white and wealthy, the other black and poor' (see Southscan 1998).[26] Here lies the essential problem: South Africa has *never* been a society in which merit was the sole criterion for the selection of professional sports teams.

South African schools cricket has always been of a high standard, and many leading players went to the top private schools.[27] These were fee-paying establishments that by definition only took those from comfortable economic backgrounds. At Hilton College ('the Eton of South Africa'), for example, the journalist Jonathan Rice wrote of 3,200 acres of fields for 470 boys – seven acres a boy (1993: 59). These pupils had role models to look up to as well: portraits of famous old boys such as M. J. Procter and R. A. MacLean hung on the walls of the Hilton pavilion. They also had the chance to play in the three or four XIs that could be fielded at senior or colts level. Most black children are excluded from these institutions, if not today by racial segregation, then by social and material circumstance. If the Hilton case sounds a little remarkable, consider the Vryburg High School, which raised its fees to a level of 1,200 rand a year (£120) – the equivalent of two months' wages for many African families (Guardian 1999). South African secondary schools remain in a dilapidated condition and these are the schools attended by the great mass of African children. Elias Mashile, the principal of the Morris Isaacson school (birthplace of the Soweto uprising), highlights a desperate situation: 'I have 1,000 pupils; we have 30 teachers, which is a good ratio.' Up to 40 per cent of secondary school teachers are under-qualified, some not even having passed 'matric' (equivalent to a British A level) (Duval Smith 1998). The black pace bowler, Makaya Ntini, recalled how there had been no kit or equipment at his village school (Owen-Smith 1998b: 31).[28] The school of his colleague Mfuneko Ngam, on the outskirts of Port Elizabeth, did not even have a cricket pitch. It still doesn't (Prior 2000). Despite the many changes and the granting of full citizenship, the black child's life chances remain poor in comparison to his/her white compatriot.

60 *Jon Gemmell and James Hamill*

Today there are areas of South Africa that appear to have missed the dismantling of apartheid. The conditions of the townships Crossroads and Khayelitsha were described by Will Hutton (1999): 'Desperate, incredible poverty; little shacks that provide one room for a family; dirt as the floor, corrugated iron as the ceiling. People having to defecate in a hole in the ground. The unemployment. . . . Five years into the ANC government the apartheid geography of South Africa remains surprisingly little touched, and the poverty of the townships virtually unchanged.' Half a million jobs have been lost since 1993. Naomi Klein wrote in 2001 how wages for the poorest 40 per cent have dropped by 21 per cent. Poor areas have seen their water costs go up by 55 per cent, electricity by as much as 400 per cent. Many drink polluted water, leading to a cholera outbreak that infected 100,000 people. In Soweto, 20,000 homes have their electricity cut off each month (Klein 2002: 109). It was only in 2001 that the combined income of black South Africans (almost 80 per cent of the population) surpassed that of whites (10.5 per cent of the population) (The Economist 2001). The increase in the crime rate has principally affected the black population (even if it is the fact that crime has reached white suburbia since 1994 that has given it added newsworthiness), while over the past ten years, spending on private security has increased 12-fold to 12 billion rand (£1.1 billion) – more than three times the housing budget of 1999–2000 (Younge 2001).

Although the government is fully committed to a programme of economic and social development, that programme is proceeding within a highly restrictive policy framework imposed by the neo-liberal economic orthodoxy to which the ANC government now fully subscribes, with its emphasis on tight public expenditure control, falling budget deficits and high real interest rates, aimed at stabilising national debt and producing low inflation. The macroeconomic policy introduced in June 1996 and known as the Growth, Employment and Redistribution (GEAR) strategy – a self-imposed Structural Adjustment Programme in effect – openly commits the government to a programme of privatisation or the 'restructuring of state assets', to deploy the ANC's more delicate description, a diminishing economic role for the state generally, the removal of tariff barriers, the lifting of exchange controls, and the introduction of more flexible labour markets. All this is designed to reassure capital at home, the financial markets, the international financial institutions and the leading Western governments of South Africa's economic 'responsibility' and its commitment to the creation of an investor-friendly climate. The price for such a strategy, however, has been paid by the very population groups that the ANC claimed would be lifted out of deprivation through the implementation of the RDP, which GEAR has effectively supplanted. That point has been repeatedly made by GEAR's critics on the South African left, particularly the Confederation of South African Trade Unions (COSATU), the ANC's formal political ally, for which GEAR is a shameless ideological retreat from the promise of the RDP, a recipe for the preservation of the inequalities currently disfiguring South African society, and a betrayal of the ANC's own impoverished constituency.[29] This begs the question: does South Africa now qualify as 'normal' in the old sense of the term? The term 'equal

National identity in South Africa   61

opportunities' refers to the removal of obstacles that stand in the way of personal development (Heywood 1994: 231). The obstacle of poverty still confines an African population to a citizenship that at best is second-class, whatever the formal position. Makaya Ntini, for instance, was selected for Border's Under-15 team, quite an achievement in itself. At the time the only footwear he possessed for playing cricket was a pair of 'takkies', which flip-flopped as he ran in to bowl. It remains the case that on current projections, and notwithstanding the emergence of a new stratum of more affluent blacks who have benefited from the government's commitment to black economic empowerment, skin colour will still largely determine the chances of playing sports at a successful level in South Africa, and while that is the case, there can be no common destiny.

Racism

> I'm not prepared to apologise for what I said because I believe it is part of cricketing terminology
>
> (Brian Macmillan, quoted in Mail and Guardian 1999b)

The extent of a homogenising national identity can be measured in a number of different ways. In a society where social, economic and political status has been structured according to race and ethnicity, it seems logical to explore the continuation of previous values. Racism in South Africa remains an emotive issue and one that will long remain on the political agenda, as people are unlikely to determine their allegiances without a sense of history. Decades of socialisation cannot be dismantled overnight. A World Cup Music Committee, for example, can still be divided over a tournament's anthem because it sounds too 'African' (Independent 2002). Racism still exists, and segregation can be enforced using methods such as separate teaching for Afrikaans- and English-speaking children in schools. This works its way into sports. The Vryburg High School, for example, at the centre of controversy for the way it has tried to exclude pupils of colour, said that it did not have the money to buy a ball for the football team, which is exclusively black; yet it spent £2,000 on 'white' sports, including rugby and golf (Guardian 1999).

Separate ethnic and racial identities, especially if built upon a feeling of injustice, will prevent the emergence of a sense of identity to which all groups can subscribe. Historically, black South Africans shunned the national sports teams on account of their association with apartheid. They will continue to do so if they feel that sport remains 'a last bastion of white dominance'.[30] A number of incidents in recent years have tarnished the efforts of those who have been concerned with the integration of cricket. Perhaps they might be dismissed as simply ignorant and insensitive. However, they do show that sensitivity is dictated by a historical value system formulated within a racial environment, and that attitudes cannot be immediately eradicated. The young spinner Paul Adams, for example, earned himself the nickname 'Goggo' for his unorthodox action, when he first broke onto the scene. In Afrikaans, 'goggo' refers to a small gnat-like insect

62   Jon Gemmell and James Hamill

that has arms and legs thrashing everywhere. Some coloured cricketers took exception to this association with clumsiness, a throwback to an era in which the temperament of black cricketers was questioned by their white counterparts. The spinner Pat Symcox was accused of using abusive language towards spectators of Indian origin during a match against Pakistan in Durban in February 1998. Twelve months later, while playing for Western Province in the SuperSport Series game against Natal in Cape Town, the international all-rounder Brian Macmillan suggested that left-arm spinner Claude Henderson bowl a 'coolie creeper' (a slow ball rolled along the ground) to Ashraf Mall, who is of Asian descent. A 'coolie' is a derogatory term used to stereotype the Asian population as being subservient and sycophantic. The UCB found the ex-international all-rounder guilty of contravening its code of behaviour and he was severely reprimanded. At the same hearing, Alan Badenhorst was suspended for the remainder of the year for using crude and abusive language when he referred to a player as a 'half-bred kaffir' during the Bowl match between Eastern Province 'B' and Griqualand West (Mail and Guardian 1999a, b).

The former national captain Kepler Wessells claims that racism is 'a problem that people have gotten used to', and that it isn't 'a problem any more'.[31] While racial discrimination has been formally removed from South African social life, it does not mean that deeply entrenched racial attitudes have been cleansed. Considering some of the comments from the Minister of Sport, Ngconde Balfour, against the UCB's move to abandon targets, Wessells' remarks suggest at the very least a lack of understanding and sensitivity, but they perhaps reflect what the white cricketing establishment believes. Yet it has to be understood that those to whom racist remarks are directed reserve for themselves the right to measure the offensiveness of such language and to determine when the issue of racism should no longer be considered a problem. Those who decry political correctness should take heed of this.

Multiracial or non-racial?

> South Africa is not a normal country at the moment and it is something we must all understand. If we don't move forward we stand the very real risk of having political protests at our cricket grounds again, and they will be made by cricket-loving people.
>
> (Ali Bacher, quoted in Owen-Smith 1998a)

Cricket was assigned a distinctive role in the development of the 'rainbow nation'. In contrast to white sporting values based on notions of competition and victory, the project for cricket was one of reconciliation and opportunity. If the nation's sports teams reflected the social and ethnic fabric then perhaps they might act as a unifier around the concept of nationhood. While it remained a nationalist ideal, it was a nationalism based on the forging of component parts, rather than the promotion and domination of one particular group – the form that nationalism had traditionally taken. The re-emergence of a political ethnic nationalism would

National identity in South Africa 63

be extremely divisive and have the potential to devastate the South African social landscape, as it had previously threatened to do between 1990 and 1993. In order to avoid further fragmentation, the social and economic environment needs to reflect real opportunities for all people, regardless of skin colour. Recognising and accommodating the distinctiveness of ethnic cultures is a worthy attribute of any political regime, but history has shown that exclusiveness and insularity on the part of certain groups, especially when accompanied by a sense of injustice and grievance, will ultimately lead to conflict.

On its readmission to the international fold, South Africa was keen to show that it could develop cricket within the disadvantaged communities. Young black players such as Abraham Sinclair, Donald Letlhake and David Makopanele were sent to Australia to receive coaching. The same Makopanele when younger had had to walk three kilometres to practise his game (Roebuck 1994: 12). The *1993 Protea Assurance Cricket Annual of South Africa* records the inclusion, on merit, of a black player in the South African Schools XI for 1992–3, together with a young coloured batsmen from Cape Town – Herschelle Gibbs, now a celebrated Test match player. At the same time an under-15 South African Schools XI that took part in a tournament against their English equivalents included five players of colour, 'all chosen on merit and all performing with skill' (Crowley 1994: 21). According to the Schools' National convener (the former Springbok captain Jackie McGlew), schoolboy cricket in South Africa is 'looking extremely healthy, and with the development programme it's looking even healthier' (Alfred 1994: 20).

Towards the end of the 1990s, though, these players were not coming through, as anticipated, at the national level. The ANC described the side selected to play against the West Indies at the beginning of December 1998 as 'lily-white'. While acknowledging that many young black players had demonstrated great potential in the fields of cricket, the ANC questioned why 'nothing has been done by . . . cricket associations to help them develop to levels where they would be considered for selection in the national teams'.[32] Steve Tshwete announced in 1999 that he felt he was unable to continue to support the national team in its current set-up. 'I am worried we will be sending white teams to the rugby and cricket world cups this year. If this is the case, it will be difficult for me to support them' (Hawkey 1999: 40). He added that the government was considering a special commission with intervening powers to promote black players into the national XI. Ali Bacher, managing director of the UCB, agreed that 'the national team must be a team of colour' (ibid.: 40). This was an astonishing acceptance of the failure to fulfil his vision after the formation of the UCB. Cricket, it appears, was failing in its historical role of reconciler.

Tshwete's comments aroused the disdain of the UCB president, Ray White, who told politicians to keep out of the business of cricket. 'As far as interference is concerned,' he announced, 'we don't want it and we don't need it' (ibid.: 41). The ANC, however, a decade after the dismantling of apartheid and by this time into its second term in office, could see that the remnants of the old system were still rooted in sport – in selection, coaching and administration. South Africa

64 *Jon Gemmell and James Hamill*

is still represented by teams that fail to reflect the racial and ethnic composition of the nation. True, it is no longer the preserve of English-speaking whites; Afrikaners have become regular members of the national side, providing the first two captains (after Clive Rice's brief stay at the helm in India in 1991) Kepler Wessels and Hansie Cronje, and also arguably South Africa's greatest post-apartheid player, Alan Donald. Ex-South Africa player Eddie Barlow has pointed out that in the 1960s Afrikaners had no cricketing facilities and no cricketing culture (1995: 6). Such a leap forward would not have been possible without the substantial economic benefits derived from apartheid. This suggests that given a sufficient investment of resources by the state, a community's potential for participation in almost any sport can be massively expanded. We return then to the question of economics, at the heart of the 'no normal sport in an abnormal society' position. Facilities, especially in the schools, are essential if players are to progress. Quick-cricket is only a substitute for the real thing and will serve little benefit if it is the only form of the sport that people play. The non-racial society envisaged by those early SACB supporters was one in which equality of opportunity did not just mean the right to vote, but was inextricably bound up with economic justice. Despite the gradual emergence of a more affluent section of the black community, the vast differences in income and wealth distribution in contemporary South Africa are still largely determined by racial category, and those differences will not produce either a country at ease with itself, or a fully non-racial national XI selected on merit. Tshwete acknowledged this when telling Parliament that the ANC had no desire to directly intervene on the sports field: 'The government's responsibility is the creation of that environment in which sport and recreation will become the property of an entire nation' (Thomasson 1999), although he may have shown a degree of sensitivity in deliberately underplaying the ANC's (very real) willingness to adopt a more intrusive policy should the need arise.

South African cricket will become a genuine force for national identity only once all its population groups believe that they are being given a fair and equal chance to compete for their schools, provinces and, ultimately, nation. In order to realise such ambitions, cricket has to embrace the positive discrimination agenda in three key areas:

- the provision of adequate facilities to play cricket;
- the provision of coaching to equip anyone interested in cricket to play the game properly;
- a widening of the opportunity to play cricket at various levels.

Cricketing development must also be situated within a broader project bringing health, education and nutrition (clean water, electrification and adequate housing) to disadvantaged communities. How can anyone say that a black player is not up to standard if he has been denied the basic facilities that would enable an observation to be made on cricketing talent, rather than on social circumstances? Imtiaz Patel, number two at South Africa's UCB, pointed out that 'If you

National identity in South Africa 65

have two equally talented bowlers, one black and one white, it's a fair bet that the black bowler has had to work a lot harder to get to that level, which probably means he's a lot more talented' (Chaudhary 1999). Does the selection of a team on merit, a principle strongly defended by the white liberal establishment, prevent selection of a side based on equality of opportunity? In a society where the distribution of economic resources remains as deeply skewed as in contemporary South Africa then it surely does. In current circumstances the call for team selection to be based on 'merit' – without an accompanying call for a wholesale transformation in the socio-economic conditions of the black majority – is an abdication of responsibility that effectively serves to shore up an unjust status quo. In the context of such extreme inequalities a genuine meritocracy is not remotely feasible and attempts to package it as such deserve to be treated with derision.

Conclusion

> Cricket it is the vehicle for something much greater . . . [it] remains today a powerful force for change.
>
> (Charles Davies, businessman[33])

The South African shares with his Australian counterpart a sporting ethos that believes in a competitive approach with an emphasis very much on winning. The middle-class English qualities traditionally applied to cricket, such as the manner in which the game is played mattering more than the result, have been shunned. It is hardly surprising, therefore, to find that victory for the national team is seen by some as more important than the role cricket might play in formulating a new national consciousness. This argument proceeds to claim that there is no room for an interventionist strategy when it comes to the selection of a sporting team; the market is the sole determinant. A statement from *The Cape Times* (1998) summarises this position:

> [T]he national selectors' prime duty must remain the choosing of the best possible team available. The moment they depart from that principle they compromise not only the country's sporting integrity at international level, but the reputations of the very players they might have put in the side at the expense of superior performers because of race. No one wants to be a token anything.

Perhaps we forget that targets have always existed in South African cricket. It is simply that before the 1990s, being white was the single most important criterion for selection to the national side. The election of an ANC government was supposed to get rid of such horrors. No longer would selection be driven and ultimately decided by social circumstance. South Africa would become a national entity, with all its ethnic groups sharing the bounty of a democratic non-racial society. Reform would affect all sectors of social and economic life, and sport would not be exempt. Such ambitions could be realised only over the

66 Jon Gemmell and James Hamill

long term, but in the short term there were measures that could be introduced to facilitate the development of disadvantaged communities. Affirmative action was one such strategy, as the market, by its very nature, is incapable of delivering equality.

The ANC was delivered to power on a historic programme of redistribution and equality. It sought economic investment in order first to stimulate the economy, and eventually to alleviate poverty. Economic growth needed to be improved in order to reduce the chronic black unemployment rate. Its adopted economic machinery was that of the World Bank and the International Monetary Fund, and ANC economic thinking, as discussed above, has endorsed the post-Cold War 'Washington consensus' on macroeconomic policy. However, the levels of direct foreign investment sought by the ANC have not been forthcoming, and this has been a major disappointment to a government that believes it deserves much better, given its commitment to 'responsible' economic policies and the fact that it has put in place an economic infrastructure specifically designed to attract investment.[34] The ANC shied away from emphasising redistribution, fearing international consequences, as any economic meltdown would be an indictment not just of itself, but of black rule as a whole. Thus, the government ignored calls for greater public spending, higher corporate tax rates and the maintenance of exchange controls, favouring policies such as privatisations, the removal of tariffs, lay-offs and wage cuts in the public sector, and corporate tax cuts. Labour-intensive industries such as tourism were emphasised. Unfortunately, these service-sector jobs lack stability and tend to be low-paid, and in the long term could further exacerbate inequality.

The government is currently criticised as drifting, in search of direction. Its economic strategy favours its new partners in the banks and big business rather than its traditional working-class allies. This has led to obvious friction within the liberation movement, especially between the architects of GEAR within the ANC leadership and the policy's critics in COSATU and at least a section of the SACP, a party that is itself drifting and 'in search of direction'. Back in 1996, Nelson Mandela stated that 'our strategy in dealing with our former enemies has been dialogue, discussion, criticism and patience. Now we have to apply that method in dealing with our own allies, the labour unions, who helped to put us in power' (Holman *et al.* 1996). This suggested that while economic policy was, in Mandela's own highly provocative phrase of the time, 'non-negotiable', the leadership still hoped to convince its trade union allies of the policy's merits. That has proved to be a futile exercise, as COSATU's opposition to GEAR – and its commitment to a socialist future – has remained steadfast, prompting Mbeki to adopt an increasingly aggressive and confrontational posture towards his leftist critics since 1999. This period of intra-alliance acrimony has led to increased speculation about an eventual split from the ANC and the formation of a new leftist party based on COSATU (see, for example, Guardian 2001a, b; 2002; Sunday Times 2002a, b). With the government struggling to find solutions to the housing problem, unemployment, crime, education and the need for social uplift – failures that COSATU attributes directly to GEAR – it has sought to manipulate other circumstances in order to maintain a semblance of its nationalist heritage. Sport provides one such opening. It costs the regime little financially, but allows an opportunity to reach out to a disadvantaged population, providing visual examples that suggest that they are benefiting from the transformation of society. This opiate, as we have seen, also has a unique ability to reconcile and unite all sections of a population, divided by historical and political tensions. Thus, through sport we witness the dual nature of the ANC's nationalism: on the one hand it seeks to promote or uplift the disadvantaged communities that gave birth to the movement; on the other it seeks things in common around which the nation's various groups can coalesce.

On no question is there greater disputation than the policy of affirmative action in sport. What constitutes merit? It is our contention that a society riddled with massive economic inequalities, still largely based on skin colour, cannot reasonably call itself a meritocracy. Indeed, the ANC's 1994 *Reconstruction and Development Programme* acknowledged that economic change was the prerequisite to success for the majority population on the sporting field.[35] True, remarkable strides have been made on the cricket pitch to provide opportunities to players from disadvantaged communities. If the object is one of creating a new post-apartheid national identity then the experiment has to continue, until race is no longer the principal determinant of inequality. Unfortunately, however, cricket is still searching for the 'parity' that Ali Bacher demanded, and is still not being played in a 'just society' where everyone has a 'common destiny'. That reality needs to be explicitly addressed by sporting bodies and by government itself, but that threatens to be hugely problematic. Sports bodies are notoriously insular and uncomfortable with even limited forms of engagement in wider political and social debates, and their instinct is to reach for the comfort blanket provided by the 'keep politics out of sport' mantra. For its part, the government has recognised, quite rightly, that socio-economic transformation is vital for the creation of the 'just society' that will, in turn, unleash the sporting potential of the majority community, but it is our contention that an economic policy rooted in the nostrums of neo-liberalism – and one that has so far has failed to reduce colossal levels of unemployment, to deliver rapid growth, or to halt the growing disparities between the richest and poorest South Africans – will endanger that noble objective.

The temporary scrapping of targets in July 2002 aroused excitement within the cricketing establishment; it also provoked alarm within political circles. An article by Mark Smit of the South African *Business Day* made a couple of pertinent points that seemed to summarise the arguments:

> For cricketers, apart from the disaffected few, some who protest the scrapping of quotas for reasons not necessarily related to cricket, the move heralds the dawn of an exciting new age in which kids of all colours will compete on equal terms for places in teams.
>
> The principles of excellence and merit will *once again* [our emphasis] become the only criteria by which players will be judged and selected. There

68   Jon Gemmell and James Hamill

will no longer be a need for some to complain that the world sees them as products of an unfair system.

(Smit 2002)

The 'disaffected few' would, we assume, include those who see a larger role for cricket than merely being the best side. 'Kids of all colours', though, will not 'compete on equal terms for places in teams'. Perhaps the small, yet increasing black middle class will compete with the white population, as they very gradually break down the barriers of a historically racist education system. What, though, of the millions in poverty, those in the large townships and 'informal settlements' who placed their faith in an ANC government to alleviate their chronic plight? While they may have the vote, they also have very limited opportunities to enjoy the 'excellence and merit' that will 'once again become the only criteria by which players will be judged and selected'. Merit reflects not just achievement, nor only ability, but potential. Perhaps it was the 'disaffected few' to whom Percy Sonn was referring when he claimed that there were some people who were failing to get behind Shaun Pollock and the Proteas? 'We have to forget what happened in the past,' said Sonn at the Mutual and Federal SA Cricket Annual dinner at the Sandton Sun. 'We have to get behind him for the World Cup' (Lichterman 2002). It is not always so easy to forget how we have arrived at the present. What is important is to use the past to prepare for tomorrow. Oppressed peoples are not going to discard a lifetime of injustice for some naïve call to rally round the flag. They will demand change. Already there are disconcerted bodies within the cricketing structure. The Concerned Group of Cricketers (COGOC) was formed out of frustration at the slow pace of transformation. Its founding document argued that the UCB 'had lost its way', and reminded those who were interested of the old slogan, adapted to reflect contemporary concerns, that there can be 'no abnormal cricket in a normal society' (Desai *et al.* 2002: 410–11).

Following a disappointing World Cup performance, the UCB now finds itself in a position to rebuild a disjointed national side. Six players of colour were selected for the 2003 tour to England. This is the second-generation post-apartheid team and it will face pressure from the ANC to incorporate the principles of reconciliation, equality of condition and a common destiny. If the South African cricket authorities adhere to such objectives then they will be making a meaningful contribution to the forging of a *truly* national identity. But the ANC must also be conscious of its own historic responsibility to deliver the 'equality of condition' that can help change the face of South African sport and build a 'common destiny'. Paradoxically, however, its continuing attachment to neo-liberal dogma may point to a more shallow and disappointing socio-economic outcome, one that on current projections threatens to fall well short of the 'transformation' envisaged by Thabo Mbeki.

Notes

1 The slogan 'no normal cricket in an abnormal society' formed the basis of the deliberate strategy of the non-racial South African Council on Sport (SACOS). The strategy, devised in March 1973, argued that the normalisation of sport in South Africa could only occur once there was political and economic equality for all South Africans. See Desai *et al.* (2002: 278).

2 *Colonialism of a Special Type*, 1977, online at http://www.anc.org.za/ancdocs/history/special.html (accessed 1 January 2003).

3 Lodge and Nasson (1991) provide an excellent summary of the numerous standpoints and discussions.

4 Statement of the Lisbon Conference, *Colonialism of a Special Type*, 1977, online at http://www.anc.org.za/ancdocs/history/special.html (accessed 1 January 2003).

5 Ibid.

6 University of the Witwatersrand Students' Representative Council, 'Working class politics and popular democratic struggle', 'Update', July 1984, pp. 8–11. Quoted in Lodge and Nasson (1991: 133).

7 The actual merger took place on 29 June 1991.

8 Statement of Intent. Quoted in The *Cricketer* (1991: 4).

9 Mackerdhuj later became appointed South Africa's ambassador to Japan.

10 Only companies with proven black empowerment policies were allowed to tender for contracts; World Cup mascots and logos were produced by rural cooperatives, rather than remote contractors; some 50,000 tickets were distributed to cricketers in disadvantaged areas; and on the field the South African team was required to be multiracial.

11 The moratorium was seen as a leverage to ensure that white cricket would remain true to black development and meaningful change.

12 Percy Sonn, president of the UCB, justifying his overruling of the selection of Jacques Rudolph and the inclusion of Justin Ontong for the New Year's Test against Australia in 2002 (Sonn 2002).

13 Lulu Xingwana, head of the parliamentary committee on sport, during the Test series against the West Indies, December 1998. Quoted in Seale (1998).

14 *Constitution of the Republic of South Africa 1996*, ch. 2, 'The Bill of Rights', 9.2, online at http://www.polity.org.za/html/govdocs/constitution/saconst02.html?rebookmark=1 (accessed 30 April 2003).

15 Ibid., chapter 10, 'Public Administration', 195 (1)i.

16 Employers are required to submit annual reports to the government outlining their progress. On the Employment Equity Act, see Financial Times (1998) and February (2001).

17 The ANC, *Reconstruction and Development Programme*, 1994 (Sixth Draft), p. 72 (point 3.5.3), online at http://www.polity.org.za/html/govdocs/rdp/rdp3.html#3.5 (accessed 1 January, 2003).

18 On that renewed polarisation, see Mail and Guardian (2000), Time (2000) and The Economist (2001).

19 There are numerous accounts of this process. The best are to be found in Beckles and Stoddart (1995), Manley (1988), Beckles (1999) and Birbalsingh (1996).

20 Wilson Ngobese became the first groundsman of colour when he took over at Kingsmead, KwaZulu Natal, in 1999. Vinny Barnes became the first man of colour to become a coach at a major province, when he succeeded Duncan Fletcher at Western Province in the same year. In October 2000 Gerald Majola was appointed to succeed Ali Bacher.

21 *Wisden Cricket Monthly*, April 2000, p. 17.

22 'Selectors forced to deselect', *Wisden.com*, 2 January 2002, online at http://www.wisden.com/news/news.asp?colid=44115066 (accessed 24 December 2002).

70   Jon Gemmell and James Hamill

23 *Poverty and Inequality in South Africa*, Report prepared for the Office of the Executive Deputy President and the Inter-Ministerial Committee for Poverty and Inequality, May 1998, p. 1, online at http://www.socdev.gov.za/Documents/2000/Docs/1998/Pov. htm) (accessed 1 March, 2003).

24 Policy Statement of the South African Council on Sport, first published in 'Souvenir Brochure of the Natal Council of Sport', 13 December 1980. Quoted in Ramsamy (1982: 17).

25 Under the multinational policy, Africans were divided along ethnic lines into eight (later expanded to ten) 'homelands', which totalled a mere 14 per cent of South African territory, consisting of the poorest agricultural terrain.

26 This inattention is all the more ironic when one considers that this more affluent section of the black community is almost entirely the ANC's creation. On the rise of that new black elite, see Southscan (2001). Francis Wilson, a co-author of *South Africa Survey*, a barometer of development trends, is quoted in *Southscan* as saying, 'Among the wealthiest 20% of South African society, a clear process of deracialisation is under way. But the base of the pyramid has stayed the same. Poverty remains to be endured overwhelmingly by African households.'

27 Michael Owen-Smith (1992: 37) estimated that there were at least 25 outstanding schools in South Africa.

28 Ntini was fortunate; he was sent to Dale College, having been 'discovered' by the development programme. His story is not common.

29 COSATU points out that GEAR has failed to deliver, even on its own terms. Growth in GDP has been consistently sluggish since 1996 and in 2003 was still barely half the 6 per cent per annum the government had promised by 2000. Unemployment remains catastrophically high in black communities at an average 40 per cent, the economy has continued to shed rather than create jobs since GEAR's introduction, and inequality is widening. COSATU sees GEAR as the route to a so-called 30–70 society in which the existing affluent section of the community expands to accommodate a new black elite, thus giving South African capitalism a multiracial flavour, while millions of people, almost exclusively black, remain mired in poverty. For an early but illuminating discussion of GEAR and its reception, see Financial Mail (1996). A general discussion of GEAR is provided by Blumenfeld (1999: 33–48). For a radical critique of GEAR, see Bond (2000). For a stridently critical view from the left, see Harvey (2000).

30 Nelson Mandela to a court hearing following the South African Rugby Union's attempt to block a commission appointed by Mandela to investigate allegations of racism and mismanagement in the organisation. See *The Examiner* (Ireland), 20 March 1998, online at http://archives.tcm.ie/irishexaminer/1998/03/20/fhead.htm (accessed 3 May, 2003).

31 Interview with Kepler Wessells, *Rediff.com*, online at http://www.rediff.com/wc2003/ 2003/feb/11kepler.htm (accessed 3 May, 2003).

32 ANC Statement on Transformation in Sport, Issued by ANC department of Information and Publicity, 30 November 1998, online at http://www.anc.org.za/anc docs/pr/1998/pr1130a.html) (accessed 1 December, 2002).

33 Charles Davies, chief executive officer of Norwich Holdings. Press release by the Transvaal Cricket Development Programme announcing Norwich Life Sponsorship launch, 26 September 1996.

34 Foreign direct investment (FDI) in South Africa since 1994 has totalled about $22 billion, 'significantly less than went to comparable markets such as Chile and Mexico'. South Africa's share of global FDI 'totals less than 1% of the total flow to developing countries'. Financial Times (2003).

35 *The Reconstruction and Development Programme*, 1994; see sections 1.4.9, 3.2 and 3.5 for the references to sport. Online at ttp://www.polity.org.za/html/govdocs/rdp/rdpall. html#3.5 (accessed 17 May 2003).

References

Agnew, Jonathan (1998) 'Never mind the other Pollocks', *Wisden Cricket Monthly*, July.

Ahmed, Qamar (1991) 'Witness to history', *Wisden Cricket Monthly*, August.

Alfred, Luke (1994) 'The last generation', *The Cricketer*, July.

Allison, Lincoln (1993) 'The changing context of sport life', in Lincoln Allison (ed.) *The Changing Politics of Sport*, Manchester: Manchester University Press.

Barlow, Eddie (1995) '25-year development', *The Cricketer*, April.

Beckles, Hilary (1999) *The Development of West Indies Cricket*, 2 vols, London: Pluto Press; Kingston, Jamaica: University of the West Indies Press.

Beckles, Hilary and Stoddart, Brian (eds) (1995) *Liberation Cricket: West Indies Cricket Culture*, Manchester; Manchester University Press.

Birbalsingh, Frank (1996) *The Rise of West Indian Cricket: From Colony to Nation*, Antigua: Hansib.

Bishop, John (1991) 'The end of isolation?', *Wisden Cricket Monthly*, February.

Blumenfeld, Jesmond (1999) 'The post-apartheid economy: achievements, problems and prospects', in J. E. Spence (ed.) *After Mandela: The 1999 South African Elections*, London: Royal Institution of International Affairs.

Bond, Patrick (2000) *Elite Transition: From Apartheid to Neoliberalism in South Africa*, London: Pluto.

Booth, Douglas (1998) *The Race Game: Sport and Politics in South Africa*, London: Frank Cass.

Cape Times (1998) 'Ali Bacher's mixed signals', *Cape Times*, 5 December.

Chaudhary, Vivek (1999) 'End of the lilywhite rainbow', *Guardian* (London), 26 February.

Cook, Jimmy (1993) *The Jimmy Cook Story*, London: Pelham Books.

Cricketer, The (1991) 'A breakthrough in South Africa', *The Cricketer*, February.

Cricketer, The (1999) 'Lily-white cloud hanging over', *The Cricketer*, January.

Crickinfo (1999) 'South African cricket aim for three-year racial overhaul plan', *Crickinfo*, 7 August, online at http://www.cricket.org.link_to_database/ARCHIVE/CRICKET_NEWS/1999/AUG/ 002408_AFP_07AUG1999.html (accessed 12 December 2002)

Crowley, Brian (1994) 'History of South African cricket', *The Cricketer*, May.

Day, Bill (1991) 'An end to South Africa's isolation', *The Cricketer*, July.

Desai, Ashwin, Padayachee, Vishnu, Reddy, Krish and Vahed, Goolam (2002) *Blacks in Whites: A Century of Cricket Struggles in KwaZulu-Natal*, Pietermaritzburg: University of Natal Press.

Duval Smith, Alex (1998) 'Cradle of Soweto uprising falls', *Guardian* (London), 16 January.

Economist, The (1997) 'Who is Thabo Mbeki?', *The Economist*, 1 November.

Economist, The (2001) 'Race in South Africa: when dogs don't bark', *The Economist*, 1 September.

February, Judith (2001) 'Legislation alone can't cure social ills', *Mail and Guardian Online* (South Africa), 31 August, online at http://archive.mg.co.za/ (accessed 4 September 2001).

Financial Mail (1996) 'Economic policy: struggle for the ANC's ideological soul', *Financial Mail* (South Africa), 7 June.

Financial Times (1998) 'South Africa's affirmative action law meets negative responses', *Financial Times*, 11 September.

Financial Times (2003) 'A less than wondrous record of attracting the cash', *Financial Times* (special report: Investing in South Africa), 6 October.

72 Jon Gemmell and James Hamill

Guardian (1999) 'Racist school asks court to back ban', *Guardian* (London), 19 March.

Guardian (2001a) 'South African unions threaten split with ANC', *Guardian* (London), 2 May.

Guardian (2001b) 'ANC fears union plot to launch rival party', *Guardian* (London), 23 October.

Guardian (2002) 'Communists row with ANC tests alliance', *Guardian* (London), 25 July.

Harvey, Ebrahim (2000) 'COSATU cannot live with the ANC', *Mail and Guardian* (South Africa), 4 August.

Hawkey, Ian (1999) 'Mandela and beyond', in Rob Steen (ed.) *The New Ball* (*Universal Stories*), vol. 2, London: Mainstream Publishing.

Heywood, Andrew (1994) *Political Ideas and Concepts*, Basingstoke, UK: Macmillan.

Holman, Michael, Lambert, Richard and Pell, Quentin (1996) 'Still dancing after all these years', *Financial Times*, 13 July.

Hutton, Will (1999) 'Can South Africa shrug off its economic apartheid?', *Observer* (London), 28 March.

Independent (2002) 'No racial split over World Cup song', *Independent* (South Africa), 16 October.

Independent (1998) 'Why I can't support the Proteas', *Independent* (South Africa), 5 December.

Klein, Naomi (2002) *Fences and Windows*, London: Flamingo.

Lichterman, Justin (2002) 'Sonn of a b!*@#', *Cricket on-line.org*, 11 October, online at http://www.cricket-online.org/news/archive/2002/October/1 1_OCT_2002_JLICHTE RMAN.html (accessed 5 May 2003).

Lodge, Tom and Nasson, Bill (1991) *All, Here, and Now: Black Politics in South Africa in the 1980s*, London: Hurst.

Mail and Guardian (1999a) 'No apology from McMillan', *Mail and Guardian* (South Africa), 24 February.

Mail and Guardian (1999b) 'Big Mac ordered to apologise', *Mail and Guardian* (South Africa), 25 February.

Mail and Guardian (2000) 'SA politics moves closer to racial polarisation', *Mail and Guardian* (South Africa), 4 August.

Manley, Michael (1988) *A History of West Indies Cricket*, London: Guild Publishing. March.

Marsden, Eric (1977) 'New wave ripples English shore', *The Times* (London), 19 August.

Miscevic, Nenad (2001) 'Nationalism', in *The Stanford Encyclopedia of Philosophy*, winter edition, ed. Edward N. Zalta, online at http://plato.stanford.edu/archives/win2001/ entries/nationalism (accessed 29 April 2003).

Murray, Martin J. (1994) *The Revolution Deferred: The Painful Birth of Postapartheid South Africa*, London: Verso.

Owen-Smith, Michael (1992) 'The Nuffield contribution', *The Cricketer*, April.

Owen-Smith, Michael (1994) 'National developments', *The Cricketer*, August.

Owen-Smith, Michael (1998a) 'Pulp fiction', *The Cricketer*.

Owen-Smith, Michael (1998b) 'Ntini steps into the limelight', *The Cricketer*, May.

Owen-Smith, Michael (1999) 'Magic worker', *The Cricketer*, October.

Prior, Marcus (2000) 'Role models for the future', *BBC Online*, 7 December, online at http://news.bbc.co.uk/sport1/low/cricket/l060068.stm (accessed 24 December 2002).

Ramsamy, Sam (1982) *Apartheid, the Real Hurdle*, London: International Defence and Aid Fund.

Rice, Jonathan (1993) 'A successful winter tour', *Wisden Cricket Monthly*, May.

National identity in South Africa 73

Roebuck, Peter (1994) 'Teenybopper quartet', *The Cricketer*, February.

Seale, Tyrone (1998) '"Apartheid lives on" in South African sport', *Independent on Sunday* (London), 13 December.

Smit, Mark (2002) 'Which is it, kicking the ladder away or a giant leap of faith?', *Business Day*, 12 July.

Sonn, Percy (2002) 'Quota, unquote', *The Cricketer*, February.

Southscan (1997) 'Mbeki says race riots ahead if whites fail to redistribute wealth', *Southscan*, 12 (41), 7 November.

Southscan (1998) 'Mbeki champions poor against black and white elites', *Southscan*, 13 (12), 12 June.

Southscan (2001) 'Few changes in wealth gap but more blacks enter the ranks of richest', *Southscan*, 16 (25), 14 December.

Sunday Times (2002a) 'Mbeki acts to stop new left party', *Sunday Times* (South Africa), 29 September.

Sunday Times (2002b) 'ANC sets out to crush dissidents', *Sunday Times* (South Africa), 1 December.

Thomasson, Emma (1999) 'South African sports bodies address "lily-white" criticisms', *Reuters*, 5 April.

Time (2000) 'The legacy that won't die', *Time*, 28 August.

White, Raymond (1991) 'South Africa's long road ahead', *The Cricketer*, August.

Younge, Gary (2001) 'Life after Mandela', *Guardian* (London), 16 May.

Part II

Cricket in the New Commonwealth

4 Play together, live apart

Religion, politics and markets in Indian cricket since 1947

Sharda Ugra

When India plays Pakistan at cricket, it's said every thing can wait. It often does. When the fractious neighbours, who have not played each other in Tests since early 1999, met in a group match in the 2003 World Cup in South Africa, everything stopped in both countries. Everyone – including former US president Bill Clinton – was made to wait. Clinton was to deliver, via satellite from New York, the keynote speech at an international conference in New Delhi where a gathering of the Indian elite from government, business and the media waited to hear him.

But only after the cricket. The India–Pakistan match was being relayed live on the large screen where Clinton was to appear and make his transcontinental address at a scheduled time. The problem was that the match had dragged on into an extra-half hour, India were on their way to a clinical win and, naturally enough, no one was ready for Clinton. His staff were told there was ten-minute delay as a traffic jam had held up dignitaries. But the penny eventually did drop in New York (perhaps there was a South Asian on the ex-president's staff). So the ex-president of the United States was made to wait as India and Pakistan finished their cricket match in South Africa. When his image finally flashed on the screen his first words to a still noisy, celebrating audience were, 'Congratulations. Yes, I know you won the cricket match.'[1]

Thousands of miles away the Indian captain Sourav Ganguly had been receiving a string of phone calls – before the game from Lata Mangeshkar, a legendary and much-revered 'playback' singer from Indian cinema, and after the match from the Deputy Prime Minister L. K. Advani and the Indian Army Chief Gen N. C. Vij.[2]

Civil society, government and the military. There wasn't, it seemed, a part of India cricket couldn't touch.

The world is frequently told that in India cricket is a religion. The affirmation of this inevitably follows on a banner held up by a spectator in a stadium, stating, 'And Sachin is our God.' It refers in third-person familiar to India's foremost batsman, Sachin Tendulkar, who also holds the record for scoring more international runs than anyone in the history of the game. It is a tall claim to make in a country with a preponderance of gods and religions. Or is it? Indian

78 Sharda Ugra

cricket, its documented history more than two hundred years old, has continued to defy capture. The inexplicable popularity of a nineteenth-century English sport in an environment that is the polar opposite of its original setting has been variously interpreted, but never satisfactorily explained.

Did the Indians seize and then subvert the game from their colonial masters? Was it, to use Nandy's celebrated assertion, 'an Indian game accidentally discovered by the English' (1989: 1)? Or like the English language, did the Raj manage to insinuate itself into the hearts and minds of Indians and thus render the very mission of Empire complete?

This chapter is not an attempt to settle that argument, which continues to occupy the attention of scholars, but merely an attempt to trace a more recent phenomenon: the transformation of Indian cricket in the past ten years from a popular sport played with much enthusiasm into a vehicle for many purposes. Or even, to use an orientalist image, a deity with multiple, contrarian heads. Indian cricket today stands for both First World market domination *and* Third World aspiration; inclusion *and* insularity; arrogance *and* open-mindedness. It represents both nation and market, and the use of one by the other. Cricket in India is a powerful tool and everything depends on who chooses to wield it.

The potency of cricket's symbolic importance to contemporary India has intensified in recent years. There remains one critical difference between the growth of Indian cricket and the growth of other older sporting cultures. Unlike soccer in Europe or South America and baseball and basketball in the United States, cricket's recent spread across India has not been the by-product of local loyalties to a club or a region. It has not even been responsible for the strengthening or rejuvenation of those loyalties. If fact, if the thin crowds at first-class matches are any indication, regional loyalties have declined.

Cricket's sweep across the landscape of popular culture in India has had little time for the growth or development of something so deep-rooted as local affiliations. All the attention, interest and popularity have had only one target: the national team. The reasons for that will be discussed a little later, but the consequences of this are now clear: the close linkage of cricket team and country, the underpinning of national identity/national pride with the performances of the Indian team. India sees cricket – and indeed an image of itself on a global stage – through its cricket team. This chapter traces the strengthening, reassertion and crystallisation of those linkages in modern India – the more so in the past decade.

In his highly original social history of Indian cricket, *A Corner of a Foreign Field: The Indian History of British Sport*, Ramachandra Guha has argued that the linkages between cricket and nation are not new: 'Cricket has always been a microcosm of the fissures and tensions within Indian society; fissures that it has both reflected and played upon, mitigated as well as intensified' (2002: xv). In the past ten years, however, in an India caught in the tumult of political and economic change, cricket's unique place in the national mind has become clearly identified. Now the main political/economic forces and mantras that gripped India in the 1990s – chauvinism and commercialisation – openly seek to embrace, and to piggyback upon, Indian cricket.

India: religion, politics and markets 79

Between 1993 and 2003, India was caught up in a period of the most rapid economic change in its existence as an independent nation, following the opening up of the economy in 1991. Until then the economy had been run on Soviet-style principles of state ownership, five-year plans, protectionism, licences and quotas. With the opening up of the Indian market the licences and quotas vanished, foreign investment was welcomed, private players could enter most areas of industry and the rupee was made partially convertible. As an adjunct, the Indian skies opened up to satellite television. Cricket was an interested party everywhere.

Since its inception in 1927, Indian cricket has been run, through a bitterly contested series of elections, by the Board of Control for Cricket in India (BCCI), a private body independent of government control. Cricket's administrators today are no longer the princes of the Raj (though Madhav Rao Scindia of the royal house of Gwalior in central India and Raj Singh of Dungarpur, a minor principality in the western Indian state of Rajasthan, served as BCCI presidents in the 1990s), but a mixture of businessmen, political strongmen and anyone who can wield financial clout – whether in the local community at the level of the state associations or at the national level in the BCCI.

Cricket has always been run by private enterprise in India and relies on the government for nothing more than Foreign Ministry clearances to undertake tours. As Bose (1990) says, 'Modern Indian cricket derives its strength from the money of the industrialist allied to the power of the civil servant.' When the market opened up in 1991, the players of the BCCI were both ready and knowledgeable enough to cash in.

Between Indian independence in 1947 and the opening up of the economy, cricket – along with the railways, post and telecommunications – was regarded as one of the more appetising leftovers of empire. The most popular pre-independence cricket competition had featured a 'European' team and Indian teams divided on the basis of religions – Parsis, Hindus, Muslims and finally, in 1937, the Rest (Christians, Jews and Buddhists). The quality of cricket was high and all of Indian cricket's pioneering and great pre-war players came through the event, but its religious divisions were contrary to the tenets of nationalist movement of the day. In the 1940s, opposition to the event grew along with the demand for a separate homeland for Indian Muslims, which was to eventually lead to partition of the country and the creation of Pakistan. After communal riots during the final push for independence claimed thousands of lives, the event was no longer viable.

Its place was taken by the Ranji Trophy, India's national cricket championships, and the sport began to reflect free India – some of its teams came from the newly formed states, and others from older cricketing powers were still allowed independent identities. The state of Gujarat contains three Ranji Trophy teams: Baroda (based around the city and its old princely state), Saurashtra (centred in Rajkot) and Gujarat (headquartered in Ahmedabad). Mumbai (Bombay) may be the capital of Maharashtra state but it continues to field its own team, the competition's most successful ever, and the Maharashtra state cricket team is administered from the city of Pune.

80 Sharda Ugra

The popularity of the game spread through two means: the staging of international matches and live radio commentary. These commentaries were made in English, as well as Hindi and three regional languages: Bengali, spoken in the state of West Bengal; Tamil, spoken in the southern state of Tamil Nadu; and Marathi, spoken in Maharashtra. Cashman believes that the introduction of Hindi commentary was part of a policy of promoting Hindi as a national language. In a young country with no fewer than 21 official languages, speaking in one voice and vocabulary was imperative – whether it was affairs of the nation or the state of play that was being discussed. The commentary panels never developed the cult status of BBC Test Match Special (that happened three decades later with the TV commentators on satellite channels), but they performed another role: helping the game 'attract an even broader mass following in urban India . . . well beyond the mass confines of the English-educated urban middle class to other social groups' (Cashman 1980: 146).

What also helped cricket along, Cashman believes, was 'the absence of competitors in the business of mass entertainment' (ibid.: 135) other than the only alternative – cinema (which was to keep its date with cricket at the beginning of the new century). The regularity of live international competition meant that the cricket match was the place for celebrity itself to be seen, whether it was film star, politician, businessman or general of the army. The status of cricket as a glamour sport only grew with these associations, and Bose describes one day in the 1960 Test match between India and Australia in Bombay when 'the great film stars of the Hindi screen – like Raj Kapoor, Dilip Kumar and Pran and others – were in the CCI pavilion trying to persuade Ramchand (the Indian captain) to declare' (Bose 1990: 218).

The crowd was restless, the match was heading for a draw when at that time another quite extraordinary event took place. One swift act proved that the demographic of people who responded to cricket, and the manner in which they did so, had become much wider and more expressive. When Abbas Ali Baig completed his second fifty, a girl from the respectable North Stand of the stadium climbed over a fence, ran onto the field and kissed the batsman on the cheek. It was an unusual, unorthodox gesture in an orthodox and largely conformist nation where public displays of affection between the sexes are still uncommon. To many it has remained just another a colourful aside in the official history of Indian cricket – and the one thing Baig is remembered for right after his century on his Test debut – but to many it seems like a signature event. It happened during the first week of the Swinging Sixties, but has seldom happened since, even though many more women attend cricket matches today. (Brijesh Patel was kissed on the field, from memory, on the sixth and final day of the fifth Test against West Indies at Wankhede in 1974–5. He scored a fifty as India collapsed in the fourth innings.)

Cricket had clearly touched parts that other sports in India could not reach. The national team's youngest captain, Mansur Ali Khan of Pataudi, was to write after India won its first overseas Test in New Zealand in 1967:

India: religion, politics and markets 81

I cannot pretend there are not many more important jobs to be done in India today, but in our huge and emergent nation, cricket does have a more than usually important role. Through it we can meet the rest of the world on near-equal terms, show our skill and express our artistry and enthusiasm. It is a game which our people love and follow with an interest unrivalled in the rest of the world.

(Pataudi 1969: 129)

In the 1970s, India won Test series overseas in England and the West Indies (a feat it has had considerable difficulty repeating) and, in all, wiped out the memory of the previous unprofitable decade by winning 17 Tests (as opposed to 9 in the 1960s). Instrumental in these wins were the combined talents of Indian cricket's first superstars in opening batsman Sunil Gavaskar and the legendary Spin Quartet (Bishen Singh Bedi, Bhagwat Chandrashekhar, Erapalli Prasanna and Srinivas Venkataraghavan). Progress against other nations became quantifiable even as Indian success in other sports began to wane.

By the time India won the World Cup in 1983, cricket had already won the contest for the status of India's number one sport. Field hockey, which has won India eight Olympic golds, is still officially India's national game. But crushed by the advent of artificial turf and the European ascendancy that resulted from it, hockey had lost its place in the public mind. Like most other Indian sports, it had a niche following and loyal regional pockets, but, once the results began to dry up, nothing like a mass appeal.

The hockey team won India's last Olympic gold in 1980 at the Moscow Games. Three years later a team led by all-rounder Kapil Dev and nicknamed 'Kapil's Devils' by the British tabloids brought the cricket World Cup – called the Prudential Trophy at the time – home. It was an unexpected result, but by beating Clive Lloyd's supremely dominant West Indians, and becoming world champions, the Indian cricket team of 1983 had kick-started the process that was to change the very idiom of the game in their country. When the team returned home to India with the Prudential Trophy they received an overwhelming welcome on the streets and within the corridors of power. The then prime minister, Indira Gandhi, held a reception for the team in New Delhi and provided the soundbite for the occasion, saying that the cricket victory had proved 'India can do it.' Mrs Gandhi was no doubt referring to loftier goals such as economic self-sufficiency and population control, but what India could certainly do from then on was take one-day cricket to heart. Until 1983, India had played 48 one-day internationals in nine years. Between 1983 and 1993 that number increased threefold, the team playing 134 one-day matches. (Since the onset of liberalisation in April 1991, it has played 357.) While this does correspond to an overall increase in the number of one-dayers played worldwide, there is an underlying pattern and a clear shift in preference.

There was a very distinct drop in the number of Test matches played in India (from 43 in the 1980s to 30 in the 1990s). In contrast, the team played 155

82 Sharda Ugra

one-dayers in the 1980s (65 at home) and in the 1990s played 257 one-day games (82 at home, 71 away). The big difference was that in the past decade the Indian team has played the majority of its one-day fixtures in 'neutral' venues such as Sharjah, Toronto, Singapore, Nairobi – that is, in random one-day competitions not forming part of an overseas tour. The figure more than doubled from 49 in the 1980s to 104 in the 1990s. The popularity of these 'neutral' venues/tournaments was driven by television revenues, which in turn fed into it.

While there is no exact moment when the great mass of Indian spectatorship flipped a switch and declared its preference for one-day cricket over the traditional variety, we could use the years 1983–93 as an era in which this 'mutation' (used here to refer to an evolutionary process rather than as a disparaging comment) in public choice began to occur. The rationale behind Kerry Packer's heavily marketed World Series Cricket (launched in 1977) – to take the sport to a wider, more diverse audience, make it more accessible, increase the numbers of cricket's 'consumers' and earn plenty of sponsorship dollars – worked its magic in India too.

Children, housewives, women, older retired people, could easily follow the game through live television and do the simple maths required by one-day games. (This was well before the Duckworth–Lewis method of adjusting winning targets, and the huge array of statistical parameters that are now set out during the broadcast of a one-day match.) When the match ended, there was, to borrow an Americanism, 'closure' and finality. Seven hours after it began, at least there was a result. There is a great irony in the readiness with which India took to the one-day game and discovered its passion for the instant form of cricket, an entertainment spectacle of runs, wickets, fours and sixes compressed into a single day, requiring neither the discernment nor the patience to follow Test cricket.

Prior to 1983, India's love for cricket was explained by the very open-endedness, the protracted nature and complexity of the game. That India, an ancient culture, loved the long, unfolding drama of a Test match and had a greater tolerance even of the tedium that some matches brought, as it mirrored the rhythms of life as lived out in the East. Indians then were perceived to have a deep-rooted and fundamental understanding of the idea of the draw because its very ambiguity (no one won, yet no one lost) suited a country where society was based on joint families, compromise and cooperation, and not on competition or individualism. The essential purposelessness and timelessness of some of cricket rituals perfectly matched a land where, in some languages, yesterday and tomorrow were the same word.

In *Cricket Wallah*, an account of the England tour of India of 1981–2 (also the tour on which the first one-day match was played in India), Scyld Berry discussed the great potential of cricket in India and in a conclusion of astonishing foresight said, 'Although the game grew up thousands of miles away, India is destined to become the capital of cricket' (Berry 1982: 157). That is indeed true today, and the reasoning used to arrive at that conclusion is still valid (a large supporter base, vast stadiums, the lack of competition from other sports, the BCCI's financial

India: religion, politics and markets 83

solvency), but the root, the starting point of his argument – 'as part of its legacy from the past cricket in India remains sensitive to the better traditions brought by the founding fathers from England . . . in batting India remains close to orthodoxy because the one-day game, which grows fast in other Test countries holds no great attraction' – was turned on its head in a very short span of time.

The falling away of batting orthodoxy remains the despair of coaches and Old World commentators. Known for its resistance to temptation, technical fortitude and the premium placed on one's wicket, the Mumbai school of batsmanship has moved on from Vijay Merchant and Sunil Gavaksar to the explosive expressive genius of a Tendulkar. In 2000, India played fewer Tests – 6 – than any other Test nation barring Bangladesh, the debutants that year.

Following the 1983 World Cup win, India travelled to Australia in 1985 to take part in another multi-nation, one-day tournament called the Benson & Hedges World Championship of Cricket and, led by Sunil Gavaskar, won the title, with Ravi Shastri winning an Audi sports car as Man of the Series. The sight of his teammates piled onto of the car as it took a victory lap of the Melbourne Cricket Ground has remained as iconic in Indian memory as that of Kapil Dev on the balcony at Lord's with the 1983 World Cup trophy in his hands.

One-day cricket was trendy, India was proving to be very good at it, and for a country starved of sporting success – India had won only one medal outside field hockey in more than eight decades of Olympic participation – it was reason enough to switch loyalties. The businessmen on the BCCI cashed in. The board began to schedule more and more one-day fixtures during tours by foreign teams, and wherever they were held, tickets sold out early and grounds were filled to capacity.

The Indian love for cricket was not, it could be confirmed, a particularly aesthetic, philosophical or cultural choice. The 'purists' would remain a handful, but for the rest, the instant thrill would be attraction enough. Indian cricket was distinct and special, but not *that* special. When the change came, Bose described the roots of Indian cricket as 'shallow'. He dismissed the Indian attachment to cricket itself as a flighty, insubstantial thing: 'One-day cricket has replaced it [the enthusiasm for Test cricket] but fortune is fickle and Indians could soon discover another tamasha [spectacle] to titillate and amuse them. I hope it does not happen but I fear it might' (1986: 167). It hasn't happened yet because market forces, having discovered their golden goose in the form of the largest audience in international cricket, will not allow it. As cricketer turned commentator and columnist Sanjay Manjrekar says, 'As a cricketing nation, India is unique: it is a poor country that spends a lot of money on cricket' (2002: 11).

Running parallel to the increase in the number of one-day matches played by India came the birth and growth of cricket's first offshore venue – in the Gulf emirate of Sharjah, keen to tap into the South Asian expatriate population in the Gulf. Between 1984 and 2000, teams from India and Pakistan were the centrepiece of tournaments that took place in a stadium in the middle of a desert. The matches were televised live on state television and the Sharjah cricket stadium was a place to be seen. Every time India and Pakistan played there (the

84 Sharda Ugra

other countries were merely invited to complete the formality of a tri-nation or four-nation series), the clubhouse stands were filled with movie stars from India, television stars from Pakistan and the rich and the famous who were flown over by the owner of the enterprise, Sheikh Abdul Rahman Bukhatir.

The organiser of these 'duels in the desert' was the Cricketers Benefit Fund Series in Sharjah. Former international cricketers were named beneficiaries, receiving purses of between $25,000 and $30,000 as overdue payment for their contribution to cricket. Indo-Pak games were played in front of highly charged and ultra-jingoistic spectators at the ground and beamed live to both countries, and a motley mix of Indian and Pakistani commentators cranked up the temperature, billing every match as a mini-battle. Rather than temper Orwell's 'war minus the shooting', Indo-Pak cricket in Sharjah was pitched as proxy war, and those echoes linger to this day every time the two neighbours meet.

India had proved it had the enthusiasm for the game (if not the stomach, as an infamous six hit by Javed Miandad in 1986 won the Australasia Cup for Pakistan off the last ball of the final versus India and earned Miandad the eternal hatred of the Indian cricket fan) and the numbers to support it. In 1987 it proved it had the infrastructure and the organisational skill to facilitate the eastward shift of the power centre of the game. The World Cup moved out of England for the first time – to the Indian subcontinent, being jointly staged in India and Pakistan and sponsored by a fast-growing Indian conglomerate called Reliance. The mascot for the Reliance Cup of 1987 was, curiously, a dove. The only two cricketing nations that had ever needed the world's official avian ambassador of peace played joint hosts. But the tournament was a financial and organisational success even if the hosts couldn't make it to the final.

Australia and England knocked heads for the title at Eden Gardens in front of a capacity crowd, who greeted the Australian victory far more warmly than crowds in Melbourne had hailed the winners two years earlier when India and Pakistan met in the final of the 1985 World Championship of Cricket. A poster at the ground had scathingly pronounced judgement on the citizenry of the two finalists: 'Bus Drivers vs Tram Conductors'. But as fireworks exploded over Eden Gardens and Allan Border and his Australian team posed with the trophy, world cricket found itself surveying a stage that was distinctly different from the balcony at Lord's. However, it had to be admitted that there was no lack of fervour or of a sense of occasion.

India's growing confidence in world cricket was evident merely in its even dreaming of hosting the first World Cup outside England. The Prudential sponsorship had run its course in England, and the Indian board now resolved to make a bid for the World Cup. To go by an account written by the then BCCI president, N. K. P. Salve, the Indian board made its first nationalist 'Us versus the old Empire' pitch back then. Salve declared that he had been refused two extra passes by the MCC for the 1983 final at Lords and he swore he would stage his own World Cup.

This has increasingly become the tone of Indian cricket administration over the years, especially as it has been discovered that it carries political currency and can be used to sway public opinion at a time of any controversy. When Sachin Tendulkar and five other Indians were penalised by ICC match referee Mike Denness for their various indiscretions on the field of play during the Port Elizabeth Test of 2001, the irascible Indian board president Jagmohan Dalmiya turned it into an East versus West battle, coupled with Old World versus New, and of course, following almost naturally, black versus white.

The Indian board first sold television rights of a test series to a private television channel in 1993, when England were touring. The first time cricket appeared on cable TV in India was during that series, when it went out via Rupert Murdoch's Star Sports. Star Sports, the cricketing pioneers of satellite television in India, and the IMG-owned television production company Trans World International (TWI), tapped into the Indian audience's demand for cricket as non-stop, year-round entertainment. They were welcomed in India because of their excellent production qualities and high-profile commentary panel, full of illustrious former cricketers. Viewership ratings were high and sponsors flocked to cricket. What satellite TV also did through its revenue-earning cameras was turn crowds at matches in India into part of the show.

Thus, India's 'passionate', 'volatile' and 'colourful' crowds (words used *ad nauseam* by commentators who may have baulked at touring India and playing in front of these very crowds during their playing careers) found themselves part of the entire production and consequently at the control of the television producer. Mark Mascarenhas, whose company, World Tel, brought the 1996 World Cup into Indian homes, described television's unwritten policy: 'In India much more time is spent on the crowd because they are so animated, so colourful. . . . If you try to do this Indian type of coverage in England, it won't go over well' (quoted by Ugra 2001: 24).

Whether this 'Indian-type' coverage, where cameras seek out spectators waving flags and banners and indulging in other telegenic acts, has actually led to a change in the spectatorship in Indian stadiums is yet to be established. What is without doubt is that Indian cricket spectatorship has changed. Other than the appearance of more national flags at stadia than in pre-satellite television days, violent reactions to impending defeat are now more common, and appreciation of the opposition team's effort has been diminishing.

Javed Miandad, in his last appearance in international cricket, was heckled off the field by spectators in the otherwise genteel southern Indian city of Bangalore during the 1996 World Cup quarter final (Marqusee 1996: 230–1). The New Zealand captain, Stephen Fleming, said on arrival for his team's Indian tour of 2003, 'The greatest challenge in India is to try and keep the crowd quiet. If we do that we know we are doing well.'[3]

The knowledgeable and generous Indian spectator seems to be a thing of the past. The Eden Gardens in Kolkata (Calcutta) has had crowd disturbances disrupt matches at least twice in the past seven years. The 1996 World Cup semi-final was abandoned and three years later angry spectators were driven out of the giant ground, and the final day of the India–Pakistan Test of 1999 was played out in front of empty stands.

86 *Sharda Ugra*

These extreme reactions are the result not of other social tensions being expressed in the microcosm of a cricket stadium, but of a low tolerance for failure and the elevation of the result of a cricket match into more than just a sporting defeat or a victory. The one-day game leaves no room for the ambiguous draw or the honourable retreat. It is confrontational, and its increasing frequency throws up 'win or die' encounters for national teams every day on television. For the Indian the end result in favour or against the national team began to occupy the mind of the spectator, especially the one newly arrived to the game, to a greater extent than the quality of the cricket played. In a developing country whose overt global triumphs are few and far between, the cricket match has become a barometer of national self-worth.

In the decade during which live cricket has been fed into India via satellite, television has also pumped up the volume on jingoism, which scholars have called 'hypernationalism'. Without a smidgen of self-consciousness, cable networks have promoted cricket series involving India as Badla (Revenge), Qayamat (Judgement Day) and Sarfarosh (Ready to Be Martyred). One advertisement for the Indian team's official sponsors c. 1996–7 showed fast bowlers hurling balls of fire, batsmen facing bowlers firing machine guns, and fielders leaping over burning tyres to get to the ball.

The fires, tyres and thick smoke looked alarmingly like news footage of riots familiar to most Indians. For a country so used to being told that its differences of religion, language, culture, wealth could pull it apart, there was another subtle message: only two things brought India together – war and cricket. Only two institutions could therefore keep the flag flying: the army and the cricket team. War and cricket were to be seen as interchangeable.

The country with which India has been to war more times than any other is, of course, its neighbour and gifted cricketing rival Pakistan. Between 1996 and 1998 the two countries played a made-for-TV tournament in Toronto, Canada, called, of all things, the Friendship Cup, until the familiar political hostility took its toll. The bad blood has intensified in the past decade as the Hindu right and its campaign of national polarisation as a means to power has taken it all the way to New Delhi.

In the interim, Bal Thackeray, a failed cartoonist turned leader of the right-wing Shiv Sena in the western Indian state of Maharashtra, asked Indian Muslims to pass his own sinister loyalty test. 'I want them [Muslims] with tears in their eyes every time India loses to Pakistan,' he said. It is a standard that India's largest religious minority has been forced to adhere to as the Indo-Pak dispute over the northern state of Kashmir has become more intractable. India has accused Pakistan of supporting separatists in the Kashmir Valley, of supplying them with arms and men and of funding terrorist strikes in other parts of India.

Months after Pakistan played an eventful three-Test series in India in early 1999, and the Indian prime minister, A. B. Vajpayee, took a peace bus from Delhi to Lahore, matters went downhill very quickly, impacting on cricket. A war between the two neighbours in the summer of 1999 in the Kargil district of Kashmir, an attack on Parliament and an unprecedented troop build-up on the

India: religion, politics and markets 87

border have meant that there could be nothing as normal as a cricket match between India and Pakistan. In this not-so-cold war, cricket was turned into a bargaining chip. The right-wing Bharatiya Janata Party (BJP) government banned 'bilateral' matches, decreeing that the two could not play each other anywhere other than in official ICC-sanctioned multinational tournaments such as the World Cup. The reason, according to the sports minister, Uma Bharti, was that 'We see cricket not as just a game but as a symbol of a nation's sentiments'.[4]

There it was. The official word from the government. India and Pakistan could play each other at hockey, tennis, soccer – any sport, but not cricket. Cricket was, the minister said, 'an extraordinary game. It has begun representing the sentiments of the people'. Cricket was special, more equal than other sports and doomed to be the field in which, it would seem, India could not allow Pakistan to gain ascendancy over it. Every time the two countries ran into one another, both nations were put into a state of high alert and high anxiety. No wonder the high and the mighty in New Delhi believed it was acceptable to keep Clinton waiting.

The freeze on India–Pakistan cricket relations has annoyed the BCCI because it knows the latent profits waiting upon a resumption of regular Indo-Pak cricket. Similarly with the Pakistani Cricket Board whose audience size in television markets is much smaller and whose finances depend on regular appearances by the national team against the one opponent every Pakistani cricket fan would want to see. Politics has hit the commerce of Indo-Pak cricket and neither side is pleased.

The other apparent consequence of the commercial success of Indian cricket was a succession of soon-to-be-proved rumours of a nexus between cricketers and illegal betting syndicates. The occasional whispers of deals struck finally exploded into cricket's biggest crisis since the Packer era when the Delhi police tapped into a telephone conversation between the former South African captain Hansie Cronje and an Indian bookmaker. Betting on any sport other than horse racing in India is illegal. But the growth of betting syndicates and the uncomfortable proximity of bookies to cricketers was linked to the spurt in one-day internationals in the 1980s and 1990s, especially at the offshore venues. Along with providing entertainment on television, the matches also kicked off a daily trade in millions of rupees per day, which was run from Dubai and neighbouring Gulf States (where the most wanted of the Indian criminal underworld also live), with bucket shops in major Indian cities acting as the hubs for Indian punters.

But only with the evidence on the Cronje tapes was an official inquiry launched by the Indian Central Bureau of Investigation (CBI) into illegal betting and the player–bookmaker nexus. This inquiry identified four Indian cricketers as having frequent contact with the bookies and assets disproportionate to wealth. The Indian board held its own inquiry on the basis of the CBI findings and banned the former captain Mohammed Azharuddin, together with Ajay Jadeja, Ajay Sharma and Manoj Prabhakar. However, it exonerated one of Indian cricket's biggest names, Kapil Dev.

88 *Sharda Ugra*

The months between April and October 2000 were confusing ones for the Indian cricket fan, whose heroes not only had turned out to have very strange friends but had not even, it seemed, been trying to win all the time. The CBI presented its report, but, because of a legal loophole, could not prosecute any of the cricketers in a court of law. But the very act of 'naming and shaming' the players forced the Indian board to act. Had the BCCI been seen to be dragging its feet on the issue, the damage to its commercial interests would have been immense. Azharuddin and Jadeja had lost their endorsement contracts almost immediately and the speed with which those actions were taken sent out a very strong message to the BCCI. If the cricketers proved unreliable brand ambassadors, corporate India could once again return to the make-believe world of Bollywood – no actor could possibly be accused of not trying to dish out a hit.

In hindsight, many factors worked in the BCCI's favour: Jagmohan Dalmiya, who had always been a big supporter of offshore cricket and had scoffed at the idea of betting syndicates, had just finished serving his time as ICC chairman, and had no say in the punishments dealt out to players by the BCCI. The BCCI president, the Chennai-based industrialist A. C. Muthiah, acted swiftly, virtually ordering the then team coach, Kapil Dev, to quit.

Also, 'Cronjegate' broke at the end of the Indian team's season, with most of the scandals emerging during the off-season months. When it took to the field again in Nairobi in the ICC Champions Trophy six months later, it had a new coach, an untainted new captain in Sourav Ganguly, a new set of players and no sign of Azharuddin or Jadeja even on the fringes. By the time the 2000–1 season ended, that same team had won a three-Test series against Australia, a series now being unashamedly sold as 'the greatest Test series ever'. Once again, all it took to win back the faith of the doubters was a few euphoric sessions of cricket.

The ugly side of Indian cricket – whether its extreme nationalism or frequent betting scandals – has tended to obscure the fact that, in this same tumultuous decade, cricket has reached into corners of small town and rural India in a way that had never previously done in its two hundred-year life in India. The traditional metropolitan hubs such as Mumbai, Bangalore, Chennai and Kolkata and the old royal heartlands of Hyderabad, Baroda and Indore continue to produce players. But so do towns like Bhubaneswar (home to S. S. Das), Allahabad (Mohammed Kaif), Jallandher (Harbhajan Singh), and even the previously unheard-of hamlet Srirampur, birthplace of Zaheer Khan.

There has been a genuine democratisation of Indian cricket in the past decade, its player, spectator and supporter base multiplying by the thousands every year. It is today in every way a pan-Indian phenomenon, more so, some people would say, than even Bollywood. Its allure for the advertiser is very clear. An executive of Hero Honda, the Indian company which is the world's largest manufacturer of two-wheelers, admitted, 'Cricket is the only sport where India can be No. 1 and hence the pull' (quoted in Goyal 2002: 51).

Modern times have given the Indian cricket advertiser not only the audience who will pay attention to his message but, it is now quite clear, perhaps even the kind of cricketer. For decades the Indian team was criticised for its lack of 'killer

India: religion, politics and markets 89

instinct' as an explanation for its failures in world sports. Rather than a failure to institute professional and systematic training, this lack of a killer instinct – and the vegetarian diet – was thought to explain why India, unlike Pakistan, has failed to produce fast bowlers.

But perhaps influenced by the growth of a palpably overt, somewhat angry and sometimes belligerent kind of nationalism, projected through the televised cult of cricket, the Indian cricketer in the past few years has been seen trying to bust the cliché. The current captain, Sourav Ganguly, often pilloried for conduct unbecoming, stripped off his shirt and waved it over his head on the balcony at Lords after India won the 2002 NatWest Trophy final in an improbable run-chase. It was his retort to a similar gesture by Englishman Andy Flintoff earlier in the year after England, trailing one-three, squared a six-match one-day series in Mumbai. As Ganguly is one of the more expressive internationals (he has been reprimanded or fined no fewer than six times by ICC match referees, three times as captain), it was a gesture expected of him.

But on the same tour, his sober, well-read and thoughtful deputy, Rahul Dravid, was asked by *Cricketer International*, 'Who would you have liked to have been in a previous life?' Dravid replied, '[O]ne of the leaders in the Indian freedom struggle.'[5] The postcolonial jibe was lost on no one. Then again, in the later stages of the 2003 World Cup, as the Indian national anthem played, many players on the team were seen mouthing the words with hand over heart. It was a gesture completely alien to most Indians, no doubt glimpsed on television and borrowed from the West as a way to express how truly moved and motivated they were. In an extensive cover story, *Wisden Asia Cricket*, the subcontinental arm of the English magazine, described Ganguly's team as standing for a 'New India'.[6]

The burden on the New India player to be a representative of the country and to conform to an image of the ideal Indian, outside even the scope of his skill at cricket, can be crushing. Nandy described it thus: 'Eleven players, with an average age of less than thirty and mostly innocent of politics and culture are expected to recover the self-esteem of 800 million Indians and undo colonial history in the southern world' (1989: 108). Of course, times have changed since then and the symbolic undoing of colonial history is no longer a priority. In cricket, India is now the financial powerhouse and can beat England often. But there is no way, for example, that any Indian cricketer could get away with the 'metrosexuality' or even the fashion choices of a David Beckham. It is what Guha calls the syndrome of Tendulkar as the 'only flawless Indian'. The onus on the cricketer is only slightly different in a new globalised India: 'Today our cricketers are expected to substitute for all our failures – they must win matches because our economy is bad. It is an unfair burden' (quoted in Ugra 2002: 39).

The team as representative of India, with members drawn from the varied regions and religions of the country, is another more sensitive theme used by groups campaigning for calm between religious communities as well as decon-structionists in the media. In 1987 a poster went into mass circulation showing pictures of four cricketers – Kapil Dev (a Hindu), Mohammed Azharuddin (a Sikh), Roger Binny (a Christian) and Maninder Singh (a Sikh) – with the slogan

90 *Sharda Ugra*

'If we can play together, we can live together.' It is a powerful message, akin to the one inspired by the multicultural French football team winning of the 1998 football World Cup. No Indian cricketer, though, has had the confidence to speak publicly against the politics of hate, as the footballer Marcel Desailly did against Jean Marie Le Pen during the 2002 French presidential campaign. The ice, they know, is very thin.

More than one cricketer (the opener Chetan Chauhan and the all-rounder Kirti Azad, to give only two examples) has upon retirement joined the BJP, whose right-wing politics are based on the principle of 'Hindutva' – that is, the rejuvenation of Hindu pride. When he was accused of being involved in a nexus with bookies to fix matches in 2000, the besieged Azharuddin, India's longest-serving and, to date, most successful captain ('for years the ultimate symbol of India's all-inclusive nationalism' – Sardesai 2002) said he was being victimised because he belonged to a minority.

But still Indian cricket remains pinned to notions of nationalism, like an insect to a board.

Two young players, Mohammed Kaif and Yuvraj Singh, struck a thrilling partnership that enabled India to successfully chase 325 at Lord's to win the NatWest Trophy final against England in 2002. When India won by two wickets with Kaif and pace bowler Zaheer Khan, both Muslims, at the crease, the symbolism proved too powerful.

Earlier that year, riots in the prosperous western state of Gujarat, fuelled by a deliberately passive government, had claimed the lives of thousands of Muslims. Here, according to one columnist, was the rebuttal:

> As Muslims huddle in fear in Ahmedabad . . . Mohammed Kaif leads the victory charge at Lords . . . for a generation growing up in the increasingly ghettoized neighbourhoods of the country, they [Kaif and Zaheer] offer some hope for a better future, for a non-discriminatory society that rewards merit, irrespective of religious afflilation . . . like the black West Indian cricketers of the C. L. R. James era, India's Muslim cricketers too have a role to play beyond the boundary.
>
> (Sardesai 2002)

But the challenge to *that*, which came from another writer, was swift, calling the NatWest final a 'short-lived, feel-good glow' and arguing that the acclaim for Kaif only symbolised Muslim isolation. His acceptance into the Indian mainstream, like that of other Muslims, was conditional on conformity: 'Only flag-holding achievers of spectacular public achievements confirm. The achievements themselves have to conform.' By contrast, the author pointed out, two prominent Muslims, a noted painter and a socialist activist, had been threatened by rioters. 'They are not ordinary Muslims but painting and social activism do not measure very high on the patriotism scale' (Mukhia 2002).

Time was to prove, however, that locating Kaif in the centre of a heated debate about nationalism and the status of minorities was a bad idea. Less than a year

India: religion, politics and markets 91

later, when India lost its World Cup league match to Australia, Kaif's home in Allahabad was one of those targeted by vandals, who flung black paint on it in protest. By all accounts his home was attacked not because he was a Muslim but because he just happened to be the only Indian cricketer from that town. In July 2002 he had won a cricket match and had been turned into a national hero. In February 2003, when his team lost a cricket match, he was a disgrace like the rest of them.

The Indian cricketer himself is trapped in this maelstrom of emotion, the only perks being a healthy annual income, the chance to see the world, and more than 15 minutes of fame. A few hours before the Indians left for the World Cup in South Africa in 2003 there was a proposal to have them visit a famous temple to Ganesha, the god of good fortune, in central Bombay. The plan was shelved, not only because it would take too long, but because some on the team argued about whether it would seem appropriate. 'Aren't we the national team of a secular India which has Muslims/Christians/Sikhs as members?'[7] It is difficult to imagine this dilemma confronting any other international sports team.

Cricket's place in modern Indian life was neatly captured by the 2001 release of a regulation 3 hour 45 minute Hindi film called *Lagaan*. The film engagingly and vividly told the tale of a cricket match played in 1893, in which a team of Indian villagers beat a team of British soldiers as a wager over the imposition of an exorbitant agricultural tax or *lagaan*. The Lagaan XI was supposed to reflect the Indian demographic: Hindus, a Muslim, a Sikh, an 'untouchable' (a low-caste leg-spinner) and, of course, in powerful echoes from Indian history, even the token traitor who provides secrets to the opposition and deliberately misfields the ball. At the end of the hour-long cricket match, the Indian team wins off a last-ball six (take that, Javed Miandad) and is freed of its *lagaan*, the British regiment being forced to withdraw its presence from the region. The film proved a critical and commercial success, turning cinema houses into stadiums where people reacted to the scenes of the match by whistling, cheering and applauding. The film was nominated for an Oscar in the Best Foreign Film category.

The twist to this whole tale lay in the past – in 1911 a barefoot team of Indian footballers from Mohun Bagan had actually beaten the Yorkshire Regiment in the final of the IFA Shield. This was hailed as a great triumph for the nationalists of the time and a blow to the pride of the Raj. Rather than immortalise a real slice of history on celluloid, the ultimate Indian dream factory, Bollywood, sought to give Indian cricket – flavour for many seasons now – its noble antiquity and nationalist credentials by creating this story of barefoot cricketers. After all, the so-called great ancestor of Indian cricket, the Jamsaheb of Nawanagar, K. S. Ranjitsinhji, did not even consider himself an Indian cricketer. When asked to help the newly formed BCCI, he is reported to have said, 'Duleep and I are English cricketers' (Rodrigues 2003: 222). During the freedom struggle, political fondness for cricket was split between those who opposed it as a British hangover (Mahatma Gandhi declared himself opposed to the Pentangular Championships because teams were picked on religious lines) and others, such as the Westernised first prime minister, Jawarharlal Nehru, who had learned the sport in Harrow and

92 Sharda Ugra

Trinity College. *Lagaan* sought to create a simpler mythology. In his book, Guha proved that the victory of a team of Parsis (the first Indians to take to cricket) over a team of Europeans in Bombay in 1906 was hailed as far away as Madras.

But to Bollywood the real story was not quite deemed worthy of an epic movie. It chose to recreate Indian cricket's folklore instead, depicting a bunch of barefoot villagers – not a group of educated merchants – as India's country's first home-grown cricket heroes. When the Denness affair boiled over in South Africa later that year, *The Week*, an English news magazine, called it a case of racism and used a poster from *Lagaan* on its cover, superimposing the faces of Tendulkar and the other five banned cricketers over those of the actors. The headline declared, 'Victims of Racism' and the cover lines read, 'Faced with a totally unfair LAGAAN [their emphasis] from an English match referee, Indian cricketers and board ponder the best way to counter this discriminatory raj.'[8] The mythology had come full circle.

Indian cricket as religion is far from a quiet, confident, somewhat personal spirituality. It is more like organised religion with all its fervour, dogma and, often, even a distinct lack of logic. Cricket has become a motif of a modern Indian identity but one that is completely at the mercy of many notions of nationalism. It can either produce the 'best' kind of Indian or show up the worst – as in the overpaid underperformer without killer instinct who cannot win everything.

In Indian public life, cricket is everything, except just the game it needs to be.

Notes

1 *India Today*, 10 March 2003, p. 19 and interview with Ranjit Sahaya, News Co-ordinator, *India Today*, on 1 August 2003.
2 Lokendra Pratap Sahi, *The Telegraph* (Calcutta), 3 March 2003.
3 Quoted by Reuters on www.cricketnext.com, online at http://www.cricketnext.com/news1/next/reutersSept03/reuters088.htm.
4 *The Hindu*, 26 April 2001.
5 *Cricketer International*, July 2002.
6 *Wisden Asia Cricket*, December 2002.
7 Interview with Amrit Mathur.
8 *The Week*, 2 December 2001.

References

Berry, Scyld (1982) *Cricket Wallah*, Hodder & Stoughton.
Bose, Mihir (1986) *Maidan View*, George Allen & Unwin.
Bose, Mihir (1990) *A History of Indian Cricket*, Rupa.
Cashman, Richard (1980) *Players, Patrons and the Crowd: The Phenomenon of Indian Cricket*, Orient Longman.
Dravid, Rahul and Mathur, Amrit (forthcoming) *Amrit World Cup Diary*, HarperCollins India.
Goyal, Malini (2002) 'Patriot games', *India Today*, 30 September.
Guha, Ramachandra (2002) *A Corner of a Foreign Field: The Indian History of a British Sport*, Picador India.

Manjrekar, Sanjay (2002) 'Spare the rod', *Wisden Cricket Asia*, December.

Marqusee, Mike (1996) *War minus the Shooting*, Mandarin.

Mukhia, Sudeep (2002) 'Kaif only symbolises Muslim isolation', *Indian Express*, 18 July.

Nandy, Ashis (1989) *The Tao of Cricket: On Games of Destiny and the Destiny of Games*, Penguin.

Pataudi, The Nawab of (1969) *Tiger's Tale*, Orient Paperbacks.

Rodrigues, Mario (2003) *Batting for the Empire: A Political Biography of Ranjitsinghji*, Penguin India.

Salve, N. K. P. (n.d.) *The Story of the Reliance Cup*.

Sardesai, Rajdeep (2002) 'The powerful symbolism of Mohammed Kaif', *Indian Express*, 16 July.

Ugra, Sharda (2001) 'The spectator as spectacle', *The Hindu Folio*, 14 January.

Ugra, Sharda (2002) 'Passion play', *India Today*, 5 August.

5 History without a past
Memory and forgetting in Indian cricket

Satadru Sen

That there is something curious, or not quite right, about the way in which Indians 'remember' cricket has been noted by at least one historian of the sport in South Asia (Bose 1991: 376–7). It is difficult to deny that as a cultural artefact, cricket has more room for memory than any other sport, including its closest cousin, baseball. There is the structure of the ritual itself: a sport in which games are played over relatively long periods of time, that is awash with recorded statistics, and that focuses attention upon individual performance even as it frames the individual player within the collective, has extraordinary potential for lasting impressions upon the modern memory. The nature of that memory is also significant. The history of team sports, since the nineteenth century, is also the history of the stable collective, with similarly stable claims upon the allegiance of the individual member (Lelyveld 1996: 253–60; Sandiford 1994: 34–52). This has been truer for cricket than it has been for most other sports, largely because cricket has been organised around collectives that, following Benedict Anderson (1983: 1–7), are limited and territorial. In other words, cricket since the Victorian era has been endowed with a historical memory that is recorded and invoked in ways that parallel the histories of that other essential modern institution: the nation-state. Indian cricket was organised 'nationally' from the very outset: as a Parsi project, as a 'pentangular' project for the regeneration and mobilisation of identifiable nations within India (Guha 2002), and then as the hyper-competitive projects of the Indian, Pakistani and now Bangladeshi national sides. Under the circumstances, Indians who follow cricket should 'remember' the sport much as they 'remember' the nation: in terms of a series of recorded events, attached to specific points on the calendar, highlighting a set of victories, defeats and revelations.

Reinforcing this expectation of a normative memory is the apparent coincidence of the normative communities of the cricket follower and the nationalist in India: both are the domains of the middle class. These are not, of course, neatly bounded domains, and the cultural 'overflow' into (and from) previously indifferent sections of Indian society has accelerated in recent years. Nevertheless, it is apparent that even within the middle-class heart of the nation, the stadium and the sports page, there is a failure of what might be called the memory requirement of cricket. How many Indians who consider themselves cricket fans remember

Memory and forgetting in Indian cricket   95

when India first won a Test match? How many remember Vijay Merchant's batting average? Those details are precisely the kind of memory that C. L. R. James's Trinidadian Puritans would possess if they existed (see James 1963), and that English cricket fans of certain classes may have possessed at one time. Why is it that India – a country in which cricket is routinely described as 'a religion' – has not produced a body of cricket literature beyond journalism that is instantly relegated to the status of yesterday's newspaper?

So far, two sets of answers have been put forward to explain this culture of amnesia. One is Ashis Nandy's hypothesis that cricket is fundamentally ahistorical, and therefore aligned with an Indian proclivity to view the past in terms of myth rather than history (2000: 58, 71). Too much need not be made of this, not least because it reduces cricket, nationhood, myth and history to crude essentialisms, eliding their mutual complicities. The other explanation is Mihir Bose's speculation that it is the *recent* past that has destroyed the historical memory of Indian cricket, by introducing the element of *tamasha* (carnival) (1991: 377–83). Appadurai has indicated something very similar in his remarks on cricket in Sharjah, with an added emphasis on the changing class base of the Indian cricket crowd (1996: 41–3). Both writers have implied that while there was a time when Indian cricket was followed by adequately modern and historically inclined middle-class fans, the broadening of the popular base of the sport – as a result of the interconnected phenomena of economic liberalisation, corporate sponsorship, satellite television, the triumph of one-day cricket over the longer version of the game, and the adoption of the game by semi-proletarian spectators – has created an environment in which cricket is consumed as instant entertainment, and the specifics instantly forgotten. The argument that I shall make is related tangentially to the Appadurai–Bose hypothesis. It is that Indian cricket has only recently arrived at a historical location at which memory is viable. This memory is different from the normative memory of English or Australian cricket, just as contemporary Indian nationalism is not identical to English or Australian nationalism. From this perspective, the memory of the older, pre-television, pre-liberalisation cricket fan in India can be seen as a 'failed' memory that coincides with a failed attempt to define the national community in liberal terms.

In the century before the 1980s, Indian cricket underwent impressive expansion, moving beyond its status as the pastime of very limited groups of Anglophiles towards a certain centrality as an 'Indian' ritual. At the same time, there was nothing hegemonic about its place in the national culture, let alone in the various sub-national and extra-national cultures that existed alongside what Partha Chatterjee has called the society of 'proper citizens' (1998: 11). In the discourse of national sports, cricket shared centre stage with hockey, and there can be little doubt that it was eclipsed in Bengal by soccer (Dimeo 2001). Those who inhabited the slums, the provincial towns and the villages did not show any consistent preference for cricket over unorganized forms of recreation such as *kabaddi*, *gilli-danda* and 'street football', or semi-organised sports such as body-building and wrestling (see Alter 2003). While 'sport' as a discourse was not alien

96 Satadru Sen

to this marginal majority (certainly it was a powerful presence in the lives of provincial groups that sought to transcend their provinciality), it was neither a dominant cultural presence nor dominated by a single pastime.

Cricket was played within shifting but limited circles of place, class, caste and political affiliation: the middle and upper classes and educationally privileged castes (such as Maharashtrian Brahmins) in major metropolitan areas.[1] In fact, it might be argued that in the decades after independence, the geography of Indian cricket actually shrank, as the older centres of princely cricket lost their sources of patronage and, with it, their significance (Cashman 1980: 24–47). I shall not enter here into a narrative history of Indian cricket. I shall point out, however, that this period and place in the history of the game are not devoid of memory. Certain things were in fact 'remembered', and these memories can be separated into two categories. On the one hand, there were statistics and memorable performances, which *were* recorded, in the sense that they were written down. Organised cricket generated documents in India just as it did in England, and this documentation surely counts as a type of 'memory'. On the other hand, there was what might be described as legend, of folk memory: a Parsi victory over a visiting English team in the 1890s, an exuberant innings by C. K. Nayudu in 1926, England losing early wickets in India's first Test match, Clyde Walcott trudging to the boundary to retrieve the ball and waste time in Bombay in 1949. This folk memory is not ahistorical or anti-historical: rooted (albeit tenuously) in time, place and collectivity, it is the very stuff of historical consciousness.

The two types of memory met with different fates. While neither was 'successful' in the short term, the second contained the potential for success over the long term. The statistical memory of cricket has little appeal in Indian society, and the documented basis of this memory has been largely buried. The value that has historically been attached in England to the statistical memory of Grace, Hammond and Hobbs is not remotely approached by the cultural significance of what is remembered in India of the batting of Merchant and Hazare during the domestic seasons of the Second World War. Those who remember such things in India are a minuscule minority. This is not a simply a matter of 'forgetting over time' as the events in question recede in relevance. It is, instead, evidence of the limited demographic space in Indian society for what might be considered the normative memory of modern sport – that is, a form of remembering in which the sport itself is privileged. I am not attempting, here, to separate athletic ritual from its cultural context. What I have in mind is a cultural perspective on cricket that focuses attention upon specific discursive aspects of the ritual, including statistical records, descriptions and demonstrations of technique, the insistence upon political innocence, and memory. Within this perspective, what is remembered is memory itself, events folding back upon themselves to provide depth to a sporting community that is deeply attached not only to its presumed historicity, but also to the value of history. An aficionado of the game might 'remember' that K. S. Ranjitsinhji – whom he has never seen, but who has become a part of the accumulated memory of cricket – had a wristy batting style, and relate that 'memory' to the batting technique of the relatively contemporary David Gower.

Memory and forgetting in Indian cricket 97

He believes not only that these relationships are natural, but also that his ability to make such connections are basic to his identity as a cricket fan. The process is much the same as the ability of a British nationalist to 'remember' and relate Agincourt and Iraq.

There is, within this historical tradition, an essential separation of culture and politics. In other words, there is a deep reluctance to concede that fundamental cultural institutions might be driven by anything so shallow and fleeting as political purpose. This is effectively the distinction that Liah Greenfeld has noted in her comparison of Anglo-American nationalism on the one hand, and Russo-German nationalism on the other: the former self-contained, innocent and based on liberal civic institutions, the latter driven by *ressentiment* or existential envy, aggressively focused on what lies beyond the national Self (Greenfield 1992: 17–25). The separation that Greenfeld makes is actually a false one; all nationalism is ultimately grounded in *ressentiment*, and to assume that English nationalism is not dependent upon existential envy directed towards 'outsiders' is to read colonialism out of the formation of the modern English Self. Nevertheless, what matters is that the idea of a self-contained and innocent national culture is *perceived* to be true by citizens, ideologues and sports fans. This conviction, or pretence, is precisely what makes 'civic nationalism' of the English variety possible. In England at the turn of the century, cricket existed at the very centre of the culture of apolitical innocence. In fact, the Anglo-Australian cricket establishment, including the mainstream media, have shown an extreme reluctance to abandon the idea that political considerations in sport are 'not cricket' – a reluctance that has contributed to a rearguard action against challenges to other cultural institutions, such as racism, sexism, class privilege and the stuffiness of Lord's (Sen 1994: 137–83 see also Marqusee 1994).

In India the culture of modernity has been overtly political, in the sense that there has been little interest in segregating ritual from the desire to demarcate the Self and the Other, or from the pleasures of competition. Tanika Sarkar (2001: 32) and John Rosselli (1980: 121–48) have noted that the Indian middle-class articulation of a physically charged masculinity has been fundamentally grounded in the desire of competing elites to establish and extend their hegemony. Because athletic activity was deeply implicated in this project, Indian cricket was played on explicitly as well as implicitly political fields, and cricketing episodes that did not convey political messages left no imprint upon the memory. The viable images, like the image of the barefooted soccer triumph of Mohun Bagan over the East Yorkshire Regiment, constitute the second type of athletic memory, which I have called 'folk' memory. Its constituting images were almost all generated at the intersection of sport and nationhood: they represented the triumph of the national collective or, alternatively, the defeat of that collective. Cricket in India, unlike cricket in England, has no cultural significance when it is divorced from political meaning of a very specific kind, which is the politics of *ressentiment*. Thus, club-level cricket or even interprovincial competition of the Ranji Trophy variety fails to generate 'memorable' episodes in the same way in which the county game does in England, or club sports do in much of the world.

98 *Satadru Sen*

It is useful to ask why this is so. Ranji Trophy sides, for the most part, represent collectivities that possess nearly all the ideological and institutional components of nationhood. Yet the matches typically attract little or no attention from crowds, sponsors or the media, and players who have secured their places in the Indian national team prefer to leave inter-state cricket to the aspiring and the unfortunate. There is an apparent disconnection between this indifference and the reality of political identities in contemporary India. To explain this disconnection we must first acknowledge that even when a sport becomes 'popular' in a society within which nationalism has become hegemonic, that sport does not automatically become a carrier of the ideology. Tamils and Punjabis who are 'nationalistic' in their particular identities do not feel any serious compulsion to take that nationalism into the stadium for a Ranji Trophy match, although the same individuals watch India–Pakistan matches primarily because the sport then functions as a combat vehicle of national identity. Under the circumstances, we can reach two possible conclusions. One is that regional identities in India are not especially competitive – no more competitive than county-based identities in England or state-level identities in post-Civil War America, which exist largely as organisational fictions with only superficial sentimental value. This seems unlikely, given the nature of India's political society, with its multiplicity of sub-histories and regional parties, not to mention its frequently confrontational politics of language. What is more likely is that the states of the Indian federation do not perfectly represent the identities to which they are attached. In other words, there is in some contexts a separation between 'Punjabi' (the identity) and 'Punjab' (the state), based on the fact that whereas the former is quite old, historically endowed and thus existentially meaningful, the latter is a relatively recent creation of the Indian Union. The Ranji Trophy team, in this formulation, represents Punjab but not necessarily the more competitive notion of being Punjabi, and thus lacks the power to generate memory even when the standard of the cricket is good by any objective standard.

Club cricket, which is even less memorable than the regionally organised sport, presents another dilemma. The question here might be posed as follows: why is club cricket in India played in a vacuum of notice and recollection? It is not enough to say that it is because the standard of play is not high enough, because second-rate club soccer has thrived in Kolkata (Calcutta) for decades and left its share of memories, doggerel and folklore (Dimeo 2001). But Kolkata soccer is club soccer only by default, being the organisational front of regional and religious stress fractures that developed in the city in the process of several generations of migration and resettlement (ibid.). It is, therefore, able to generate the athletic memory of *ressentiment* in a way that club cricket – which lacks communal affiliations – cannot. It is not that Mohun Bagan and East Bengal do not have cricket teams, but the identities of the clubs are not attached to cricket in the way that they are linked to soccer. Under the circumstances, club cricket in India remains either a private pleasure or an afterthought, and neither can be transmuted into 'public memory' – that is, memories that are shared, in some form or other, by significant numbers of people.

Memory and forgetting in Indian cricket 99

The public memory of cricket in postcolonial India until quite recently, then, was generated within fairly narrow limits. While the culture of statistical memory and 'apolitical' nostalgia was essentially stillborn, there was a space within which moments that were overtly connected to the politics of competing national identity could be remembered, reproduced and disseminated. This latter space, however, was restricted by the practical economy of Indian cricket. While there is no doubt that the demographics of the sport in India expanded in the decades after independence,[2] the new cricket fan was still primarily urban, middle-class and male. The Indian middle class may have been large in terms of absolute numbers, but even if the concept of the 'middle class' is interpreted generously, it enclosed a very small segment of a larger population whose interest in the athletic memory of nationhood was either superficial or altogether absent. Moreover, the middle class consumed cricket under circumstances that handicapped the production of memory. The most crucial of these is that it did not possess significant reserves of disposable income. This did not necessarily keep fans from attending the 'big' events: Test matches in India were routinely among the best-attended in the world, with spectators filling giant arenas such as Eden Gardens in Kolkata, with seating for eighty thousand.[3] Nevertheless, it did impose restrictions upon how often fans could afford to pay for matches, and this ensured that only certain kinds of games – that is, Test matches – attracted public patronage. The number of international matches that India played was not very large in the decades between the 1930s and 1970s, either in comparison with the frequency of such matches today, or compared with the frequency of 'major' cricket matches in England and Australia. This low frequency reflected the limits of the Indian consumer, as well as the marginal status of India and Pakistan in the international cricket bureaucracy in the decades before Sunil Gavaskar emerged as a star batsman and Jagmohan Dalmia as a powerful bureaucrat. Consequently, opportunities for the generation of memory continued to be limited.

Infrequent matches and frugal fans existed in a state of mutual complicity with what was perhaps the biggest obstacle in the way of a culture of memory: underdevelopment of the sports media. In comparison with the highly developed industry of cricket gossip in late-Victorian and Edwardian England, which revolved around an extraordinarily prolific cricket press, the journalism of Indian cricket in the decades after independence was severely restricted in its ability to generate memory. Unlike in the Caribbean, where the local could coexist with the communal among relatively small island communities, the geographic realities of South Asia required effective modern media to disseminate any durable notion of shared cultural and political concerns. Before the Asian Games of 1982, television broadcasting was accessible only in the largest Indian cities, and even there the coverage of cricket was rudimentary at best. For months or even years at a stretch, cricket would not be mentioned on television, except for a ten-second report of the latest Indian defeat. The local Test match would be broadcast live, but with a near-total absence of 'frills' – that is, of imagination. There was very little visible corporate involvement in the form of advertisements before Palmolive put Kapil Dev in front of the camera to sell shaving cream. Radio broadcasts of Test matches, which had a much wider audience than television, were in fact much livelier and more 'imaginative', but their impact was reduced by the infrequency of matches and, I would suggest, by the non-visual nature of the medium.

The print media were similarly impoverished. While newspapers provided excellent coverage of Test matches when these were in progress, they paid little attention to 'lesser' games. The secondary print media, such as sports magazines and especially the industry of books about cricket, were badly attenuated in a market with a limited readership and without surplus income. The nature of the newspaper coverage of cricket was also critical. It provided information about statistics and technique, and it was oriented towards the action on the field. It was not geared to stimulate the imagination of those who were less interested in the cricket than in the soap opera that surrounded it: the personal lives of the players, their financial fortunes, their sunglasses and cars, and so on. In any case, in the pre-Packer era the financial fortunes and clothes of Indian cricketers tended to be relatively modest and uninteresting. Not only did this mean that less knowledge was being produced, but it also meant that what was produced was remembered only by a very few.

The change came in the early 1980s, but it was not entirely sudden. The ideological and economic groundwork was laid in the 1970s. On the one hand, what has been described as the 'Gavaskar era' (Bose 1991: 289) reflected and reinforced a new emphasis on triumphalism – that is, a situation in which Indian victories came to be awaited with a mixture of confidence and anxiety. There can be little doubt that Test victories of the 1970s – against the West Indies (1971, 1974–5, 1976), England (1971, 1972–3), Australia (1977–8) and Pakistan (1979–80) – had come with a frequency and a conviction that exceeded anything witnessed in the 1950s and 1960s. Several of these victories, including the series victories of 1971, had come on 'enemy territory', where the erstwhile Indian record was notoriously poor. Bose has noted that these victories were received differently from the occasional win of the pre-Gavaskar years: whereas the latter were accepted as a kind of bonus in a narrative composed primarily of defeats, the victories of the 1970s marked a new sense of 'arrival' in the ranks of the great powers (ibid.: 260–9). The two experiences were not entirely different, however, because the feeling of arrival was extremely brittle, marked not only by the heightened expectation of victory, but also by an exaggerated fear of defeat.

This combination has generated numerous incidents of 'overreaction' on the part of Indian cricket fans confronted with lost matches, series and competitions, from the defacement in 1974 of the cricket monument in Indore (erected to remember the victories of 1971) to the riot in Eden Gardens during the India–Sri Lanka semi-final in the World Cup of 1996. Such overreactions are not simply evidence of enthusiasm for cricket, or of the excitability of natives. They reflect a particular stage in the development of the Indian nation-state, at which certain expectations had been badly frustrated and others imperfectly achieved. After a quarter-century of independence and in the aftermath of the Bangladesh War of 1971 and the Pokhran nuclear test of 1974, the continued marginality of India

Memory and forgetting in Indian cricket 101

in the structures of global power and significance, not to mention the precarious economic circumstances of middle-class life, international cricket could provide a forum for assertive celebration of power as well as deeply anxious acknowledgement and anticipation of failure. In no other country, not even Pakistan, has the national cricket team had to carry the burden of a fraudulent superpower status. The narrative of victory that began in the 1970s did not erode the importance of *ressentiment* in the memory of Indian cricket, but amplified it to an unprecedented level.

There were other changes that occurred in cricket in the 1970s that affected the Indian memory either indirectly or belatedly. Kerry Packer's World Series Cricket (WSC) was undoubtedly one. This might appear curious, since no Indian player played on the WSC circuit. Nevertheless, WSC – with its floodlights, unorthodox attire, 'souped-up' media coverage and, above all, its money – went a long way towards revolutionising how the Indian middle class consumed the images that accompanied cricket. The impact was not perceived immediately; I would argue, in fact, that a change in the culture of the sport did not become apparent in India until 1979–80, when the Pakistan team toured India. Some of the Pakistan players, most notably Imran Khan, had participated in WSC. Their images had been transformed by the experience; the 'sex symbol' persona that Imran brought to India in 1979 was a product not of his looks alone, but of the media circus that surrounded Packer's enterprise. During the tour, Imran, Zaheer Abbas and their teammates made a further transition that had been enabled by the 'memory' of WSC: they became the performative equivalents of Indian film stars, shadowed by paparazzi off the field, sought out not only by 'serious' and male cricket journalists like Kishore Bhimani and Dicky Rutnagar but also by 'lifestyle columnists' and by women reporters such as Tavleen Singh (who did not usually write about sport), escorted to parties by assorted movie stars and starlets, and captured by the cover-page editors of dedicated magazines such as *Sportsworld* as well as of news magazines such as *Sunday*. As a result, Indians who followed cricket, and even those who did not, learned to remember a kind of knowledge that was usually associated with the gossipy, personality-driven and widely popular world of Mumbai (Bombay) cinema.

This glamour was actually the beginning of a democratisation of the culture of the sport in India – that is, its emergence from the confines of the field and the world of male experts. It was nevertheless a continuation of the older search for a powerfully assertive national self. The archetypal new celebrity cricketer in India – ironically, a Pakistani – was not simply an entertainer in a ripped 'Big Boys Play At Night' T-shirt. He was also the symbol of a cosmopolitan self that – again, ironically – is deeply imbedded in the desires of nationalist modernity. The nationalist does not want only to draw borders that will establish a geography within which he is powerful. What he (and increasingly in Indian cricket, she) wants also is the power to eliminate those boundaries by which the relatively powerful segregate the marginal. As a way of participating in a selectively desegregated culture of power, cosmopolitanism is integral to middle-class nationalisms in the Third World. Because 'globalised' cricketers such as Imran Khan and

102 Satadru Sen

Sachin Tendulkar allow the marginalised middle classes of South Asia to walk and play upon a stage that is not restricted to the margins of the world, the images that convey their centrality in the culture of 'big boys' and international glamour are extraordinarily appealing and memorable.

What we see by the early 1980s, then, is the convergence of partially new desires and entirely new opportunities for the sustenance and multiplication of those desires. At the same time, it is important to keep in mind that these desires and opportunities were still played out within the same, fairly narrow, segment of the metropolitan middle class. In this context the dramatic expansion of Indian television after 1982 marked a major movement. First, by taking coverage of cricket matches into new 'viewing publics', the TV revolution exposed entirely new segments of the population not only to the esoteric rituals of cricket but also to the culture of athletic nationalism. By the end of the decade, over 80 per cent of the country was covered by Doordarshan (the national broadcaster), and from the 1990s this reach was exponentially supplemented by the rapid expansion of satellite channels, including ESPN and Star Sports. The new channels in particular were responsible for introducing in India various technical developments in the journalism of televised sport that can be traced not only to Packer, but to US innovations such as Monday Night Football (Patton 1984; see also Chandler 1991). These included the shifting of focus away from the 'field' to what used to be the 'background': the players as media personalities, and the media themselves, including the journalists. In other words, the soap opera of cricket that became evident in the print medium in the early 1980s was adapted for a television audience that was 'national' in more than one sense of the word, and made many times more influential in the process.

This process was inseparable from the economic policies that were put in place in India by the Narasimha Rao government in 1991. Collectively known as 'liberalisation', these policies involved opening the economy to greater levels of foreign investment, and the partial or complete deregulation of certain sectors. The effects of liberalisation and rapid economic growth upon Indian society have been enormous, and it is probably too early to put forward any sweeping hypotheses. Nevertheless, it is apparent that the Indian middle class has changed very considerably over the past decade: in its size, its membership, its spending power, its spending priorities, its political attitudes, and what might be described as its cultural proclivities. For my present purposes the most significant developments are the affluence of segments of the metropolitan middle class, their access to images and products of global capitalism, and the inclusion in 'middle-class culture' of small-business-oriented groups and segments of the urban underclass that had hitherto been marginal to it. Taken together, these have not only expanded the existing scope for remembering cricket, but determined the content and the context of memory.

The emergence of a relatively flush new market for cricket in India in the 1990s eliminated much of the practical difficulty in the way of disseminating culture. While it has not created a huge new cricket press, it certainly has created a market with greater room for English-language sports magazines, new vernacular journals

Memory and forgetting in Indian cricket 103

such as the Hindi *Kriket Kriket*, more elaborate sports sections in the daily newspapers (which now cover cricket year-round), and semi-academic work such as Ramachandra Guha's recent books. The spread of the Internet, with its proliferation of news portals, marks an expansion of this market, since most websites for established Indian newspapers and online journals such as Rediff.com place at least one cricket story on their 'front page' every day. The online medium has been especially powerful in sustaining the sporting memory of the Indian diaspora, particularly among affluent immigrants in North America who would otherwise be isolated from cricket and 'home'. Endowed with the flexibility of the Internet, online newspapers not only keep chronically anxious expatriate nationalists informed of the national score, but submerge them in the 'new journalism' of Indian cricket, providing gossip and commentary, some of it 'expert', much of it decidedly plebeian. Perhaps most crucially, the Internet provides the Indian middle class and their expatriate and foreign-born ('non-resident Indian', NRI) cousins with the ability to 'play' vicariously by participating in online polls, wishing Sachin Tendulkar a happy birthday, and expressing their opinion without having to get past editors with elitist expectations of literacy.

In spite of their location within the 'middle class', many of these consumers of cricket are a new demographic in Indian sport, and are in many ways closer to the semi-proletarian cricket crowds of Sharjah and the provincial cities than they are to the 'old' middle class (Appadurai 1996: 41–3). These are men and women from the provincial cities and the smaller towns, from the less prestigious educational institutions, and from that sector of the economy which is loosely described as 'export–import'. They have benefited from the liberalisation of the economy and now claim to belong to the middle class, but their cultural codes – including the meanings and priorities that they attach to cricket – differ from those of the pre-liberalisation elites, sometimes subtly, sometimes not. They embrace cricket as part of their movement into the metropolitan, university-educated, middle-class lifestyle, but the movement is never in only one direction. It would be accurate to argue that the Indian middle class has been partially colonised by the moneyed newcomer in many areas of the popular culture of liberalisation, and the cricket crowd (extended to the Internet portal) has not been immune to this transformation. Those who participate in online polls on 'Will India win the World Cup?' or 'Should Ganguly be sacked as captain?' probably do not assume that the question poses a worthwhile intellectual challenge or requires a deep technical knowledge of the game. It is unlikely that many believe that Tendulkar cares about their birthday greetings. They proceed from the expectation of certain interrelated pleasures: of an interactive new national community in which their voices carry, and of entry into a forum upon which they can subvert authority (of players, administrators, umpires, journalists, experts, intellectuals, men). The process marks the creation of not so much a discourse of athletic knowledge as a cacophony of modern self-advertisement – that is, the announcement of the hitherto silent individual's arrival in the midst of a vocally performed community. The pleasure of this participation, more than the scorecard, is basic to the modern memory of Indian cricket.

104 *Satadru Sen*

The biggest changes in how cricket is followed and remembered in India have been in the area of television coverage; in fact, it is television, rather than the old print medium, that has provided the templates for coverage of cricket on the Internet and in the new press. The 2003 World Cup attracted record television audiences in excess of one billion people,[4] with the greatest concentration being in South Asia. Needless to say, such audiences attract corporate sponsorship, and cricket – especially Indian cricket – today is so flush with advertising revenue that it makes WSC appear unorganised and small scale in comparison. Sachin Tendulkar's current five-year contract with the advertising giant World-Tel pays him more than US$20 million dollars, which is an unprecedented level of prosperity and public exposure. My point is that it is not simply the audience that draws the advertisers; the advertisements also draw and shape the audience, and this dynamic profoundly affects what the audience remembers. People who tune in to watch cricket do not simply do so to watch the game. Like Super Bowl audiences in the United States, they do so to watch the advertisements too, not least because consuming images of global products such as Pepsi and Adidas when those products have been attached to Indian national icons like Tendulkar (and thus domesticated, without being stripped of their cosmopolitan glamour) is an experience of the pleasure of being a modern consumer-citizen. Their memories of cricket, then, include the products that are associated with the cosmopolitan stars of the national game, as well as the stark facts of big money: the statistics of batting averages have been reduced to near-irrelevance by the statistics of players' contracts (Ananthanarayanan 2002).

The new crowd in Indian cricket also consumes – and thus remembers – the crowd itself. The panoramic eye of the television camera produces a visual memory of one's fellow spectators that is significantly different from the observed recollection of the ticket-holder in the stands. The crowd is at once expanded, rendered spectacular and incited to perform as spectacle. Without television, there would be little incentive for the painted-face carnivals of present-day cricket, which survive as a continuous trace in the memory of the watcher when the specifics of the game itself have faded. I am reminded of the appearance in the World Cup in South Africa of the so-called 'Bharat Army': British Asian soccer fans moonlighting as cricket enthusiasts and India supporters, decked out in tricolour T-shirts and Gandhi caps, waving giant Indian flags and chanting 'Hoo, haa, Tendulkaa' (The Telegraph 2003). As a televised phenomenon, the Bharat Army are a part of the Indian's consumption of the NRI. In the cricket crowd, as in the cinema, the 'resident' Indian confronts the 'non-resident' not as an autonomous entity but as a projection of his or her own fantastic desires (and anxieties) amid globalised products, images and 'lifestyles'. In this context the appearance of the boisterous, foreign-yet-familiar, and rather 'un-cricketing' NRI in the television audience provides the Indian fan not only with entertainment and amusement, but with a way of remembering what he or she wants to be, is afraid of becoming, and has already become.

The Bharat Army are also noteworthy because they simultaneously imitate and parody the 'Barmy Army' of England supporters, as well as their own 'English'

Memory and forgetting in Indian cricket 105

selves as soccer fans.[5] In spite of the growing numbers of Asians in county-level and national-level cricket in England, British Asians have their own reasons to be invested in the memory of Indian cricket. In a political climate in which the British-born continue to be viewed as 'immigrants', Sachin Tendulkar and Indian performances not only produce the imagination and nostalgia that is essential for an alternative sense of 'roots', but also provide a forum for remembering the racial tensions of British society. The Bharat Army are an Indian fantasy of the NRI; they are, at the same time, NRIs acting upon their fantasy of India, performing 'Indian cricket' as an ironic remembrance of soccer and of 'English cricket', in the context of the Tebbit test and the chicken tikka masala controversy.[6]

While discussing the memory of the new spectator in the Indian crowd, it is necessary to raise the phenomenon of women, television and cricket in contemporary India. While small numbers of women have long shown some interest in the sport, the dramatic expansion of the female audience for Indian cricket – both in the stadium and in front of the television – is something quite new. I recently had the pleasure of meeting a middle-aged matron of a distinctly 'traditional' sort, who does not pretend to know the difference between a square cut and a hook but idolises Tendulkar and literally prays for him to score runs, 'so that India can win'. Watching the World Cup final in a room crowded with the fashionable and inebriated wives of slovenly and inebriated Indian men, it occurred to me that the cricket – if the word is used to describe the game itself – was of minimal interest to most of those present. Like the matronly well-wisher of India's star batsman, these fans were more interested in the possibility of a national victory. They were, however, also invested in the glamour of their own roles as consumers of nationalism and modernity, designer clothes and television advertisements, martinis and the sex appeal of Rahul Dravid.

Women cricket fans in India are both different from and similar to female fans of American football. In India as well as in the United States, there is now a significant 'female demographic' in the audience for sports that women generally do not play. In the United States, women who follow football often begin (and end) as supporters of high school or college teams. In India, where school and college sports generate little attention from those not actually playing, female interest is generated through other means, and television programming is the most significant of these. The tactics used are not fundamentally dissimilar from the methods pioneered by the architects of Monday Night Football, but Indian networks have improved upon those innovations by introducing the glamorous female ingénue in the role of cricket journalist. I refer here to actress Mandira Bedi's highly successful (and Ruby Bhatia's less successful) career during the 2003 World Cup: male 'purists' of the game were openly contemptuous, but others were thoroughly entertained. More importantly, the Sony television network calculated, explicitly and accurately, that female viewers would identify with Bedi's attempt to learn something about the game without being concerned with esoteric technical details or statistical arcana (Banerjee 2003; Sen 2003).

106 *Satadru Sen*

Mandira Bedi represents trends in Indian middle-class culture that are both reactionary and subversive. She epitomises the idea of women as silly, giggling creatures who must be indulged (with various types of pleasure and forbearance) by the male athletes, journalists and viewers who actually own the sport and the profession. She personifies a kind of modernity – that of the liberated yet feminine woman who might share some of the interests of her husband and male friends – that has been deeply attractive to the Indian middle class since the late nineteenth century, when companionate marriage first became an ideal within a narrow segment of the colonised elite (Forbes 1996: 62, 86). Bedi represents also a further feminisation of the culture of the sport, which is recognised by the 'female-oriented' television advertising that accompanies the coverage of one-day cricket. The result might be described as an explosion of memory that has no precedent in the history of the sport in India: not only do middle-class women now share the collective knowledge of Indian cricket, but Mandira Bedi herself has become a part of what Indians remember about cricket, as have her fashionable clothes, and the fact of women's interest in the game.

The reaction that is both buried and manifest in the phenomenon of the female cricket 'personality' is closely related to the crisis of liberalism in contemporary India. In its naked affiliation with capitalist forces, its rampant emotionalism and its aggressive nationalism, the present-day culture of Indian cricket is very far removed from the Puritanical world of James's Trinidad, and from the liberal Englishness that James imagined, absorbed and deployed. In his insightful analysis of *Beyond a Boundary*, Ian Baucom has implied that what was liberal – and liberating – about James's vision of cricket and empire was his erasure, within the space of the cricket field, of the 'boundary' of Englishness (1999: 155–62). Within this space, by which Baucom means not only 'place' but also gestures (such as a cover-drive, or the refusal to challenge an umpiring decision), the distinction between white pedagogy and black performance broke down, the line between nation and empire wavered, and the communal identity became charged with inclusive possibilities.

It is quite possible that James's memory of the Trinidadian cricket field is the desperate reproduction of a middle-class fiction, and there is no doubt that it was exclusive in its own way: towards poor blacks, towards women, towards anybody who declined to make the necessary gestures or made gestures that were proscribed by 'the code' (James 1963: 39–46)· There is no doubt, either, that the code that James eulogised was deeply implicated in English nationalism and racism. Because James attempted to retrieve it from those associations, his vision of sport, team and community is ultimately incompatible with *ressentiment.* It cannot survive in an environment in which identity and pastime have both been nationalised. Nor can it flourish in an environment in which the pedagogical has been circumvented by the performative – that is, in which the processes of teaching and learning the discipline of the ritual have been rendered superfluous by the carnival.

While the public school code was imparted quite effectively to generations of Indian cricketers and their middle-class fans, cricket as a *memorable* ritual has

Memory and forgetting in Indian cricket 107

never been played 'beyond a boundary' in India. The sport is played, watched and remembered as a part of the boundary between Self and Other: imposed not only by the repressive Other, but also by the assertive Self. James's code is essentially the athletic counterpart of the ideology of the Nehruvian state, with its rhetoric of secularism, manly asceticism and nationalist internationalism. Both are based on the hope that discrete communities will subordinate themselves to a higher authority, behave with restraint and equity in the present, and merge honourably in the future. Each is elitist, contemptuous of dissent, convinced of the possibility and desirability of pedagogy, and adamant that dissidents play by 'universal' rules even when the rules were made by others. Not surprisingly, each has been swept away by those who derive their pleasure and their identity from other, less liberal, but more productive and memorable forms of exclusion.

Thus, while certain 'old' patterns of recollection persist in Indian cricket, their significance has been both magnified and altered by the changes in the crowd that remembers, and in the mechanisms of remembrance. The attention paid to on-the-field heroics and catastrophes has not passed: the victory in the 1983 World Cup is still cherished, Chetan Sharma's hat-trick in the 1987 tournament has not been forgotten, neither has the come-from-behind victory against Australia in 2001, and Javed Miandad's last-ball six at Sharjah is probably indelible in a historical memory that reserves a special place for defeat at the hands of the Muslim. But other episodes have vanished from public consciousness, even though their loads of political meaning are just as 'inspiring': Vijay Hazare's two centuries in a lost Test match against Australia in 1948, Vinoo Mankad's performance in the midst of another defeat, this one against England in 1952. This is not because the political significance of each event is radically different. Each is viewed through the filter of *ressentiment* nationalism. However, the creation of public memory requires infrastructure, and it requires a certain critical mass of knowledge. In the process of accumulating the infrastructure and the critical mass, the nature of the knowledge has changed. The new Indian cricket crowd, gazing through the new press, satellite television and the Internet portal, does not so much see a series of games as it sees itself, and it experiences the vision as a set of anxious fantasies about nationhood, modernity, power, isolation and connection. The 'Indian' – and not the 'cricket' – is the primary content of the modern memory of Indian cricket.

Notes

1   On caste and cricket, see Guha (1998) and Anand (2003).
2   Radio played a major role in this expansion (Bose 1991: 218–19).
3   It is worth noting that while admission at Test matches in India was free in the 1930s, the subsequent move towards ticket sales has not reduced attendance in any way. Eden Gardens has been refurbished to seat more than 100,000 spectators.
4   'South Africa's cricket World Cup will dazzle', www.safrica.info, 18 April 2003.
5   On the politics of cultural imitation, see Bhabha (1984: 127).
6   In 2001 the British foreign secretary, Robin Cook, stirred up a public debate on the ethnic content of British identity by calling chicken tikka masala 'a true British

108 *Satadru Sen*

national dish'. The 'Tebbit test' refers to the English parliamentarian Norman Tebbit's well-known complaint that Asian immigrants to Britain and their children do not support England in international sports, and his insistence that such support is a critical test of national identity. See Sen (1994).

References

Alter, Joseph (2003) 'The wrestler's body', in James Mills and Satadru Sen (eds) *Confronting the Body*, London: Anthem.

Anand, S. (2003) 'The retreat of the Brahmin', *Outlook*, 10 February.

Ananthanarayanan, N. (2002) 'ICC row brings focus on India's endorsement-rich players', Cricinfo.org, 20 August.

Anderson, Benedict (1983) *Imagined Communities*, London: Verso.

Appadurai, Arjun (1996) 'Playing with modernity', in Carol Breckenridge (ed.) *Consuming Modernity*, Delhi: Oxford University Press, 1996.

Banerjee, Sudeshna (2003) 'Get a woman, but a cricketer', *The Telegraph* (Calcutta), 10 March.

Baucom, Ian (1999) *Out of Place: Englishness, Empire and the Locations of Identity*, Princeton, N.J.: Princeton University Press.

Bhabha, Homi (1984) 'Of mimicry and man: the ambivalence of colonial discourse', *October*, 28 (Spring): 127.

Bose, Mihir (1991) *A History of Indian Cricket*, London: André Deutsch.

Cashman, Richard (1980) *Players, Patrons and the Crowd*, Delhi: Orient Longman.

Chandler, Joan (1991) 'Sport as TV product: a case study of Monday night football', in Paul Staudohar and J. A. Mangan (eds) *The Business of Professional Sports*, Urbana: University of Illinois Press.

Chatterjee, Partha (1998) *Wages of Freedom: Fifty Years of the Indian Nation-State*, Delhi: Oxford University Press.

Dimeo, Paul (2001) 'Contemporary developments in Indian football', *Contemporary South Asia*, 10 (2): 252–64.

Forbes, Geraldine (1996) *Women in Modern India*, Cambridge: Cambridge University Press.

Greenfield, Liah (1992) *Nationalism: Five Roads to Modernity*, Cambridge, Mass.: Harvard University Press.

Guha, Ramachandra (1998) 'Cricket and politics in colonial India', *Past and Present*, no. 161, November.

Guha, Ramachandra (2002) *A Corner of a Foreign Field: The Indian History of a British Sport*, London: Picador.

James, C. L. R. (1963) *Beyond a Boundary*, London: Stanley Paul.

Lelyfeld, David (1996) *Aligarh's First Generation*, Delhi: Oxford University Press.

Marqusee, Mike (1994) *Anyone but England*, Delhi: Penguin.

Nandy, Ashis (2000) *The Tao of Cricket: On Games of Destiny and the Destiny of Games*, Delhi: Oxford University Press.

Patton, Phil (1984) *Razzle-Dazzle: The Curious Marriage of Television and Professional Football*, Garden City, N.Y.: Dial Press.

Rosselli, John (1980) 'The self-image of effeteness: physical education and nationalism in nineteenth-century Bengal', *Past and Present*, 86: 121–48.

Sandiford, Keith (1994) *Cricket and the Victorians*, Aldershot, UK: Scolar Press.

Sarkar, Tanika (2001) *Hindu Wife, Hindu Nation: Community, Religion and Cultural Nationalism*, Bloomington: Indiana University Press.

Sen, Ayanjit (2003) 'Indian females bowled over', www.bbc.co.uk, 18 March.

Sen, Satadru (1994) 'The peasants are revolting: race, culture and ownership in cricket', in Paul Dimeo and James Mills (eds) *Sport in the South Asian World*, London: Anthem.

Telegraph, The (2003) 'Cacophony in Gandhi cap', *The Telegraph* (Calcutta), 21 March.

6 Cricket in 'a nation imperfectly imagined'

Identity and tradition in postcolonial Pakistan

Chris Valiotis

The history of cricket in Pakistan is both fascinating and enigmatic. As an offshoot of the pre-1947 Indian variant of the game, it has developed from an insignificant and obscure pastime of mostly urban educated players and endured any number of obstacles and intrigues to become a commercially successful sport and a nationally contested dialectic in Pakistani society. This chapter assesses why an essentially successful international culture of cricket has developed in Pakistan when numerous internal upheavals and controversies have bedevilled its domestic game, and why these may in the end have worked to the advantage of the national team. The history of Pakistani cricket and its significance in the postcolonial world will be examined under four broad headings: the development of a specific Pakistani cricket tradition; popularisation and the emergence of the 'vernacular' cricketer; the political appropriation of cricket in Pakistan; and, by way of summary, Pakistani cricket identity in a global space.

The development of a specific Pakistani cricket tradition

Pakistani cricket history cannot be understood without reference to the historical growth and development of the game in the pre-partition period. It is not a *sui generis* outgrowth of Pakistani independence, but a variant of India's cricket history that found itself stranded in a new separate, imagined community. The Muslims that adopted the British game in the colonial era did so, like their Parsee and Hindu counterparts, for complex motives, but it is reasonably certain that they did not see themselves as Pakistani cricketers. They shared the general assumption of the wider Indian community that the unity of the subcontinent was a given that would continue however the conflict between the British and the nationalists played itself out. Until the 1940s even the political elite had taken the integrity and unity of India for granted. Since popular culture followed political trends at a respectful distance, it is scarcely surprising that the non-political masses were even more surprised by the extraordinary rapidity of the endgame of British rule and the suddenness with which the Pakistani option emerged as a serious possibility than were the politicians of the Congress Party and the Muslim League. As part of this non-political milieu, most cricketers thought that their careers would remain bound up with the substantial cricket infrastructure that they were a part of in India.

Pakistan: identity and tradition 111

Cricket in colonial India had set out on its own trajectory developing indigenous traditions and regional peculiarities devoid of the nationalist ideals of both the Congress and League. Arjun Appadurai writes, 'Rather than being a spin-off of the imagined community of nationalist politicians in India, nationally organized cricket was an internal demand of the colonial enterprise and thus required cognate national or protonational enterprises in the colonies (1996a: 99). In other words, the cricket authorities and players of India were independently forging their own national sports culture that was inclusive of all ethnic and communal groups that had taken to the game in the colonial period. This was consistent with the logic of Indian historical tradition, which offers numerous examples of communal coexistence. Thus, cricket, like many other popular cultural enterprises in India, conformed to the Indian *mohalla* tradition that provided for the participation of diverse communities – each characterised by multiple foci of identity – in the wider economy and society.

This is crucial for an understanding of the difficulties that have plagued the organisation of domestic cricket in Pakistan. Having been embedded in the framework of Indian cricket, which relied almost exclusively on its domestic competition in Bombay[1] and its imperial and indigenous patrons, Muslim cricketers from the regions that became Pakistan found themselves orphaned at partition. This was because cricket in the colonial era had not itself consciously been partitioned. Instead, its administrative and cultural links with the rest of India were severed because of political events that it did not control and that left it bereft of funds, patrons and organisational structure.

Karachi and Lahore provide good case studies of the problems encountered by Pakistan's first cricket organisers. In the colonial period both were by far the most advanced cricket-playing centres of north-west India, and remained so after their inclusion within Pakistan. However, the traumatic events of 1947 disrupted and, for some time, impaired the development of the game in both centres. First, partition adversely affected the established patrons and players of cricket in both Karachi and Lahore. In pre-partition Karachi, Hindus and Parsees were the most important local cricketers. Guha writes of the fierce rivalry generated by the cricket teams of these two communities: 'the two communities were rivals in business, in the professions, in politics – and on the cricket field' (2002: 41). Moreover, partition resulted in the exodus of the city's majority Hindu population. In other words, the most influential and established organisers and players of the local game were lost to Karachi after 1947. Furthermore, the Muslims from north India who emigrated to the city during the same period had learned their cricket and honed their playing skills in Aligarh College and the local competition of that region. Ignorant and disapproving of the cultural traditions of Sind, they avoided social contact with the local population and concentrated entirely on setting themselves up as Pakistan's earliest political leaders.

The Muslims of Lahore made a very strong and crucial contribution to cricket in colonial India. Lahore had a vigorous collegiate system modelled on the educational institutions of Britain. Three of its colleges, Aitchison, Government

112   *Chris Valiotis*

and Islamia, promoted the disciplinarian approach to cricket and other sports that they inherited from British muscular Christian educators. Many of the Muslim cricketers in Lahore were graduates of these colleges. They became competent and able players; a few of them were selected to play Test cricket for India before partition. Furthermore, the success of the University of Punjab in winning the first three national Rohinton Baria Trophy inter-university finals in succession from 1935 to 1937 (Cashman 1980: 85) further attested to the strength of the region. However, Lahore's success was equally attributable to its strong Hindu and Sikh organisational and participational presence. Both these communities were lost to it after partition, which disrupted cricket in both Karachi and Lahore, leaving it in a state of disarray in a country that had no historical tradition of political and cultural unity.

Two years elapsed before the preliminary steps were taken to develop a new Pakistani 'national' cricket culture. The Board of Control for Cricket in Pakistan was established on 1 May 1949 after organisers had met the previous year to discuss its development and that of a domestic cricket structure geared towards international acceptance (Kardar 1954: 97; Bowen 1967: 157).[2] From its inception, the national governing body for cricket encountered numerous difficulties in developing and promoting the game in Pakistan. First, the ICC had rejected its submission for membership in 1948 and 1950 on the grounds that there were 'insurmountable difficulties' for the new nation to overcome.[3] However, in July 1952 the ICC, on the recommendation of Anthony de Mello, the president of the Board of Control for Cricket in India (BCCI), recognised the BCCP's right as a national organising body and awarded it full membership (de Mello 1959). Second, the BCCP was not the most efficient and amicable of associations: intrigue, dispute, power conflicts and lack of unanimity characterised its earliest meetings (Akhtar 1953) and have continued to do so since.[4] Finally, the indecision of board members and the lack of any substantial funding has left cricket in Pakistan with a weak domestic structure and few facilities of first-class standard.

Domestic cricket in Pakistan has encountered many organisational and structural problems. These range from an initial absence of substantial infrastructure and funding to a later conflict of opinion over the direction the game would take and the type of leadership it was to have. Pakistan found itself in the unusual position of playing official Test matches in 1952 before it had developed a recognised domestic structure. This frustrated early attempts to develop the playing talent of local cricketers and inhibited the growth of the game nationally.

In 1951 an unsuccessful attempt to revive the Pentangular Tournament model of colonial India was tried, with teams representing the Muslims of Lahore and those of Karachi, Europeans, Parsees, and a side chosen from minority ethnic and religious groups. This competition failed to arouse the interest of patrons and the public, and folded after two years. It was also a strong reminder of many of the recent communal divisions of the pre-partition period that cricket itself had condoned. In the 1953–4 cricket season the BCCP organised the Quaid-i-

Azam Trophy – a regional competition that was modelled on the English County Championship. It was named after the founder of Pakistan, Muhammad Ali Jinnah, to legitimise the BCCP's right to call itself a national body. This was done at a time when the cult of personality associated with Jinnah was used by any number of individuals in professional and institutional positions to validate their organisations as national enterprises (Talbot 2000: 201; Al Mujahid 1981: 424–35).[5] The BCCP sought to further justify its national image by making the head of state for Pakistan its chief patron, thereby associating its position with the official nationalist discourse.[6]

The Quaid-i-Azam Trophy has not been able to emulate the success of the English County Championship or the Australian Sheffield Shield. From its very inception it lacked funds, suitable playing facilities, and strong regional and grass-roots foundations. It was also short in duration, and the players were poorly paid.[7] As a result of these numerous obstacles, the BCCP has tried to find an appropriate structure for this competition, adding, removing and amalgamating sides even while experimenting with its playing format to include zonal, group and round-robin matches at different times and in different years. For 25 years, none of this challenged the dominance of Karachi and Lahore. If anything, the playing and administrative strength of these two cities was further reinforced in 1975 when private corporations were formally invited[8] to develop their own domestic teams by the Zulfiqar Ali Bhutto government. These company teams were meant to underwrite the game financially. By the 1990s, company and regional teams were divided into separate competitions: the Patron's Trophy for the former and the Quaid-i-Azam Trophy for the latter, played at different ends of the cricket season so that regional associations could use the services of the more established domestic cricketers who were contracted to the country's largest financial and commercial industries.

Pakistan's cricket administrators hope that the post-1990 domestic game will grow to become truly national and regionally inclusive: the best cricketers will be financially rewarded by the companies through contracts that in many instances tie them to long-term career positions, and the regional competition will grow because of player availability and the strategic spread of talent to all parts of the country. In the long term it is envisaged that the domestic competition in Pakistan will comprise regional associations that will have strong commercial and promotional arrangements with the private sector.[9]

Several trends can be discerned from the way in which cricket has been organised and controlled in Pakistan. In the absence of any substantial infra-structure and resources, authoritarian leadership has been influential in the direction the game has taken. A small number of mostly senior players and prominent public and military figures have historically been given a free rein by the BCCP to develop and promote the structure, culture and symbolism of the game for themselves. This corresponds with the traditional South Asian pattern of political authoritarianism and systems of patronage that invest absolute author-ity in the hands of a few individuals who, for one reason or another, have been able to win the – sometimes tenuous – support and recognition of constituencies

114 *Chris Valiotis*

at the local, regional or national levels. Authoritarian leadership and patronage of cricket is linked with patriarchal socio-cultural norms of loyalty. In this context, leaders expect nothing less than the unreserved support of those they are in charge of to facilitate their own personal success and recognition at the national and domestic levels. In Pakistan the likes of Justice R. A. Cornelius, Abdul Hafeez Kardar, General Nur Khan and Imran Khan have all, at one time or another, found themselves in positions where they have exercised complete control over many cricket issues. Both Kardar and Imran showed their hand at identifying and selecting players for the national team – many with little or no formal experience of the game. The successful transition of players from relative obscurity to international cricket stardom under their respective captaincies procured for both of them respect and authority within the ranks of cricket officialdom.

The shortcomings of the domestic game and the subsequent rise of authoritarian leadership have left cricket in Pakistan in a precarious organisational position. The structure of the game is top-heavy, dealing, as it does, with international issues, and has little capacity for the development of a strong club and grass-roots culture. Having historically been a less developed cricket region of colonial India and indelibly attached to its domestic structure and the BCCI's organisational umbrella, the game as it developed in Pakistan lacked the arrangements it needed to successfully negotiate its unexpected removal from the Indian cultural milieu.[10] This saw Cornelius and the earliest members of the BCCP encourage successful public and private figures to organise cricket clubs throughout the country to provide a necessary fillip to the growth of the domestic game. This initiative inadvertently, and unbeknown to the earliest organisers of the game in Pakistan, engendered enormous administrative and financial intrigue that has hampered attempts to reform the organisation and structure of cricket in the country.

In 1980, divisional and city cricket associations were made members of the BCCP council at the expense of provincial associations. This gave greater power to the two traditional strongholds of cricket in Pakistan, Karachi and Lahore. This change allowed both city associations to have one member appointed to the council for every 65 clubs within their jurisdictional boundaries (Salahuddin 1999). The number of clubs from Karachi and Lahore registered with the BCCP since the time of Cornelius's initiative was enormous. Many of them lay defunct, and in order to prevent their surreptitious representation, or the 'rise to enrolment of [other] bogus clubs', the BCCP was prompted to scrutinise the records and activities of all clubs claiming active legitimacy. According to Brigadier (retd.) Salahuddin, this investigation was carried out rather liberally, and failed in its attempt to identify and remove clubs with fraudulent claims to existence (ibid.). From 1979 to 1999 no checks were carried out on club activities to ascertain whether they were still active and playing cricket. In 2000, Salahuddin himself was appointed as the head of a scrutinising committee to determine which clubs were active and in existence, and thereby legally authorised by the 22 February 1995 Pakistan Cricket Board (PCB) Constitution to participate in elections for

Pakistan: identity and tradition   115

the council.[11] The inability of the PCB to detect and police unscrupulous activities in its formal structures, and in many instances its assisting in their emergence and prolongation through policies with little long-term vision, have inhibited the growth of equitable and accountable institutions for the organisation of cricket in the country. This has exhausted much-needed resources of energy and capital and diverted their use from the crucial task of developing the game at the domestic and grass-roots levels.

Popularisation and the emergence of the 'vernacular' cricketer

Broader networks of communication and capitalisation as well as changes in the education system provided an incentive for more lower- to lower-middle-class Pakistanis to play first-class cricket. In the immediate post-partition period few paths existed for the dissemination of cricket in Pakistan. Cricket commentator and journalist Chisty Mujahid claims that cricket in the 1950s was a 'social outing' for the college and university alumni of both Lahore and Karachi; they attended matches 'to be seen' and to mix with each other. Many of them organised, or were present at, numerous friendly matches played in Pakistan prior to, and after, the introduction of the Quaid-i-Azam Trophy.[12] However, the game's popularity did gradually increase as media technologies promoted the game more widely.

The growth of newspaper, radio and television coverage has been crucial to the popularisation of the game. However, it must be stressed that the media's role in the popularisation of cricket was gradual, tentative, and often fraught with controversy and uncertainty. Muslim newspapers were few and they were mostly located in Delhi and Calcutta before 1947; only two Muslim newspapers[13] were printed in areas included within Pakistan in 1947 (*Twenty Years of Pakistan* 1967: 539–40). Many other newspapers, mostly owned by Hindus and Sikhs, ceased operating or transferred their operations to India (ibid.).[14] To counter the loss of its Hindu and Sikh newspaper operators, Pakistan welcomed the addition of newspapers run by Muslims that were formerly based in India (ibid.).[15]

Throughout the 1950s and early 1960s the newspaper industry in Pakistan suffered from a scarcity of printing facilities, machine operators and journalists, as most of these positions had previously been filled by Hindus or Sikhs (ibid.). Furthermore, in the same period, newspapers were low revenue-generators because of their low readership levels. Some 86.2 per cent of Pakistanis were estimated to be illiterate in 1951 (ibid.) – and the figures subsequently improved only slightly. While large levels of illiteracy existed in the urban centres, the problem was still more acute in the rural areas. This severely restricted newspaper sales and provided little incentive for cricket's popularisation in Pakistan. For instance, *Dawn*'s cricket coverage grew as the game in Pakistan became more significant, though it and *The Pakistan Times* were read predominantly by the minority urban elite of Pakistan who had acquired a Western education. Both papers represented the views of the educated and affluent political and industrial sectors of society. They were better financed and maintained than the vernacular

116 *Chris Valiotis*

press. Similarly, the Urdu press had a restricted readership confined to that of immigrants into Pakistan from India and some sections of the Punjabi elite.

Radio Pakistan began with just three medium-wave stations in Lahore, Peshawar and Dacca on 14 August 1947. Staff numbers at these stations were small, and equipment was old, over-used and worn out (Dawn 1950). In July 1951, Radio Pakistan's headquarters were moved to Karachi, where a new facility housed modern radio technology that made it the equal of radio stations world-wide (Khalil 1951).[16] By 1960, Pakistan had radio stations in Lahore, Karachi, Peshawar and Dacca, as well as Rawalpindi, Hyderabad, Quetta and Multan.[17] Radio became an effective mode of communication in a society the majority of whose people lacked any formal education.

Early cricket commentary had its limitations: it was broadcast exclusively in English by two staunch proponents of English-language commentary, Omar Kureishi and Jamshed Marker (Dawn 1975).[18] Despite these imperfections, both Kureishi and the current cricket commentator Shahzad Humayun claim that commentary in English did facilitate a popular understanding of the game, and thereby provided a basis for its adoption by other Pakistani communities. The transmission of cricket matches to those who previously had little or no knowledge of them came about in two important ways. First, the development of cheap transistor band radios meant that poorer members of the population could afford to listen to cricket broadcasts for themselves; and second, radio coverage of the game was superimposed on traditional village and urban market cultures where shopkeepers provided a public space for broadcasts. Humayun describes the growth of a collective community-centred audience for cricket in this way:

> [I]n the rural areas . . . access to radio was always there . . . they didn't have too many radio sets but still it [cricket] continued to flow to the rural areas. . . . [In] the urban areas . . . I remember when I was a child listening to radio commentary; and roaming around the streets of Lahore I could see the shops with scoreboards and blackboards with [the] latest scores [written on them] . . . I would say that if radio commentary had not been there, cricket would not be where it is today in Pakistan.[19]

Universal cricket parlance and the broadcast etiquette of English-language commentators such as Kureishi and Marker facilitated the popularisation of the game in Pakistan. Cricket idioms such as 'googly' and 'howzat' became familiar terms (Aziz and Salam 1983: 18);[20] and Kureishi's style and delivery became a benchmark for succeeding cricket commentators on radio and television[21] – including those broadcasting in Urdu, such as Munir Hussain, Hassan Jalil and Bashir Khan. The introduction of Urdu commentary contributed to cricket's growing popularity. As an adjunct to English cricket commentary, it provided an additional impetus for the game's adoption by those who spoke Urdu exclusively. Furthermore, Urdu's official validation as the national language of Pakistan, even in the face of staunch opposition from regional groups, increased its capacity as a cricket language, particularly as it came more and more into general use.

By the late 1960s, Pakistan Television began its coverage of cricket matches, drawing on the knowledge, skills and workers of Radio Pakistan – often recruiting writers, producers, technicians and commentators. Television provided greater scope than radio for the popularisation of cricket. In Pakistan, televisual footage of cricket matches has given to the non-English and non-Urdu speaker a greater observation of the game's rules and structure, as well as its subtleties, intricacies, disputes and outcomes – indeed, it has done the same for those proficient in English or Urdu.

Television reached the people in much the same way radio had: through traditional urban and rural market cultures. Instead of turning to radio for match updates and scores, many shopkeepers purchased television sets and began screening cricket matches from their premises. Blackboards used as scoreboards were still maintained for passers-by who had little or no time to sit and watch games. In this way, customers could see events on the cricket field transpire in real life and real time, and begin to identify with the nation's players irrespective of their ethnic and political affiliations or their disdain for and disapproval of their political leaders. This process heightened with the development of colour television and the advent of one-day cricket. The crescent and the colour green found on the one-day uniform were symbolic representations of nationalism. In shops or bazaars they reinforced national identity during the telecast of cricket matches to an audience often at odds with the political vision of their leaders, and with little empathy or attachment to other ethnic, cultural and sectarian groups in Pakistan.

With very few exceptions, the cricket that Radio Pakistan and Pakistan Television have covered is that of the international game. As such, it is the national team that Pakistanis in bazaars, shops and homes in cities and villages throughout the country identify with. This may help explain why there is little community interest shown in the domestic game, even when pertaining to regional teams. Televised cricket, like radio, has popularised the players and symbols of the national team, and this has coincided with the nationalist politics of its leaders. The advent of television coincided with the declining years of Ayub Khan's leadership, but this did not stop him from using the medium for propagandistic reasons to attempt to save his political career. Both Bhutto and Zia were also notorious for using television to underpin their political objectives and undemocratic policies (Page and Crawley 2001: 53–7).

A lesser but important contribution to the popularisation of cricket in Pakistan has been the development of a sports goods industry. Sialkot, which lies to the north-east of Punjab, is the centre of a thriving sports goods industry that dates back to the late nineteenth century. Sports equipment produced in Sialkot is exported to numerous countries, mainly Western ones such as the United States, Britain, Germany and Australia. Pakistanis boast of the craftsmanship of their sports goods workers, and of the 'superior' quality of their wood and tanned leather (Aslam Hayat 1949). Many of the factories that manufacture sports products were under the ownership of Hindus prior to partition. These factories have since come into the hands of Muslims,[22] many of them immigrants from India.

118   *Chris Valiotis*

The sports goods industry provided opportunities for less affluent Pakistanis to familiarise themselves with cricket, as well as other sports. Many of Sialkot's workers were skilled or unskilled lower-class citizens who lacked the finances to put themselves or their children through college and university. In these circumstances it was not uncommon for many children to follow their parents into the trade. The craftsmanship of the sports goods trade was a skill handed down from generation to generation; it was not unusual to find numerous members of individual families working in the manufacture of sports products (Aslam Hayat 1949). Many of the workers learned about the game through their trade; others still were to learn it from the workers themselves. Over time, and with the early success of the Pakistani cricket team on the international stage, Sialkot's sports goods industries provided an outlet for poorer youth to develop an appreciation for the game that they might not otherwise have done.

The popularisation of cricket through media outlets and the sports goods industries and changes in the socio-economic conditions and educational expectations of Pakistani elites, who shifted their allegiances and occupational preferences away from traditional professions like that of the army, and cultural pastimes like that of cricket, and on to the professional services, allowed many lower-class and predominantly non-English-speaking cricketers – what Richard Cashman (1994) refers to as 'vernacular cricketers' – to play cricket for Pakistan's national team. Cricketers began to be recruited from poorer urban areas or small villages and towns contiguous to big cities such as Lahore to take the place of mostly educated and affluent players from Lahore and Karachi. This mirrored the changes experienced in the most traditional of colonial India's elite professions, the army. The post-1947 Pakistani army recruits differed from their Sandhurst-trained predecessors in two distinct ways: first, they mostly came from 'the small towns and villages of Central Punjab' (Burki and Baxter 1991: 7) and were traditional and more religiously devout in their outlook; and second, they had no prior historical association with the military and possessed meagre resources, having accrued little or no material gain from colonial policy (ibid.).[23] However, once they inherited traditional positions of authority through their leadership of the army, their identity and status began to change. They acquired power and prestige that ranked them alongside or above the traditional elites of Pakistan.

Pakistani cricket has not transcended the socio-economic limitations that have affected professions like that of the army. In the past three decades it too has come to realise that its traditional player market would gradually become negligible. Those belonging to the network of college alumni steeped in the traditions of British education, language, and culture were relegated to the role of onlookers – or at least, critical onlookers, as many of them have over the years been commissioned to write articles on the state of cricket in Pakistan – as vernacular players and commercial and industrial patrons replaced them. The modern Pakistani economy with its gradual shift to urban commercial and industrial markets has engendered an economic culture at variance with the traditional military landholding structure, which was intrinsically tied to the cricket landscape of colonial India and early postcolonial Pakistan. With graduate employment shifting to the professional services from the 1970s – and more recently to the information and communications industries of the home economy and those of Western industrialised countries through immigration and educational exchange programmes – domestic cricket players from less privileged backgrounds have emerged to take their place.

Majid Khan (a Pakistani Test player from 1964 to 1983) believes that the deterioration of college cricket had as much to do with the neglect shown to sport and sports facilities by educational authorities from the mid-1960s as it did with the changing economic milieu in Pakistan. These authorities decided that the construction of more buildings and classrooms in existing schools and colleges would accommodate the larger student intake brought about by increasing levels of affluence in Pakistan. This decision led to a drastic reduction in the number of playing fields in schools and colleges. Thus, a changing educational philosophy with its emphasis on preparing students for the professional services offered little incentive for sports participation. This, according to Majid, led to a shift in the recruitment policies of domestic cricket clubs, which looked to poorer rural and, to a lesser extent, urban youth to fill the absence brought about by the virtual disappearance of sport in schools and colleges.[24]

Poorer youth played improvised games of cricket in spontaneous settings where space could be found. Their familiarisation with cricket came from radio and television broadcasts, which had gradually penetrated previously neglected rural and urban zones where the game was little known. Their recruitment by club teams led to changes in the organisation of grass-roots cricket. The school and college system was replaced by under-age championships. In the latter, young players were invited to trial for club teams, and the best of them were then sent off to trial for regional and national under-age teams.[25] Of course, the difficulties of travelling to urban centres for trials, as well as the cost of playing competitive cricket on a permanent basis, may explain why those closest to urban centres have made the transition to the domestic game more frequently than those further away.

There is also much that remains to be said about the flamboyant and improvised style of cricket that these players develop in their original surroundings and its significance to the national team. The majority of them encounter formal training programmes, proper cricket pitches, and suitable attire and equipment when they first make their way into domestic teams. The village and urban cricket of poorer youths is far removed from that of the domestic game – and more so from international cricket. It is an improvised version of the international game, frequently altering its formal arrangements and rules, and with numerous regional and spacial variations. The demise of traditional grass-roots cricket, along with a lack of infrastructure, sustainable coaching programmes, and a domestic competition that has historically encountered numerous organisational and financial problems, has meant that vernacular cricketers from poorer backgrounds are given little opportunity or incentive to alter the playing skills of 'informal' village and urban cricket. The sudden rise from obscurity that many of them make – an outcome of traditional patronage patterns where senior players with some authority are free

120 *Chris Valiotis*

to select and recruit players of their choice – has given rise to a distinct Pakistani style of cricket that challenges the traditional norms of international cricket. This style of cricket is risqué and flamboyant, and it has coincided with the advent of the one-day game. It shares much in common with the cricket of other 'Third World' playing nations/teams such as the West Indies (particularly in the 1970s and 1980s), India and Sri Lanka. The style of cricket played by the modern Pakistani cricketer is a hybrid of the 'informal' indigenous game and the formal international one, with more of an emphasis on the first. This is why the style of cricket exhibited by the Pakistani team on the international stage has often been unpredictable and unconventional.

The political appropriation of cricket in Pakistan

The appropriation of cricket in Pakistan by authoritarian politicians controlling the state is the contemporary outcome of a political culture based on the myth of Muslim homogeneity and exclusiveness. The recognition and success given to Pakistan on the international stage by its cricket players, especially from the 1970s onwards, has encouraged the state's active involvement in the cricket affairs of the country. In seeking to tap into the prestige of the Test team and its 'superheroes', unpopular authoritarian political leaders have made it their civic duty to manage the cricket culture. It is, after all, one of the few institutions to have generated a sense of Pakistani rather than ethnic, linguistic or sectarian identity and to have thereby validated the Muslim separatist discourse. Political leaders' attempt to fulfil the role of patrons and managers is both a symbolic gesture acknowledging cricket's internal mass appeal and a political strategy to procure domestic approval of their authority and vision by associating themselves with the game. Additionally, it provides the basis for the perpetuation of the official national discourse and the validation of their established political power at the domestic level to a larger world audience. The projection of a separate cricket tradition in support of the 'two-nation theory' that validates the need for the Pakistan project runs contrary to the historical origins and development of the game in the subcontinent.

From the mid-1950s, civilian and military politicians in Pakistan have involved themselves in cricket board affairs. Between 1954 and 1963 three of Pakistan's earliest political leaders, Mohammed Ali Bogra, Iskander Mirza and General Muhammad Ayub Khan, became president of the BCCP (Salahuddin 1999). Thereafter, the first BCCP constitution (1963) recognised the head of state as its patron. The earliest authorities for cricket, particularly Cornelius, made a conscious effort to involve the government in the affairs of the cricket board to validate both the game and its organising body as nationally important. It was also a way to generate resources, financial and otherwise, which the game and the board were critically short of at this time. However, active government involvement prior to Zulfiqar Ali Bhutto's rise to power was at best half-hearted.

On its independence, Pakistan had to deal with a vast shortage of funds (Talbot 2000: 198),[26] industry and skilled workers (Robinson 1992: 33–4),[27] a severe

Pakistan: identity and tradition 121

refugee problem, and diverse ethnic, cultural and linguistic traditions. Under these circumstances the politicians of Pakistan in the immediate post-partition period were preoccupied with developing suitable political and economic institutions to validate the nation's existence. The concentration of meagre resources into these crucial areas meant that a growing number of socio-cultural activities and pastimes, including cricket, had to fend for themselves. The most noticeable act of political significance that affected cricket in some way prior to 1971 was the adjournment of India–Pakistan Test matches from 1960–1 until 1978. If anything, the use of cricket as a political instrument in this period came from an entirely different source altogether.

Crowd disturbances and riots at international cricket fixtures in Pakistan have occurred regularly. During February–March 1969, the last year of President Ayub Khan's political leadership, a three-Test match series against England was continuously disrupted by opponents of the political regime. The political crisis that befell the Ayub Khan government in its decline had reached a climax of sorts on the cricket field in early 1969. Many dissenters and protesters used Test match venues as a public forum for political agitation against the government. The socio-political turmoil that afflicted Pakistan on the eve of the Lahore Test match included 'railway and dock strikes for wage rises, power blackouts, students' protests against academic stagnation and financial rigidity, processions, mass demonstrations flaring into violence, fanatical assassinations, all aimed against the authoritarian regime of President Ayub Khan' (Robinson 1972: 91).

The Test match in Lahore and those in Dacca and Karachi that followed it all lost valuable playing time because of frequent crowd disruptions. Chairs and debris were thrown onto the playing arena and at police officers. The crowd's abuse levelled at Ayub Khan, including the chant of 'Ayub is a dog', reached fever pitch and led to numerous outbreaks of uncontrollable rage (ibid.: 92). In response to expected disturbances in the lead-up to each of these Test matches, the cricket board made crucial decisions in an effort to reduce – if not completely eliminate – their potential to disrupt play and escalate into violence. These included the selection of Aftab Gul, of the rebel Students' Action Committee, in the Test team for Lahore as 'insurance that riots would not stop the match' (ibid.: 92);[28] and the selection of East Pakistan's first ever, and only, Test match player for Pakistan, Niaz Ahmed, in the Dacca Test in preference to the more appropriate choice, Asif Masood (Noman 1998: 129). These disturbances reached their apogee during the Karachi Test, when play was abandoned owing to on-field demonstrations in support of a teachers' general strike for better wages and working conditions,[29] leaving the MCC team manager, Leslie Ames, to respond to BCCP president Syed Fida Hassan's request for the crowd to be given 'one more chance' with 'The [MCC] team will catch the first available plane to leave for home'.[30]

It was under the leadership of Bhutto that cricket was first brought into the political mainstream. Unlike his predecessors, particularly Ayub Khan, Bhutto was a 'populist' leader who saw himself as a spokesman and democratic representative of the people, releasing them from the restricted and oppressive

122   *Chris Valiotis*

rule of authoritarian politicians. In the light of this, Bhutto identified with, and subsidised, certain popular cultures, particularly sports such as cricket, to procure the political support and approval of large sections of the population. The establishment of the Z. A. Bhutto Institute of Sports and Culture was, according to Shahid Javed Burki, driven 'on essentially political grounds' to develop 'a political rapport between himself and the people' (1988: 152). However, like many of Bhutto's plans, this project, whose aim was to generate the support of the masses, was driven by underlying political concerns. Bhutto sought to control a burgeoning national sports culture that was developing links to other parts of the Third World that were otherwise closed to him because of Pakistan's membership of SEATO (the South-East Asia Treaty Organisation) and CENTO (the Central Treaty Organisation) (ibid.: 153). These were both Cold War treaties organised by the United States and directed against the Soviet Union. Membership of them ran counter to the non-alignment principle that was at the heart of the idea of the Third World. Pakistan's membership of both treaty organisations, especially as it was a developing nation itself, acquired for it the disapproval of other Third World nations.

The growing importance of sport as a symbol of nationhood in the 1970s saw Bhutto appoint his own government ministers and party members as executives of the more established sports governing bodies. This created a precedent for his successor, General Muhammad Zia ul-Haq, to do likewise. The sudden need from the 1970s for politicians to manage the affairs of sports bodies, particularly that of cricket, coincided with the game's growing commercial appeal worldwide, and the influx of a sizeable Pakistani presence in English county and league cricket. The higher international profile that Pakistan acquired as a result of the changes that the game as a whole underwent in this period provided a substantial basis for its national politicians to legitimise their authoritarian positions. The politicisation and control of cricket gave them international exposure and a national framework that could underpin their political longevity and vision. In other words, the success of the national cricket team and its international players in English domestic cricket was seen to justify the national discourse and political process of Pakistan.

Two of Bhutto's most important appointments were Kardar, who at the time was the minister for food and education in Punjab, as the President of the BCCP, and Abdul Hafeez Pirzada, the minister for education in the Bhutto government, who was the president of the Sports Control Board. In 1977 the two of them came to loggerheads over player payment disputes that called for Bhutto's intervention. Bhutto sided with Pirzada and this led to Kardar's resignation. Kardar, a long-time friend of Bhutto (Kardar 1987: 283),[31] was appointed as the head of the cricket board because of his disciplinarian and meticulous approach to cricket organisation, which was a product of his days as a charismatic leader and ambassador for Pakistani cricket in the 1950s. His undying devotion and loyalty to the national team had long been unquestioned and unchallenged. He was seen by many as being the right person to steer Pakistani cricket back onto the rails after its disappointments in the 1960s.

Pakistan: identity and tradition 123

For the first time in its short history the BCCP was given an official headquarters at Qaddafi Stadium in Lahore. From here Kardar presided over vast changes to the domestic game, bringing it into line with professional sport elsewhere in the world and providing a greater incentive for local cricketers to continue playing the game. Financial institutions and commercial houses were given permission to organise cricket teams to revive the sagging state of the domestic game. However, the steps taken to commercialise the game and improve player remuneration and career prospects in Pakistan during Kardar's tenure as BCCP president (1972–77) were deemed to be insufficient and not on a par with developments elsewhere in the cricket world by several of its more established players. This set Kardar on a collision course with the players in question, with Pirzada, and ultimately with Bhutto.

Kardar had been offended by Imran Khan, Majid Khan, Mushtaq Muhammed, Sadiq Muhamed, Wasim Bari, Asif Iqbal and Zaheer Abbas over their insistence that Test match allowances be increased to facilitate the loss of income that they stood to incur when on national team duty. His authoritarian outlook and obstinacy in the face of this challenge threatened to derail cricket relations between the players and the establishment. Kardar saw this issue in nationalist terms, questioning the players' loyalty to Pakistan, particularly since he felt that he had done much to improve their lot in the game during his presidency; on the other hand, the players' time in England had made them conscious of the contractual and organisational arrangements of cricket there, where the game was more lucrative and competitive, its facilities much better and more plentiful, and the rewards and publicity arising from it more substantial and enticing.

Pirzada's reversal of Kardar's decision to reject player payment increases created conflict within cricket's administration and in media circles. The press coverage in the period reflected a universal approval of Pirzada's actions that stemmed from the country's highest office, where the decision to overrule Kardar was first made, and included many BCCP members alienated by their president's approach to leadership, and numerous journalists, who felt that the game in Pakistan needed to keep abreast of cricket procedures in other parts of the world. On Kardar's side stood many old cricket teammates such as Fazal Mahmood and Munawar Ali Khan, the nephew of the Nawab of Mamdot. Fazal described the demands of the players as those of 'Money-sick' cricketers;[32] Munawar, on his part, described events leading to Kardar's resignation in political overtones, pointing to the impropriety on the part of Bhutto as an act of revenge for a 'betrayal' by Kardar:

> [Bhutto's decision to overrule Kardar, which had been carried out by Pirzada] was a sinister political plot, or a classic tale of conspiracy to stab Kardar in the back, Brutus style, by his old partymen, with the dual purpose of cutting him to size for the resounding popularity he had gained and as a reprisal for his quitting the party as Minister in the Punjab Government. It was then commonly known that Z. A. Bhutto, the all too powerful autocratic ruler of the time, did not take kindly to resignations from his party, so that it could

124 Chris Valiotis

well be construed as a set-up for Kardar's gruesome murder through a political coup of sorts.

(Munawar Ali Khan 2000)

Zia hardened executive control of cricket in Pakistan by appointing retired generals to the presidency of the BCCP. This was an adjunct to his reforms in political, bureaucratic, commercial and legal organisations and departments that placed 'senior military officers' in crucial administrative positions of power to strengthen and consolidate military rule and authoritarianism in Pakistan (Baxter et al. 1998: 236). His position in relation to the administration of cricket in the country was similar to that of traditional Islamic civilian rulers in their dealings with religious authorities (Von Grunebaum [1963] 1970; Coles 1968: 33–76)[33] – a position Zia himself adopted to win the support of Pakistan's religious clerics. Zia intervened in the affairs of cricket only when there were disputes to resolve and diplomatic scores to settle. Otherwise, cricket patrons and players, like the ulema (Muslim scholar-jurist elite), were free to cultivate their own traditions and practices so long as they did not clash with the political authority of Zia.

Zia inherited the cricket crisis that arose out of the commercial and professional challenges that the game's international authorities and national governing bodies confronted in the late 1970s. His patience and diplomatic skills were called upon to resolve the conflict that emerged in domestic circles when the organisers of the breakaway World Series Cricket competition procured the services of essentially the same group of players[34] who had previously demanded greater financial rewards for their Test match appearances. Zia was categorically at odds with Packer's World Series Cricket and informed Pakistan's 'rebel' cricketers of this in no uncertain terms. In a meeting he held with Mushtaq, Imran and Zaheer in January 1978 he questioned the loyalty of the players to Pakistan and advised them that playing for 'the highest bidder' was unethical, particularly when 'jobs and other incentives' were open to them in their home country.[35]

Under Zia the military presidents of the BCCP were given every chance to exercise control and leadership in the affairs of cricket. While some of them proved more capable than others, all were criticised by members of the press, and cricket players and administrators both past and present. Air Marshal (retd.) Nur Khan, who had a background in sports administration and corporate manage-ment with the Pakistan Hockey Federation and Pakistan International Airlines respectively, was seen to be the most efficient. He and his cricket board secretary, Arif Ali Khan Abbasi, began commercialising the game through corporate sponsorship and merchandise agreements with national and regional commercial organisations. This process reached its apotheosis in the 1990s under the latter's treasureship and presidency of the PCB, when sponsorship deals with multi-national corporations such as Pepsi and Coca-Cola were reached, and when the cricket board itself was fully privatised.[36] However, Nur Khan's presidency was volatile and often criticised by members of his own board. Both he and Abassi were accused of 'high-handedness' and numerous financial misdeeds. The BCCP council disapproved of arbitrary decisions, taken primarily by its secretary, that

Pakistan: identity and tradition   125

resulted in 'serious irregularities and misuse of funds'. The council requested Zia
to intervene and bring an end to such practices.[37]

Other criticisms of the long list of military presidents of the BCCP under
Zia included Kardar's unflattering remarks concerning Major-General Safdar
Butt's ability to manage cricket in Pakistan. Kardar wrote to *Dawn* that the
BCCP

> is mistakenly persisting with the notion that enthusiasm can be a substi-
> tute for knowledge and talent . . . I should have thought that a Chairman
> of WAPDA [Water and Power Development Authority], which demands
> whole-hearted attention to meet the challenges of the energy crisis and
> arresting the spread of the cancer of waterlogging and salinity of the agri-
> cultural life of this country would have kept him [Safdar Butt, who at the time
> of his BCCP presidency was also the WAPDA chairman] fully occupied
> 24 hours of the day.[38]

Other noted critics of military interference in cricket organisation and game
strategy – a significant issue for cricket players, especially in the 1980s – have
included Imran Khan (1988: 156–68) and Wasim Akram (1998). Both were
critical of the appointment to official positions of individuals lacking knowledge of the game, and both stressed the need for greater regional development
that will promote a stronger community supporter base than that generated by
the restricted popular appeal of a domestic game centred around corporate and
commercial organisations.

Zia's timely interventions were many and have been referred to as 'cricket
diplomacy' by Omar Noman. An example of the political importance that cricket
began to acquire during his leadership – and that of Bhutto before him – was his
constant need to be seen publicly as the chief patron and authority of the game
in Pakistan, particularly when competitive matches against India commenced
again from late 1978. He admonished Pakistani players to be at their best when
playing against the Indian team and rebuked them if they fell short of his expectations. However, when they did well, as they did in wrapping up the 1982–3
home series against India by winning the fourth Test in Hyderabad, Zia was at his
most gracious and benevolent, and showered the team with gifts and words of
praise:

> Throughout the present series the Pakistan team showed consistent and
> exemplary team spirit, discipline and stamina which deserves the highest
> praise of all cricket lovers in the country. On this occasion the whole nation
> joins me in extending warmest felicitations to Captain Imran Khan and
> members of the Pakistan Cricket Team.[39]

Zia's cricket diplomacy was also on show when addressing India's cricket
players. During the Lahore Test match between Pakistan and India in the 1984–5
home series, Zia commemorated Sunil Gavasker's 100th test appearance by

126 Chris Valiotis

awarding him a silver tray and a pictorial book, *Journey through Pakistan*.[40] Zia also made an unexpected appearance in Jaipur, Rajasthan, to watch the second Test between India and Pakistan in 1987. His visit to Jaipur came at a time of increased diplomatic tensions between the governments in Delhi and Islamabad, and was meant to be a gesture of goodwill and of the hope for peace in the region (Noman 1998: 222). This was a politically symbolic trip and an ingenious diplomatic manoeuvre on the part of Zia. It also showed the level of diplomatic importance that cricket had acquired in South Asia, especially in Pakistan, by 1987, and the need for Zia to use it as a forum for political discussion and as a symbol for his political validation as a national leader.

Pakistani cricket identity in a global space

The idea of Pakistani cricket identity in a global space offers an insight into the essence of Pakistani cricket nationalism in the context of a global sports environment. Contemporary Pakistani cricket identity and national cricket culture can be divided into two broad categories: official Pakistani cricket nationalism, and Pakistani cricket nationalism from below.

Official Pakistani cricket nationalism is now intertwined with the policy objectives of the central government. The political appropriation of cricket has meant that the game has come to underpin the official nationalist discourse of its ruling authorities. As a result, Pakistani cricket at the international level is synonymous with its fierce rivalry with India, its assiduous promotion and support of 'Third World' cricket nations, and its advocacy of Muslim assertiveness in the face of unjust criticisms from Western cricket nations.

Pakistan's cricket rivalry with India is an example of what John Hoberman has referred to as 'sportive nationalism' (1993: 18).[41] Its ruling authorities have used Pakistani cricket success against India, particularly in the one-day game (Marqusee 1996: 211),[42] to justify their national vision and political legitimacy to an international audience and to the various regional and ethnic groups within Pakistan who disapprove of their claims to power. This strategy has been supported by extensive media campaigns that identify India as the 'enemy' while perpetuating the jingoistic rhetoric of nationalist solidarity. Interestingly, the notion of national regeneration in defiance of a perceived and contiguous threat is now reciprocated by Indian politicians such as Bal Thackeray and the Shiv Sena, who see Pakistani cricket as ridiculing the Indian game and Hindu virility (ibid.: 212).

In the past twenty years, Pakistan has been proactive in its endorsement and assistance of 'Third World' cricket nations such as Sri Lanka, Zimbabwe and Bangladesh in their pursuit for ICC Test match status. It also strongly supports the development of the game in Kenya and the Middle East, where many Pakistanis reside and play cricket, to make cricket more representative internationally. This stance is also considered a means to redress the strong and conspicuous Western orientation of the ICC. Pakistan has long resented England's monopolistic control of world cricket.

Pakistani cricket authorities and players have developed religio-cultural safeguards to shield themselves from the pejorative and defamatory remarks that Western cricket players and officials have made about their country, playing facilities and integrity over the years. In response to accusations vilifying the ethical standards of Pakistani umpires and players for unfair dismissals and match fixing, and criticism of local hospitality standards, including standards of food, hygiene and accommodation, the cricket authorities and players of Pakistan have become self-sufficient and forged their own distinct way of doing things. One of these ways has been to identify themselves more readily with Islam and to see themselves as the Muslim representatives of a game controlled by Anglo-Europeans. However, the *ulema* continue to distance themselves from the game, as they have done with many other British traditions.[43] Islam as practised by Pakistani cricket authorities and players is of both religious and symbolic value, and its purpose is to solidify team unity and cohesion against those who object to the way in which they organise and play the game.

Pakistani cricket nationalism from below helps provide an anchor for Pakistanis both within the country and abroad in a postcolonial world of overlapping and disjunctive global cultural processes where the certainties of the modernist project, including clearly defined political, institutional and personal identities, have fragmented and, in many instances, been made to appear irrelevant (Appadurai 1996b: 32–7, 42–3). Pakistan provides a suitable case study for an examination of multiple postcolonial identities in the vastly integrated world of the early twenty-first century, where traditional ethnic and more recently constructed national identities are but a 'small fraction' of the quotidian realities of many in the world (Werbner 1996a: 1). The problematic of postcolonial realities in the contemporary world sees many Pakistani nationals and diasporic communities readily identifying with the Pakistani cricket team even as they disapprove of authoritarian regimes in Pakistan and the logic of their national discourse. Much research remains to be done within the Pakistani context itself and that of the Gulf States and Kenya; however, some preliminary work has already been carried out on the youth cultures of Pakistani diasporic communities in England (Werbner 1996b: 98).[44] This type of analysis will hopefully provide the means for a better understanding of the concept of identity, national or otherwise, as a term symbolising a complex set of meanings and permutations, and not one that is simplistic and rigid in its logic and characterisation. In the context of the global sports milieu it will offer a more thorough appreciation and understanding of Pakistani cricket identity as the multi-layered and heterogeneous concept that it has become.

Notes

1 The premier cricket competition in colonial India was the Bombay tournament. Its success encouraged the development of replica, though substantially subordinate and ancillary, competitions in other parts of India. By 1930, Karachi, Lahore and Madras, among others, had similar communal tournaments of their own.

128 *Chris Valiotis*

2 Also, Fazal Mahmood, the Pakistani seam bowler of the 1950s and early 1960s, when interviewed by me recalled the initial meeting in 1948 in the WAPDA building of Lahore. This meeting was organised by the likes of the Nawab of Mamdot, Justice Cornelius, Keki Collector – all early cricket board officials – and included Fazal himself and other cricketers. The topic of discussion for all assembled was the organising of an unofficial test match against the West Indies – who were then on their way to play in India, to impress the ICC panel of its credentials for international recognition (interview with Fazal Mahmood, Lahore, 31 October 2000).

3 *Dawn*, 13 June, 1950. The BCCP vice-president responded to this decision by informing the sitting members of the ICC that 'We get the impression that we are not wanted in the world family of cricket' (ibid.). Members of the English press, including the *Times* of London and the *Manchester Evening News*, were also dismayed by this decision. A letter to the editor of the latter newspaper commented that '[The] procedural and legislative objections [to Pakistani admission into the ICC were] . . . unnecessarily insensitive to the feelings of a new dominion. . . . [Furthermore, Pakistan is a] legitimate member of the ICC [as it] represented an integral part of the territory previously under the jurisdiction of the board of undivided India which has now gained full membership of the Conference' (letter to the editor of the *Manchester Evening News*, 18 August 1950).

4 On 15 May 1953, BCCP board members from Lahore representing both Lahore and North-West Frontier Province (NWFP) elected themselves to the board in the absence of the members for Karachi and Bahawalpur, who had moments before stormed out of the meeting because they opposed Lahore's overarching numerical strength. (An agreement had been reached between both Lahore and NWFP for the former to select its delegates as spokespersons and representatives of the latter. In actual fact, all Lahori delegates came from the one club, Mamdot. This further irked the delegates from Karachi and Bahawalpur.)

5 The earliest benefactors of political and economic power in Pakistan set out to consolidate and entrench their authority by increasingly using Jinnah's name to rubber-stamp their investments and policies. This extended to educational and other research-based institutions, commercial ventures, sports competitions and events, and infrastructural facilities in cities and towns, such as roads, buildings and parks. They were ably supported by the media.

6 The national discourse of Pakistan was an extension of *the two-nation theory*: whereas in the colonial Indian context it had been used to justify the imagined validity of communal 'national' differences between Hindus and Muslims, its postcolonial variant called for opposition to be shown to India at both the national and international levels to perpetuate the legitimacy of Pakistan as a nation.

7 Interview with Qamar Ahmed and Chisty Mujahid at the Gabba, Brisbane, 5 January 2000. Qamar Ahmed told me that cricket in 1950s Pakistan was financially in disarray; few games were played, and there were few incentives for people to play. Furthermore, Qamar himself, then a domestic cricketer in Pakistan, played on average three first-class games a season, earning the equivalent of two dollars a day. In one seven-year period from 1956–7 to 1963 he played only 17 first-class matches.

8 Private teams such as Pakistan Railways and Pakistan International Airlines had long fielded teams in local championships, but this was not at the request of government, nor was there a systematic policy to include company teams.

9 Interview with Arif Ali Khan Abassi in Karachi, 25 November 2000.

10 Hassan Shah (the chairman of the organising committee of the BCCP) and K. C. Collector (the Secretary of the Board of the BCCP) in *Dawn*, 2 December 1948. The situation was so critical and unexpected at the time of partition that one solution offered at the end of 1948 was for India, Pakistan and Ceylon to combine as a single Test-playing entity, rather as did the West Indies. However, this was at a time when the organisation of cricket in Pakistan began to gain momentum, and under these

circumstances the earliest officials of the game in the country began to think it wise to develop their own playing traditions. Subsequent attempts by the BCCI to poach Pakistani players in the period when the ICC continued to reject its membership were met with indignant disapproval by the BCCP and the Pakistani press. Both ultimately applauded the loyalty of these players for turning down all such contractual approaches.

11 Interview with Brigadier (retd) Salahuddin at the National Stadium in Karachi during the third Test match between Pakistan and England in 10 December 2000. At the time of this interview the findings of Salahuddin's committee had not yet been disclosed. Nor, to my knowledge, have they been since. *The Constitution of the Pakistan Cricket Board* (22 February 1995) was issued by the Government of Pakistan: the Ministry of Culture, Sports and Tourism in Islamabad on 16 March 1995. The previous BCCP constitution was revised and included a name change (it is now the PCB) and structural modifications that allowed it to be organised and registered as a company.

12 Interview with Chisty Mujahid, 6 January 2000 at the Gabba in Brisbane.

13 The English morning daily *The Pakistan Times*, and its Urdu equivalent the *Nawa-i-Waqt* (both from Lahore).

14 Two that did not were *The Civil and Military Gazette* in Lahore and *The Sind Observer* in Karachi.

15 These included two Urdu dailies, *Jang* and *Anjam*, and the English daily *Dawn*, all from Delhi.

16 Previously the Radio Pakistan employees had worked mostly out of tents (Dawn 1950).

17 Radio Pakistan website, www.radio.gov.pk.

18 In relation to this, Kureishi has remarked that 'It is an English game and therefore the commentary has to be in English.'

19 Interview with Shahzad Humayun, Lahore, 25 October 2000.

20 Early Urdu commentators encountered difficulties in translating much of the terminology of cricket. The word 'googly' was initially translated literally by Urdu commentators as *dhuke baaz gaind*, meaning 'treacherous, deceitful ball'; later, Pakistanis of all regional dialects became so familiar with the English spoken popular idiom of cricket that there was little reason for words such as 'googly' or 'howzat' to be translated into Urdu.

21 Shahzad Humayun.

22 *Sports Guardian*, 1 (4) (September 1951): 1, 18. In 1951, Sialkot exported 95 per cent of its sports goods. In March 1950, Australia imported sports goods to the value of £6,833, £834 from Pakistan and £5 from India; in cricket bat sales alone, Pakistan exported £16 worth to India's nil. The corresponding figures for September 1950 saw Australia import £23,851, £315 from Pakistan and £135 from India; Pakistan's cricket bat exports were worth £1,407 to India's £61.

23 There were some exceptions to this: the Arains as a group benefited considerably from the British.

24 Interview with Majid Khan, Zaman Park, Lahore, 2 November 2000.

25 Ibid.

26 Pakistan received 17.5 per cent of the total assets of undivided India, and lost the fiscal contributions of Hindu and Sikh entrepreneurs, who had withdrawn some three billion rupees prior to partition.

27 Robinson (1992) describes how Pakistan at its independence had no governmental infrastructure and no political figures with a tradition of representing the country as a single unit, and lost traditional manufacturers, customers and ports at Bombay, Ahmedabad and Calcutta for its raw materials.

28 This did not prove successful, as riots and other crowd disturbances were noticeable, particularly on the afternoon of the fourth day, when Pakistan was battling to avoid defeat.

130 *Chris Valiotis*

29 *The Sunday Tribune*, 9 March 1969.
30 Ibid.
31 Kardar writes: 'As an administrator of cricket I was his [Bhutto's] favourite. He took my word as final and would always tell me, "Who knows cricket better than you?"' However, by 1977 Bhutto was beginning to question Kardar's authority on cricket and for the first time took issue with him over his running of the game.
32 Fazal Mahmood in Ahmed (1977).
33 Traditional Islamic civilian rulers recognised the importance of political and religious institutions working together as an understood compact even though the two kinds of institutions had different and specific societal duties to fulfil. Thus, political rulers governed on a consultative basis with the *ulema*. For their part, the latter were awarded patronage by political rulers for staying out of politics. These awards included the appointment of *ulema* as political advisers, judges under *Shariat* law, inspectors of markets, and schoolteachers at various *madrassahs*.
34 In this case Mushtaq Muhammed, Imran and Majid Khan, Asif Iqbal and Zaheer Abbas.
35 *Dawn*, 20 January 1978.
36 Interview with Abassi.
37 *Dawn*, 10 January 1983.
38 *Dawn*, 6 February 1984.
39 *Dawn*, 19 January 1983.
40 *Dawn*, 18 October 1984.
41 Hoberman writes that 'sportive nationalism exists, not as an inchoate mass emotional condition, but as the product of specific choices and decisions made by identifiable political actors'.
42 Mike Marqusee writes of Pakistan's one-day dominance over India in a ten-year period beginning in April 1986 when Javed Mianded hit a last-ball six to win the Austral-Asia Cup Final in Sharjah for Pakistan. Of 26 one-day matches played, Pakistan won 21.
43 *Dawn*, 20 July 1983. Dr Asrar Ahmad, 'a distinguished religious scholar', denounced cricket because 'it paralysed all constructive activity throughout the duration' of a game, and its television coverage was 'likely to arouse an erotic sensation among feminine spectators'. He, like many other religious authorities, calls for the game to be banned.
44 Werbner's article looks at how the hybrid cricket culture of British-Pakistani youth challenges the family structure and traditional beliefs of the parent culture. British-Pakistani youth, it is argued, develop multiple identities by borrowing from both parental traditions and Western popular culture. These borrowings are selective and together they provide a basis for individual and collective expression in a world of global exchanges.

References

Ahmed, H. (1977) 'Fazal says our top cricketers are money sick', *Dawn*, 2 October.
Akhtar, M. (1953) in *Dawn*, 24 May.
Appadurai, A. (1996a) 'Playing with modernity: the decolonization of Indian cricket', in *Modernity at Large: Cultural Dimensions of Globalization*, Minneapolis: Minnesota University Press.
Appadurai, A. (1996b) 'Disjuncture and difference in the global cultural economy', in *Modernity at Large: Cultural Dimensions of Globalization*, Minneapolis: Minnesota University Press.
Aslam Hayat, M. (1949) *Dawn*, 14 February

Aziz, R. and Salam, A. (eds) (1983) *Pakistan Test Cricket 1982–83*, Karachi: Sports World Publications.

Baxter, C., Malik, A., Kennedy, C. and Oberst, R. (1998) *Government and Politics in South Asia*, 4th edn, Boulder, Colo.: Westview Press.

Bowen, R. (1967) in *Wisden Cricketers' Almanack*, Guildford, UK: Wisden.

Burki, S. J. (1988) *Pakistan under Bhutto*, 2nd edn, London: Macmillan.

Burki, S. J. and Baxter, C. (1991) *Pakistan under the Military: Eleven Years of Zia ul-Haq*, Boulder, Cob.: Westview Press.

Cashman, R. (1980) *Patrons, Players and the Crowd: The Phenomenon of Indian Cricket*, Delhi: Orient Longman.

Cashman, R. (1994) 'The paradox of Pakistani crocket: some initial reflections', *The Sports Historian*, 14: 21–37.

Coles, P. (1968) *The Ottoman Impact on Europe*, London: Thames & Hudson.

Dawn (1950) 'Propap', *Dawn*, 20 August.

Dawn (1975) 'Goodbye to cricket commentary', *Dawn*, 17 February.

de Mello, A. (1959) *Portraits of Indian Sport*, London: Macmillan.

Grunebaum, G. E. Von ([1963] 1970) *Classical Islam: A History*, trans. K. Watson, London: Allen & Unwin.

Guha, R. (2002) *A Corner of a Foreign Field: The Indian History of a British Sport*, London: Picador.

Hamid Khalil (1951) in *Dawn*, 29 July.

Hoberman, J. (1993) 'Sport and ideology in the post-communist age', in L. Allison (ed.) *The Changing Politics of Sport*, Manchester: Manchester University Press.

Imran Khan (1988) *All Round View*, London: Chatto & Windus.

Kardar, A. H. (1954) in *Wisden Cricketers' Almanack*, Guildford, UK: Wisden.

Kardar, A. H. (1987) *Memoirs of an All-Rounder*, Lahore: Progressive Publishers.

Marqusee, M. (1996) *War Minus the Shooting*, London: Mandarin.

Al Mujahid, S. (1981) *Quaid-i-Azam Jinnah: Studies in Interpretation*, Karachi: Committee on Quaid-i-Azam Biography, Quaid-i-Azam Academy.

Munawar Ali Khan, M. A. (2000) 'Who killed Kardar and our cricket?', *The News on Sunday*, 27 August, Sports 15.

Noman, O. (1998) *Pride and Passion: An Exhilarating Half Century of Cricket in Pakistan*, Karachi: Oxford University Press.

Page, D. and Crawley, W. (2001) *Satellites over South Asia: Broadcasting Culture and the Public Interest*, New Delhi: Sage.

Robinson, F. (1992) 'Origins', in W. E. James and S. Roy (eds) *Foundations of Pakistan's Political Economy*, New Delhi: Sage.

Robinson, R. (1972) *The Wildest Tests*, London: Pelham.

Salahuddin, Brigadier (retd) (1999) 'Ad-hocism in cricket over the decades', *Dawn*, 18 August.

Talbot, I. (2000) *Inventing the Nation: India and Pakistan*, London: Arnold.

Twenty Years of Pakistan, 1947–67 (1967) Karachi: Pakistan Publications.

Wasim Akram (1998) *Wasim: The Autobiography of Wasim Akram*, London: Piatkus.

Werbner, R. (1996a) 'Multiple identities, plural arenas', in R. Werbner and T. Ranger (eds) *Postcolonial Identities in Africa*, London: Zed Books.

Werbner, R. (1996b) 'Our blood is green: cricket, identity and social empowerment among British Pakistanis', in J. McClancey (ed.) *Sport, Identity and Ethnicity*, Oxford: Berg.

7 Sri Lanka
The power of cricket and the power in cricket[1]

Michael Roberts

Cricket is the one single game through which Sri Lanka has performed on the stage of world sport in consistent and striking fashion. It is now a national pastime for a sizeable section of the population. But the story of cricket in Sri Lanka or Ceylon is not one of rags to riches. There are many skeins in the history of the game in this lovely island, the brilliance and the verve of some moments being matched by threads sordid, vindictive, factious and topsy-turvy. To display the seamier side of cricket politics is beyond the capacity of a single historian. But some glimpses of this facet will be provided here amid the glitter of Sri Lankan cricketers' triumph in securing the World Cup at the one-day competition in the subcontinent in 1996. This essay will not cleave to a chronological line. As this preamble suggests, it begins beyond the cricket field in the terrain of power set in geographical space.

Problems of governance and political economy

The cricket scene in Sri Lanka today, as in the past, is a lopsided one. This imbalance is a product of political economy. Because the island lacks significant deposits of industrial raw material and because it developed into a modern state as a plantation economy, its orientation from way back in the 1830s has been towards the hub of the transport and administrative network, namely the city of Colombo. Colombo's dominant centricity was compounded when its port facilities were transformed from the 1870s onwards to make it a major harbour and entrepôt. Thereafter, Colombo became the leading city and a hegemonic centre. All roads, so to speak, led to Colombo. Internal migration flowed in its direction and virtually all media outlets have been within its confines from the 1850s to the present day.

Subject to some critical provisos, Colombo's dominance and pull continue today – in ways that bedevil the field of cricket. Most of the leading cricketers in the 1940s and 1950s were from Colombo schools or from two colleges in Kandy (itself the mini-hub of the hill country plantation economy). But as the increasing democratisation of politics and the widening of cricketing opportunity enabled talented lads from the seaside towns of Matara, Galle, Ambalangoda, Kalutara, Panadura, Moratuwa and Negombo on the one hand and Kurunägala in the hinterland on the other to reach the highest rungs of local cricket,[2] the fact remains that even now all roads lead to Colombo. Budding cricketers from these towns mostly end up playing for Colombo clubs and living in the Colombo metropolitan area.

The problem does not lie in the structure of cricket so much as in the character of Sri Lanka's political economy. The firms that can recruit cricketers as public relations faces are all located in Colombo. So are the best clubs: the SSC (Sinhalese Sports Club), NCC (Nondescripts Cricket Club) and Bloomfield head the pecking order at the moment, with the Colts, CCC (Colombo Cricket Club) and Tamil Union next in line. Indeed, most of the clubs in the Premier League are located in Colombo or its urban fringe.

The two caveats attached to this contention arise from contrasting circumstances, the one (A) an outcome of the electoral process for cricket governance, the other (B) from the history of conflictual politics in the island dating from the 'revolution of 1956', as the electoral shift in that year is sometimes, albeit controversially, called (M. de Silva 1967; Pieris 1958; K. M. de Silva 1981: ch. 36; 1998: 47–63, 67–8, 88–93, 305–6).

Let me take Point A first. The leading Colombo clubs may continue to lead the pack in recruiting a substantial proportion of the top cricketers. However, they do not *make*, or dominate, the governing body of cricket, once known as the Board of Control for Cricket in Sri Lanka (BCCSL), but recently (late 2003) rendered corporate under the name 'Sri Lanka Cricket'. From 1948 till 2003 this governing body was – in normal circumstances[3] – elected annually. Once cricket became a business and a centre of attraction from 1996, its governing positions attracted entrepreneurs of various types. The voting system gave (gives) even a parlous club the same voting power as the most famous. With largesse available to the winners at these elections from 1996 onwards, an American-style spoils system has taken root in recent years. This has favoured the election of wheeler-dealers and populist politicians rather than patrician notables ready to dig into their personal pockets.

The outcome has been a regular turnover of supremos every year, with the roller-coaster changes exacerbated further by periodic crises leading to ministerial interventions and the establishment of interim committees (in most cases staffed by honourable men). But created by ministerial fiat, such interim boards have also been subject to removal every time the sports minister is displaced or has a row with the chairman of the board. In sum, Sri Lanka has had about five different regimes over the past seven years! It is a wonder that any cricket tours actually take place in the midst of all these musical chairs and dodgem games.

A new board usually means a new selection committee. By good fortune, Brendon Kuruppu, T. B. Kehelgamuwa and Amal Silva remained on the selection committees, serving through the years mid-1999 to 2002 so that some element of continuity in fostering players was maintained. The imposition of a new interim committee under Hemaka Amarasuriya in April 2002 and a new selection committee led by Guy de Alwis altered matters. The choice of one-day international (ODI) teams for the tours of England, South Africa and Australia as well as the World Cup in 2002–3 was a tale of disaster upon disaster. As a result, the

134 Michael Roberts

opportunity provided by favourable wickets and events at the World Cup in South Africa could not be seized (see Roberts 2002b–d, 2003).

The message here is simple. Since 1996 the process of annual cricket elections, the politics and rivalries within the domain of cricket, ministerial interventions and the politics outside cricket that impinge on cricket – all these factors together have made for continuous turmoil. It has hindered long-term policies in the building of infrastructures and held back the progress of emerging players. That the Sri Lankan cricket team has continued to be competitive in such circumstances is something of a miracle and speaks volumes for the pool of talent available and the wonderful bowling arms of Muttiah Muralitharan and Chaminda Vaas.

Now to Point B: the cloud over cricket because of political conflict-become-war. Though the causes are several, one major development arose from the political transformation through the vote that occurred in 1956. The year 1956 represents the upsurge of two allied forces: first, underprivileged and socialist forces attacking the privileges of the English-speaking, Westernised middle class and, second, the vernacular-educated social strata hostile to the dominance of English-speak. By and large the latter represented the voice of Sinhalese linguistic nationalism. Though led by a maverick faction of the middle class centred upon S. W. R. D. Bandaranaike and his Sri Lanka Freedom Party (SLFP), this coalition began an assault on the dominance of English through a process that also enthroned the Sinhala language as the official language and thereby rendered Tamil secondary.[4]

One consequence was the alienation of some Sri Lankan Tamils, whose political demands then escalated. Disenchanted with the political weight they were afforded, growing discrimination in the government services and unfolding events, these Tamils began to jettison their Ceyloneseness: by the mid-1970s they were demanding a separate state, while some Tamil youth set up underground liberation organisations. Seeking to 'teach the Tamils a lesson', in July 1983 some state functionaries and some populist elements initiated a pogrom against Tamils residing in the south. This horrendous event was counter-productive: it multiplied the support for the militant Tamil liberation forces among the Tamil peoples as well as international bodies. From then on, Sri Lanka has been effectively divided into two nations. As a hot war developed and moved beyond guerrilla struggles to a complex military situation wherein the Liberation Tigers of Tamil Eelam (LTTE) have had *de facto* control of large swathes of territory in the north and east from 1986 onwards, Sri Lanka became a war-torn state (Narayan Swamy 1994, 2003; Wilson 2000: chs 6, 7, 9).

In effect, little tournament cricket was played in the northern and eastern reaches of Sri Lanka from the mid-1980s. Indeed, when C. E. Anandarajah, the principal of St John's College in Jaffna, organised a cricket match between his school and the army as a gesture of goodwill, he was assassinated by the LTTE on 25 June 1985 because they considered the army to be an occupying force and his act one of collaboration.[5] Cricket in Sri Lanka, then, is imbricated with politics.

The war between the Sinhala-dominated state and the Tamils sometimes impinged on the cities in the south. Indeed, the metropolitan area around Colombo was a war zone from 1987 onwards. The New Zealand cricket team was on tour when two bombing attacks occurred, one a horrendous atrocity involving a car bomb at the Central bus station in the Pettah on 4 April 1987 and the other an attack on the navy commander's car by a suicide bomber opposite the hotel at which the Kiwis were staying on 11 November 1992 (Roberts 2002a; Perera 1999: 517–18).

The political circumstances worsened further when an indigenist and socialist force known as the *Janata Vimukti Peramuna* (JVP, or People's Liberation Front) launched an underground war in 1987 intended to oust the ruling United National Party. The JVP was virtually wholly Sinhalese in composition and its threat led to what was in effect a civil war in the southern and central heartlands of the island. In this situation both tourists and international cricket teams avoided Sri Lanka. The period April 1987 to mid-1992, therefore, was a kind of hiatus and a distinct setback for Sri Lankan cricket.

In overview, therefore, it will be evident that the Sinhala–Tamil conflict has resulted in the energies of Tamil youth being lost to the cause of cricket. Let me qualify this remark by noting that in the era between 1945 and the 1970s few Tamil cricketers from the Jaffna Peninsula or the eastern regions climbed into the highest ranks of cricket; indeed, C. Balakrishnan in 1969 is the only instance. Tamils who achieved success were usually from the schools in Colombo and Kandy. This outcome was due to infrastructural factors and the Colombo-centred character of the game in that era.

As the political gulf between Sri Lankan Tamils and the rest of the island widened from the mid-1970s, moreover, even young Tamils residing in the south-western regions began to lose interest in cricket. Their focus has been on educational achievement and jobs abroad. Thus, the Tamil Union has had only a handful of Tamils in its ranks from the late 1970s. In short, the limited number of Tamil cricketers in the ranks of international cricketers since, say, 1980 has been due to the paucity of Tamil cricketers. As for the most famous of them, Muttiah Muralitharan, he is of Malaiyaha Tamil ('Indian Tamil') background because his patrilineage had its roots among the plantation foremen who moved into small business. His father was able to initiate a small factory and educate his sons at St Anthony's College, Kandy.

The ethnic conflict has had other effects, however. The loyalty of many Tamils, both those living abroad and those remaining in Sri Lanka, has been compromised. This is difficult terrain for conclusive verdicts. But Nirupama Subramaniam's evaluations and my casual enquiries lead me to the opinion that whenever Sri Lanka face India, a goodly majority of Tamils in all parts of Sri Lanka favour an Indian victory. When Sri Lanka face other sides, however, it seems that local Tamil sentiments are divided: one section of the local Tamil peoples root for Sri Lanka, but another part, quite considerable, seem to favour any side playing against Sri Lanka.[6] The principle in operation here is simple: the enemy of your enemy is your friend. No better illustration of this sharpening of

136   *Michael Roberts*

identity and enmity can be provided than an anecdote from the National University of Singapore (NUS). Mustapha, a Sri Lankan Muslim lad studying at the NUS, was introduced to a Sri Lankan Tamil girl at the same campus who promptly told him, 'You are our enemy.' As significant as the statement is the fact that Mustapha was shocked numb.[7]

But there is also a faint thread of silver lining provided by cricket amid the stormy landscape of ethnic hostilities in Sri Lanka. Since peace overtures commenced in December 2002, cricket has been one of the forms of bridge building. Some of the schools in Jaffna and Royal College in Colombo have played each other recently on a reciprocal basis. Janashakti, a leading insurance firm headed by Chandra Schaffter (a former Ceylon cap and a Tamil), took a team that included Muralitharan, Kaluwitharana and Ruchira Perera to play a match against the Jaffna District Cricket Association on 1 September 2002.[8] The Australian High Commission saw to it that the Australian Cricket Board's coaches, Buchanan and Nielsen, conducted a coaching clinic on 20 September 2002 in the Jaffna Peninsula[9] – that is, the centre of Sri Lankan Tamil culture and the movement for Eelam. As I have said, cricket in Sri Lanka is imbricated with politics.

British colonialism, sport and cricket

Cricket did not begin in Sri Lanka with any obvious political ramifications. It was mere pleasure. For a few British males. These blokes were not tourists. They were part of the imperial machine that had taken over the island in two bites, 1795–6 and 1815–18, the latter involving the suppression of a massive rebellion in the hill country regions in 1817–18. As one would expect in such circumstances, the military establishment was a significant part of the British order at the outset of British rule in 'Ceylon', as the island was called then.

It is likely that it was the military personnel who introduced the game of cricket to British Ceylon and British India (Perera 1999: 3). That it was part of recreational activity in the Indian subcontinent is illustrated in an oil painting by Thomas Daniell of a game on the *maidan* (open space for recreation) at Madras about the year 1792.[10] Thus far, the recorded data on cricket in Sri Lanka in the first 70 years of British rule are negligible and we are mostly indebted to S. S. Perera (1999) for the little that we know.[11] The first recorded game was played between the NCOs and privates of the 97th regiment, and the CCC in November 1832. The CCC, a club for British gentlemen, had been initiated in September that year, but may have declined subsequently, for it had to be resuscitated in 1863 (ibid.: 26, 28).

The subsequent attractions of cricket for the indigenous elites can only be understood through attention to its significance for the British ruling class in the imperial scheme of things. The British in the colonies commanded a large number of menial workers to service many sports, including hunting, shooting, horse racing and games of all types. The colonial body of leisured gentlemen and ladies pursued the full panoply of British games. In taking up more energetic pastimes, moreover, the British believed that they were counteracting the debilitating influence of a tropical climate (Mandle 1973: 526), while also sustaining the building of character. Such games as cricket, polo and soccer were, at least by the mid-nineteenth century, considered symbols of 'pluck' and 'manliness' (Mandle 1973; Mangan 1981).

Such pastimes called for organisation. They were institutionalised as clubs and associations (with their ranking distinctions and colour bar). The annual calendar was arranged to cater for ritual occasions of race meets, sporting events and ballroom dances, while the urban space was reshaped to cater for such activities. In enjoying themselves with such gusto, the British ruling class provided a model for emulation. Their racial arrogance may have been disliked, but most of their enjoyments proved attractive to the emerging indigenous elites of urban Ceylon. Such pastimes, whether cricket, cards, carrom and other board games, or soccer and athletics later on, were FUN

In such a colonial setting, cricket helped induct the indigenous elites into the Westernised life-ways of their masters. Indeed, it entered school activities in order to train character in the manner pursued in the best public schools in Britain (see Mangan 1981). Cricket seems to have been introduced to schoolboys of the elite government-run school known as the Colombo Academy (which became the Royal College in 1881) by the Reverend Brooke Bailey in 1832, and St Thomas' College figures among records of games in the 1860s. Regular school encounters do not seem to have commenced till the Royal–Thomian series began in 1879.[12]

What is striking, however, about the earliest local cricketers of the 1860s and 1870s was the degree to which they were drawn mostly from two indigenising immigrant bodies domiciled in Colombo in particular, namely the Malays and the Burghers. Malays had served in the Dutch (and Kandyan) armies in the eighteenth century and were incorporated into the Ceylon Rifle Regiment (CRR) in 1827. Malay soldiers took to cricket and the community eventually set up their own club, the Malay Cricket Club, around 1871–2, a year or two before the CRR was disbanded (Roberts et al. 1989: 102). But most of the club teams of the 1860s were Burgher in composition.[13]

Burghers at the cutting edge

As understood in the twentieth century, the term 'Burghers' refers to those believed to be descendants of representatives of the colonial powers, namely the Portuguese, the Dutch and other Europeans serving the Vereenidge Oost-Indische Compagnie (Dutch East India Company) and the British.[14] The Burghers of Ceylon had a much greater role in the history of Sri Lanka than the Eurasians and Anglo-Indians of India did in that country. Residing mostly in urban centres, they were quickly recruited into the middling echelons of the British administrative order. They found it easier to pick up English and were clearly more attuned to Westernised life-ways. Their capacities were such that the liberal English journalist William Digby felt that they could be a bridge between West and East

138   *Michael Roberts*

and mediate the self-improvement of the island colony.[15] Events were to prove him overly optimistic – not least in the year 1956. However, he was partially correct. The Burghers were a central force in effectively transmitting the repertoire of British sports to the rest of the island peoples. From the 1860s to the 1930s, and even into the 1950s, they were the island's leading sportsmen in numerous fields – from angling to hunting, cricket and rugby football.

Their sport was not only fun. It was a kind of politics. However versed in English-speak and the virtues of Shakespeare, in the mid-nineteenth century the Burgher middle class found that they were viewed as 'half-caste' and 'natives'. They began to stress their indigenous stakes. Taking their cue from Mazzini's Young Italy movement, a handful of remarkably talented young Burgher lads established the journal *Young Ceylon* (1850–2) as a literary engine for what I would call 'Ceylonese nationalism'. A few years later this same group was at the heart of a syndicate that bought the *Examiner*, a local English-media newspaper, from its English proprietor so that they could prove that 'Ceylon has arrived at a position when her children can speak for themselves.'[16]

Direct confrontation with British dominion was still not feasible, however, because it would be treated as 'sedition'. In this circumstance the cricket field provided an alternative venue for challenges to white supremacy. The competition inherent in games was proper, a jolly good show, legitimate. Thus, on 26–28 May 1881 a team of youth assembled as 'Young Ceylon' ranged against the CCC (Perera 1999: 42–4). They lost badly, but the gauntlet had been laid down. The challenge was renewed in 1882. Then, on 29–30 June 1887 there occurred a contest between 'the best eleven European cricketers and the picked representatives of the Ceylonese'. This game aroused 'unusual interest in Colombo' because it was viewed as a Test match and a test of superiority (Foenander 1924: 157). The Ceylonese team was as follows: Dr Edgar Kellaart (captain), Collin Kelaart, 'Banda' Kelaart, Edward Weinman, 'Jillah' Weinman, Oswald Van Hoff, E. H. Joseph, W. de Fransz, C. Wilkins, Charles Heyn and Patrick Thomasz. It was a Burgher team (Roberts *et al.* 1989: 122ff.).

It was also an eleven drawn from the Colts Cricket Club. Formed in 1873 and located in the Pettah, this club dominated the cricket scene during the last three decades of the nineteenth century. But as the leading schools encouraged cricket, one saw middle-class men from the Sinhalese, Borah, Colombo Chetty, Tamil and Moor communities taking up the game. By the 1890s, indeed, the internal migration of Tamils to Colombo had developed in such proportions that the Tamil Union CC was inaugurated on 2 December 1899.[17] Thus augmented, the Ceylonese teams during the twentieth century were usually superior to the sides that the local Europeans were able to pit against them in what was called (from 1905) the 'European–Ceylonese Test'. By the 1920s the local Europeans were being regularly pulverised, and the last match in this series was played in 1933 (Roberts 1985: 425; Foenander 1924: 157–68; Perera 1999: 172–4), by which time the colony was well on the road to self-determination by virtue of the new Donoughmore constitution brought into effect in 1931.

Sealane and empire cricket, 1900–47

The nationalist lining to some cricket contests should not obscure the fact that the game was sponsored during the nineteenth century by a number of Englishmen. Ashley Walker, a schoolmaster, and George Vanderspar, a businessman, are identified by S. S. Perera as leading promoters of the game in the late nineteenth century. The organisational roles were soon taken up by Ceylonese, such as Col. Dr John Rockwood (Tamil), S. P. Foenander (Bharatha, considered Burgher), P. Saravanamuttu (Tamil) and E. M. Karunaratne (Sinhalese) of Galle, during the first half of the twentieth century. When the Ceylon Cricket Association (CCA) was established on 13 July 1922, Dr John Rockwood became president while the British businessman O. B. Forbes became Honorary Secretary (Perera 1999: 141; Foenander 1924: 131–3).

The ethnic mix in the CCA denoted by these names is of significance in a political context in which the Ceylonese middle class was challenging British overlordship and demanding constitutional devolution – for the early 1920s was replete with verbal wrangles and political brouhaha.[18] Along one dimension, the trans-ethnic cooperation shows that cricket transcended politics. Along another dimension it reveals how doors were opened to some Ceylonese because of their wealth and Anglicised manners. Indeed, the genteel civility of the upper layers of the Ceylonese middle class in the 1920s had proved a great asset in persuading the British Raj to transfer a considerable measure of political power by 1927–31 (following the Donoughmore Commission of 1927).

Ceylon's junction location in the grid of international shipping lanes and its links with the British upper classes through the plantation trades also encouraged cricket teams from several parts of the British Empire to tour the island. Among the many, let me note three contrasting instances: the Reverend E. F. Waddy's team of Australians (December 1913 – January 1914), St Peter's College of Adelaide (1928) and the MCC at the end of their tours of India in early 1927 and early in 1934 (Foenander 1924: 89–91; Perera 1999: 177–8; Colin-Thome 2003: 83).[19]

Perhaps the most colourful of these visits was when the MCC, Australian and New Zealand teams played 'whistle-stop' matches over one day when their P&O ships called at Colombo on their way to or from England. Radio Colombo (established 1922) transmitted the BBC's external service broadcast of the famous Fifth Test at the Oval in 1938.[20] Once the Ashes series were renewed after the Second World War, such radio broadcasts generated legendary fervour among cricket devotees in Ceylon for a long time thereafter – at least till local heroes entered the global circuit of cricket. When famous cricketers dropped in at their doorstep for the whistle-stop games, therefore, enormous crowds were drawn to the matches. In the result, too, Sri Lanka derived one satisfaction that was denied to the Indian devotees of the game: they were able to see Bradman bat on their soil in 1930 and 1948.

For reasons of proximity and affinity, however, the trans-imperial links were strongest with British India. The first of these friendly encounters, involving a five-week tour to Bombay to play its Gymkhana sides in 1903, was perhaps the

140 *Michael Roberts*

most significant. Though organised by the Colts CC, the money required for the trip (Rs 29,317) was collected by public subscription, while the team included five players from the SSC, four from the NCC and A. C. Ahmath from the Malay CC in addition to leading Colts players (Perera 1999: 89–90).

The 'ecumenical' character of imperial cricket was illustrated when Tommy Kelaart and D. L. de Saram were asked to attend the trials to select an Indian team in December 1903 for a planned tour of England in the summer of 1904, a tour that did not eventuate (Perera 1999: 90–1). Thirty years later the Maharaj Kumar of Vizianagram (MKV) attempted to persuade the Indian authorities to include Edward Kelaart, a marvellous off-spinning all-rounder, in the Indian squad for England, but failed (ibid.: 164–5). Such trans-national affinities were not surprising in an era when Indian princes such as Duleepsinhji, Ranjitsinhji, Iftikar Nawab of Pataudi and Yuvraj of Patiala played for England – that is, the MCC.

The Tamil Union toured Madras in the Christmas season of 1911, 1913 and 1918; the Malay CC toured Bombay in December 1907, while John Rockwood organised a two-week tour of Bombay in December 1919. This team included one Malay (Ahmath), two Tamils, five Burghers and seven Sinhalese (Foenander 1924: 106–7, 208–11; Perera 1999: 136–7). As noticeably, the team played four matches against the Islam Gymkhana, Parsee Gymkhana, Hindu Gymkhana and Bombay Gymkhana – three ethnic teams and one trans-ethnic. Thereafter, a team from Bombay made a reciprocal visit and played three matches in Colombo in 1926 versus a European XI, a Ceylonese XI and an All-Ceylon XI. Again, in 1930 MKV promoted an eight-match tour of Sri Lanka by a team that included England's Jack Hobbs and Herbert Sutcliffe as well as the two Nayudu brothers, C. K. and C. S. (Perera 1999: 152–3, 163–4).

Such exchanges with India, clearly, promoted the game in Sri Lanka. Five significant moments in this relationship need marking. One: the 'All-Ceylon' tour of India in late 1932/early 1933, when the team was led by Dr C. H. Gunasekara (Perera 1999: 170–1). Two: the invitation extended to Edward Kelaart to play for MKV's side in 1930–1, 1933–4 and 1935, the second of these being against the MCC (ibid.: 164–5). Three: Indian invitations to outstanding Sri Lankan players such as F. C. de Saram, S. S. Jayawickrema, Pat McCarthy, George Pereira and M. Sathasivam to play for the Rest of India in the Bombay Pentangular tournament or the capstone game against the Ranji Trophy champions (ibid.: 165, 230–1). Four: the tour of Sri Lanka in 1945 by the Indian side under Vijay Merchant for a set of five matches, including an 'unofficial Test' versus 'All-Ceylon'. This Test was witnessed by a crowd estimated at 15,000 – an indicator of the popularity of the game in the urban south-west (ibid.: 221–2). Five: the CCA's trip to Madras to play South India in January 1947, a triumphant occasion when Sri Lanka scored 521 for 7, with Sathasivam playing what many considered to be the finest innings ever seen at the Chepauk grounds up to that date, 215 runs in 248 minutes; and then dismissed the local side for 197 and 200, with R. L. de Kretser (off spin) and L. E. de Zoysa (right arm leg spin) as main destroyers (ibid.: 229–30).

For all its lustre, cricket in the first half of the twentieth century remained an elite game confined for the most part to the urban centres of the southern and central parts of the island and Jaffna town in the Peninsula, but supplemented by the inputs from the British planters as well as British personnel in the main towns. Highly talented cricketers were emerging from the ranks of all the indigenous communities. A few families also had the wherewithal to send their sons to England for cricket and study. Dr C. H. Gunasekara played cricket for Middlesex (1919–20 and 1922) and S. G. A. Maartensz for Hampshire; while J. A. de Silva and T. E. Tweed played for Cambridge in 1925–6 and F. C. de Saram for Hertfordshire and Oxford University in the 1930s. Young de Saram had an outstanding season for Hertfordshire in the minor county league in 1933, scoring 479 runs in 8 outings for an average of 68.42. This feat earned him a belated place in the Oxford University XI, where he scored a brilliant 128 out of Oxford's total of 218 against Woodfull's Australian team in 1934.[21]

By 1945, then, as the end of the Second World War ushered in a new era, Sri Lanka had a handful of talented cricketers who were capable of performing well *occasionally* against the best international sides. This talent was more evident in batting than in bowling. Sathasivam and de Saram stood out amid this pool of talent. Derrick de Saram has been described by one of his protégés as 'the complete batsman', one with 'a granite defence . . . blended with punitive orthodoxy' (Gunasekara 1996: 34–5). He made 50 and 122 not out for the Rest of India versus the Muslims in 1937, and scored masterly centuries for the SSC when they played Madras and Baroda on their tour of India in 1945 (ibid.: 48–9; Perera 1999: 165).[22] The debonair 'Satha' was twinkle-toed, all class and finesse. Indeed, folklore suggests that Ghulam Ahmed considered him the best batsman he had ever bowled to and that Worrell thought him 'the best batsman he had ever seen' (Gunasekara 1996: 57). Statistics support the interpretation: before his classic innings at the Chepauk grounds, he made 101 runs in 1944 for the Rest of India versus the Hindus (the All-India champions in that year); a masterly 111 runs in difficult conditions against the full complement of Indian bowlers under Merchant at the unofficial Test match of 1945; and a remarkable 96 runs out of a total of 153 when the Ceylon side struggled against a visiting Commonwealth team on a rain-affected pitch in February 1950 (ibid.: 48–9; Perera 1999: 221–2, 165, 229–31, 251–2).

In overview, therefore, one could say that by the second quarter of the twentieth century cricket had a vibrant place in the hearts of many middle-class males living in the main urban centres. This was never more evident than on the occasions when the leading colleges in a city played each other in their annual blood match. These games attracted large crowds from across the social spectrum in and around each urban centre. Whether it was Mahinda playing Richmond at Galle, St John's playing Jaffna Central at Jaffna, or Trinity playing St Anthony's at Kandy, the townsfolk could not but take note of the boisterous activities generated by roving bands of schoolboys; while older alumni assembled in droves to consume booze in gargantuan proportions.[23] This spirit, so to speak, also flowed over to the annual Law–Medical match in Colombo, where some of the highest in the land let their trousers down in festive mood.

142 *Michael Roberts*

Independence in 1948: towards change

Despite such traditions and the playing talent on hand, Sri Lanka's cricket stepped forth into the postcolonial era in 1948 with many limitations. For one, cricket being a game played with a leather ball, the pool of players was wholly amateur and largely drawn from middle-class families, though lads from an urban lower-middle-class background were soon entering the ranks. The working class in the towns were not strangers to the game. Tennis ball cricket was popular, and the big matches drew crowds from all the urban strata; and indeed they attracted betting. Second, little or no cricket was played in the outlying rural hinterlands of the north-east, north-central, south-east and Uva regions. As a pastime that drew popular attention, cricket was still limited in its reach and market value. Third, there were few turf pitches and most of the cricket was played on matting. This was but one sign of the limited facilities in support of cricket.

The securing of sovereign status by Ceylon in 1948 was accompanied by an organisational transformation in cricket. The CCA was replaced by the Board of Control for Ceylon Cricket in June 1948. It was at this moment that the ridiculous practice of annual elections seems to have been established. But its problematic potentialities were not felt immediately. At the annual AGM, club representatives went into a huddle and chose a president by haggling and consensus. Few crises arose, because powerful and/or wealthy personalities had already put their hands up for an onerous job with few perquisites. The Royal–Thomian network of influence, moreover, appears to have called the shots. By and large it ensured that the presidency for many decades rested in the hands of a few notables from United National Party (UNP) families: J. R. Jayewardene (1952–5), Robert Senanayake (1957–75), T. B. Werapitiya (1980–1), Gamini Dissanayake (1981–9) and Tyronne Fernando (1991–4).

Such individuals as Senanayake and Werapitiya sometimes dipped into their own pockets to assist the cricketing activities. Privilege meant *noblesse oblige*. This cabalistic character as well as Robert Senanayake's long tenure of office ensured a relative continuity of policy over the years. But such a structure may have encouraged an element of myopia as well as elitist conceptions of the island's cricketing needs between the 1940s and the 1960s. It was not till Gamini Dissanayake took over the reins in 1981 in a move engineered by Abu Fuard[24] that a major change occurred – helped by the achievements of the Lankan cricketers as well as shifting currents in the global management of cricket.

Tentatively, one can identify several developments that transformed cricket in Sri Lanka and enhanced its popularity over the course of the years 1948–2000.

1   The beginning of broadcasts in the Sinhala medium around 1967 because of the initiative taken by Neville Jayaweera in his capacity as director-general of the Ceylon Broadcasting Corporation (CBC) to broadcast the annual big match between the former Buddhist denominational schools, Ananda and Nalanda. He called on Palitha Perera, a former Nalandian cricketer, an employee in the Sinhala section of the CBC, to take up this task. A whole

new vocabulary had to be devised for the purpose, with Dr Vinnie Vitharana and Karunaratne Abeysekera assisting Perera in this innovation.[25] This breakthrough provided the foundation for Sinhala coverage of international matches in subsequent years, with Premasara Epasinghe achieving fame in this work in subsequent decades. These accounts disseminated knowledge and interest in the game among many to whom it had been quite unfamiliar. What one sees here, therefore, is the ramifying effect of the socio-political transformation of 1956 – so that its democratising effects only began to penetrate the cricket world some 10–15 years later. Though Jayaweera and Vitharana were solidly middle-class and Western educated, their ideological leanings were towards the underprivileged; while Perera, Abeysekera and Epasinghe were from Buddhist schools and typical of the lower-middle-class strata of the 1950s and 1960s which were the motor force behind the SLFP-led movement of Sinhala nationalism.

2   The advent of television to the island in 1979 – in colour form, unlike in India, where early television was in black and white – and TV coverage of international cricket matches from c. 1982 increased enthusiasm for the game.

3   Sri Lanka's success in July 1981 in securing entry to the highest echelon of international cricket administered by the ICC, an event that calls for further detail later in the chapter.

4   The subsequent expansion of facilities for cricket as a result of this step and the initiatives of Gamini Dissanayake and Abu Fuard – a programme that was materially assisted by the fact that Dissanayake headed a UNP ministry supervising massive construction works.

5   The gradual widening of opportunity that enabled cricketers beyond those educated at the best schools in Colombo and Kandy to penetrate the ranks of the teams representing Sri Lanka. This expansion encompassed individuals from less prestigious schools at these centres (e.g. Dharmaraja, Thurston) as well as young men from the towns further afield, such as Kurunägala and Ambalangoda. Among the classic illustrations of this process has been the tale of the brothers de Silva, D. H., D. P. and D. S., from Mahinda College in Galle during the period spanning the 1960s and the 1980s; and the meteoric rise in the 1990s of Sanath Jayasuriya, a lad nurtured among the fisher folk in the locality of Matara. Such success stories inspired local interest and widened networks of influence.

6   The winning of the World Cup in 1996 and the gigantic increase in the financial coffers of the BCCSL flowing from this event (see pp. 151–3).

Tensions, rivalries, conspiracies

Even in the era before 1983 the elitist character of cricket governance did not erase the potential for rivalry. Trouble emerged at the birth of the new era. With Bradman's team due to play a match in March 1948, it was expected that F. C. de Saram, captain of the SSC, the most senior player and star, would captain. But

144 *Michael Roberts*

a close vote (9 against 7) within the selection committee saw the captain of the Tamil Union, M. Sathasivam, chosen to lead the side. This choice rankled. In the weeks that followed the Australian match, de Saram and five other SSC players expressed their displeasure by declining to play for the CCA when selected to represent Ceylon against the visiting Ranji Trophy Champions, the Holkar Cricket Association.

This unproclaimed boycott immediately drew a chorus of criticism from a number of voices, Sinhalese, Burghers and local Britons among them. It says much about the ethos of the time that 'ill-mannered' was one of the charges hurled at these SSC men. That was not all: in April 1948 the CCA suspended all six players for a year. However, a rapprochement was soon brought about and the ban was removed by the new BCCSL in October 1948. The reason was simple: the great West Indian team was due to tour Sri Lanka shortly. The island could ill afford to lose its best cricketers – for the SSC had by far the best squad of players at that time (Perera 1999: 236–41).

Though at face value it would appear that this controversy was motivated by ethnic rivalry, an unimpeachable Tamil source claims that de Saram was the logical choice and the displacement was due to Sathasivam's personal ambitions and ability to mobilise key support.[26] Whatever the validity of this evaluation, ethnic dimensions were attached to the cricket scene by the cricketing public. For all Sathasivam's brilliance as a player, there were elements in the crowd who teased him with the epithet 'fifty/fifty' when he played for Ceylon against Vijay Merchant's India XI in 1945; and in 1948 both the Tamils in the side, Sathasivam and Nagendra, had to endure this bantering abuse.[27]

The slogan 'fifty/fifty' was an eminently political one, indeed a notorious phrase. In the 1930s the Tamil Congress, led by G. G. Ponnambalam, had argued that the division of parliamentary seats should be organised so that the Sinhalese received 50 per cent and the diverse minority communities together made up the other 50 per cent – so 'fifty/fifty' summed up this political programme. In a context where the Sinhalese made up 69 per cent of the population and where most people in that period considered the island's history to be largely a Sinhala one, the Tamil Congress demand was deemed ridiculous, even by non-Sinhalese. In short, it was a 'joke'. But since the Tamil Congress and its demands also served as an obstacle in the push for complete self-determination, the deployment of the joke in most contexts, cricket field included, had some bite in it.

The next major controversy over team selection – in 1968 – was rather more disastrous in its consequences: it is arguable that it delayed Sri Lanka's ascension to Test status by 5–12 years. To understand the manner in which some Sri Lankan cricketers shot themselves in the foot, one has to comprehend the cricketing circumstances of the early to mid-1960s. Two sets of cricketing achievements came into play.

For one, by the 1960s several Sri Lankan cricketers had shown their mettle on the English county circuit. Laddie Outschoorn (Worcestershire, 1946–59) was an early 'outrider', but it was the cumulative effect of performances by Stanley Jayasinghe and Clive Inman for Leicestershire, Gamini Goonasena for

Nottinghamshire (1952–64) and Cambridge University (1954–7), P. I. Pieris (1956–8) and Mano Ponniah (1967–9) for Cambridge, and Dan Piachaud for Oxford University (1958–61) and Hampshire that would have impressed English cricketing circles. 'Ceylon' was placed on their map.

Their ability to penetrate the English world of cricket at this point of time is a little story that demands its little historian. Cricketing talent, of course, was one requisite. But how did these unknowns from the colonial boondocks break the ice and get decent trials? Jayasinghe had to do the hard yards in the Penzance and Lancashire Leagues (1956–9) before making his mark in the Leicestershire Second XI, though grapevine gossip suggests that Len Hutton's recommendation helped him at one point. By 1960 he had cemented his place in the Leicestershire side. Jayasinghe in turn paved the way for Inman (1960–8). In most of the other instances, considerable familial wealth, upper-class connections and intellectual capacities enabled these talented young men to make the university XIs. Goonasena was even supported by a public collection of funds and financial support from the Sri Lankan government when he entered Cambridge in 1954 after a short spell at Cranwell RAF College (1950). His success made it easier for the other university men from Sri Lanka who followed, the more so because he captained Cambridge, performed the double of 1000 runs and 100 wickets in two county seasons, and was one of Wisden's Cricketers of the Year in both 1957 and 1959 (Perera 1999: 269).

The other achievements were back in South Asia. Led by Michael Tissera, Sri Lanka had defeated Pakistan in an 'unofficial Test' at home in August 1964 and then engineered a remarkable victory over India at Ahmedabad after bold cricket in January 1965 (Perera 1999: 298–302).[28] Such factors, therefore, may have induced the ICC to make Sri Lanka an Associate Member of the ICC in 1965 and led S. C. Griffith, secretary of the ICC, to intimate that they were ready to host the Sri Lankan team in England in 1968.

This was a major breakthrough. But there remained the question of funds. The island was racked by a severe foreign exchange crisis, while the BCCSL was impecunious. Though the prime minister was brother to the president of the Board, the government, harassed by the Communist Party as well as some of its populist members and the media, refused to release foreign exchange for such a trivial activity as cricket. Cricket enthusiasts, however, proceeded to make plans from 1966 onwards and began to collect funds for the tour, in particular by arranging for the donation of air fares from institutions connected with the tea trade in London. The 1968 tour was on course.

It was anticipated that some of the stars in England at that time in 1968, notably Goonesena, Inman, Piachaud and Ponniah, would be part of the team because of their capacities as well as the saving of air fares. But voices could already be heard in complaint against this suggestion because it 'denied' those at home opportunities to advance. Suspicions of a conspiracy strengthened when Abu Fuard engineered a selection committee comprising Sam Abeysekera (chairman), C. Schaffter, Dhanasiri Weerasinghe and H. I. K. Fernando. The latter two (and Fuard himself) were Ceylon caps. The next step was when

146   *Michael Roberts*

Fernando was made captain of the side facing Joe Lister's team as they toured Sri Lanka in 1968. The meeting to select the team for the tour of England was held in April 1968: Schaffter stormed out of the discussion in disgust; the rump committee proceeded to make Fernando captain and Tissera vice-captain, and included both Weerasinghe and Fuard, while omitting D. H. de Silva, who appears to have been part of the 'conspiracy'.[29]

Predictably, a storm erupted. The promise of air fares was withdrawn. At an emergency meeting the BCCSL declared the decisions *ultra vires* because one selector was not present. The tour was cancelled. The incidents of 1948 and 1968, therefore, reveal that it is not only money and big business (post-1996) that encourage manipulative action. Indeed, stories about the machinations of Abu Fuard when he was a kingmaker and kingpin in the 1980s are legion.

The attempted 'captaincy coup' of 1968 had class jealousies among its inspirations. Here, then, on the cricket scene was a whiff of the 1956 revolution: a tale of those on the fringes of power attempting to seize the throne. The cricket world in the 1960s, as in the decades before, was still dominated by the Westernised set drawn from Christian denominational schools and Royal–Thomian networks. Though proficient in English, such individuals as Weerasinghe (Ananda) and D. H. de Silva (Mahinda) represented the elite Sinhala-Buddhist schools, which resented this dominance.

The sharpness of status/class differentiation in the first six decades of the twentieth century requires underlining for those unfamiliar with the island's social order. Fluency in English speech and sophistication in life-ways were part of status differentiation and class dominion (see Roberts *et al.* 1989). Where these assets were exercised arrogantly, a superior gent would make remarks about the 'sarong-johnnies' and 'yakoes' (the Sinhala word for demons, used to denote 'rustics' or 'primitives'). The epitome of this mentality was F. C. de Saram, 'the most English of [Sri Lanka's] cricketers in style, speech and demeanour' (Gunasekara 1996: 23).[30] De saram was a true leader of men who commanded deep loyalty from those of his sort around him, but his disdain could be monumental. Take the anecdote about Arjuna Ranatunga's first encounter – presumably in the early 1980s – with old man de Saram. As a rising schoolboy star, Ranatunga had been snaffled by the SSC and was introduced to this doyen of the club. As Ranatunga responded to the occasion in (presumably halting) English, de Saram looked down his nose and said, 'It speaks English.'

This said, one must not take the point too far. By the 1960s, most of the Royal–Thomian and other elite cricketers had experienced the transition brought about by the '1956 revolution'. Though English-speaking, such individuals as Darrel Lieversz, T. C. T. Edwards, A. E. De Silva, Buddy Reid, Nihal Gurusinghe and Michael Tissera were unassuming and amiable men.[31] That so many of them gained representative honours for Sri Lanka was due to their talents rather than the power of old boy networks.

The nurturing of such talent was in part the cumulative result of good ground facilities at their schools and the chain of example and inspiration from their elder peers. In short, heritage had a compounding effect. In the case of St Thomas'

College, moreover, this heritage included the exceptional coaching talents of Lassie Abeywardena at a critical stage, the Under-16 level, over a period extending from the 1940s to the 1960s. If a single hand is to be discovered behind the strength of Thomian cricket in the 1960s, it is to this man that we must look. But he also stands here as a symbol for a long line of coaches, known and unknown, who have laid the foundations for so many Sri Lankan cricketers. It was on this foundation that the foreign coaches, including Captain F. C. Badcock and Learie Constantine early on, and subsequently Garfield Sobers, Don Smith, Peter Philpott, Dav Whatmore, Bruce Yardley and John Dyson, added their inputs. Sobers says as much of his coaching stint in 1984:

> [w]hat a pleasure it was to coach them . . . when I saw the quality of the players in the nets for the first time, I couldn't understand what I was doing there. Their technique was so good it looked as if they had already enjoyed the best of coaching.
>
> (2002: 171–2)

No better illustration of the impact of a specific line of coaching heritage is provided than a glance at the Sri Lankan team that defeated Pakistan A, virtually its Test side, by 41 runs in a low-scoring match at the Oval in Colombo on 28–30 August 1964. T. C. T. Edwards, Mano Ponniah, Buddy Reid, Michael Tissera, P. I. Pieris, Neil Chanmugan, or six out of eleven, were Thomians. Led by Tissera, three of them (and Lieversz from Royal) were also part of the team that defeated India at Ahmedabad on 2–5 January 1965. Again, an epitome of this line of Thomian talent was soon witnessed in the person of Anura Tennekoon, a technically perfect batsman in classic mould. Unfortunately, Tennekoon, like Tissera before him, retired from cricket prematurely in 1979 – in both cases partly because of a conflict between the demands of the game and the demands of their mercantile firms, itself a sign of the shaky amateur foundations on which Sri Lankan cricket was structured.

A further illustration of the 'streams of possibility' that stood Lankan cricket in good stead in subsequent decades can be provided by a relatively obscure event associated with the tour of Sri Lanka by the Hyderabad Blues in 1967, a side that included Jaisimha, Brijesh Patel and Abbas Ali Baig. Though the Blues defeated an XI representing the Central Province Cricket Association at Asgiriya (CPCA) in early April 1967, the CPCA scored 303 in the first innings because of an impressive 113 runs by Randy Morrell and a scintillating 61 by T. B. Marasinghe 61. Morrell was right-hand opening batsmen and a planter, but had been schooled at St Thomas' College – 'partly made by Lassie' at the Under-16 level (in the late 1950s), one could say. Marasinghe was from Dharmaraja College in Kandy, a left-hand batsmen with pulverising strokes tailored elegantly.[32]

Neither Morrell nor Marasinghe quite made it into the highest reaches of Sri Lankan cricket because they were residing beyond Colombo and not involved in premier Sara Trophy sides. This, then, was the difference between the 1960s and the 1980s and 1990s. It took the changes that I have outlined earlier for provincial

148   *Michael Roberts*

youth to climb into the centre of things. For all that, the schooling trajectories of Morrell and Marasinghe in the 1950s and 1960s also mark the lines of promise that crystallised into a body of talented cricketers in subsequent decades, namely a solid cricketing heritage in elite Colombo establishments on the one hand and raw regional talent on the other.

By the 1970s and 1980s, moreover, the elite schools of cricketing talent were not Royal–Thomian or Christian denominational. The best cricketers were emerging from Ananda and Nalanda. Bandula Warnapura from Nalanda succeeded Tennekoon as captain in 1980. Sidath Wettimuny from Ananda replicated Tennekoon's perfection in technique and revealed an ability to cope with all manner of wickets; while the apple of coach Garfield Sobers's eye in the 1980s (see Sobers 2002: 171) was Arjuna Ranatunga from Ananda, who made a debut 90 runs in difficult circumstances against the Australians at Asgiriya in 1984, eventually led Sri Lanka to victory at the World Cup in 1996 and stood up to the Australian umpiring fraternity in January 1998.

Securing ICC Test status

Sri Lanka had been endeavouring to secure full Test status from the ICC from 1975, but been rejected every time. It was the cricketing talent of its players, and the batsmen in particular, that eventually eroded the conservatism and vested interests within the ICC establishment and secured full Test status for the country in July 1981. These talents were first displayed to the wider world in July 1975 when the Lankan batsmen scored 276 runs for 4 in reply to a massive Australian score of 328 for 5 during their ODI game at the first World Cup in England. Sri Lanka had confirmed its leading position among the minnows once again by winning the ICC Trophy for Associate Members for the second time when it was held in England in 1979; and then went on to defeat India comfortably in the World Cup of 1979 (Perera 1999: 372–6). These signals were confirmed when Kim Hughes's Australian team played matches in Sri Lanka on their way to the Ashes in 1981. The Australians were matched and/or outplayed in the three one-day games, while the unofficial 'Test' ended in a draw (ibid.: 372–6).

The support of Australian officials and the Australian Cricket Board (ACB) may have been another critical factor in swaying the ICC. Bob Parish and Fred Bennett from the ACB seem to have backed Sri Lanka's claim. Parish was linked with Prahran CC in Melbourne, where both Owen Mottau and Dav Whatmore were leading players. Unconfirmed stories suggest that Parish and Sam Loxton of Prahran initiated a long history of support for Sri Lankan cricket from that club.

And last but not least, there was the advocacy and sophistication of Gamini Dissanayake, president of the BCCSL, who went to London in 1981 to argue Sri Lanka's case and seems to have done so persuasively. The fact that he held an important ministerial post and had connections with British companies involved in construction projects for the Mahaweli Development Board under his ministry may have been another background factor: for the ICC was concerned about the number of cricket grounds of Test standard and other infrastructural facilities.

The years 1981–96

No sooner had Sri Lanka attained elite status and begun playing Tests than its cricketing ranks were split asunder by the attractions of the South African rand. The cricketers were all amateurs and were relatively easy targets once the South African Cricket Union (SACU) decided to extend its sponsorship of rebel tours. This programme was a retaliatory move on the part of the SACU. The ICC had excluded South Africa from its ranks in the early 1970s because of the apartheid policy of its government. Sponsoring rebel tours of South Africa was conceived by the SACU as a way of undermining world cricket while sustaining South Africa's own standards. A body of Englishmen led by the former England captain Graham Gooch served as its first catch in February/March 1982. Its next seductions were directed towards the Sri Lankans and West Indians.

Tony Opatha[33] acted as the principal intermediary with the Sri Lankan personnel. While touring India under Warnapura, sections of the team held several clandestine meetings. The original plan centred on Duleep Mendis (vice-captain) and Roy Dias, who were the team's outstanding batsmen as well as close mates. A day or so before the team was due to embark secretly for South Africa, President Dissanayake brought pressure to bear on these two and/or offered carrots. In the event, Mendis and Dias became captain and vice-captain of the Sri Lanka side, while the rebel squad under Warnapura and Opatha (now vice-captain) left the island with a pot-pourri of players from a range of clubs, towns and class levels[34] to South Africa in September 1982. The tour was a financial flop for the South African Board, but its cricketers had all the joys to be derived from roundly spanking the Sri Lankans whenever they stepped onto the field. More to the point, the 13 Sri Lankan cricketers were immediately deemed pariahs and banned for 25 years by the BCCSL.[35]

Needless to say, the capacities of the Sri Lankan cricket team were severely weakened by these defections – with the loss of their spinning duo of Ajit de Silva and Lalith Kaluperuma being particularly damaging. While they lost the majority of their Test matches in the period 1982–96, there were some excellent performances on occasions, notably (a) in August 1984 at Lord's, when they outplayed England and amassed 491 runs and 294 for 7 in their two innings, with three century-makers all told; (b) beat India by 149 runs after declaring in their second innings at the Oval in Colombo on 6–11 September 1985; (c) beat Pakistan by 8 wickets at the CCC grounds in Colombo on 14–18 March 1986; and (d) scored heavily in a high-scoring series in New Zealand in 1992 where all three Tests ended as draws. What might have been a sweet and marvellous moment, the game against Australia on 17–21 August 1992 at the SSC grounds in Colombo, where Australia was on the hop throughout the game, turned sour during the last session. An unholy collapse by the Lankan batsmen (8 wickets for 37) enabled the Australians to seize victory (by 16 runs) from the very jaws of defeat.[36]

Sri Lanka's cricketing prowess, however, lay in the shortened form of the game. Its lack of penetrative bowlers counted for less in this domain and its team's

150 *Michael Roberts*

attacking batsmanship could pay dividends. As early as 1984, Greg Chappell's Australians were put to the sword in all three ODI matches. It is not necessary to provide a more detailed history of this strand of activity except to mark four 'moments' along what can be called 'the road to Lahore, 1996'.

1   During the World Cup in the Antipodes in 1992, Sri Lanka began the series with two remarkable victories against South Africa and Zimbabwe in New Zealand, even chasing a target of 312 runs at Napier on 23 February to defeat the latter by 3 wickets.

2   In one of the preliminary games during the Triangular Champions Trophy competition at Sharjah in October 1995, Sri Lanka was confronted by a West Indian total of some 333 runs, the highest in the history of ODI cricket till then. They proceeded to score 329 runs in reply and lost gamely after 49.3 overs when Hashan Tillakaratne was caught on the boundary seeking a winning six.

3   As one of the two visiting sides in the ODI series in Australia in 1995–6, the Sri Lankans were considered also-rans because the West Indians and Australians were expected to make the final. They had not read this script, however. They sneaked and screamed their way to the final post by beating the West Indies at Perth and the Australians at Melbourne. They may have lost the two finals that followed, but gave Australia a good run for their money in the midst of some home-town umpiring and the occasional twist in TV commentary.

4   This particular ODI series was sandwiched amid the Sri Lankans' tour of Australia, itself a landmark because their schedule included three Tests for the first time. But the tour became another sort of landmark for other reasons, the wrong ones. The Sri Lankans were subject to unprecedented psychological warfare from the Australian media, accused of ball-tampering by a Pakistani umpire on the first day of the first Test and then had to undergo the traumatic experience of Muralitharan being branded a thrower by Darrell Hair on the first day of the second Test on 26 December 1995 in what is now known to have been a pre-considered move. After he was called a second time at Brisbane,[37] he did not bowl again – so that the team's battles in the latter part of the ODI series were staged without his aid. It is widely reckoned that the pressures and experiences of this tour, not least the unrelenting Australian strategy of verbal intimidation, gave the Sri Lankan cricketers the necessary steel to withstand all comers during World Cup in February–March 1996.

The signs were there. It was feasible for perceptive observers, such as Mike Marqusee and Richard Hadlee, to suggest that the Sri Lankan team were dark horses and could win the World Cup.

The Cricket World Cup, 1996

There was, of course, another factor helping the Lankans. The matches were all on the Indian subcontinent, mostly away from home, it is true, but on slower, lower subcontinental wickets for the most part. And then, on 31 January 1996, the Tigers (LTTE) struck. A truck bomb outside the Central Bank, which held the island's gold reserves, devastated the central business district and killed large numbers of people. The target was a strategic one, the aim being to terrorise the administrative centre, and the timing was directed against the notion that 4 February was a day of celebration (for the Tamils, it is held to be a mark of oppression and a denial of their self-determination) (Roberts 1998b).[38]

The ACB and the West Indian Board quickly decided that their teams would not play the first-round matches of the World Cup scheduled for Sri Lanka. Concerns for player safety were paramount, but they also reasoned (correctly) that the system in place would enable them to reach the second round despite the forfeit of one match. These decisions were politically myopic as well as unfortunate (Roberts 1998a). The Sri Lankan public and players were denied contests they were looking forward to. But the forfeits also distributed the top teams over the subsequent stages of the competition in ways that assisted the Sri Lankan team.

That granted, the team's march to victory was a remarkable one, perhaps matchless. For one, virtually all their victories were comprehensive, and the final triumph over Australia was comfortable. Second, batsmen 8–11 batted only once during the whole series, while Mahanama at seven batted only three times. Third, they scored at 5.99 runs per over and 56.24 runs per wicket and bettered all previous rates on these scales. Fourth, Aravinda de Silva secured four man-of-the-match awards, and Sanath Jayasuriya walked away with the award for 'Player of the World Cup' because his strike rate was 131.5 over 100 balls on top of other specific contributions (Roberts 1998c: 152–3).

Among the cricketing factors that I would pinpoint as the foundation for this emphatic march to victory are the following:

- the close rapport between Ranatunga and de Silva as captain and vice-captain;
- Ranatunga's leadership;
- the experience that all the players had garnered on the international circuit in the early 1990s and the fact that they had been playing together as a team since 1992, if not earlier;
- the resolve that had developed, especially after the 'assaults' they had encountered from all sides in Australia in December–January 1995–6;
- the balanced bowling attack, centred upon four spinners suited to sub-continental conditions;
- a superb batting line-up right down to number seven;
- competence fielding, with Mahanama and Jayasuriya as sharpshooters in the inner ring;

152   Michael Roberts

- Dav Whatmore's input as coach, specifically man-management and the professionalisation of training methods (weight training, nutrition, etc.);[39]
- Whatmore's choice of Alex Kontouri as physiotherapist and the transformation of the team's fitness levels by this intelligent, hardworking and approachable man;[40]
- the fact that basic homework on climatic and pitch conditions at Lahore was conducted – leading in turn to the unusual, but masterly, decision to field first because it was expected that dew would hinder the fielding side at night.

Much has been made of Dav Whatmore's role as coach, and the influence he had on the side after he was made coach in mid-1995 (see, for example, Nicholas 1996). However, the side was already well equipped before Whatmore's advent. That said, his insertion of modern sport science into the preparation of the cricket team was a significant factor in the mix of forces. Evaluating the relative weight one should attribute to each factor is impossible without having been a fly on the wall of the Sri Lankan changing rooms over the years 1994–6; and even such a fly would be hard put to make precise assessments.

Post-1996 consequences and ramifications

The finances of the BCCSL expanded a thousandfold as a result of the World Cup victory. Cricket became big business within Sri Lanka and an attractive investment for sponsors. But as noted above, these attractions and the existing constitutional scheme generated sharpening competition for posts, debilitating manipulations associated with a spoils system and organisational instability.

That was not all. Arjuna Ranatunga emerged from the World Cup as Man Mountain in Lankan eyes. His style of leadership became even more autocratic, a combination of boss man and *walauwwa mahattayā* (manorial lord, in Sinhala mode). When, moreover, Thilanga Sumathipala was elected president of the BCCSL in 1997, one found an SLFP network at the centre of power, with S. B. Dassanayake as sports minister[41] and Dhammika Ranatunga appointed chief executive of the BCCSL. By the time the next World Cup came around in 1999, Arjuna Ranatunga was given the freedom[42] to select the team with Duleep Mendis[43] at his side. Some of Ranatunga's acolytes benefited, as did the old stalwarts. The side chosen for the series in England was an ageing body of personnel, with several quite unsuited to English conditions. It was easy to predict that the side would not secure a spot in the second stage of the contest (Roberts 1999). In the event, the performance of the team was an utter shambles, accentuated by poor captaincy, de Silva's manifest unfitness, and the distance between Ranatunga and de Silva on the one hand and many of their colleagues on the other. Prima facie, one can conclude that '1996' had gone to some heads.

Remarkably the '1996 syndrome' continued to cloud judgement in subsequent years, notably in 2002–3. Thus, in 2002 when specific heroes from the year 1996 produced good scores on the local circuit or in international matches on Lankan grounds, they were automatically deemed good enough for selection even when the side was slated to encounter early summer conditions in England (Roberts 2002b, d). The 'disease' extended beyond local commentators and vested interests. During the World Cup in 2003 some foreign TV-callers kept referring to the events of 1996 without any recollection of the disastrous performances in 1999. Even now, the phrase 'little Kalu' denotes explosive innings and an assured place in the side for this lovely fellow – without reference to the fact that he only played one explosive hand during the 1996 World Cup and without any evaluation of his ODI statistics tabulated according to country.

It was precisely because of the cricketing failures of 1999 that the interim board of mid-1999 under Rienzie Wijetilleke and the selection committee under Sidath Wettimuny secured Whatmore's services once again[44] and revamped the composition of the side. This process, however, was arrested by a radical transfer of the reins of power in March–April 2002. The new interim committee under Amarasuriya included many of Sumathipala's men. To judge by subsequent events, it was designed to pave the way for the 'democratic' system of elections to be reinstated – in effect ensuring that Sumathipala would take office in June 2003 (see Austin 2003). By January 2004 the situation was in flux because of yet other events outside cricketing terrain.

Social change

Amid this flux, one major transformation in the order of political society, and thus of cricket politics, can be registered. The 'class/status' struggle of the 1940s to the 1960s between the English-educated elite and the vernacular underprivileged has diminished considerably. English has not been dethroned by the political platform of 'Sinhala only' launched in 1956. It retains its central significance for jobs and communication, but it now shares this political space with Sinhala speakers (and with Tamil in Tamil majority districts). The Anglophile pukka sahibs of the past have passed away, aged or moved abroad. Thus, the inferiority complex of the mid-twentieth century coursing through the sentiments of those lacking fluency in English has mostly disappeared. In recent decades, notables from business, political, media, cricket and other circles speak English on television without one hundred per cent proficiency, yet without hesitation. Allowing for significant exceptions, for the most part the new Sinhala-speaking generations do not express the type of antipathy to English-speak that one found in the mid-twentieth century.

But powerful undercurrents of nativist Sinhala nationalism remain. The strident outcry in recent months against the alleged expansion of Pentecostal churches has been accompanied by arson attacks on more than 100 churches, 'mostly Evangelical but a scattering of RC churches as well'.[45] This strand of politics is reminiscent of the anti-Christian campaign that accompanied the 'revolution of 1956'. Behind all this is the anxiety generated by the military success of the LTTE and the prospect that they will gain near-total autonomy and international recognition through the ongoing peace negotiations begun in early 2002. At least three forces embody these tendencies. First, there is an articulate

154 Michael Roberts

coterie of intellectuals known as *Jātika Chintanaya* (Nationalist Thought). Second, there is the revamped JVP, an indigenist Marxist force that launched insurgencies in 1971 and 1987–9 and has now adopted a parliamentary veneer. Third, there is a wing of the SLFP that remains strongly attached to the values of 1956.

Enter Arjuna Ranatunga the politician. As an MP since December 2001, he is among the SLFP hardliners. His entry into politics was in familial footsteps: his father has been a MP since 1989, while his elder brother Prasanna has been a member of the Gampaha Provincial Council since 1993. The Ranatunga family itself hails from Gampaha District in the immediate rural hinterland of Colombo. That Arjuna should cleave to the values and prejudices of the 1950s is hardly surprising.

Such prejudices also intruded into his cricket politics. As a folktale has it, when Russel Arnold, an English-speaking youngster from St Peter's College, gained entry into the pool of Sri Lankan players in the late 1990s and entered the changing rooms, Ranatunga 'welcomed' him with an acid greeting. Here, then, was F. C. de Saram turned on his head: the boot rammed home was a Sinhala boot, the victim someone 'Westernised'. More significant, however, is the fact that Ranatunga has been a prominent participant in the cross-party gatherings of a new coalition, the Patriotic Front, which was set up in September 2003 and has been described by a socialist critic as 'an umbrella organisation that brings racists together'.[46] The Patriotic Front also challenges the directions taken by the present peace process under UN peacekeeping aegis. Such chauvinist moves imply a return to war – even though that subject is never addressed in their protestations.

In brief, the silver lining arising from the ceasefire of the past two years has dark clouds threatening it. Instability, alas, has been a feature permeating the cricketing scene as well as the political scene for many a year.

Notes

1 This chapter has been written at short notice. I have been assisted by the email responses of many friends. I thank all of them warmly. They are too numerous to list! Likewise, space limits decreed that citations should be minimised.

2 For those unfamiliar with Sri Lanka, let me note that virtually all these towns are in the south-western quadrant, while Kandy is in that part of the Central Highlands adjacent to this segment of the island.

3 Governmental interventions in 1999, 2002 and 2003 saw the creation of interim committees, so normality was less than usual.

4 English continued to be of importance as *a* language of communication.

5 Grapevine information. The date is from Hoole (2001: 406).

6 Ms Subramanium is a Tamil from India who was a correspondent in Colombo for different Indian newspapers throughout most of the 1990s. I also tapped the views of three-wheeler drivers based on one street in Wellawatte (a Tamil quarter, by and large) whom I use regularly when visiting the island. This 'cricket test', needless to say, is not full proof. It is a really a guesstimate on everyone's part.

7 Information transmitted during email correspondence on other matters in late 2003.

8 'Murali appearance puts Jaffna into a spin', *Daily News*, 3 September 2002, on the Internet.

Sri Lanka 155

9 See *Daily News*, 30 September 2002, on the Internet.
10 *Cricket Match in India* is the title of this painting (information from Ismeth Raheem, who has a booklet called 'Images of early history of cricket in Ceylon and south India' awaiting publication).
11 As one would expect in a book of such magnitude, one chances upon errors in Perera's book. It follows that I may be repeating some errors whenever I deploy his material.
12 In the first match in 1879, English schoolmasters also played. But from 1880 this series featured only the respective schoolboys (Perera 1999: 38–41). Also see Wijesinghe (2004).
13 Data supplied by S. S. Perera and incorporated in appendix 11 in Roberts *et al.* (1989: 239).
14 The Burghers included a far higher proportion of British descendants than is popularly recognised – because some British personnel, especially those widowed, married resident European descendants (that is, Burghers) as well as Sinhalese and Tamils. For greater detail, see Roberts *et al.* (1989).
15 Digby believed the Burghers could be 'a medium of civilisation' and a bridge between West and East. He argued his case strenuously for the European descendants in India as well as Ceylon. See Digby (1877; 1879, vol. I: 6, 23–4) as well as Roberts *et al.* (1989: 48–9).
16 Letter from Lorenz to R. Morgan, 14 March 1859, in the Lorenz MSS, RAS Library, Sri Lanka. For elaboration of this argument, see Roberts *et al.* (1989: 58–61, 127–9, 140–75).
17 The first club formed by the migrant Tamils in Colombo was the Lanka Sports Club, established in November 1895 (Perera 1999: 73), but it must have declined. For the Tamil Union, see (Foenander 1924: 59–65).
18 See de Silva (1981: chs 27, 28), especially details on the political manoeuvres of Governor Manning (pp. 390–5). Also note the strikes and labour agitations of the period 1919–29 described by Jayawardena (1972).
19 *St Peter's College Magazine*, 1928. See also Foenander (1924: 89–91), Perera (1999: 177–8) and Colin-Thome (2003: 83).
20 Email memo from Neville Jayaweera, 16 January 2004.
21 This paragraph is based on Perera (1999: 135–6, 151, 174–6), Gunasekara (forthcoming) and Gunasekara (1996: 24–5).
22 It was only after the game against the Hindus at the Bombay Pentangular in 1944 that someone remarked that Sathasivam was ineligible to play because he was a Hindu.
23 For a hilarious account, see Levine (1996: 36–7). Perhaps the juiciest tale is that a tipsy old gent told this British lass that what she saw before her eyes was 'a hangover from the British days'.
24 Fuard is a Sri Lankan Moor who was educated at Wesley College. An outstanding off-spin bowler who could bat, he played for Wesley and various clubs and represented Sri Lanka in the 1960s. He was a dominating figure in the BCCSL administration in the 1980s and still wields influence from his home. For other comments, see the text that follows.
25 Email memo from Neville Jayaweera, 16 January 2004 and Perera (1999: 193–4). Commentaries in Tamil are now interspersed amid English and Sinhala accounts; but this may be a recent development.
26 Email note, 19 January 2004: 'Absolutely no ethnic angle, just that Satha was a man whom everybody loved to hate. They loved him for his cricket and hated him for everything else.'
27 Information from Neville Jayaweera, who, as a Thomian schoolboy, was in the crowd and admits – to his 'shame' in his own words now – to being one of those participating in this joking abuse.
28 I have also profited from conversations with Mano Ponniah.

156 Michael Roberts

29 My account is based on Perera (1999: 320–6) as well as conversations with several cricketers from that era. The consensus is that Fuard and Weerasinghe were the driving forces behind the takeover bid, though one individual at the centre of things also identified D. H. de Silva as part of the scheming. H. I. K. Fernando was from St Peter's and Fuard from Wesley, and both were senior to Tissera in the Ceylon squad when he was made captain.

30 In the description that follows, Channa Gunasekara affirms that de Saram 'was likewise the most nationally oriented in bearing' and that he had the capacity to laugh at himself.

31 Personal knowledge, mostly in and around the cricket fields.

32 News cuttings and information conveyed by Morrell in Sydney and my memories of a set of cricket trials in Kandy and Peradeniya in the late 1960s in which I participated.

33 Opatha represented Sri Lanka at cricket between 1973 and 1979, and may have established links with South African cricket during his coaching stints in the Netherlands.

34 From the Lankan side that had toured India in 1982 Madugalle, Sidath Wettimuny and Asantha de Mel were not approached or declined to join.

35 This account is based on Chesterfield (forthcoming) and Perera (1999: 415–18). However, the published details are skimpy and inadequate. Note that the ban on the cricketers was rescinded in early 1990 (Perera 1999: 416).

36 Details from Perera (1999) and www.cricketarchive.co.uk/Archive/.

37 By both Emerson and McQuillan, sometimes when he was bowling leg-breaks. It is therefore significant that the ACB's umpiring committee chose Emerson and McQuillan to stand together at Adelaide Oval on 23 January 1998.

38 For the Tamil's self-perception of themselves as a 'nationality', their claims to self-determination and other facets of their political history, see Roberts (1999b: 34–7), Nesiah (2001), Wilson (2000) and de Silva (1998: 119–58, 297–332).

39 This point has been refined in conversation with Sidath Wettimuny, who was part of the team's official entourage during the World Cup. Whatmore is not a coach who works a great deal on technique.

40 This point was impressed on me by Sidath Wettimuny (telephone chat, 20 January 2004) who noted that 'the players swear by him [Kontouri]'.

41 Dassanayake and Sumathipala have been a 'partnership' of sorts for some time. When Dassanayake and a few other Ministers became unhappy with their leader Chandrika Kumaratunga's political moves in 2002, Sumathipala negotiated their crossing over to the UNP and thus assisted the victory of the UNP-led coalition in late 2002. This step consolidated the split between Sumathipala and the Ranatunga clan – a clash that appears to have originated earlier from affairs internal to cricket administration.

42 'Arjuna was given the freedom to make his moves as he had a wealth of experience like no other player in the business,' said Sumathipala in May 1999 in a reference to the situation in 1995, but which we can reinterpret to be the line he took in early 1999 (interview with Channaka de Silva for the Sunday Times World Cup Supplement, 16 May 1999).

43 Former Sri Lankan captain and chairman of selectors in 1998–9.

44 Whatmore did not continue as coach of Sri Lanka beyond 1997 because he received a lucrative offer from Lancashire, while the BCCSL was, typically, prevaricating in preparing a new contract (possibly because some cricketing personalities had their own aspirations?). His readiness to return to the lion's den of Sri Lankan cricket politics in mid-1999 was due to his Sri Lankan patriotism. It was also facilitated by Skanda Kumar's trip to Manchester and Whatmore's trust in the personnel of the interim committee under Wijetilleke.

45 Email memo from Neville Jayaweera, 17 January 2004. Jayaweera notes that only a fraction of these atrocities have been reported in the newspapers. For a brief note

on the attack on St Michael's Church at Katuwana, Homagama, see *Daily News*, 16 January 2004. Also see K. M. de Silva (1998: 88–93).

46 Email note from Ananda Wakkumbura, 1 February 2004. Note that the Sīhala Urumaya (Sinhala Heritage Party) is not an affiliate of the PNM. Also see www. pnmsrilanka.com.

References

Austin, Charlie (2003) 'Sumathipala as new president: hero or villain?', Wisden Cricket Comment, 8 June 2003, www.cricinfo.

Chesterfield, Trevor (forthcoming) 'The politics of isolation: South Africa's rebel era', in M. Roberts (ed.), *Essaying Cricket*, Colombo: Vijitha Yapa Publications.

Colin-Thome, David (2003) 'A bat, a ball, a herb', in Sri Lanka Cricket, *England vs Sri Lanka, 2003*, Colombo: Sri Lanka Cricket.

De Silva, K. M. (1981) *A History of Sri Lanka*, Delhi: Oxford University Press.

De Silva, K. M. (1998) *Reaping the Whirlwind: Ethnic Conflict, Ethnic Politics in Sri Lanka*, New Delhi: Penguin Books India.

De Silva, Mervyn (1967) '1956: the cultural revolution that shook the Left', *Ceylon Observer Magazine Edition*, 16 May.

Digby, William (1877) 'The Eurasians as leaven in India and Ceylon', *Calcutta Review*, 64: 180–208.

Digby, William (1879) *Forty Years of Official and Unofficial Life in an Oriental Crown Colony, Being the Life of Sir Richard F. Morgan*, Madras: Higginbotham.

Foenander, S. P. (1924) *Sixty Years of Ceylon Cricket*, Colombo: Ceylon Advertising & General Publicity Co.

Gunasekara, C. H. (n.d.) 'My cricket in England during the early twentieth century', in M. Roberts (ed.) *Essaying Cricket*, Colombo: forthcoming.

Gunasekara, Channa H (n.d. [1996]) *The Willow Quartette*, Colombo: Sumathi Publishers.

Hoole, Rajan (2001) *Sri Lanka: The Arrogance of Power. Myths, Decadence and Murder*, Colombo: Wasala Publications for the UTHR.

Jayawardena, V. K. (1972) *The Rise of the Labor Movement in Ceylon*, Durham, N.C.: Duke University Press.

Levine, Emma (1996) *Cricket: A Kind of Pilgrimage*, Hong Kong: Local Colour.

Mandle, W. F. (1973) "Games people played: cricket and football in England and Victoria in the late nineteenth century', *Historical Studies* (Australia) 15: 511–35.

Mangan, J. A. (1981) *Athleticism in the Victorian and Edwardian Public School*, Cambridge: Cambridge University Press.

Narayan Swamy, M. R. (1994) *Tigers of Sri Lanka*, Delhi: Konark.

Narayan Swamy, M. R. (2003) *Inside an Elusive Mind. Prabhakaran*, Colombo: Vijitha Yapa Publications.

Nesiah, Devanesan (2001) 'The claim of self-determination: a Sri Lankan Tamil perspective', *Contemporary South Asia* 10: 55–71.

Nicholas, Mark (1996) 'Australian downfall plotted by one of its own', *Daily Telegraph*, 18 March, p. S14.

Perera, S. S. (1999) *The Janashakthi Book of Cricket, 1832–1996*, Colombo: Janashakthi Insurance.

Pieris, Denzil (1958) *1956 and After*, Colombo: Associated Newspapers of Ceylon.

Roberts, Michael (1985) 'Ethnicity in riposte at a cricket match: the past for the present', *Comparative Studies in Society and History*, 27: 401–29.

158 *Michael Roberts*

Roberts, Michael (1998a) 'Fundamentalism in cricket: crucifying Muralitharan', in Michael Roberts and Alfred James, *Crosscurrents: Sri Lanka and Australia at Cricket*, Sydney: Walla Walla Press.

Roberts, Michael (1998b) 'Avoiding Lanka: Australia and the World Cup', in Michael Roberts and Alfred James, *Crosscurrents: Sri Lanka and Australia at Cricket*, Sydney: Walla Walla Press.

Roberts, Michael (1998c) 'The World Cup on field and newsprint', in Michael Roberts and Alfred James, *Crosscurrents: Sri Lanka and Australia at Cricket*, Sydney: Walla Walla Press.

Roberts, Michael (1999) 'Seaming turfs: the lottery of the World Cup', *Lanka Monthly Digest*, World Cup Supplement, May, pp. 17–18.

Roberts, Michael (2002a) 'Bomb blasts and cricket', *Sunday Observer* (Sri Lanka), 26 May 2002.

Roberts, Michael (2002b) 'Choosing our cricketers: the 1996 syndrome', *The Wicket.com* and www.ozlanka.com.

Roberts, Michael (2002c) 'Await embarrassment? Sri Lankan cricketers in Australia', www.ozlanka.com, 13 December.

Roberts, Michael (2002d) 'ODI teams. Messy selections', www.ozlanka.com, 21 December.

Roberts, Michael (2003) 'Shortcomings in Sri Lanka's team at stage one, World Cup', March, Colombo: Vijitha Yapa Publications.

Roberts, Michael, Ismeth Raheem and Percy Colin-Thomé (1989) *People Inbetween*, vol. 1, *The Burghers and the Middle Class in the Transformations within Sri Lanka, 1790s–1960s*, Ratmalana: Sarvodaya Book Publishing.

Sobers, Gary (2002) *My Autobiography*, with Bob Harris, London: Headline.

Wijesinghe, Mahinda (2004) 'The longest uninterrupted match in the world', *Sunday Leader* (Sri Lanka), 8 February.

Wilson, A. J. (2000) *Sri Lankan Tamil Nationalism: Its Origins and Development in the 19th and 20th Centuries*, London: Hurst.

8 One eye on the ball, one eye on the world

Cricket, West Indian nationalism and the spirit of C. L. R. James

Tim Hector; compiled and with editorial commentary by Stephen Wagg

Editor's foreword

I began putting this book together in the spring of 2001. Tim Hector was one of the last authors to be recruited and I felt quietly proud when he came to the telephone, somewhere on the island of Antigua, and said that he'd write the chapter on West Indies cricket.

Tim Hector was widely, and rightly, regarded in the Caribbean as the inheritor of the intellectual and political mantle of C. L. R. James. Like James, Hector was a Marxist and polymath who wrote copiously about politics, culture, literature, art and cricket. He also edited the *Outlet* newspaper on Antigua and led the radical opposition to the Bird family dynasty that has governed the island since independence.

After his initial acceptance I was unable to contact Tim Hector again. This was principally because he was undergoing open heart surgery in the United States. Sadly, he died in November 2002 (Stewart and Chamberlain, 2002). Later I resolved, with the approval of his family and executors, to compose a chapter from his own writings. To do this I have culled a good deal of material from Tim's website, *Fan the Flame*. Most of what follows appeared on that site between 2000 and 2002.

The chapter is therefore is expressed largely in Tim Hector's words, but I have selected the words, configured them and linked them with editorial commentary, so ultimate responsibility for this essay is, effectively, mine.

> The house still stands with its bird's eye view of the world in miniature, in Tunapuna, which allowed C. L. R. James to keep his eye both on the ball and on the world, at one and the same time.
>
> (Tim Hector, 2001)

Introduction

Tim Hector wrote copiously on cricket and West Indian nationalism and he always placed Caribbean cricket culture in the context of imperial settlement and

160 *Tim Hector with Stephen Wagg*

of the racialised oppression that the British Empire brought with it. He wrote in April 2000:

> The myth that the English planters and merchants brought cricket with them as part of their colonising baggage should now be laid to rest. The culture they brought, in these small islands, where they were very few in number, was the culture of terror. The terror of a terrified minority faced with an overwhelming majority, not as human beings, but as fearful even frightening property, listed along with the mules, horses and asses in the planter/ merchant inventories. . . . Cricket came not by way of the planters. But by way of the English military which sought to repel Napoleon's conquering forces in these islands. These English soldiers, wrote the very fine historian Professor Hilary Beckles 'entertained themselves with bats and leather balls within garrisons while taking respite from bowling cannon balls at the French'. When the colonial wars of conquest ended it was replaced, so to speak, by contests off the field of play between the English merchants and planters and their white employees, and their white military protectors.
>
> ('The OECS in time, space and sports', *FtF* 21 April 2000: p. 2)

In the first of his two-volume history of West Indian cricket, Beckles talks of the emergence of black cricketers in the Caribbean of the nineteenth century; this he calls 'a popular cultural transracial expression'.

> The desire of coloured and black communities to play cricket their own way seemed to have grown in direct proportion to the white elite's determination to establish it as the exclusive sport of the propertied, the educated and the 'well bred'.
>
> (1998a: 4)

Hector, like his mentor C. L. R. James, always saw this development as a gesture of self-emancipation in a context broader than the Caribbean or the British Empire. It was, for him, an expression of Pan-Africanism. 'Cricket and Pan-Africanism met overtly', he observed in 1998, 'in the 1895 English tour of the West Indies under Slade Lucas.' This stimulated the work of Marcus Garvey, 'who followed cricket throughout his life' and 'must have had no small effect on C. L. R. James, then 22, who was to write one of the great anticolonial tracts, *The Case for West Indian Self-Government* in 1932. . . . The same C. L. R. James was to write the first *History of the Pan African Revolt* in 1934' (Hector 1998: 49–50). This perspective caused Hector later to reflect on the whole relationship between sport and black people:

> [Both] colonialism and racism deny the humanity of black people. Therefore through sports black people assert that: **To win is to be human.**
> In other words, the official view, widely accepted that black people see sports as a vehicle, practically their only vehicle to fame and fortune, I did

West Indian nationalism and C. L. R. James   161

and do not accept. On the contrary, a more plausible view was that since we were losers, and therefore given to the blues and the consequent sorrows of the spirituals, sports offered the avenue, perhaps the only clear avenue, **to assert a new style different from the established style** in the first place. And in the second stage, arising out of the first, not only a new style, a black style, but to win in black style, as opposed to the oppressor's style, which was and is hegemonic, is to be human.

('Why do blacks big-up in sports at this point in time?',
FtF 28 August 1998: 1)

Sport, in other words, was a means to a positive self-identity for black people; it was 'self-humanising', as Hector saw it. And Hector never lost sight of the achievement of West Indian cricketers, especially in the second half of the twentieth century. Then, for a 15-year period (1980–95), a succession of teams from these small and economically undeveloped islands became acknowledged as the world's finest exponents of the formerly imperial game. Hector was keen to remind his readers of this when, during the late 1990s, Caribbean cricket culture became beset by low morale and public recrimination among players, officials and commentators:

Unprecedented is this fact in world sport. No other people for so long – a decade and a half – so completely dominated an international sport. Especially when it is understood that this dominance, this excellence, was produced based on a small, a tiny, a minuscule population of 5 million souls. The smallest cricketing nation in the world, was the greatest!

In the light of that all-important and radiant fact, no one, just no one, and no circumstances, however dire, not even 10 consecutive brownwashes, or whitewashes, could ever get me to berate a West Indian cricket team. Never happen.

('Lara, the captaincy and West Indies cricket'),
FtF, 16 January 1998, pp. 2–3)

Elsewhere, Hector proudly contrasted the success of West Indies cricket, which 'represents the genius of the West Indian people', with the minute villages that spawned some of its leading players:

No cricketer from any other country has come from a village as poor as Curtley Ambrose's Swetes, or Stuart Williams' Gingerland, or Richie Richardson's Five Islands, or Chanderpaul's one-phone-village in Guyana. Yet against all odds, these cricketers make it up, and over, from under. Not just on the national stage, but on the world stage.

('Cricket is More Than Meets the Eye', *FtF*, 20 February 1998: 4)

The path towards this historic cultural achievement was, as Hector always recognised, paved with heroism. In this he liked to cite not only the great West

162 Tim Hector with Stephen Wagg

Indian Test players, but pioneers such as 'Sir' Sidney Walling, whose early exploits made later triumphs possible. Hector lovingly recounts the story of how in 1920, at the age of 13, Walling used his only white shirt and trousers to play cricket for Antigua Grammar School. In doing so, he defied his devout mother, who had decreed that these clothes were for church on Sunday. She flogged him for this transgression, but supported his cricket career thereafter. Sidney Walling went on to become the first black man to captain a West Indian territorial team when he was appointed to lead the Antigua side in 1934. Walling (who was also made Post Master General in 1953) was thus, as Hector pointed out, one of the first to challenge, through cricket, Kipling's notion that men such as he came from 'sullen peoples / Half-devil and half child' ('"Sir" Sidney Walling – the Quintessential Antiguan. Part 1', *FtF*, 5 September 1997). (The first black West Indian cricket captains were, as Hector later pointed out, selected on the smaller islands, such as the Leewards and the Windwards – Hector, 1998: 54.)

Those two little pals of mine: cricket and the struggle for Caribbean nationhood

In 2000, Hector summarised the progress toward black captaincy and political emancipation as follows:

> By 1842, not ten years after the abolition of slavery, the Trinidad Cricket Club was established. By 1891 there was an intercolonial tournament between Barbados, Jamaica and British Guiana, now Guyana. By 1897 a team of nine black men and two white men represented Antigua against MCC. The whites, small in number in the Leewards, were declining cricket-wise, though not in the economy, and blacks were taking over in cricket, in Antigua, even before the 20th century!
>
> From the very beginning cricket in the West Indies exposed with near exactitude the social relations of the islands. Originally the whites, the owners, 'the gentlemen,' batted. The black plebeians were at first bowlers, ground attendants, who bowled often without shoes, let alone boots. Later the brown skin or black middle class produced a few good batsmen who challenged the English planter/merchant class and toppled them from their batting pedestal.
>
> CLR, as always, and undoubtedly the finest sociologist of cricket, expresses the social development with astonishing fidelity. CLR wrote:

> > Between 1900 and 1939 the development of West Indian society improved the status and conditions of the coloured middle class with effective organisation of cricket **as a national expression**. In addition to clubs, exclusively white [Antigua Cricket Club (ACC) in Antigua, Queens Park in Trinidad, Pickwick in Barbados, and so on] with perhaps a few coloured men of distinction the brown skinned middle class also formed their own clubs [St John's in Antigua, Maple in Trinidad,

Spartan in Barbados, etc.]. So did the black middle class. In time the black plebeians also formed their own clubs [Rising Sun and Rivals in Antigua, Shannon and Stingo in Trinidad, and Empire in Barbados, with the Barbados Cricket League (BCL) completing the picture]. These divisions (not always in every island iron-clad) were not only understood but also accepted by players and populations alike. All these clubs played in club competitions and not infrequently a white member of the Legislative Council or President of the Chamber of Commerce . . . would be playing amiably for his club against another most of whose members were black porters, messengers or other similar social types.

Cricket was therefore a means of national consolidation. In societies very conscious of class and social differentiation, a heritage of slavery, **it provided a common meeting ground of all classes without coercion or exhortation from above.**

And, continued CLR James, 'Though for a long time in the West Indies the value of the services and the authority of [white] men like H.B.G. Austin was unquestioned, **cricket was a field where the social passions of the colonials, suppressed politically, found vigorous if diluted expression.**

There are few passages in West Indies history, which so concisely and so precisely sum up the movement and development of our sojourn in time and place under the stars.

('Will we continue to be annihilated and humiliated?', *FtF*, 1 December 2000, pp. 2–3)

Thus, Caribbean cricket, like cricket for long periods back in England, was a social theatre in which the classes mixed in comparatively relaxed circumstances. Since this meant mingling of the 'races' also, it was possible in West Indian cricket for black expertise to be pitted against white. Cricket became linked to notions of black struggle in the 1930s. Cricketers such as Learie Constantine began to question white leadership of the national team (Beckles 1998a: 52–6) and cricket, along with strikes and politically triggered disturbances, became part of what Tim Hector identifies as a '[n]ationalist upsurge' and a 'revolution from below' during 1937–8 (1998: 53).

After the Second World War, cricket helped to spur the final push for independence in the Caribbean territories and to strengthen support for some kind of confederation, under the banner of West Indian nationalism, of these territories once independent. A milestone, in this regard, was the West Indies' first Test victory on English soil, at Lord's in 1950, and their subsequent winning of the series of that year. As Hector recognised over fifty years later:

[T]his cricket in 1950 was a social metaphor for political history. In 1948, West Indian leaders, 'convinced that each separate territory was not a viable economic entity' met at Montego Bay to decolonise the English-speaking Caribbean by uniting in a Federation. Nothing else would do for these

164 *Tim Hector with Stephen Wagg*

separately economically non-viable territories. They were prepared to get rid of the old colonial masters. The West Indies, in a manner of speaking, being the only place in world history created by genocide and by colonialism, were rejecting both and affirming its own authenticity. The majority of the West Indian population, African and Indian, had no previous or independent history in these islands. Colonialism created us. Now in 1948 we would venture forth as a Federation of islands, rather than be deranged by foaming channels. So in 1948, after the historic upheavals by the mass of the population against colonial rule in 1938, the West Indian leaders met to create a new nation out of former slave colonies. Nothing of the like had ever happened in the world before, save in Haiti in 1804 where slaves declared the first independent Black Republic in History, and the United States and France in particular systemically reduced Haiti to penury, because it dared to be black, proud and free.

It follows logically that the West Indian team victory in England in 1950 according to the remarkable Michael Manley in his **History of West Indies Cricket** [(Manley 1988)] was more than a sporting success. It was the proof that a people was coming of age. They had bested the masters at their own game on their own home turf. They had done so with good nature, with style, often with humour, but with conclusive effectiveness. Rae, Stollmeyer, Worrell, Weekes, Walcott had made hundreds to the delight of thousands and to establish the foundations upon which victory was to rest. The victory itself was produced by **'those two little pals of mine', Ramadhin and Valentine.**

Indian and African spinners were 'pals' not only for Lord Kitchener [a well-known calypso singer] but for all the English-speaking Caribbean.

I beg to note too that an Afro Indian spin pair had spun West Indies to an historic victory 'over the masters at their own game on their home turf.' Afro-Indian unity as a metaphor in cricket was vital to West Indian success in politics and in particular Federation. Cricket had shown the way.

('More than talent is required', *FtF*, 10 May 2002, pp. 2–3)

Hector had in 1997 paid particular tribute to Ramadhin and Valentine. Drawing on the work of American academic Michael Eric Dyson (Dyson, 1993) he reflected:

Dyson argues most credibly, that the nature of oppression of blacks in the United States produced in 'African-American cultural practice the ability to flout widely understood boundaries through mesmerisation and alchemy, a subversion of common perceptions of the culturally or physically possible, through the creative and deceptive manipulation of appearance.' The important thing was for blacks to go beyond the established limits.

I could and do argue here that Ramadhin applied the same 'mesmerisation and alchemy' to his bowling, which made it impossible for Englishmen to 'pick' him. It seemed as if, by mesmerisation and alchemy, Ramadhin bowled

West Indian nationalism and C. L. R. James 165

the off-break and the leg-break with the same action. But, and this is crucial, the sub-soil, the cultural unconscious, so to speak, from which Ramadhin came, East Indian indenture, was essentially different from that of Afro-Americans. Simultaneously, Valentine, had developed orthodoxy to its Zenith.

('How does Michael fly?', *FtF*, 21 March 1997, pp. 2–3)

The West Indies' historic victory had been achieved, however, under a white captain – the Barbadian John Goddard. As support both for independence and for the appointment of a black captain grew, the West Indies cricket authorities stood firm:

> The West Indies Cricket Board of Control, then **anti-nationalist** and representing the powerful planter-merchant class, appointed **two** tour managers, N. Pierce and Cecil de Caires, each with equal authority for the 1957 tour of England. It was a management recipe for friction and disaster.
>
> Then sticking to the formula of the white captain, since according to the logic of the rulers, whiteness alone could lead, John Goddard who had not played against England in 1954 at home, nor Australia in 1954–55 at home, was brought back as player-manager for the first West Indies tour to New Zealand in 1955–56, and re-appointed captain in 1957 at age 38. Worrell who was vice captain against Australia in 1955–56 was relegated to player in 1957. These shenanigans, all performed in the unstated service of racism, no doubt had its effect in the rout of the West Indies in 1957 in England.
>
> ('It is the West Indies that is in peril, NOT West Indies cricket',
> *FtF*, 12 December 1997, pp. 2–3)

West Indies lost to England three times in their tour there of 1957, having also lost in Australia in 1953 and 1954–5.

The first black man to captain West Indies was Frank Worrell. Worrell, a middle-class Barbadian and graduate of the University of West Indies, had already captained a Commonwealth side in India during the winter of 1951–2 and been vice-captain of the national side. Hector reflected later that

> a tremendous campaign led by C.L.R. James and in which Worrell himself participated, so much so, that he was referred to as a 'Cricket Bolshevik,' toppled the white leadership in West Indies cricket. This overt racism in West Indies cricket crashed like Stalin's statue in Budapest had done just before. With Worrell's ascent to the captaincy West Indies cricket appeared in its own true colours, shorn of racism for the very first time.
>
> ('Cricket is more than meets the eye', *FtF*, 20 February 1998, p. 2)

But Hector was careful to look beyond 'race' when appraising the significance of this event. Worrell, he suggested, brought discipline and sound strategic thinking:

166 Tim Hector with Stephen Wagg

In that independent style, West Indian batsmen often played with dash and panache. The idea of strokeless West Indian batsmen seemed a contradiction in terms, and a definite affront to our own independent style. Sometimes we were cavalier *in extremis*.

And then came 1960, the first Black captain was appointed and Worrell changed all that. The cavalier was replaced by the consistent, without any loss in the desire to put opposing bowlers to the sword. Gone was the cavalier individualist approach. But the panache remained. Sobers and Kanhai embodied what can really be termed the satyric passion for the expression of the natural man, bursting through the restraints of disciplined necessity. Both Sobers and Kanhai showed the creativity of the great Jazz musicians in their marvellous improvisations, which *improvs* in Jazz were **the** innovation in 20th century music. European classical music was all disciplined necessity though tinged with romanticism.

('Will we continue to be annihilated and humiliated?',
FtF, 1 December 2000, pp. 1–2)

This strategic awareness was often lost on (albeit sympathetic) observers, and Hector gently rebuked the (white) English cricket writer Scyld Berry on this score:

[I]t is passing strange that whenever black men penetrate some field, overcoming racism, or white supremacy, always it is said we bring 'light, excitement and energy,' never intelligence and knowledge. I want to suggest to you, dear reader, that it is a habit of mind, a mind-set, a way of seeing the world, fostered by the Welfare State and before that, the imperial state. The same was said of the Brazilians in football. It is a mind set. A setting of the mind which states that one race, and only one, possesses a monopoly of intelligence and expertise.

However, when the white captain in cricket was firmly in place, West Indians did not and do not like to admit that racism existed and still dominates their life. Only CLR James, Learie Constantine and Worrell had the courage to speak out about it. West Indians do not like to deal with the racism which shaped their historical life, and still determines it.

('Cricket is more than meets the eye',
FtF, 20 February 1998, pp. 2–3)

Worrell, Garfield Sobers (a working-class black Barbadian and virtuoso cricketer), Rohan Kanhai (a Guyanese batsman of Indian descent) and others effectively laid the foundation for the prolonged period of West Indies dominance of world cricket from the mid-1970s to the early 1990s. This dominance, as Hector always argued, had huge political significance in the Caribbean, and beyond.

High tide: cricket, West Indian nationalism and the black diaspora

First and foremost, successive generations of West Indian cricketers were nationalists who saw the West Indies team as a flagship for independence and nascent nationhood. For Tim Hector, and others in the vanguard of this movement, it therefore carried the hopes of many for a successful federation of Caribbean nations after independence. The West Indies Federation, which briefly united ten island territories in the English-speaking Caribbean, lasted only from 1958 and 1962 and did not, in any event, grant full internal self-government. Although supported by the British government (on the grounds that it would make for administrative efficiency and economic strength) and by Caribbean labour unions (who thought it would speed the arrival of self-rule), federation had been opposed, historically, by the white planter class on each island. It broke up largely because the governments of its two biggest constituent islands – Jamaica and Trinidad – judged that they would be more prosperous by seceding (Rogozinski 2000: 321–3).

Looking back, forty years on, spokespeople for the Caribbean left, such as Tim Hector, tended to regard the great West Indians sides of the 1970s and 1980s as the only lasting expression of federation:

> It took Sobers' incredible all-round abilities, Worrell's unequalled leadership, Andy Roberts' scientific method, Holding's poetry in motion, the wizardry of Lance Gibbs and Malcolm Marshall's pyro-technics to establish the West Indian personality in the international arena free of past encumbrances. Free at last! In a Federal State, created by all three races namely, African, Indian and European, **in cricket**, though not in economics and politics.
> ('How does Michael fly?', *FtF*, 21 March 1997, p. 5)

'Our politics,' Hector wrote on another occasion, 'pales into insignificance against our cricket. Our economics fares even worse. In science and technology we have done little of note. In literature and music alone, do we have achievements matching our cricketers' ('It is the West Indies that is in peril', *FtF*, 12 December 1997, p. 1).

Among all the West Indian cricket heroes thrown up by this period of dominance, Hector singled out the Antiguan Vivian Richards, who captained the side throughout the 1980s. Here Hector addressed Hilary Beckles' well-known division of West Indian cricket into three paradigms. Beckles has suggested that the history of West Indian cricket divides roughly into three epochs, each seen as a paradigm because it carried with it a specific set of assumptions. These three periods were defined, respectively, by colonialism, nationalism and globalisation (see particularly Beckles 1998b: 1–30). Hector differed politely with Beckles over Richards. Beckles suggested that Richards typified the second, nationalist paradigm. Hector perceived a greater political significance in his fellow Antiguan. Viv, he argued, straddled all three paradigms. He set out his case in March 1998:

168   *Tim Hector with Stephen Wagg*

Says Beckles in his illuminating and ground-breaking piece.

> Richards, then, was undoubtedly a highly developed product of the
> second paradigm in West Indies cricket. The first paradigm was that
> of the nineteenth century in which cricket was the **instrument of
> colonial exclusion**, used by white elite society to distance itself from the
> black majority. By the 1930's this model was under attack and the rise
> of the three W's, Weekes, Worrell, Walcott, against the background of
> Learie Constantine and George Headley signalled the rise of the second
> paradigm. During the 1950's and 60s cricket became hinged to the
> process of anti-colonial reforms and the movement to independence.
> The political project – rise of nation states and cricket as a symbol of
> West Indian liberation – grew hand in hand and together accounted for
> the ideological positions taken by Viv on a number of issues.

This is an amazing historical schema. And like all philosophical schemas it
is what it yields that matters. And I am going to surprise you. Marvellous as
Hilary Beckles is here, I beg to disagree.

Viv undoubtedly represents the first paradigm, as well as the second, and
in my view, the third unstated by Beckles.

Viv was a representative of the first paradigm, in that he was the embodiment **of Leewards exclusion** from first class cricket and Test cricket. His was
the passion of the excluded announcing himself on the world stage, at long
last, after long and merciless exclusion. If size, smallness of size was a factor
in that exclusion, then the grandeur of his efforts, would lay that to rest, with
Andy Roberts' feats having served as fore runner.

Viv represented the second paradigm. The anti-colonial paradigm.
He himself said the issue 'was quite central for me, coming as I do from the
West Indies at the end of colonialism. I believe very strongly in the black
man asserting himself in this world.' If this is not Aimé Cesairé's **negritude**,
the overcoming of inferiority, the overcoming of colonial subordination,
the assertion of our natural and acquired abilities, without apology to those
who had a vested interest in our continued marginalisation and irrelevance,
except as cheap labour in their foreignising and globalising schemes, then
negritude has no meaning.

And now to the third paradigm. Viv was not a Rastafarian, but he wore
his Rastafarian sweat band on all the Test grounds of the world as a statement. He himself said that 'It was perfectly natural for me to identify, for
example, with the Black Power Movement in America, and to a certain
extent with the Rastafarians. I cannot say that I ever reconciled myself totally
to Rastafarianism.'

The point was and is, that Viv saw the Rastafarians as downtrodden
sufferers, who had dared to be different, in that they broke sharply with
English colonial mores, which had at first been enforced, and then adopted
in the Commonwealth Caribbean. As such, the Rastas human rights were

constantly violated, with the silent approval of the silent majority. Viv could not abide that.

Viv knew that the Caribbean could not be the wealthiest country in the world. Nor the most dominant. It could not encircle the world with military bases and weapons of mass destruction. We could not be more than bit players in modern world trade. But in Antigua, there had emerged in Viv's youth and maturation, the third paradigm, a Movement, of which his eldest brother Donald 'Donnymitch' Richards was a founder. This Movement held that we could, with a new system of social ownership and control, become a model to the world, in terms of human development, in a society with the most advanced Human Rights, not as abstract declaration of the Rights of Man where some were more equal than others. But as concrete manifestation, where every race and class finds an equal place, freed from racial and class oppression. That position went well beyond American Black Power. It manifested itself, though originating in Antigua, in the Grenada Revolution only to be destroyed by Old World Stalinism.

Viv in 1993, was to put himself on the line, when he observed in Antigua, the police firing tear-gas rockets into an unarmed crowd, on what became known here as Terror Thursday. He at once joined the protesters, bringing his enormous prestige to bear, in defence of human rights. And too, against those who felt that power and authority conferred on them the right to suppress and repress, to sedate and humiliate. All that repressed and humiliated was Viv's mortal enemy. He wanted a New World in the new world, freed from governor and governed, but one in which the people in council owned and controlled a region.

It was the same spirit which manifested itself in Viv's duels with [Australian fast bowlers] Lillee, Thompson and Pascoe; [Indian bowlers] Bedi, Venkat and Chandra; [English bowlers] Willis, Old and Underwood, [Pakistani bowlers] Imran Khan or Abdul Qadir. It was old, it was new. It cannot be separated from the old colonial exclusion which led to the Leewards exclusion. It cannot be separated from the naïve nationalism, which said put the colonialists out, run up a flag, and sing the anthem, in the same old, same old order, and all will be well, if not swell. It cannot be separated from the new regionalism, which saw new forms of social ownership and economic organisation — hence the improvisation or 'a hitting across the line' in Viv's batting – as the key to a regional society of the most advanced Human Rights, freed from racial oppression and social humiliation, with the people in council, going well beyond ancient Greek democracy. That is the Third paradigm, laid down by the Movement of which his brother was a founder like this writer.

Viv bristles at any form of insularity. . . . As the great artist he embodied and personified the **new** in the womb of the old. The great artist, which any super batsman is, and which he undoubtedly was, represents both the past and present in a new future.

('The spirit of excellence', FtF, 20 March 1998, pp. 3–4)

170 *Tim Hector with Stephen Wagg*

This crystallises Hector's view of the James legacy. The federation had foundered and the nationalist dream had lived on principally through cricket. But in their cricket, Caribbean people had shown each other, and the expropriated black people of the world, the best of what they could do. The team had been a continuing metaphor for the West Indian nation and, at its zenith, it had been led by a proud black man from the periphery even of Caribbean society (the marginal island of Antigua). This man mastered the white man's game while playing it his own way and he enjoined all black people to do likewise. In doing so he straddled the worlds of colonial subjection, nationalist struggle and the striving of small countries in the bleak, deregulated global marketplace. Beckles, whose intellectual differences with Hector on matters of West Indian cricket seldom seemed to be substantial, wrote later:

> Caribbean social scientists are in general agreement on one point at least. That the excellence achieved in the region's cricket culture, masterfully demonstrated in the two decades that came crashing down in 1995, represents one of the finest expressions of efficient human resources mobilisation since the fulfilment of the national independence agenda.
>
> (1999: 81)

After the fall: the crisis in West Indian cricket

Hector, like Beckles and others, sought to explain and to address the decline in the team's fortunes and, with it, the apparent unstiffening of the sinews of West Indian cricket nationalism:

First, some history was needed, to provide perspective. There had, after all, been previous occasions when darkness had followed the dawn. For example, despite their triumph in England in 1950, the West Indies went on to incur a series of heavy defeats during that decade. During this period, Hector recalled, the team 'were as soft as pap' ('It is the West Indies that is in peril . . .', *FtF*, 12 December 1997, p. 3).

Nor was Hector sympathetic to the argument, canvassed in several quarters, that cricket had been superseded by basketball as the Caribbean's favourite sport. Cricket would remain a West Indian thing. Once again he cited history in support of his argument:

> Cricket and cricket alone provided the medium in popular sports, through which we could take an English institution, and transform it, re-create it in our own image and likeness and stamp our personality on it, liberating ourselves from impositions which the heavy weight of centuries had re-inforced with the limitation of spirit, vision and self-respect . . .
>
> . . . It is for that reason that I am convinced that no amount of basketball can dethrone cricket. A mode of expression, of national expression, is not created by chance or by whim. It is the product of history and historic striving, conscious and unconscious. Michael Jordan 'flies', Vivi Richards

West Indian nationalism and C. L. R. James 171

'hits across the line', each expressing his particular genius, in their own specific mode of national expression. Cricket is ours, not basketball.

Our participation in basketball is, in the main, a celebration of the new universality created by Michael Jordan – the first truly global sportsman.

('How does Michael fly?', *FtF*, 21 March 1997, p. 5)

But there were clear and acknowledged difficulties. The West Indies lost heavily to Australia at Sabina Park in Jamaica in 1995 (when West Indies were bowled out for 51). They lost to Kenya, a country with negligible cricket pedigree, the following year. The successor to Richards as team captain, Richie Richardson, had been scapegoated and Brian Lara, the most talented Caribbean cricketer of the new era, was frequently at odds both with his teammates and with the West Indian cricket authorities. Hector saw the problems but was reluctant to lay responsibility for them at the door of individuals. 'There is a West Indian tendency', he suggested in January 1998, 'to level downwards. A crab-in-the-barrel syndrome, bred and fostered by plantation slavery and plantation colonialism, which mutilates, militantly, against any and every exceptional achiever, especially when born to the humble' ('Lara, the captaincy and West Indies cricket', *FtF*, 16 January 1998, p. 5).

Besides, for Hector, the root of the present difficulties lay primarily in the material circumstances of the Caribbean islands in the colonial and postcolonial eras. These circumstances must be confronted.

Our economies are externally controlled, managed and directed be it in oil, natural gas, bananas, bauxite, sugar or tourism. The same people do not campaign against that external control. So it is. So it was. So it has been. So it must **not** always be. Our cricket too, has been externally dependent. That is a shocker I suppose. The West Indies cannot support its own cricketers, professionally. That puts it baldly and clearly. Our cricketers are dependent on English Leagues, or English County Cricket, and for a time, Packer, to survive professionally. Even now after oil booms, bauxite booms, tourism booms, we cannot find a sponsor for our own first class domestic competition! A game, which encapsulated a way of life, is withering on the vine. Even in the age of Television financial windfalls for cricket, we see less and less cricket, on television, and more and more U.S. basketball and even U.S. Football, and by the time we get to the Superbowl I suspect more interest will be generated in that, than even Test Cricket.

That in itself speaks volumes. We are more interested in the activities of the alien Other than in our own. That cannot be disputed. A population is being made to accept that the ways and sports of the Other are far more important than their Ways and their Sports. A people are being [led] down a blind alley by spineless leaders.

I want to be more emphatic. In 32 weeks in Bangladesh of telecast time 8 hours were devoted to cricket. In South Africa over the same 32 weeks, there were 23 hours of major cricket. Over the same period in Jamaica, in

172   Tim Hector with Stephen Wagg

Trinidad & Tobago along with Barbados there were 2½ hours, of live cricket, combined. No one bothered with Antigua & Barbuda. That is accepted as the American outpost.

I hope you are getting the point. Traditionally we have a lot of interest in cricket. Actually that interest is being undermined systematically as well as constantly. What is ours, is not on our TV. The major means of electronic communication alienates us further, in an alien controlled society . . .

. . . To be succinct, West Indian Test cricket has been largely, superstructural. That is not rooted in Shannon, Empire, Spartan, GCC [Georgetown Cricket Club] in Guyana or Melbourne in Jamaica or Rising Sun in Antigua. Now we have to put our cricket on a self-sustaining basis, rooted in the Clubs, with the best games televised across the region, showing the up-and-coming players. That way, we strike the ultimate blow against our own insularity, which has been structured, geographically, economically, and not least, politically, to our external detriment.

And now I end, with the greatest of them all, C.L.R. James, of course.

He wrote in 1966 this: 'The West Indies Cricket Board of Control has always been sustained by **clubs** in each territory which are lineal descendants of the old aristocratic clubs of the plantocracy and commercial magnates. Their services in West Indies cricket, all proportions strictly guarded, can legitimately be compared to that of MCC in Britain.'

That, true then, is no longer true. The plantocrats have gone, and the new industrial or commercial magnates, mainly American, are least of all interested in cricket. The cricket clubs then have faltered. And, without English County cricket, will continue to falter, if Clubs do not become the nursery of West Indies cricket.

But, the plantocrats have gone, and the new alien magnets are not native, but globalising Americans.

(ibid. pp. 1, 6–7)

Not that this would be easy. Hector sensed and often identified a demoralisation in the Caribbean, brought on by the depredations of global trade and financial bodies. The term 'structural adjustment' appears in a dozen or more of his essays for *Fan the Flame*. This term is now widely accepted as a euphemism for programmes, usually framed by the International Monetary Fund, which entail 'the liberalization of foreign exchange policies, the devaluation of national currency, anti-inflation programmes based on credit restriction, reduction in state expenditure, wage controls and the ending of price controls' (Grugel 1995: 182). But there was hope.

I should pause here too, to remind that the dominance of West Indies cricket began in 1977 and precisely the point that Jamaica was structurally adjusted and put under the thumb of IMF surveillance, or if you prefer external impositions. Trinidad and Tobago went the way of structural adjustment in 1988, Guyana was next. Barbados followed the same course in 1991.

Yet it is precisely at this point **1977** as the West Indies slid into structural adjustment that the West Indies in the same 1977 became dominant in world cricket after its 5–1 drubbing at the hand of Australia in 1976.

('Crisis in society and cricket –women to the rescue',
FtF, 25 June 1999, p. 4)

Nevertheless, Hector did not underestimate the impact of these programmes on West Indian society and thus on its cricket. They had brought, he argued, a culture of fear:

'Structural adjustment totally undermined all of our nationalist assumptions, about **'we'** being as good as 'Them' and therefore holding our own, independently, in good times or in bad. It is responsible for the gangster behaviour in our society at **top** and bottom. We, at top and bottom, are holding on to nothing. Everything has been adjusted and undermined. Hence 'the culture of fear.'

('How can I be insular to say Sir Vivi deserves better?',
FtF, 10 March 2000, p. 5)

So, structural factors – and, more specifically, the ravages of 'structural adjustment' – were the key to the crisis in West Indian cricket. But one individual failing on the part of the players Hector was not prepared to forgive. In 1998 the West Indies test players staged a strike and refused to travel for their forthcoming series until they received more money. These players and their manager, Clive Lloyd, perhaps the chief architect of the West Indies' period of dominance, received a stern rebuke. For a West Indian team to demur on the threshold of its first visit to a South Africa now under black government was a betrayal:

When Vivian Richards, refused $1 million US to play cricket in apartheid South Africa, I felt that as the son of poor parents from tiny Antigua and Barbuda, and a citizen of the Caribbean, Vivian Alexander Richards, like Anderson Montgomery Roberts before him, had made an imperishable statement, that not by money alone do people live, but by their faith in human freedom. Freedom as the free and full development of the human personality freed from race, class and gender domination. How comes it now that on the first tour of a West Indian cricket team to a free South Africa, where the great Nelson Mandela rules, the tour was beginning in utter disgrace, a wild-cat strike over, not present, but future fees. It seemed to me that the entire West Indies team, Manager Clive Lloyd, former captain Courtney Walsh, all lacked a **sense of occasion**, a sense of history, a sense of the defining role of cricket in a Caribbean civilisation.'

('This cricket fiasco and South Africa', *FtF*, 6 November 1998, p. 1)

Few among the leading Caribbean spokespeople would have dissented from this. But the debate about the way forward, led by Beckles, Hector and others, mostly

174 Tim Hector with Stephen Wagg

assumed that contemporary West Indian cricketers now knew little of the nationalist tradition, and maybe cared less. Lara, Hooper and the others wanted the best deal they could get as sportsmen in the global marketplace. Where to go from here?

The future of West Indies cricket: the appliance of science?

Beckles, among West Indian nationalists, has led the way in trying to reconcile West Indies cricket culture to the exigencies of the global economy. In this regard, he has written, there must be better marketing, and full use should be made of the expertise and facilities of the University of the West Indies. This latter provision would cover the scientific aspects of the task as well as the political and historical contextualising of it. Young Caribbean cricketers must be taught the importance of their own political heritage (see particularly Beckles 1998b). Science – the application of computer technology, sport psychology, nutritional advice, and so on – has been an important part of the argument. Beckles calls, for example, for captains, managers and specialist players to be equipped with databases and for information technology and data processing to become central to West Indies cricket preparation. Art, he argues, has been replaced by science in the twenty-first-century game.

For those of the nationalist/pan-Africanist intellectual tradition, this has not, ultimately, been an easy circle to square. Could a skill that expressed the virtuosity of Caribbean – and, by extension, all – black people really be enhanced by computer programming and the analysis of statistical data? Hector, in essence, believed that it could: 'Acquired abilities through the application of science to West Indies cricket is a vital need', he wrote in April 1999 ('Crisis in cricket? Or crisis in society? Or both?', FtF, 2 April 1999, p. 4). A few months later he observed:

> Coaches provided by the WICB [West Indies Cricket Board], will work with coaches in each territory on a uniform approach. The Cricket Committee supervises this cricket programme, the coaching, the practice sessions, **the preparation** of the players in each territory. The science of the game, in which we are lacking, will be developed. What is required for fitness in cricket, what is the optimum level of nutrition, how to develop concentration, how to react and to respond to mental or psychological pressure, and more important how to apply pressure, how to regain lost form, etc, etc, all this and more will be worked upon by the West Indies Board Cricket Committee, with a branch in each territory working with the local Association.
>
> Let me be empirical here. Watching the current rounds of our Busta Competition, I saw most of the teams still at the old, out-dated level. The water breaks were bottled water breaks. No player was being supplied with a nutritious drink to restore lost energy. As energy and oxygen levels sank, concentration lapsed or collapsed.
>
> ('Dear Mr President', FtF, 11 February 2000, p. 3)

West Indian nationalism and C. L. R. James 175

But science, Hector soon realised, would be no good unless it was allied to the democratic and civic enthusiasms that had fired James movement for independence and nationalism through cricket. Brian Lara, he argued, had had periods of estrangement from the West Indian side

> not because of any personal weakness. But, because neither the working class, or if you prefer, the lower-middle class into which he was born, nor the society in general could give him any sense of direction, any sense of purpose. A purposeless society cannot produce purposeful cricket.
> What Sobers, Kanhai, Richards, Kallicharan and Lloyd, Greenidge and Haynes inherited from the nationalist movement, its sense of commitment to overcoming our lowly place in cricket and the world of production and achievement, was undermined and lost as Lara and Hooper succeeded the past greats. It is not Lara and Hooper's fault. I repeat, a purposeless, structurally adjusted society, cannot produce purposeful cricketers.
> ('Will we continue to be annihilated . . . ?', *FtF*, 1 December 2000, p. 5)

Moreover, when an actual coach – ex-West Indian test cricketer Roger Harper – delivered his (no doubt, scientifically endowed) report on West Indies' unsuccessful tour of England in 2000, Hector was scornful. Harper, 'highly certificated' as Hector wrote, 'and meeting all the academic vanities, which substitute themselves for real achievement' (ibid., p. 5) had, in his report, lamented the lack of grit and determination particularly on the part of his batsmen. Hector, in his riposte, called for socialism and a return to the spirit of resistance typified by James and those who, like himself, had carried the torch thereafter on the various islands:

> Harper's method, alien to the West Indian temper, and independent style is to 'graft', 'occupy the crease' and 'play within our limitations'. This is proof of our batsmen structurally adjusted. Improvisation, when set, to get on top of good bowling, is gone, dead and buried.
> Fredericks method, like Sobers, like Kanhai, was to fight fire with fire, to improvise in order to release 'limitations' placed on them, and not 'to occupy the crease' **to set bowlers**. But to occupy, **to unsettle bowlers**. It is this reversal of method, this decline and fall, which Harper represents, though certified. He himself was a grafter, whose bowling action collapsed without remedy, as Sir Gary Sobers so pointedly reminded. Finally, and a point which escapes Harper altogether in his ceaseless empiricism, losing himself in the labyrinth of detail, and therefore seeing all trees and no forest, is this: A people who have seen all their leaders from William Bramble in tiny Montserrat to Norman Manley in larger Jamaica opt for some form of socialism, and then by 1988 all their successors had by osmosis adopted for neo-liberalism without the people being aware of this sea change, this absolute betrayal had bothered, bewildered and belittled the people of the Caribbean while governing meant swaying and ducking, rather than

176 Tim Hector with Stephen Wagg

hooking all the bouncers hurled at the government and people by the First World; who saw their leaders destroy their best hope, a Caribbean nation, and then rewarded the very Destroyers with longevity in office; who saw these very leaders make deals with the racist Klu Klux Klan; saw their leaders connive to send arms to racist South Africa or the narco-terrorists in the Medellin Cartel; saw their leaders plunder Bauxite and the wealth of Guyana, reducing it to a shambles; saw their leaders when 'money was no object' and unemployment was still high, propose to spend hundreds of millions on air-conditioned horse stables; or joined with America to harass their own Grenada Revolution which overthrew the Gairy–Mongoose-gang democracy; who connived with America and Britain to have Cheddi Jagan freely and fairly elected removed from power, and then approved the CIA provoking race riots in Guyana; and then the IMF structurally adjusted the entire West Indies into the margins, definitely lost the will to struggle, to be committed to any goal or any new arrangement of society.

How then do we expect our cricket team to struggle when we ourselves have lost the will to struggle, and seek only to collaborate or to succumb. Such will be 'annihilated in humiliation' to use Coach Harper's very own apt determination.

(ibid.: p. 6)

This, then, is James's, and Hector's, political legacy. The struggle for the dignity and self-determination of the people of the English-speaking Caribbean goes on. Cricket, in the past the principal flagship of this struggle, can again become a beacon of West Indian nationalism. To do so it must avail itself of all academic and professional assistance. But the answers cannot lie solely, or even primarily, in the seminar room or the computer suite. The defining context must, as always, be political contention – in the parliaments, in the villages and out on the streets of the Caribbean itself.

The prefacing quotation is taken from 'CLR James, the Contemporary World and World Revolution. Part 1', which was placed on the *Fan the Flame* website on 12 October 2001. It's on page 1.

Acknowledgements

I should like to thank the executors and family of Tim Hector, Conrad Luke, *Outlet* newspaper, and Jon Gemmell, who commented on the first draft, for help in the preparation of this chapter.

References

Beckles, Hilary (1998a) *The Development of West Indian Cricket*, vol. 1, *The Age of Nationalism*, Kingston, Jamaica: University of the West Indies Press; London: Pluto Press

West Indian nationalism and C. L. R. James   177

Beckles, Hilary (1998b) *The Development of West Indies Cricket*, vol. 2, *The Age of Globalization*, Kingston, Jamaica: University of the West Indies Press; London: Pluto Press.

Beckles, Hilary (1999) 'The strife of Brian', in Rob Steen (ed.) *The New Ball*, vol. 2, Edinburgh: Mainstream.

Dyson, Michael Eric (1993) *Reflecting Black: African-American Cultural Criticism*, Minneapolis: University of Minnesota Press.

Grugel, Jean (1995) *Politics and Development in the Caribbean Basin: Central America and the Caribbean in the New World Order*, Basingstoke, UK: Macmillan.

Hector, Tim *Fan the Flame* website: http://www.candw.ag/~jardinea/fanflame.htm.

Hector, Tim (1998) 'Pan-Africanism, West Indies cricket and Viv Richards', in Hilary Beckles (ed.) *A Spirit of Dominance: Cricket and Nationalism in the West Indies*, Kingston, Jamaica: Canoe Press/University of the West Indies.

Manley, Michael (1988) *A History of West Indies Cricket*, London: André Deutsch.

Rogozinski, Jan (2000) *A Brief History of the Caribbean*, New York: Plume Books.

Stewart, Lucretia and Chamberlain, Greg (2002) Tim Hector: Obituary, *Guardian* (London), 26 November.

Part III
Cricket in the Old Country

9 Calypso kings, dark destroyers
England–West Indies Test cricket and the English press, 1950 –1984

Stephen Wagg

The fellows from Brixton will be a help at the Oval ... that is a home fixture for us.

(Clive Lloyd, West Indies cricket captain, July 1984[1])

This chapter is about the ways in which Test cricket between England and West Indies was represented on the sports, and other, pages of the British press during the second half of the twentieth century. It is thus inevitably also about the shifts in the political relationship between Britain and the Caribbean and about the corresponding ebb and flow of public discourse apparently occasioned by these shifts. It was conceived and written with three important assumptions in mind. First, for most British people during this period, cricket and cricketers were very likely their principal sources of knowledge of the Caribbean: the 'West Indies' were, for the most part, a nation only in white flannels, and the main means of understanding this 'nation' and its people was through representations of the men who wore these flannels and of their activities. Second, the political relationship between Britain and the peoples of the English-speaking Caribbean altered radically during the time in question. In 1950, Britain still held colonies in the Caribbean and welcomed West Indian migrants to the United Kingdom as bearers of dual nationality. By the 1980s, successive Acts of Parliament had long since withdrawn this welcome, access to British citizenship had been severely curtailed, and the presence in British society of Caribbean and Caribbean-descended people had been widely redefined as baleful (see, for example, Fryer 1984: 373–99; Sivanandan 1982: 101–40). (The notorious 'Tebbit Test' of 1990 – see my chapter with Tim Crabbe (Chapter 10) in this book – was just one way in which this impinged upon, or was played out within, cricket culture.) Third, for most of the time in question the West Indian team were the undeclared world champions of the sport of cricket. Various writers (notably Manley 1988; Beckles, 1998; and Hector in Chapter 8 of this book) have noted the paradox (and the outstanding achievement) of the emergence from these small islands of a succession of world-class teams during a time of growing postcolonial strife, both at home, with mounting poverty and inter-island political rivalry, and in the erstwhile 'mother' country.

182 *Stephen Wagg*

The chapter assesses the extent to which, and the ways *in* which, these factors were reflected in reportage of West Indian cricket (chiefly, matches between England and West Indies) on the pages of the British sports press. While I review a range of papers in their coverage of the watershed Test at Lord's in 1950, I concentrate thereafter principally on *The Times*, the *Daily Express* and the *Daily Mail*. *The Times* was chosen because of the popular view (reliable, in my judgement) that it in part reflects British ruling-class thinking – in this instance, on sport, wherein cricket is always accorded a high place, and on home and colonial affairs. The *Express* and the *Mail* were also selected for the prime place that they afforded to cricket and for their anticipation of their assumed middle-/lower-middle-class suburban readership on matters of 'race', ethnicity and migration. 'Race', as Jack Williams has argued, 'was at the heart of cricket throughout the twentieth century' (2001: 1). Here the *Express* and the *Mail* might be expected to be blunt, but nevertheless more nuanced than the British tabloids, which from the 1960s onwards were in progressively more heated pursuit of a younger, more working-class and celebrity-oriented audience and were likely to be less concerned with cricket than with other sports. The coverage of most, but not all, of the Test series contested by England and West Indies between 1950 and 1984 is considered here.

Friends of mine? Lord's, 1950

When the West Indies beat England for the first time in a Test match, at Lord's cricket ground in June 1950, the islands from which their players had been recruited were all still colonies within the British Empire. Moreover, the British government of the time – the Labour administration of Clement Attlee, which had first gained office on a huge popular mandate in 1945 – was minded that they should remain so. Indeed, although the Labour Party's annual conference had in 1942 accepted a 'Charter of Freedom for Colonial Peoples' – calling for democracy in colonial territories, based on indigenous institutions, communal land owner-ship and the nationalisation of all natural resources – it had the following year nevertheless adopted a statement drafted by Arthur Creech Jones that 'for a considerable time to come these peoples will not be ready for self-government' (Fieldhouse 1984: 84–5). The Empire had not even been mentioned in Labour's manifesto of 1945 and, once in government, Labour ministers remained convinced that Britain's continued status as a world power should be bulwarked by its imperial possessions (Saville 1993: 96–9; Callaghan 1993). Moreover, the colonies are seen by historians to have subsidised Britain's comparatively high standard of living in this immediately post-Second World War period (Fieldhouse, 1984: 96). While the territories of the West Indies were among those deemed 'most ready for self government' (ibid.: 85), Labour contented itself, in the Caribbean as elsewhere, with the encouragement of regional groupings – as at the conference at Montego Bay, Jamaica, in September 1947, chaired by Creech Jones, by then Colonial Secretary. The Colonial Office was also mindful of growing opposition to British rule and of the part played in this opposition by

England–West Indies and the English press 183

emergent trade union movements in the Caribbean. It hoped nevertheless to encourage 'responsible' trade unionism and to 'contain the demagogues and wild men' (Saville 1993: 97).

It is not surprising, then, that West Indies' massive defeat of England (by 326 runs) at Lord's in 1950 should be greeted with magnanimity and unthreatened paternalism on the pages of *The Times*. West Indies, observed a *Times* editorial on 30 June, had had their triumphs before, but

> yesterday was their finest hour. They have handsomely laid An All England XI low at Lords. JOHN GODDARD and his men have made a new mark in cricket history. To win by 326 runs at the headquarters of cricket, in spite of the brave English recovery led by WASHBROOK on Wednesday, puts these West Indians for good among the great ones. There have been giants before in West Indian cricket – GEORGE CHALLENOR, LEARIE CONSTANTINE and GEORGE HEADLEY, each of them among Wisden's best through the ages. This is the first West Indian team to bring the promise of so many fine cricketers to full fruition.
>
> Only patience and the dourer experience of more sober cricketers have been lacking before. This time the West Indians mixed the elements right. Under GODDARD's long-headed leadership West Indian cricket has come of age. There will no doubt be a calypso about it all. Perhaps it has already been composed by the knot of gleeful islanders on the stand behind the sight-screen, with their cries and calls, their songs and music sounding pleasantly strange in the Lords hush. It will be sung as a battle-honour wherever West Indians bat and bowl.
>
> (p. 7)

Fifty or more years on, the subtext to this tribute is clear enough. The West Indies are imperial children come partially of age. In their cricket they have now wedded adult sobriety to boyish enthusiasm. The instrument of this marriage has been John Goddard, the white captain of a largely black team. All this has taken place within the framework of the imperial family, currently under no apparent threat. This notion of imperial self-assurance is strengthened on another page (p. 4) of the same issue, where only fleeting mention is made of the England football team's defeat by the United States in the World Cup finals in Brazil: 'Probably never before', writes the *Times* correspondent, 'has an England team played so badly.'

E. W. Swanton in the *Daily Telegraph* expressed a similar magnanimity. 'There could be no possible question of the justice of today's result,' wrote Swanton after the Lord's Test (*Daily Telegraph*, 30 June 1950, p. 3). Later, reflecting on the final Test and a series victory for West Indies, Swanton also cautiously endorsed the more expressive Caribbean way of appreciating cricket:

> As at Lords the final scenes were enlivened by the impromptu, spontaneous rejoicings of the West Indies supporters and again the law brought them

184 *Stephen Wagg*

sternly to heel. We could well have borne another calypso and a few hand-springs, for it was a victory handsomely and sportingly earned.

(*Daily Telegraph*, 17 August 1950, p. 3)

Other newspapers, however, while still generous in their praise of West Indies cricket, were anxious also to apportion blame to the vanquished and to raise doubts about the state of the British nation-in-its-sport. The *Daily Express* coverage, for example, is neatly weighted in this regard. On 30 June 1950 its front page carries the unconcealed disgust of 'Express Staff Reporter' at England's football defeat in Brazil: 'US footballers – who ever heard of them? – beat England 1–0 in the World Cup series yesterday. It marks the lowest ever for British sport.' Next to this condemnation is a photograph of a black man in a trilby hat playing his guitar in celebration of the West Indian cricket victory at Lords. The accompanying text reads, '[T]he West Indians had won their first Test match in England. . . . And when West Indians celebrate they sing and dance. Calypso at Lords! The Turkey Trot on the hallowed turf! "Outrageous, sir", said an old member. "Just outrageous."' Here, mindful no doubt of its lower-middle-class constituency, the paper symbolically plays off one object of suburban resentment (the sensuous black man) against another (the MCC toff, born to privilege, with his 'hallowed turf' and affronted cry of 'outrageous').

Elsewhere in the same edition Pat Marshall pays tribute to Goddard and his team: 'And a big hand for those 20 year old spinners Sonny Ramadhin and Alfred Valentine for capturing 18 England wickets between them. These two must be ranked as world class' (p. 6). Two pages earlier, the *Express* makes a brittle attempt to have fun with the calypso form. The *Opinion* column (p. 4) contains this verse, headed 'Eclypso':

The West Indians have beaten England at cricket
And even the English critics can't put it down to the wicket
Instead they will say that the English team stinks
But maybe the West Indians are better than anyone thinks

This is perhaps a limp and friendly parody of the calypso composed at the game by Lord Beginner in celebration of 'those little pals of mine / Ramadhin and Valentine' (Phillips and Phillips 1998: 95–103).

During the series, Ramadhin and Valentine bowled 790 out of the 1,115 overs sent down by West Indies and took 59 of the 77 wickets taken. It is possible to argue that the key role in England's defeat of the guileful art of spin, as opposed to the overt physical power of the Caribbean fast bowlers, helped to minimise any alarm that West Indies victory might raise in the ruling circles of English cricket. This angle was certainly noted by Alex Bannister in the *Daily Mail*. Beneath the headline 'Nice work, skipper Goddard: BETTER SIDE, AND NO ARGUMENT', Bannister observes that the 'irony of England's downfall is that it was not brought about by the much-vaunted speed battery, but by two 20 year old "unknown" spin bowlers' (30 June, p. 7). In the summer of 1950,

England–West Indies and the English press   185

generous praise for the West Indies cricket team was the norm on the English sports pages, but, as I suggested earlier, space was occasionally found for the attribution of blame and the sounding of national alarm bells. After Lord's, Charles Bray in the *Daily Herald*, alone and obliquely, raises the spectre of class in the English team, calling for the dismissal of England captain Norman Yardley (an amateur) and his replacement with his fellow Yorkshireman Len Hutton (a professional) and only latterly allowing that 'West Indies deserve the highest praise for their decisive and magnificent victory' (30 June 1950, p. 6). And, at the conclusion of the 1950 series, Frank Rostron in the *Daily Express* is noticeably more concerned with English shortcoming than with Caribbean prowess: 'England's cricket reached its nadir yesterday afternoon when West Indies, with a degree of simplicity bordering on the farcical, took the rubber (the first one they have won here) by three matches to one' (17 August 1950, p. 6).

The most enduring press image of this Test series is probably in the *Daily Mail* (27 June 1950), which carries on its front page a photograph of West Indies wicketkeeper Clyde Walcott with a broad smile. The image, with text from Bannister to the effect that Walcott has 'the widest grin in cricket', confirms the dominant depiction of West Indies as essentially happy-go-lucky characters, with an attendant band of revelling supporter-minstrels recently resident in the English capital – all cheerful members of the British imperial family.

Flying bottles and the 'colour question', 1954

The first public signs of discord in this family to appear in the English press came in 1954. England visited the Caribbean in January of that year for a Test series. *The Times* during this period carries a number of matter-of-fact reports ('Great victory over Jamaica', 7 January, p. 9; 'M.C.C. morale high', 14 January, p. 3 . . .) but, as if sensing the need for reassurance among its readers on the matter of social and political stability on the islands, in mid-February it prints the following reflections on Caribbean society by the Archbishop of York:

Island impressions: sunshine and shadows in the West Indies

The loveliness of the islands, their history and the friendliness of their people are the chief impressions carried away by most visitors. There is another aspect of the islands. In different degrees in each island there exist the problems of colour, nationalism, poverty, malnutrition, unemployment and bad housing.

Colour problem

It can be said of the colour problem that it has been practically solved. . . . Nationalism is found in most of the islands. The coloured people wish to manage their own affairs and they are rapidly doing so. Already a great part of the administration is in their hands. But desire for self-government is

186 *Stephen Wagg*

combined with devoted loyalty to the Queen and with the wish to remain in the Commonwealth. But the electorate needs further education before complete self-government can be granted with safety; it is very illiterate . . .

The greatest and most general of all the problems is poverty. With the possible exception of Trinidad, where the oil fields and the pitch lake supplement the revenue from sugar and citrus, the economic position of the colonies is doubtful and insecure . . .

. . . I made many inquiries about the threat of communism. In British Guiana it is serious. Throughout the Indies there was strong approval of the action the British government had taken, but there is still much tension, with the possibility of further trouble . . .

. . . The coloured people are instinctively religious. They throng the churches and are most reverent in their worship.'

(15 February 1954, p. 7)

The action mentioned by the archbishop had been taken the previous year when the Conservative government of Winston Churchill had suspended the Guianese constitution and imposed martial law in the colony, following an election victory by Dr Cheddi Jagan's People's Progressive Party. Churchill told the Conservative Party conference of 1953:

Her Majesty's Government are not going to allow a Communist State to be organised within the British Commonwealth. Our friends can take that as a definitive statement, and our enemies can attach to it all the importance that I think they should.

(quoted in Carr, 1999: 183)

A fortnight after the archbishop's guarded assessment, *The Times* reported, almost in passing, an incident at the third Test at the Bourda cricket ground in Georgetown, British Guiana, under the heading 'West Indies need 45 runs to avoid follow-on' and the sub-headings 'Bottles in the outfield' and 'Incident follows giving out of local player McWatt by (replacement) umpire Menzies': 'It is reported that W. S. Jones, President of the British Guiana Cricket Association, had suggested to England captain Len Hutton that he take his players off the field, but that Hutton had refused' (1 March 1954, p. 10). Later, on 25 March, *The Times* carries a statement from Sir Errol Dos Santos, president of the West Indies Cricket Board of Control, apologising for crowd behaviour in the Caribbean on this tour and suggesting that Hutton had prevented an 'ugly scene' by staying on at the Bourda (p. 8).

However, on the pages of the *Daily Express* and the *Daily Mail* an altogether more fractious tour is being portrayed and considerably more doom-laden inferences drawn. As early as 14 January, Frank Rostron reports in the *Express* that Karl Nunes, president of the Jamaica Cricket Association, has protested unofficially about the behaviour of MCC players – in particular, the questioning of umpires' decisions. Hutton, it's suggested, has had a quiet word with fast bowler

England–West Indies and the English press   187

Fred Trueman about this. 'I am a lover of England and an admirer of English cricket,' says Nunes. There is also visible impatience with England's performance against West Indies: the following week a dyspeptic headline announces 'Pathetic England flop in 35 mins' (22 January 1954, p. 8) and the clearly accusatory 'Five England ducks' following England's defeat in the second Test match at Bridgetown, Barbados.

Reaction to the Bourda disturbance in the 'suburban' British papers may be interpreted in part as a reaction both to these further on-the-field setbacks for the England team at the hands of the West Indies and to the growth of nationalist feeling on the islands. Trevor Bailey, Hutton's vice-captain on the 1954 tour, later recalled his irritation with white West Indians and expatriate Englishmen who told MCC players that they had to win: 'Their reason was that their life would not be worth living if the West Indies were victorious because it would disturb the balance of power, or, as a Victorian would have put it, "make the natives uppity"' (Bailey 1986: 186). On 2 March the *Daily Mail* ran an article by cricket correspondent Alex Bannister on page 4. Titled 'Is this cricket?', like the Archbishop of York's earlier observations in *The Times* it invokes the 'colour question': 'Ever since the M.C.C. went to Bermuda as a stepping-stone to the West Indies tour the colour question with its political background has followed them around like an evil shadow.' 'The English players', he adds, 'have been shocked by the intensity of anti-British feeling here', and they 'are counting the days until they can come home'. Bannister talks of violence in Jamaica and floats the question of whether the People's Progressive Party (PPP) were 'behind the bottle-throwing incident'. A picture of Hutton accompanies the article. He has his bat under his arm and is pulling on his batting gloves, ready for action. Beneath the photograph is the caption 'LEN HUTTON When told: "This bottle throwing is getting ugly. You should come off the field", replied "No, we want another wicket or two this evening".'

Here Hutton stands, ultimately, for the West – he is the no-nonsense British subaltern dealing laconically with excitable colonial subjects. Little has been said directly about West Indian cricketers in the coverage of this tour, but their homelands are now depicted as places where angry and intemperate people live – places where the safety of a cricket match, a key benchmark of 'civilisation', can no longer be guaranteed. Moreover, there is a more visible impatience on the sports pages with British failure, defeat at sport, with British rule now openly challenged, being seen increasingly as a threat to national self-confidence.

The last calypso?, 1963

The West Indies came to England in 1957 and were soundly beaten in the Test series. The cricket correspondent of *The Times* reflected that he had expected 'a great deal more determination' from these 'popular, cheerful cricketers':

> For the crowd, though, the days were rather hollow. Massacres are never fun to watch and this was nothing else. But Englishmen since the war have had

188 *Stephen Wagg*

their share of seeing their own side badly beaten. Indeed, when Goddard first brought a team here seven years ago the boot was on the other foot.

(26 August 1957, p. 4)

The West Indies were back in England in the summer of 1963, under the captaincy of Frank Worrell. Worrell was the first black man to be given the job on a permanent basis and was the consummation, therefore, of an important element in the nationalist struggle in the Caribbean. The series of 1963 was judged by some at the time to be the best Test series they had ever seen. This section principally discusses coverage of that series in the *Mail* and the *Express*: here, as ever, the rhetoric is more expansive and less guarded than that of the broadsheet press.

In early June, articles by Alex Bannister in the *Daily Mail* are at pains to stress the respectability of members of the West Indies team. On 6 June he reports that

Senator Frank Worrell of the Upper House of the Jamaican House of Representatives, BSc graduate of the University of Manchester, Warden of the University College of the West Indies has, in his more familiar role of Test captain, the simplest of plans to beat England.

(p. 16)

The following day, readers are informed that opening batsman Conrad Hunte is giving all his tour earnings to the conservative Christian campaigners Moral Rearmament. Bannister, apparently no longer anxious about the 'colour question', is clearly satisfied that the team is under educated and moderate-minded leadership, although he laments the lack, early on in the tour, of the cavalier batting of old. After day 1 of the first Test, the West Indies are 244 for 3, with the devout Hunte 104 not out. 'Certainly, apart from Kanhai', observes Bannister, 'it was not calypso style' (7 June 1963, p. 16).

On 10 June the *Mail* columnist Ian Wooldridge, beneath the headline 'Cricket wins back its crowd appeal', refers to West Indies fast bowler Wes Hall as a 'cheerful executioner'. There are two important significations here. One is of the West Indies as potential saviours of a commercially threatened game in a world of diversified leisure options. The other is of the Caribbean fast bowler as still unequivocally within the tent of acceptable cricket practice. This judgement is shared by Crawford White of the *Daily Express*, who, reporting on the first day of the first Test, calls on readers to 'salute the courage of England's new opening batsmen, John Edrich and Mickey Stewart for the way they stood up to the bumper fire of Wes Hall and Charlie Griffith' (*Daily Express*, 7 June 1963, p. 18). This remains the dominant view throughout the summer, although in the minds of some cricket reporters of the 'suburban', 'middlebrow' press this acceptability has become open to question by the end of August. This can be seen, in retrospect, as another watershed. On 11 June the *Mail* is derisive of England's performance in the first Test, as shown in its headline on page 16 claiming England to have been 'out – bowled – batted – fielded – thought'.

Nearly a fortnight on, the *Daily Mail* of 24 June carries a photograph of five cricket captains – England's Ted Dexter (Radley and Cambridge), Richie Benaud of Australia, Worrell, the white South African Jackie McGlew and Indian aristocrat the Nawab of Pataudi – enjoying a drink together in a pub near Lords. This an image of postcolonial harmony, with key Commonwealth nations in cricket, bonded across class and 'race'. (It is worth remembering that South Africa's apartheid system was fully entrenched at this time and that the participation of its whites-only team in Test cricket was virtually unchallenged within world cricket governance. Some protestors had, however, greeted the South African cricket party that arrived for a tour of Britain in 1960, a few weeks after 69 black demonstrators had been killed by police in the Sharpeville township near Cape Town in March that year (Gemmell 2004: 120).)

The second Test at Lord's found these cricket writers trying to balance crucial considerations – the threat of West Indian fast bowling, British heroism, the joys of membership of the international cricket family, and so on – as never before. The England batsman Colin Cowdrey has had his wrist broken by a ball from Hall. Wooldridge employs the vocabulary of 'Trench war!' to describe prospects for the final day: 'The superb second Test is no longer a fiesta. Today's six-hour last act will be trench warfare, with England facing the most ruthless barrage in world cricket.' The language here stresses primarily the excitement expected from this finale and, despite the evocation of the First World War, it imputes no malign intention to England's opponents. On the same page, Bannister considers closely the morality of the West Indies fast bowling:

Worrell ends the violent spell

Wes Hall bowled some of the most violent and frightening overs ever seen on any ground in the Second Test at Lords yesterday. Though I do not think he was guilty of persistent intimidation, umpire Eddie Phillipson could have been justified in giving Frankie Worrell, the West Indies captain, a hint to put a brake on the short pitchers. In one ugly over in which Colin Cowdrey was felled, there was not one ball of normal length. But it is difficult to define which are bumpers or deliveries of intimidation . . .

Bumpers and short pitchers – which can be far more dangerous – are common tactics for fast bowlers in the West Indies to defeat their good pitches.

(*Daily Mail*, 25 June 1963, p. 12)

This assessment tentatively identifies a problem, but deliberately falls short of accusing anyone of wrongdoing; indeed, in conclusion, it contextualises the practice of bowling short by saying that it's only to be expected in West Indian circumstances – 'their good pitches'. In the *Express*, the aggressive, New World voice of ex-Australian Test cricketer Keith Miller is more forthright. Referring to the incident in which Cowdrey has fractured his wrist, Miller asks, 'Should Hall, bowling from the pavilion end under a leaden sky, have eased his pace? Certainly

190 *Stephen Wagg*

not. This is a Test match and Test matches are fought bitterly.' Crawford White, on the same page, while more circumspect, is similarly loath to indict the West Indian fast bowlers:

> [T]he ball that hit Cowdrey was the eighth successive delivery pitched short of a length. I do not blame Hall. His job was to blast out the England batsmen, and a terrifying sight he was as he set about it. I do blame the Lords authorities for not providing sight screens at the pavilion end.
>
> (*Daily Express*, 25 June 1963, p. 16)

The final day of the Test is generally accepted to have featured fast bowling from Hall that was every bit as formidable as on previous days, but press reports of this day are nevertheless couched primarily in terms of the grit of the home side in resisting this bowling and do not question the legitimacy of the bowling itself. England have held on for a draw in circumstances that evoke popular images of English heroism. These images are rooted in class and masculinity. The resistance of England's batsmen has been led by the Yorkshireman Brian Close, who has batted for nearly four hours and taken much of Hall's bowling on his body. Vice-chairman of England selectors Doug Insole accentuates the masculinity of Close's performance when he says, jokily, that, of the ten bruises Close received, '[h]e rubbed only one – when he was hit in the groin by Hall' (*Daily Mail*, 26 June 1963, p. 16). Cowdrey, a privately educated Southerner from Kent, perceived as effete by many northern cricket people, has come out to bat in the final over with his arm in plaster, in order to save the game for England. On the front page of the same edition of the *Mail* Wooldridge describes it as 'the most fantastic over Lords has ever seen'.

On these sports pages, England and the West Indies are now seen to be engaged in some epic struggle that draws heavily on preferred national myths. When England win the third Test and Fred Trueman takes seven wickets in the West Indies' second innings, the *Mail* affectionately adapts Caribbean popular imagery to announce 'Trueman collapso'. Wooldridge styles Trueman as a diffident English working-class hero: 'At 3.05 pm . . . Trueman was taking his hat from umpire Laurie Gray and walking off like a plumber who had just fixed the pipes' (*Daily Mail*, 10 July 1963, p. 12). During the next Test, at Leeds, Wooldridge describes the dismissal of West Indian batsman Garfield Sobers as 'a great warrior' going 'gloriously to his doom' (*Daily Mail*, 26 July 1963, p. 14) and on the 29th the same paper quotes the chairman of the England selectors, Walter Robins, as saying that 'this is now the greatest Test series I have ever known. If you can say that, then does defeat matter?' (p. 10). The following day Wooldridge notes that, although it was clear that there would be little play on the final day, 20,000 people have nevertheless paid to watch it. The West Indies, he observes, are 'now rightly one up with one to play'. 'In the meantime,' he suggests, 'English batsmen should not seek to excuse their frailties' by doubting the legitimacy of West Indian fast bowler Charlie Griffiths' action (p. 9). This view is vigorously endorsed by Miller in the *Daily Express*, also on 30 July (p. 11).

By the end of the series the determination on the part of the 'suburban' press to claim these matches as a collective symbol of postcolonial amity is plain. Crawford White's headline back in early June had described the West Indies as 'Calypso cricketers' (*Daily Express*, 7 June 1963, p. 18) and, on the pages of the *Express* and the *Mail*, calypso cricketers is what they remained. There were some caveats. Wooldridge points out that, in the final Test, 'England have had to withstand as frightening a blitz of bumpers and bouncers as an Oval crowd has seen for many a cricket campaign', and on the same page the veteran populist sports writer J. L. Manning calls for more courage on the part of umpires in dealing with 'the unfair fast bowling that threatened to be the only unpleasantness of this very good series'. 'English cricket's acceptance of world-wide condemnation of Jardine's bodyline in 1933 should', argues Manning, 'have been the end of the problem. It is curious to note that Australian and West Indian cricketers are willing to drift back to the bad old days when the ball was the thing you aimed at the batsman's head.' The word 'savagery' appears as a sub-heading, although not in Manning's text (*Daily Mail*, 23 August 1963, p. 4). This implies, perhaps, that it was not used by Manning in his original copy, but was added, for effect, by a sub-editor.

Generally, though, there is a will to retrieve the apparent spirit of 1950 when London's new Caribbean settlers had, along with their team, intimated to uptight white English cricket watchers that the game could be fun. 'The Test series that has made cricket live again ended yesterday,' wrote Wooldridge, whereupon

> The crowd came down the grey, old ground to chant and cheer the captains. An hour later they were still there. That is what they thought of the series that closed last night in victory for the West Indies, defeat for England and triumph for the game itself.

On the same page, Gerard Kemp notes how at the Oval the sky had been 'filled with hats, cushions, briefcases, even shoes' and celebrates the tea interval performance of 'Mr Carlton Constantine from Trinidad [who], wearing a string vest, bright orange shirt and black bowler, demonstrates with his furled umbrella how Rohan Kanhai hit a six'. 'Two Englishmen stroll by in city suits,' notes Kemp. 'One says: "It's all quite, quite unbelievable."' And J. L. Manning reflects:

> What was unique about this summer was that West Indian crowds seemed to have achieved as much as Frank Worrell's players. They stopped Test cricket becoming exclusively the white man's war-game and turned it into something everyone could enjoy.

(All the above quotations are from the *Daily Mail* of 27 August 1963, p. 12). An editorial in *The Times* is similarly confident of a cultural shift in the making: 'Thanks to the West Indians, fresh air and light have moved over the face of cricket in England. Our visitors have reminded us that cricket is a game to be played seriously and skilfully indeed, but always for fun' (*The Times*, 27 August

192   *Stephen Wagg*

1963, p. 9). But the most unbridled intervention here comes from Peter Black, best known as the television critic of the *Daily Mail*, who contributes an article in late August based on his experiences at the Oval. It's entitled 'We had a rough day yesterday – my guilt complex and I', and it's accompanied by a cartoon by Illingworth in which a beaming black West Indian cricketer is striking a ball labelled 'RACIALISM'. 'I'd say there are 5,000 West Indians here', writes Black,

> to judge from the blobs of darker colour in the crowd; and they spread a partisan joy and bustle that Tests haven't imparted in England since the 1953 series against Australia . . .
>
> These people have been maltreated for 300 years in their own islands, which they left because the exploiters had flogged the economy to death. They had to change a hot sunny island for a cold, damp one which didn't want them anyway. They've been conned, fleeced, badgered, misunderstood, patronised and insulted to the last – and this must be the hardest to bear – out of ignorance as much as hostility.
>
> As workers, they have been tolerated only as long as they accept generally second rate status. . . . By doing the pinks this good turn [of invigorating Test cricket] the browns must have let quite a bit of the poison out of racialism. And the claims for cricket as a kind of international marriage bureau suddenly make more sense.
>
> (*Daily Mail*, 23 August 1963, p. 8)

On the face of it, this article seems extraordinary. It appears in a right-wing newspaper whose readership and editorial stance had often been antagonistic to migrant groups. Moreover, with independence for the islands either achieved or accepted in principle and the demand for labour receding, anti-immigration politics in Britain had just begun to make an impact at national level: the openly discriminatory Commonwealth Immigration Act had been passed the year before (see Layton-Henry 1992: 70–99). However, a certain kind of imperialist paternalism still commanded support in ruling circles in Britain – Enoch Powell, for example, later the self-appointed leader of the racist, anti-immigration lobby in Britain, had voted against the 1962 Act (see Foot 1969) – and this paternalism probably encompassed many of those running, or writing about, British cricket at the time. The article, along with the other euphoric commentary in these newspapers, is also, in retrospect, absurdly optimistic about 'race' relations, both within cricket culture and beyond. This was clear by the middle of the following decade.

Please keep off the grass, 1976

By the mid-1970s, tensions within the British colonial family are apparent from the cricket reports of the English sports pages. In April 1976, during a Test match between the West Indies and India in Kingston, Jamaica, India manager Polly Umrigar accused West Indies fast bowler Michael Holding of intimidatory

England–West Indies and the English press   193

bowling: 'Holding bowled three to four bumpers in every over, and that's intimidatory. This was not in the true spirit of the game. It was almost like war and the whole charm of the game is being lost.' The Indian captain and spin bowler Bishen Bedi added, somewhat without originality, that this 'was not cricket' (*The Times*, 24 April 1976). This controversy was, of course, noted on sports desks in England, where West Indies were due a few days later. Pat Gibson of the *Daily Express* was among the press pack that met them and announces that in the forthcoming series:

> [T]he slightest sign of weakness against the short pitched ball will be exploited to the limit of the law. No one said it in so many words but this was the clear message from manager Clyde Walcott and skipper Clive Lloyd when the dark destroyers flew into London yesterday.

Walcott tells the cricket reporters: 'India are suspect to pace'. He adds:

> I don't think we are known to be hostile in our cricket, but we may be a little harder now. These days are tough and you have to play hard if you want to win. If a fast bowler is not allowed to bowl bouncers the games loses something. He is not trying to hit the batsman, but to get them out.
>
> (*Daily Express*, 5 May 1976)

Three weeks later the same paper carries an analysis of Holding's action, which is photographed in five stages. Although the article (by Malcolm Folley) has the ambiguous title 'Anatomy of a demon', far from marginalising Holding, it links him, in technique, to English cricket culture: veteran coach Alf Gover likens him to Fred Trueman (*Daily Express*, 28 May 1976, p. 20). Elsewhere in the same issue, James Lawton calls for Brian Close to be restored to the England team. 'Certainly', he asserts, 'I cannot think of anyone better qualified to deliver a meaningful "V" sign to the theory that English cricketers have lost the heart to fight' (p. 24). This is plainly atavistic talk, calling up the spirit of 1963 in a time of national cricket emergency. The West Indies pace attack must be met with English masculine resolve, and Close, the mythical man-who-stepped-into-the-breach in the equally mythical series of 13 years earlier, will provide it. Close, however, is now 45 years old and last played for England in 1967. Three days later, with Close's selection confirmed, *Times* cricket correspondent John Woodcock observes:

> Mingled with one's respect for Brian Close, the iron man of English cricket, who has been called upon to play in the first Test match against West Indies starting at Trent Bridge on Thursday, is a greater feeling of despair that it should have been considered necessary to choose him.
>
> (*The Times*, 31 May 1976)

Here Woodcock recognises the futility of reaching for the imagined national glories of the past. (I say 'imagined' because some cricket people thought Close's

194 *Stephen Wagg*

batting at Lords in 1963 had been tactically *in*appropriate. Certainly Worrell told the *Daily Mail* so at the time – see 'Close failed you', 26 June 1963, p. 16). Indeed, there is a notable attempt, during this summer, on the part of Woodcock and others, to come to terms with the decline in English cricket's competitiveness and the corresponding growth in the West Indies' power. This is done, for the most part, within a paradigm of admiration for Caribbean cricketers and a good-humoured exasperation with English failure. There are clear attempts to maintain the 'calypso consensus' of the previous decade but, by August 1976, especially in *The Times*, this consensus is plainly beginning to dissipate.

On the eve of the first Test match, Michael Holding goes down with glandular fever. Woodcock is laconic in anticipating the effect of this on a contest widely expected to be uneven:

> The England players heard the news that Michael Holding was out of the first Test match on their car radios as they converged on Trent Bridge yesterday. No wonder they were in high spirits when they came out for practice in the afternoon. . . . I believe we will have a less acrimonious match without Holding, not for any personal reason, but simply because less blood is likely to be drawn. Holding's lovely rhythm will be very much missed, by all but the English batsmen. He is a great sight and to West Indies a great loss.
>
> (*The Times*, 3 June 1976)

The generous and gentlemanly tone of this tribute clashes, however, with noises now being made in other parts of the forest. Three weeks later *The Times* prints an article by Marcel Berlins telling how Eddie Phillipson, one of the umpires in the Lord's Test of 1963, denies being told by the then chairman of the England selectors not to no-ball Charlie Griffith for fear of racial tension and a possible riot in London (*The Times*, 24 June 1976, p. 4). (Walter Robins, the chairman in question, and Sid Buller, the other umpire, are both now dead.) The claims have been made by Fred Trueman in his book *Ball of Fire* (1976) and he writes to reassert them on 28 June (p. 15). It is perhaps significant that this accusation is investigated, and re-presented, in *The Times*, where it might previously have been thought 'poor form', and not in the *Mail* or the *Express*, where it might, conversely, have been expected to get a sympathetic hearing. As a further reminder of the changed politics of migration and ethnicity in England, on the front page of the same edition Robert Parker reports that in Leicester, where the proportion of New Commonwealth immigrants is the highest of any British city, the racist National Front has more support than anywhere else in the country.

While Trueman and others are revising history, the cricket writers of the *Express*, dominated by ex-England Test players, are simply lamenting that it cannot be repeated: there will be no return to the thrilling cricket and apparent cultural exchange of 1963. When England have been dismissed for 71 in the third Test at Old Trafford, Pat Gibson writes, 'as the Caribbean drums beat out their triumphant message in the Manchester gloom, the scoreboard made its own sad comment on England's despair' (*Daily Express*, 10 July 1976, p. 14). The following

England–West Indies and the English press 195

day, in the *Sunday Express*, the former England batsman Denis Compton calls for a stiffening of sinews in the national side: 'England, please end this humiliation of complete surrender to the West Indies'. He notes in passing that Holding has been warned for intimidation by umpire Bill Alley, but stresses the huge gulf in technique and determination between the two teams:

> It must be a great temptation to these fast bowlers to give our batsmen more than a fair share of these deliveries because of our pathetic method of dealing with them. . . . In contrast, when the West Indies batted it was like using pea shooters against tanks.
>
> (*Sunday Express*, 11 July 1976, p. 27)

The next day another ex-England player, Jim Laker, notes that Holding has received a further warning and he warns darkly of 'open warfare' (*Daily Express*, 12 July 1976, p. 14), but his colleague Pat Gibson mocks such talk in his praise for the West Indies in the following Test:

> All the nasty things they were saying about the West Indies fast bowlers at Old Trafford could have been applied to their batsmen yesterday. Only this time they were superlatives. Talk about intimidatory bowling! It was little short of intimidatory batting. The Caribbean cavaliers treated England's full strength attack with utter contempt in the Fourth Test.
>
> (*Daily Express*, 23 July 1976, p. 16)

Five days later, Gibson celebrates this 'magnificent Test' that has 'ended as a Caribbean carnival at Headingley' (*Daily Express*, 28 July 1976, p. 16).

No doubt to their credit, Gibson and the other *Express* writers do not yet register the turning of cricket's political tide against West Indies and their exuberant supporters. *The Times*, however, does. On 22 July the paper reports that the International Cricket Conference

> last night gave full backing to umpires in an effort to control the use of bouncers in Test matches. Secretary of M.C.C. Jack Bailey says: 'Now this is a matter for the West Indies. I could not guarantee what they are going to do tomorrow [in the fourth Test at Headingley]. What happens next is up to member countries with players under their control. All individual countries now have a duty . . .
>
> (p. 11)

A fortnight later *The Times* notes the deliberations of the Test and County Cricket Board (TCCB). The TCCB will ask Clive Lloyd to appeal to West Indies supporters to cut down the noise at the fifth Test at the Oval: 'The Board after their meeting said they were very concerned at the noise which at times they considered could be intimidatory' (7 August 1976, p. 15).

196 *Stephen Wagg*

In his reporting of this match, the *Express*'s Gibson is still accentuating the positive. The expressiveness of West Indian supporters has been curtailed, but the man from the *Express* meanwhile welcomes one of their heroes into the pantheon of great batsmen:

> They silenced the Caribbean drums at the Oval yesterday but they could do little about the Caribbean beat and absolutely nothing about that magical rhythm of Vivian Richards's bat. On his way back to the dressing room he passed the bust of W. G. Grace in the Oval Long Room and I hope it smiled at him. Because in all the years since the good doctor was playing, Test cricket has never known scoring like this.
>
> (*Daily Express*, 13 August 1976, p. 16)

On 14 August, however, West Indian supporters came onto the field of play after Holding had taken the wicket of Tony Greig, England's South African-born captain. In the *Sunday Express* the following day, Compton accused them of 'trampling on the wicket and leaving beer cans and other debris all over the field' (15 August 1976, p. 24), and on the Monday, Gibson condemns this 'loutish stupidity' (*Daily Express*, 16 August 1976, p. 13).

On the English sports pages of this year, then, there have been vain appeals for a return to the English cricketing courage of a mythical past and a continued and optimistic use of the vocabulary of carnival and calypso. There has been frank admiration for West Indian exponents of the art of fast bowling, an admiration plainly not shared by cricket's English-dominated legislature. There are clear signs, however, that, once again at the behest of administrators, the cheery black folk who in 1950 and 1963 taught stiff white spectators to party are being redefined as louts and worse. Their drumming is no longer perceived as the welcome soundtrack to a joyous event; it is seen as intimidation.

The bombardment has only just begun: the 1980s

England and the West Indies played four Test series during the 1980s. The first two series of the decade were in 1981, in the Caribbean, and in 1984, in England. (England returned to the West Indies in 1986 and the West Indies played in England in the summer of 1988. All the series of the 1980s were won by the West Indies, but it is principally the first two that lie within the scope of this chapter.) In the early 1980s the immigration to Britain of black Caribbean people became virtually impossible under the British Nationality Act of 1981 (Layton-Henry 1992: 191–8), which confined British citizenship, and therefore right of residence, to those with an historic family connection to the United Kingdom – a definition overwhelmingly favourable to whites. Indeed, following Tony Greig (born in Queenstown, South Africa, and given his England debut in 1972), a number of white South Africans, born to British migrants, were granted British citizenship in order for them to play cricket for England: Allan Lamb, for example, born in Cape Province, who first played for England in 1982, and Chris Smith, born

England–West Indies and the English press 197

in Durban, who received his first England cap the following year. Meanwhile, riots convulsed a number of areas of black settlement in British cities in the early 1980s, beginning with the St Paul's area of Bristol in 1980 and Brixton in south-west London in 1981. Relations between British black people and the police became deeply problematic (see Keith 1993). Press reportage during the Test series of 1981 and 1984 in *The Times* and the *Daily Express* generally unites around a number of themes: the characterisation of the Caribbean as a place where disorder reigns and politics intrudes into sport; frequent reference to the continued 'bombardment' of the British batsmen by West Indian fast bowlers, the legality or appropriateness of which is sometimes questioned; the presence of black people in Britain, although a connection is almost never drawn between British black people (and their obvious discontent) and the West Indies cricket team; and (very occasional) nostalgia for colonial times. I now consider each of these themes.

In mid-January 1981, England's tour manager, Alan Smith, secures agreement from the West Indies board that extra time will be played 'should a Test be held up by anything other than the weather'. 'There is obvious concern with any series in the Caribbean', continues the *Times* correspondent, 'that crowd disorder could disrupt a match – as it did twice on the 1967–68 tour' (*The Times*, 17 January 1981, p. 17). A month later, John Woodcock reports from the first Test at Port of Spain, Trinidad, that 'the first full scale riot of the tour' has been 'only narrowly averted' and the pitch has been interfered with overnight (*The Times*, 14 February 1981, p. 17). In the *Express*, Pat Gibson claims that damage to the pitch, apparently inflicted because Trinidadian player Deryck Murray has not been selected for the match, has been acknowledged only 'after pressure from myself and other pressmen' (*Daily Express*, 14 February 1981, p. 44). This is a classically postcolonial image, in which cheating and factionalised former subjects *still* have to be taught fair play by a vigilant representative of the former imperial power.

Later that month a *Times* editorial responds angrily to the refusal of the government of Guyana to admit the England player Robin Jackman, who has played cricket in South Africa in defiance of a world ban on sports links with apartheid. The paper says the call for Jackman to leave Guyana is an 'insulting demand' and compares it to the refusal in 1968 of the South African Prime Minister John Vorster to admit the England cricketer Basil D'Oliveira, born a 'Cape Coloured' but by then qualified to play for England. 'On the issue of personal liberty Britain cannot give way, even if cricket suffers' (*The Times*, 27 February 1981, p. 15).

On 11 April, in the fifth and final Test at Kingston, Jamaica, the England batsman Graham Gooch scores 153. Woodcock stresses that while Gooch has compiled his innings, police have been 'present in strength' to keep anti-apartheid demonstrators at bay (*The Times*, p. 15). When the England party arrive back in London, *The Times* include a statement by tour manager Smith that cites the political impasse in Guyana as a mitigating factor in the team's lack of success: 'The death of Ken Barrington [Smith's assistant manager] and the trouble in Guyana were severe blows and the bad weather didn't help. We all felt the tour

198 *Stephen Wagg*

had to go on despite what happened in Guyana' (20 April 1981, p. 11). Here, the MCC and *The Times* render a matter, defined in the Caribbean as one of 'race' and politics, simply as a regrettable obstacle that came the team's way. It is equated with naturally occurring mishaps (the death of the assistant manager and the bad weather) and has, runs the strong implication, been borne with typically English fortitude. (Five years later, on 28 February 1986, with the English cricket team once again struggling to cope with West Indian fast bowling, the *Daily Express* will use its front page to demand that the party be brought home, rather than go to Trinidad, where 'insults and humiliations' are being planned for England's cricketers by 'anti-apartheid zealots'.)

At the culmination of a series of five Tests in England in 1984, all of which have been won by the West Indies, the *Express* correspondent Colin Bateman revisits the now well-worn journalistic theme for these occasions: West Indian-spectators-on-the-field-of-play. Once again their intervention is seen as troublesome, but this time there is a 'human interest' angle. The thoughtless West Indian supporters have spoiled an England's cricketer's day: 'Jonathan Agnew's Test debut for England ended in fear yesterday as the West Indian celebrations turned to a chaotic carnival at the Oval . . . he was attacked as hundreds of fans charged onto the field' (*Daily Express*, 15 August 1984, p. 36). Noticeably, the language has become more damning still. In 1950 and 1963, West Indian supporters celebrated; in 1976 they made intimidating noise and left debris; now, in 1984, they 'attacked'.

During the early 1980s (and for years to come), English cricket correspondents had to find ways to render the central fact of these encounters: the superiority of the West Indies fast bowlers. Sometimes they did so by challenging the legitimacy of this bowling. Reporting from the England tour of 1981, for instance, John Woodcock observes of the fast bowler Colin Croft that he 'quite frequently breaks the return crease with his back foot in the delivery stride. By the laws of the game, this is a no-ball' (*The Times*, 17 February 1981, p. 10). And when England batsman Andy Lloyd has been struck on the head by a ball from Malcolm Marshall in June 1984, Woodcock once again draws attention to the rules of engagement:

> All right, he made the crucial mistake of taking his eye off the ball and it was not an out and out bouncer. At the same time this may be the moment to spell out the law: 'Umpires shall consider intimidation to be the deliberate bowling of fast, short-pitched balls which by their length, height and direction are intended or *likely* to inflict physical injury on the striker'. The italics are mine and the wishes of the law-makers are as unmistakeably clear as they are widely ignored.
>
> (*The Times*, 15 June 1984, p. 20)

There is also, from time to time, the implication that the West Indies are now bullying lesser opponents. On one occasion in the 1984 series, the umpire 'Dickie' Bird, according to Pat Gibson, 'considered five bouncers in two overs was

England–West Indies and the English press 199

overdoing the brutality' (*Daily Express*, 18 June 1984, p. 30). Here the word 'brutality' appears not as an accusation, but as an assumption – something that we all 'know'. Ten days later, Gibson applauds Chris Broad's innings of 55 for England: 'He for one was clearly not going to be intimidated by the likes of Joel Garner and Malcolm Marshall' (*Daily Express*, 29 June 1984, p. 34). At still other times there are expressions of boredom and nostalgia. By March 1981, John Woodcock was saying of the four West Indian fast bowlers:

> It makes for painful batting and, because of the monotony of it, for tedious watching. No longer can England's batsmen look forward with much enthusiasm to playing in a Test match. When it comes to putting on all the protective gear available the fun goes out of it. . . . The best thing for cricket in general – even, in the long run, for West Indian cricket – would, I believe, be for the four fast bowlers syndrome to be sent sky high by a strong batting side in consistently good form on consistently good pitches.
>
> (*The Times*, 27 March 1981, p. 12)

Sometimes the 'politics', in the form of fallout from the continuing controversy over cricketing relations with apartheid South Africa, is invoked as a mitigating factor in the enduringly one-sided nature of these contests. On 19 June 1984, Woodcock laments in *The Times*:

> Indeed, if the sport were boxing and not cricket, the Board of Control would say that on no account must these same protagonists be allowed back in the same ring. That is how much of a mismatch it seemed. . . . Most of the experienced players on whom the England selectors might like to call, in an attempt to strengthen the side, are still banned [following a 'rebel' tour of South Africa in 1981; see Gemmell 2004: 163–78].
>
> (p. 26)

Beyond this, there is an acknowledgement of Caribbean prowess. England competed, wrote Woodcock, for example, of the second Test of 1984, '[b]ut in the end Richards' genius and Lloyd's experience told' (*The Times*, 30 June 1984, p. 27). However, this often goes, once again, with a questioning of English attitude and technique:

> England's batsmen must overcome a mental barrier if they are to keep this series alive. Their technical problems against a formidable West Indies attack are caused as much by psychological complexes as any real shortage of the ability to cope.
>
> (Jim Laker, *Daily Express*, 27 March 1981, p. 46)

With scarcely a flicker of defiance, England lost the Third Test against West Indies, sponsored by Cornhill, and the series with it. . . . Congratulations to [the West Indies] on their victory. They have done with high skill and the

200   Stephen Wagg

dash that comes so instinctively to them what they came here for. England would benefit, I believe, from a more animated attitude from [captain David] Gower. When his own shoulders sag, so do the side's.

> (John Woodcock, *The Times*, 17 July 1984, p. 25)

As England slumped to a fourth humiliating Test defeat, Peter May [chairman of England's selectors] was posing the most critical question of the summer. . . . *Do we try hard enough?*

> (Ken Lawrence, *Daily Express*, 1 August 1984, p. 36)

Here England's cricketers and their failures become a metaphor for a nation in (widely unacknowledged) decline. This metaphor has an enhanced resonance because of cricket's historic designation as the imperial game, gifted to its colonies by Britain at the height of its power in the nineteenth century (Stoddart and Sandiford 1998) and because the public culture of Britain during this period has been characterised by a hubristic nationalism. This expressed itself, among other things, through the prosecution of the Falklands War by the prime minister, Margaret Thatcher, and her subsequent claim, in a landmark speech at Cheltenham racecourse in 1982, that the war had banished fears 'that Britain was no longer the nation that had built an Empire and ruled a quarter of the world' (Barnett 1982: 47). The manifest failure of English cricket to maintain the 'Great' in Great Britain when taking on the West Indies occasionally prompted the evocation of earlier, more palatable defeats, sustained with dignity within the imperial family. In June 1984, John Collis of *The Times* seeks out Sonny Ramadhin, now landlord of a pub in the Manchester area, where he has lived since his triumphs of 1950. These triumphs, along with those of his fellow spinner Alf Valentine, are 'surprising to recall', remarks Collis, '[a]fter a decade of wall-to-wall fast bowling.' Ramadhin will only partially concur: 'It's all fast bowling now. But it's not *genuinely* fast. Even Marshall – he's not as fast as Wes Hall or Roy Gilchrist' (*The Times*, 29 June 1984, p. 24).

In conclusion: calypso kings to dark destroyers; smiling settlers to enemies within

Reading through these sports pages of the British press, one is, from time to time, struck by the juxtaposition of references, implied or otherwise, to British people of Caribbean origin and the (often critical) coverage of events in the cricket world. In the spring of 1981, for example, Pat Gibson in the *Daily Express* wrote of how the 'tall, graceful Jamaican' Michael Holding 'sprang straight for England's jugular . . . striking [England batsman Geoffrey] Boycott a glancing blow on the helmet' (18 February, p. 36), while two weeks later the same newspaper, on its front page, carried a story headlined 'Police injured in clash with demo blacks RAMPAGE OF A MOB'. The article refers to a demonstration by West Indian people in London following the death of a number of young Caribbean people in a fire in New Cross, south London, back in January. It refers indignantly to

England–West Indies and the English press 201

'an organisation calling itself "The Campaign against Racism in the Media"'. The symbolism here would not have been lost on many black observers, in either London or the Caribbean: while the Thatcher government's Nationality Act is passed and Britain's inner cities burn, the fast bowler known in the game as 'Whispering Death' who, like many Jamaicans, probably has relatives or friends settled in the United Kingdom, rattles the helmet of the avowed Thatcherite Geoffrey Boycott (Wagg 2003–4). Two weeks after *The Times* refers to the 'insulting demand' of the Guyanese government that an England player leave their country, the same paper reports that the EEC Commission is examining the UK government's Nationality Bill to see if it contravenes the European Convention of Human Rights (*The Times*, 14 March 1981, p. 13). For England's sports journalists, the politics of 'race' and the transaction of cricket matches take place in separate, if parallel, social worlds. Only occasionally, and perhaps unwittingly, do they suggest a connection. For instance, John Woodcock is clearly attempting to be ironic when he writes from the Caribbean in 1981 that 'newsmen from England "here for the bullets" must be surprised to find that the only provocative material in the local press takes the form of letters from Birmingham and London' (*The Times*, 9 April 1981, p. 10). Four days later, Woodcock reports that

> The only effective protest against Jackman's presence in Jamaica has been made so far by Holding when yesterday morning he was finishing off England's first innings. . . . After greeting Jackman with a bouncer, he hit him two stinging blows on the left hand.
>
> (*The Times*, 13 April, p. 10)

Many a true word, as the saying goes, has been spoken in jest. On the front page of the same issue, the Home Secretary, William Whitelaw, announces an inquiry into the riots in Brixton.

Thus, over a 35-year period in England, press and public discourses about the cricketers of the Caribbean and the people who cheered them were subject to a good deal of change and nuance. There was no absolute change from one definition of Caribbean cricket folk to another; nor can it be said that the objective behaviour of West Indian cricketers or their public did not itself change during that time. But whereas in the 1950s and early 1960s these people were often said to spread joy and win respect wherever they went, in the 1980s they frequently became people who played to win, dropped beer cans and demanded that political agreements (such as the ban on sport link with South Africa) be honoured. The reasons for these shifts in vocabulary seemed to lie in the changing political relationship between the British state and its former territories in the Caribbean. New political and sport circumstances provoked different recourse to particular rhetorics – although these rhetorics (of calypso king, dark destroyer, and so on) were not themselves new. All this accords quite closely with the notion presented by Peter Hulme of 'stereotypical dualism' (1986: 49–50; see also Hall 1992), whereby numerous characteristics are collapsed into one simplified figure

202 Stephen Wagg

that stands for a whole people, and this stereotype is then split into 'good' and 'bad' sides – carefree revellers, for example, as against mean-spirited bowlers of bouncers or parties to political riot. These 'good' and 'bad' sides are then deployed as is thought appropriate.

Note

1 The Clive Lloyd quotation that prefaces this chapter appeared in *The Times* on 1 August 1984 on page 21.
I should like to thank Kathryn Dodd, Jon Gemmell, James Hamill and Dil Porter for help in the preparation of the chapter.

References

Bailey, Trevor (1986) *Wickets, Catches and the Odd Run*, London: Willow Books.
Barnett, Anthony (1982) 'Iron Britannia', *New Left Review* (Special Number) no. 134 (July–August).
Beckles, Hilary McD. (1998) *The Development of West Indies Cricket*, volume 2, *The Age of Globalization*, Kingston, Jamaica: University of the West Indies Press; London: Pluto Press.
Callaghan, John (1993) 'In search of Eldorado: Labour's colonial economic policy', in Jim Fryth (ed.) *Labour's High Noon: The Government and the Economy 1945–51*, London: Lawrence & Wishart.
Carr, Matthew (1999) *My Father's House*, London: Penguin.
Fieldhouse, D. K. (1984) 'The Labour governments and the Empire–Commonwealth, 1945–51', in Ritchie Ovendale (ed.) *The Foreign Policy of British Labour Governments*, Leicester: Leicester University Press.
Foot, Paul (1969) *The Rise of Enoch Powell*, Harmondsworth, UK: Penguin.
Fryer, Peter (1984) *Staying Power: The History of Black People in Britain*, London: Pluto Press.
Gemmell, Jon (2004) *The Politics of South African Cricket*, London: Routledge.
Hall, Stuart (1992) 'The West and the rest: discourse and power', in Stuart Hall and Bram Gieben (eds) *Formations of Modernity*, Cambridge: Polity Press, in association with the Open University.
Hulme, Peter (1986) *Colonial Encounters: Europe and the Native Caribbean 1492–1797*, London: Methuen.
Keith, Michael (1993) *Race, Riots and Policing: Lore and Disorder in a Multi-racist Society*, London: UCL Press.
Layton-Henry, Zig (1992) *The Politics of Immigration*, Oxford: Blackwell.
Manley, Michael (1988) *A History of West Indies Cricket*, London: André Deutsch.
Phillips, Mike and Trevor Phillips (1998) *Windrush: The Irresistible Rise of Multi-racial Britain*, London: HarperCollins.
Saville, John (1993) *The Politics of Continuity: British Foreign Policy and the Labour Government, 1945–51*, London: Verso.
Sivanandan, A. (1982) *A Different Hunger: Writings on Black Resistance*, London: Pluto Press.
Stoddart, Brian and Keith A. P. Sandiford (eds) (1998) *The Imperial Game: Cricket, Culture and Society*, Manchester: Manchester University Press.

Trueman, Fred (1976) *Ball of Fire: An Autobiography*, London: Dent.
Wagg, Stephen (2003–4) 'Muck or nettles: men, masculinity and myth in Yorkshire cricket', *Sport in History*, 23 (3): 68–93.
Williams, Jack (2001) *Cricket and Race*, Oxford: Berg.

10 'A carnival of cricket?'
The Cricket World Cup, 'race' and the politics of carnival

Tim Crabbe and Stephen Wagg

Every four years, the cricketing world takes a step back from its globetrotting agenda and settles in one centre for the game's ultimate carnival – The ICC Cricket World Cup. In 1999, England will host the party. For just six weeks in May and June 1999, cricket's greatest roadshow will travel through England, Wales, Scotland, Ireland and Holland and become, in the words of Prime Minister Tony Blair, a focus for 'national pride, international co-operation, happiness, heartache, excitement and triumph'. The theme for the 1999 Cricket World Cup will reflect the excitement and vibrancy of the one-day game and the colourful 'new faces' of cricket – international, cosmopolitan and, above all, fun. The 1999 Cricket World Cup will, indeed, be 'A Carnival of Cricket' – with this application form you too can join the Carnival.

(England and Wales Cricket Board 1997)

Who should they cheer for now? Marketing English cricket after 'Tebbit'

This adoption of carnival imagery by the England and Wales Cricket Board (ECB) to market the World Cup of 1999 was savagely ironic. International cricket had grown out of the British Empire (Holt 1989; Searle 1990; Marqusee 1994; Beckles and Stoddart 1995), where it had been, among other things, a site of struggle on which colonial peoples, especially in India and the Caribbean, sought to beat the British at 'their own' game (James 1994; Bose 1986, 1990; Cashman, 1980). After the Second World War, various Test-playing colonies successively accomplished this aim and did so with their own styles of cricket. None was more spectacular in this regard than the West Indies, where cricket culture was most obviously touched by elements of carnival.

Little (see Stephen Wagg's chapter in this book, Chapter 9) was made by the British press of England's first defeat by the West Indies (at Lords in 1950), but since the 1960s English cricket has been widely perceived to be in crisis and increasingly characterised by malign and gloomy introspection. English cricket officials and commentators were wont by the 1980s to view the ex-colonial teams with suspicion and hostility: the 'real quick' fast bowlers of the West Indies were seen as 'intimidators' (see McLennan and Savidge 1996), their Pakistani

The Cricket World Cup, 'race' and carnival   205

counterparts as ball-tampering 'cheats' (Oslear and Bannister 1996), and so on. Most importantly, in this context, an inward-looking nationalism entered English cricket discourse, bringing with it a preoccupation with 'the enemy within'.

Within cricket there were mutterings about 'too many overseas players' in the county championship (McLennan 1994), while in 1995 the prestigious *Wisden Cricket Monthly* gave an obscure malcontent called Robert Henderson a platform from which to argue that the England team was failing because too many of its members were born abroad (Henderson 1995). Beyond the game itself, in 1990 the Conservative politician Norman Tebbit invoked an image of black cricket lovers from all over south London flocking to the Kennington Oval to see the West Indies play England. 'Which side', he had asked in sinister fashion, 'do they cheer for?' (Marqusee 1994: 137). (For a full account of this affair, see Marqusee 1998.) Furthermore, throughout this period the banners, drums and improvised percussion beloved of many West Indian cricket fans were banned from English test grounds.

Yet it was precisely these cultural symbols that the ECB sought to mobilise in the context of the Cricket World Cup of 1999. The headline on the tournament's ticket application form was 'A carnival of cricket?' accompanied by a caricatured image of an African-Caribbean man with brightly coloured shirt and beaming smile. The use of the language of carnival in this context is concerned with promoting and utilising the notion of ethnic diversity. In short, carnival is invoked as a 'non-British' cultural signifier in a call to Britain's ethnic minority communities to become involved in the spectacle and ultimately to buy tickets for matches. While young white people were included in the publicity materials, it was unambiguously black people, and particularly black men, who appeared most prominently in publicity material. At the media launch, steel bands and calypso music were provided, to add weight to the message, although, pointedly, there were no pictures of Asian-English cricket fans: for advertising purposes, only Caribbean people can signify carnival and carry its connotations of spontaneous amity and social integration (Cohen 1993: 129).

In many ways the reliance on the terminology of carnival as a metaphor for racial diversity missed the point, since in the main, we suggest, it was the British Asian community, rather than the steel bands and the sound systems associated with Caribbean carnival, that was central to the tournament's success. While seeking to be inclusive in its appeal, the tournament publicity utilised a largely discredited and narrowly defined appeal to multiculturalism (see Gilroy 1987, Solomos 1998) which was completely divorced from cricket and even from the cultural forms associated with those communities most animated by the game. The strategy was also dependent upon a refusal to recognise the varying meanings that the game has in terms of identity formation, so that the 'new faces of cricket' were dissolved into the amorphous notion of carnival through which the tournament was defined.

Whose carnival?: The 1999 Cricket World Cup

Carnival capers: two faces of English cricket

The billing of the 1999 Cricket World Cup as 'a carnival of cricket' was backed by the promise that:

> In an effort to extend the carnival beyond the field of play, the organisers will encourage communities to become involved in activities around the Tournament, through culture, music, food and other events for the whole family – particularly for the young.
>
> (England and Wales Cricket Board 1999)

In reality, there was not much evidence to support this claim. Indeed, rather than encouraging any transgressive or liberating carnivalesque features, the conditions of entry supplied with match tickets established an air of prohibition, stating that:

> The following items are prohibited and may not be taken into any 1999 Cricket World Cup Match:

- Knives and other offensive weapons
- Fireworks and smoke or gas canisters
- Flares
- Sticks and poles (including flagpoles)
- Klaxons, megaphones and compressed air or gas-operated horns
- Face masks
- Banners
- Fancy dress, or oversize headwear, of a nature which has the potential to cause injury to its wearer or other spectators, or which could severely restrict the view of, or be construed as 'offensive' to, other spectators
- Bands, other than those with prior agreement in writing from the organisers
- Any dangerous article or substance not referred to above.

The instructions go on to note that 'National flags (without flagpoles) will be permitted, however, their use must not restrict the view of other spectators. Continued use of musical instruments, which causes annoyance to other spectators, will result in them being confiscated.' Furthermore, a total ban on the importation of alcohol was applied at all but seven of the host venues.

Contrary to convention, then, this carnival was apparently to take place without any of the 'abandonment to hedonistic excesses, and the psycho-social jouissance of eating, drinking, singing, joking, swearing, wearing of stylised attire and costumes' typically associated with sporting notions of the term (Giulianotti 1995: 194). The organisers' one concession to their own marketing seems to have been to book a handful of bands, which, it was hoped, might have the necessary multicultural feel. These included a Caribbean steel pan band and an (all-white)

The Cricket World Cup, 'race' and carnival   207

jazz quartet, the Bob Bates All Stars. Furthermore, the food on sale in the stadium concourses seemed only to re-emphasise the unitary ethnic symbolism of English cricket. Spit-roasted pork conjured up images of white, rural, 'merrie' England in Canterbury, while the fish and chip stall at Headingley in Leeds fried its fare under a banner declaring 'Cooked in the Old Fashioned Way'. Even the *Sun* newspaper, usually the standard-bearer for an unreflecting, white Englishness, felt obliged to complain, declaring in the aftermath of India's clash with Pakistan at Old Trafford in Manchester, 'Much of the Asian population of North England descended on Manchester, but the food was strictly Western. Burgers and bacon butties aplenty, but not a bhaji or bhuna to be bought' (*Sun*, 9 June 1999).

The attitude of the cricket establishment in many ways seemed to be fairly hostile towards both spectator behaviour and the tournament in general. At several matches, and particularly those staged at Lord's, there was a noticeable absence of 'members' in the pavilion and those who did attend were visibly reluctant to become involved in the more expressive forms of spectator interaction. At Headingley during the match between Pakistan and Australia a middle-aged white steward, dressed in blazer and tie, passing some celebrating Pakistan supporters, called out, 'Gents, can you put your flags down. People are watching behind', adding, 'You can wave them if there's a wicket.' The fact that the supporters behind were as animated as those waving the flags and that Pakistan were *batting* seemed to be lost.

The tension between the World Cup's public face and the attitude of its more traditional guardians was most dramatically illustrated by an announcement made at Trent Bridge, when India played New Zealand, midway through the Indian innings, presumably to the Indian supporters celebrating their side's impressive performance. The PA announcer declared that 'There have been many complaints about the excessive noise at the bottom of the Radcliffe Road stand. You are spoiling the enjoyment of the cricket.' This one-dimensional interpretation of cricketing pleasures was followed a little later by a further declaration:

> This announcement applies particularly to those at the bottom of the Radcliffe Road stand. By not sitting in your seats you are contravening the safety regulations and obscuring the view of the people behind. Unless you comply with the regulations you will be removed from the ground and you will not see any further play.

While cricket's traditional match goers may have felt some alienation from these minor cultural insurgencies, the reality is that little appeared to have been done by the tournament organisers to transform one-day cricket into a truly multicultural, mass-market game. From the organisers' and sponsors' perspective the tournament was primarily a marketing opportunity and one that was clearly marked out on racial lines. As Tim Lamb, chief executive of the ECB, put it after England's departure, 'The World Cup is very exciting, very colourful, and it has done a great deal to promote the game among ethnic communities' (*Guardian*, 31 May 1999, p. 1).

208   *Tim Crabbe and Stephen Wagg*

Reading the carnival: the media, the Cricket World Cup and sporting stereotypes

Despite the apparent contradictions, the television and print media readily adopted the concept of carnival as their framework for discussion of the tournament, recognising the populist value that the slogan offered. Ultimately, however, full-hearted use of carnival terminology was mitigated, largely by frustration at the failure of the cricket establishment to embrace their own promotional rhetoric. From the cynical tone of the *Independent on Sunday*'s weekly 'Carnival' anecdotes to B. C. Pires' polemical 'Who forgot the razzmatazz?' in the *Guardian* (3 June 1999, p. 32), there was a steady stream of writing that derided the less than carnivalesque attitude of the tournament organisers and of the country's 'white' cricket followers. Reporting on the England versus Kenya match at Canterbury, Paul Weaver reported in the *Guardian*:

> If they transported the Rio Carnival to this city it would perish before the starchy stare of English middle-classness and yesterday felt as flat as a Jim Davidson joke; the whole place had the put-out, self-conscious expression [that the actor] Derek Nimmo might have worn if he had been invited to an acid house party.
>
> (*Guardian*, 19 May 1999, p. 28)

This did not prevent the use of carnival imagery in the reporting of the cricket itself, though. While the *Independent on Sunday* alliterated with a 'banquet of batting, bazaar of bowling and fiesta of fielding' (13 June 1999), the *Express* lamented Bangladesh's early defeat with 'Carnival capers can't lift new boys' (18 May 1999). Nor was there any failure to recognise the potential that Britain provided for precisely the kind of carnival that had been promoted, as an ironic consequence of the game's colonial roots:

> The logic of England's old position at the centre of the cricketing world has re-asserted itself. Sure there are bigger grounds elsewhere. But nowhere else can draw in so many supporters from all the competing countries. It is hard to believe that anywhere else could stand back, as places like Hove, Bristol, Worcester and Chelmsford have done, and act as a benignly neutral setting for all cricket's different cultures.
>
> (*Guardian*, 19 May 1999, p. 28)

Yet it is in precisely such contexts, where the language of carnival is invoked as a metaphor for racial diversity, that the media can themselves unwittingly help to generate racial, national and cultural stereotypes in the mould of Gilroy's notion of ethnic absolutism (1987, 1993). In terms of both the reporting of spectator behaviour and the adoption of national sporting archetypes, the tournament produced a catalogue of stereotypical media images.

Reporting on the India versus Pakistan match at Old Trafford, the *Sun* invoked and mocked notions of Eastern mysticism with the headline 'Indian rope trick'

The Cricket World Cup, 'race' and carnival 209

alongside a picture of an Indian player tripping over the boundary rope (9 June 1999). Equally, the *Observer*, reporting on the first World Cup match to be played in Dublin, portrayed the classic stereotype of the lazy, drunken Irishman, declaring that 'The Irish have the right temperament for cricket. They have few peers when it comes to whiling away a day, or however long it takes, with drink and conversation' (*Observer*, 23 May 1999, p. 13). Even B. C. Pires' assertion that 'The next most important requirement [after sunshine] for a true carnival is black people' (*Guardian*, 3 June 1999, p. 32) does little to move beyond the racialised motif of the uniquely undisciplined, non-intellectual, sexually promiscuous black male.

Perhaps more benign, though, was the construction of a typology of contemporary national sporting characteristics. The gloomy introspection of English cricket, articulated in comments such as 'When the going gets tough, England, it seems, barely turn the engine over' (*Guardian* Sport, 31 May 1999, p. 1), sits alongside the representation of isolated, historically grounded, 'positive' archetypes such as Darren Gough. A cheery, affable, passionate and gifted Yorkshireman, in many ways Gough represents the personification of an uncompromising, white, Northern working-class 'British bulldog' ethnicity.

The concern with this kind of perspective is that it creates a sympathy for pseudo-biological rationales that all too readily fall into line with deeper-lying racial stereotypes. As Dr Zafar Altaf, manager of the Pakistan side, put it,

> Our cricket is more indigenous. By that I mean it is more about the pleasure of hitting the ball with the bat and knocking the stumps out of the ground than being coached in the appropriate and proper way. It is a devil-may-care approach rather than a cautious approach and it is what gives our cricket so much variety.
>
> (*The Times*, 19 June 1999, p. 41)

Even in this self-analysis there is an implied sense of the inconsistency and lack of temperament often applied both to Asian participation in sport (Bains and Patel 1996) and to sport in the developing world more generally (O'Donnell 1994). This notion was even more starkly illustrated in the media reporting of Pakistan's performance in the World Cup final, which was contrasted with the solid sporting temperament of the Australians:

> Those in the know were always worried that Pakistan would be either brilliant or brittle. In the event, and sadly, they were very much the latter. Shot to pieces. Australia were just Australia. They mixed and muddled through the early rounds but in the past week, when everything mattered in sudden-death bold relief, they were simply terrific.
>
> (*Guardian* Sport, 21 June 1999, p. 3)

While there is no disputing the quality of performance by the Australians, within this framework of reporting there is a readiness to apply characteristics uniformly

210   Tim Crabbe and Stephen Wagg

on the basis of nationality which can all too easily be read along racial lines. After all, international cricket originally grew out of the modernist, 'rationalised' sports project associated with the British Empire of the nineteenth century (see Holt 1989; Birley 1993: 328–9). In the racialised culture of this empire, white settlers ruled indigenous 'coloured' populations, and part of the pretext for this political arrangement was the supposedly greater rationality of white people, as against the sensuality, lack of emotional restraint or intelligence of the 'native'. In what Gilroy terms 'the historic folk grammar of British racism', 'animal blacks enjoy an excess of brute physicality and wily oriental gentlemen conversely display a surfeit of cerebral power, while only the authentic Anglo-Brit is able to luxuriate in the perfect equilibrium of body and mind' (1993: 89).

Within these terms, what is important is not so much the fulfilment of the respective roles but the Anglocentric designation of desirable 'sporting' characteristics and their mapping out within a framework defined on the lines of race and nation. Interestingly, O'Donnell (1994) has suggested that in an era of globalised sporting and industrial developments, such typologies reinforce and exalt the images of Western rationality and technological superiority that sustain the domination of world economic and political relations by 'white' Western nations and corporations. What is denied within this outlook is what Morgan has described as 'the unmistakable presence of Western values and meanings in international sports and the equally unmistakable ability of indigenous cultures to cull different values and meanings from those same sports' (1998: 193).

> It is this 'textual' plasticity, and not so much the oft noted celebrated ability of formerly colonised nations to beat their masters at their own games, that gives subaltern cultures the opportunity to mould Western-minted sports in their own images, to load them with their own meanings and values, to stamp them with their own identities.
>
> (ibid.: 193)

Having a carnival: spectators, identity and regulated behaviour

'Inzamam ate my paratha': re-defining the cricket crowd

In keeping with the perspective of the ECB, Giulianotti suggests that the modern carnival is dominated by the perceived need to organise and the identification of particular spaces in which fans can perform, but he also notes that 'the carnivalesque always threatens to transgress the authorised boundaries granted to it' (1995: 194).

In line with this interpretation, the pre-eminent feature of spectator behaviour at the 1999 Cricket World Cup was the distinction between the performative styles of those supporters following South Asian teams and those who were not. The games involving Pakistan, India, Bangladesh and Sri Lanka were invariably played out before capacity crowds, which were dominated, with the exception of the final, by their own followers.

The Cricket World Cup, 'race' and carnival 211

We conducted participant observation at matches involving two of these sides,[1] including Bangladesh versus New Zealand at Chelmsford in Essex and Pakistan versus Australia at Headingley in Leeds. For each of the sets of supporters following these two countries the games represented an important cultural space in which to celebrate both a love of cricket and distinctive elements of their ethnic identities.

In contrast to the quintessentially stoic image of English cricket, Pakistani fans approaching Leeds on the day of the Pakistan versus Australia game were adorned in replica shirts and the green of Pakistan and Islam, flags streamed from car windows and, as the Headingley ground appeared, the noise was audible from several streets away. Hooters were sounding and drums banging in the midst of frequent loud chanting.

Pakistan's support had been drawn from all sections of the community. Geographically we came across supporters who had made their way from Glasgow, Newcastle, Manchester, London and Birmingham, in addition to those from the Yorkshire area and Pakistan itself. While they were predominantly male, there were families present, including mothers and daughters, and the age profile extended from young children through to senior citizens. Socially, there was just as much diversity. We met manual labourers, storekeepers, university students, housewives, professionals and entrepreneurs. Most striking, though, was the fact that although sections of the crowd, which was overwhelmingly (possibly by as much as 3:1) supporting Pakistan, had a younger profile, the performative, celebratory style of the fans was relatively uniform across generations and social backgrounds.

Seated at the Cardigan Road end of the Northern Enclosure before the start of play, a group of young Pakistani supporters began to shout at a well-built grey-haired old man with a full white beard dressed all in green with the Pakistan national emblem on his breast. He turned, while standing, raised his arms full into the air and, at the top of his voice, cried out a long nationalist chant in Urdu, to which the whole crowd within earshot replied '*Pakistan zindabad*' ('Pakistan forever'). As he was answered, he would chant again and receive another communal reply, and repeat this process before ending with his arms in the air, prompting cheers and excited laughter all around.

This was a highly dramatic affair and it was to be repeated many times during the Pakistani innings. Pakistani supporters seemed to hold this man in some regard, shaking his hand and urging him to sit with them. A storeman from Bradford sitting beside us said that the man, who became something of a celebrity during the tournament, is known as 'Abdul' and attended every match that Pakistan played. He has a revered status among the Pakistan supporters, regardless of their age or background, partly as a consequence of the complete lack of reserve in his expression of Islamic and nationalistic sentiment. His self-assurance and cultural confidence in this arena were total and he was almost oblivious to the presence of anyone attempting to make their way past him or anyone who was not part of this celebration.

While celebratory, passionate and humorous, the Pakistan support was also

212 Tim Crabbe and Stephen Wagg

partisan and conscious of the significance of national identities. Individual, particularly younger, supporters were quite willing to be overtly offensive towards Australian players, fans crying 'Shane Warne's a fat bastard', 'Aussies you're going XXXX out of the tournament' and booing Australian fans parading their national flags. Invoking the continuing hostilities between India and Pakistan, heightened by the two countries' recently proclaimed nuclear capacity, Pakistani banners also declared 'Danger – demolition in progress' and also, more pointedly, 'Pakistan's nuclear weapons – Wasim & Showaib – Tested in England'.[2]

These forms of behaviour were largely taken in good humour, illustrated by the ironic intervention of a middle-aged Australian who, after sitting through a prolonged period of impassioned nationalistic chanting, began singing, in solo, 'Onward Christian Soldiers'. In this way the significance of the reaffirmation of Islamic identities was to some extent emptied of its meaning beyond the Pakistani fan collective. The self-effacing recognition of the lack of any meaningful collective Australian (or, by extension, Anglo-Saxon) equivalent inevitably handed the definition of the day's dominant cultural norms to the followers of Pakistan.

The Pakistani fans' cultural domination of the event became more and more apparent as the day progressed, with supporters parading banners along the footpath around the ground to ecstatic cheers around the stadium. Similarly, at the Bangladesh versus New Zealand game we observed a column of Bangladeshi supporters with flags, scarves and bongo drums careering around the ground chanting 'Bangladesh! Bangladesh!' in clear contravention of the 'conditions of entry'. Furthermore, in Leeds at least, such behaviour emerged as the cultural norm to be adopted, with growing animation (largely alcohol induced) on the part of Australians, who in turn began to parade their own banners and flags, as if to join the Pakistani party. As Australian wickets began to fall in the afternoon, the Pakistan supporters celebrated more and more wildly. Hundreds of fans would jump down into the communal walkways to cheer, run around, hug one another, wave flags, chant, blow hooters and join human conga chains. As Thompson has suggested, in such contexts the 'tension between the anticipation of a pleasurable experience and the possibility of the experience being painful lends a peculiar intensity to the consumption of pleasure' (1983: 128). Where identification with the Pakistani team had been so complete and desire for victory so great, this intensity was overwhelming. It was an even more intense version of the spectacle witnessed during Eid celebrations in Rusholme, Manchester, when young Muslims drive their cars while sounding horns and waving flags (see Werbner 1996: 107).

For these supporters, this was a day when they could truly enjoy a sporting event in an atmosphere not stifled by the restrictive normative codes of English cricket or the white, working-class masculinity that can dominate expressive supporter culture in English football grounds (see Back et al. 2001). Furthermore, this was a cultural space in which they could express their loyalty to Pakistan and Islam without deferring to the controlled, rule-bound formulations of Islamic high culture. As Werbner has argued, 'it is in the field of sport, through support of the national team, that young British Pakistanis express their love of both cricket and

The Cricket World Cup, 'race' and carnival   213

the home country, along with their sense of alienation and disaffection from British society' (1996: 101). However, for many supporters the celebration of support for Pakistan and other South Asian teams appeared to be as much to do with the restrictive and repressed nature of English cricket, both on and off the pitch, as a rejection of England and the English *per se*.

After the crowd had loudly celebrated a boundary by Saeed Anwar, those young supporters who had earlier been waving to 'Abdul' had a mocking conversation about the marketing of the World Cup. One of them looked up at an advertising hoarding and declared 'Carnival of cricket – ha, if it was England it would be "Jolly good shot, well played."' His friends laughed, two of them chipping in with 'Anyone for strawberries?' and 'I say, what a good delivery' in simulated 'posh' accents. While exaggerated, these readings of 'Englishness' were being rejected by young British Pakistanis who, at the same time, were embracing other, less racially coded elements of English culture, including an ironic humour, regional accents, references to domestic football and Western attire.

Despite the remark from Bob, a middle-aged white man from just outside Bradford with a heavy West Yorkshire accent, 'It's what it's all about this – cricket at Headingley', expressed without a hint of irony, it was clear that this was certainly not what cricket at Headingley had been about in the past, and it is doubtful that the ECB saw this as part of its vision of cricket's future. The cultural forms in this shrine to traditional Yorkshire values were being completely transformed within a carnivalesque context that made no concessions towards English cricketing norms.

It was in contrast to the emphasis placed on the social function of carnival and festivity by writers such as Durkheim and Van Gennep (see Bristol 1985) that Bakhtin (1973) focused on the role of the carnivalesque in similar processes of 'transgression'. Gardiner makes the point that Bakhtin's 'interest in Carnival indicates a definite (if largely unarticulated) politics of culture that expressed the desire to understand and encourage the "popular deconstruction" of official discourse and ideologies' (1991: 38). In Gardiner's interpretation, for Bakhtin,

> popular festivals and rituals carved out a 'second life' for the people within the womb of mainstream society, a world where the normal rules of social conduct were (at least temporarily) suspended and life was 'shaped according to a certain pattern of play.
>
> (1991: 33)

Nevertheless, the carnivalesque practices described here did not preclude the embracing of broader non-establishment notions of Englishness as illustrated by the fans chanting of 'Aussies going home' to the tune of the rather Anglocentric Euro 96 English football anthem 'Football's Coming Home'. Indeed, for some supporters, and more particularly supporters of Bangladesh, there was even surprise at the degree of interest in the cricket. As one British-born Bangladeshi, who lived in Bedford and supported Liverpool, remarked, 'I'm surprised at the Bangladeshi turnout. We're mostly into football.' Indeed, Morgan has argued that

214 *Tim Crabbe and Stephen Wagg*

what makes [international sport] a curious cultural language is that it is difficult to categorize, at least by our conventional (Western and Eastern) cultural standards. For it is too steeped in those disparate cultural traditions to be passed off as a kind of Esperanto and yet too diffusely constituted from them to be sloughed off as a sectarian cultural expression.

(1998: 187)

Carnival? What carnival?: Cultural boundaries and the capacity for carnival

In contrast to the vibrancy experienced elsewhere, at the Australia versus the West Indies match at Old Trafford the abiding image was one of general disenchantment, frustration and even boredom. This was fuelled by a number of factors, including the complete failure of the cricket to live up to expectations, with the West Indies all out for 110 and the Australians manipulating their own run rate.[3] It was tedious stuff and soon led even committed supporters of the competing teams to become distracted. The West Indian supporters in particular bore few of the carnivalesque features that had typified their engagement with the game in the 1970s and that had re-emerged in other forms among British-based followers of Jamaica during the 1998 football World Cup (see Back *et al.* 1998).

The tournament did not enthuse Britain's African-Caribbean community in anything like the same manner that it did with South Asian cricket followers. The majority of spectators at this game were white England fans, and it is easy to see how the cultural identifications being made in this context would not necessarily be attractive to the local black community, despite their general support for the West Indies.

Historically, cricket played a defining role in the construction of Caribbean identities (James 1994; Beckles and Stoddart 1995). However, West Indian cricket has been in decline for some time, particularly among younger generations of supporters, who are increasingly drawn by the rival attractions of English football and American basketball (Beckles 1998). Furthermore, while beating England, or even Australia, may once have had some cultural significance for descendants of oppressed colonial people, that relationship now has less meaning, particularly in a context where the England team has fallen outside cricket's elite. Equally, while the flamboyant performances of Pakistan and, to a lesser extent, India continue to inspire and generate a passion for the game, the West Indies are nothing like the dominant force in world cricket that they were for much of the 1970s and 1980s. The notion of 'a carnival of cricket' might also have been particularly galling to cricket followers who had witnessed the systematic efforts of the English cricket establishment to destroy the carnivalesque features of West Indian support during those earlier periods of sporting success.

The behaviour of England's 'Barmy Army' (see Williams 1998), who indulge in the wearing of floppy hats, cross-dressing and coordinated fancy dress, rejecting the reserve and tradition associated with English cricket, has not overcome those suspicions. Such styles are still far removed from the self-regulated dance hall

The Cricket World Cup, 'race' and carnival   215

culture and characteristics of carnival witnessed among revellers in Notting Hill and Port of Spain. Their relationship with certain features drawn from normative English football fan cultures can create its own ethnically marked exclusive feel which remains unattractive to the 'reggae boyz and gyals' who travelled to France for the football World Cup (see Back *et al.* 1998).

In this respect it is worth noting that 5,000 black fans had braved the rain and cold in Cardiff to watch a nil–nil draw between the Jamaican national football team and Wales in March the previous year, and

> the reason they were [there] in these terrible conditions was that they felt this to be *their* team and *their* game. As the mass of black fans looked out onto Ninian Park and the Jamaican team, on this cold wet night they saw themselves.
>
> (Back *et al.* 1998: 24)

The cultural insularity and contingent racial inclusions that characterise British spectator sports are what discourage a greater commitment by black fans to cricket in England and the establishment of an emotional bond between them and the English game.

What is interesting, however, is that for South Asian cricket fans, even those Bangladesh supporters who profess to follow football more closely than cricket, the Cricket World Cup seems to provide precisely the cultural space that France 98 provided for supporters of the Jamaican football team. Werbner has argued that

> Just as male elders create the cultural genres and social spaces where Pakistani nationalism is celebrated officially or religious worship is conducted in the utmost seriousness, so too young men and women create the cultural agendas and social spaces for fun and amusement, for consumption and imaginative artistic expression, which also celebrate nationalism and religiosity, but through unofficial genres of parody or sport.
>
> (1996: 105)

This process might extend beyond Pakistan, one supporter commenting during the Bangladesh versus New Zealand match that 'this is the first time we have been able to wave our flag in this country. This is a matter of identity and pride and we're trying to make the players feel at home' (*Express*, 18 May 1999, p. 64).

'And Abdul's made it': the contingent inclusion of racialised others

Thompson suggests that 'carnival challenges the authority of "social laws". It is a rebellious event in which prohibitions and their transgression co-exist and so specify an ambiguous representation' (1983: 133). The ambiguity of this relationship could not have been clearer than when the organisers of the Cricket World Cup simultaneously gave licence to the carnival while establishing the prohibitions that would govern it. Guilianotti has suggested that it is in precisely

216 Tim Crabbe and Stephen Wagg

such circumstances, where the authorities attempt to organise and gain control of the festivities, that the very essence of carnival is neutralised (1991: 520), since there can then be no prospect of an 'inversion of the rules that discipline everyday life' (Fiske 1989: 139).

In the event, the tournament 'conditions of entry' were routinely ignored, although a form of 'moral panic' did blow up in relation to a series of peaceful, if exuberant, pitch invasions, predominantly by Asian spectators, at the end of a number of games. The reporting of the Cricket World Cup was largely sympathetic to the role played by Britain's ethnic minority communities, but these concerns were in some senses emblematic of a deeper insecurity on the part of the cricket authorities about the direction in which cricket is moving and the kinds of supporter behaviour that are emerging.

In the build-up to Pakistan's showdown match with India at Old Trafford, the *Sun* published images of an Indian cricket crowd on the run from police above the headline 'Indian chaseaway . . . baton wielding riot police charge in Calcutta as defeat gets fans upset' (8 June 1999, pp. 38–9). The paper went on to report that 'the game at Old Trafford will be backed by the biggest security operation ever at a cricket match in England'. Even more sensationally, the *Guardian* reported that 'War is often used as a metaphor for sport but rarely can it have been as accurate as for today's World Cup Super Six match between India and Pakistan' (8 June 1999, p. 28).

In the event, the game passed off without incident, but behind the predictable hype, given the domestic tension between the two nations, lay a deeper insecurity on the part of the cricket establishment. Jim White reported from the game that

> Old Trafford was a wonderful sight. The crowd loud, colourful, ceaselessly good natured, a timely reminder to those who would seek to orchestrate things by playing Queen hits at maximum volume that the best atmosphere is always self regulated. . . . Everywhere the ground was packed. Everywhere, that is except on the upper tier of the pavilion, where Lancashire members of what might be termed the *Telegraph* letter-writing tendency stayed away.
>
> (*Guardian* Sport, 12 June 1999, p. 5)

However, it was not just hidden faces within the cricket establishment that silently expressed concern about these cultural shifts. There were also lines of discontinuity within the broader cricket-supporting public. During the match between Pakistan and Australia at Headingley, at one point we were sitting beside two white supporters, Steve and Paul from South Yorkshire. Steve had just been in a dispute with a Pakistan supporter. He commented with incredulity, 'I can't believe it. I've never bin digged [punched] by a Paki before, some poor cunt's gonna cop for that, someone'll get it by end't day. I'll be kicked out before long now.' His friend Paul, who was wearing an England football shirt, was trying to settle him down but Steve went on: 'One of 'em hit me in't side of head and then pulled back his jacket like this [simulates the drawing of a weapon] as if to say,

The Cricket World Cup, 'race' and carnival 217

"come and 'ave a go".' Paul replied, 'Tha's the problem, they [Pakistanis] all carry a blade or a stick, don't the'.'

These young men were deeply resentful both of the Pakistan supporters' domination of the event and of the behavioural norms that had been established in the course of this domination. They were continually asked to sit down by supporters sitting behind them and, in Steve's case, were very aggressive in manner, using offensive language without concern for who might hear it. Steve in particular seemed determined that he would make no concessions. It became clear that he had a deep animosity towards Asians and, in the context of this game, towards Pakistan and Pakistan supporters. As hooters were sounded and cheering and celebrations met the fall of an Australian wicket, he asserted, 'These Pakis have been pissing me off all day. We should get stuck right into 'em. Problem is, it's just one of thousands of 'em.' He then began to illustrate his support for Australia. This was, however, clearly caged within a racial matrix of opposition to Pakistan and support for their white opponents, best illustrated by the starting up of a variation of an England football team song by Steve, Paul and four friends who had joined them:

Keep St George in my heart, keep me English
Keep St George in my heart, I pray
Keep St George in my heart, Keep me English
Fuck the *Pakis* and the IRA
No surrender, no surrender, no surrender to the IRA

In the football context there is no reference to 'Pakis', but on this occasion a specific emphasis was placed on the word. They sang the verse several times and followed it with a rendition of a number of Sheffield Wednesday Football Club supporter songs less obviously concerned with race or nation. Before long, Steve decided to stand up behind his seat, apparently in order to provoke a confrontation. He was assailed with requests to sit down but stubbornly refused to do so. He kept stating that 'I'm not being told to sit down by a Paki in my own country.' Eventually a Pakistan supporter with a heavy London accent came over and asked him to sit down, to which he replied 'Fuck off.' Several other Pakistan supporters then came over as an argument ensued and Paul intervened to tell them that he would get Steve to sit down. Within a few moments another Australian wicket fell, pandemonium broke out and Steve again jumped up. He seemed to be almost willing someone to give him the opportunity to strike them and eventually picked on an innocent-looking, slender young man whose flag he grabbed and verbally abused, declaring, 'This is fucking England, not Pakistan.' The supporter appeared unintimidated and held his flag in front of Steve's face, repeatedly chanting, 'Pakistan, Pakistan, Pakistan . . .' until Steve eventually walked away.

This behaviour was in marked contrast to that of a group of white Yorkshire fans sitting nearby, several of whom got up to dance around and chant with the Pakistan fans as the Australian wickets fell, despite their own nominal support for Australia. Their enjoyment of the day was not contingent upon cultural

218 *Tim Crabbe and Stephen Wagg*

domination. It was not even contingent on sporting success. Nevertheless, these various forms of behaviour all emerged out of a context in which the white supporters and supporters of Asian extraction were implicitly assumed to be, and largely adopted the role of, sporting adversaries, whether that opposition was explicitly racialised and aggressively played out or not.

Ultimately this was the dilemma faced by the Cricket World Cup 'carnival'. The tournament was reliant upon support for each of the competing countries emerging from descendant and expatriate communities living in Britain. Indeed, much has been made of the contribution that those communities, and particularly those supporting sides from the Indian subcontinent, brought to the tournament. However, this was at all times played out within a framework that established those communities as the exotic, transgressive element. While Abdul could be celebrated as a carnival 'character', with David Gower commenting on the day of the final as the camera focused in on him, 'And Abdul's made it', there remains an apprehensive attitude towards the young Pakistani supporters who look up to him. There is a fear and alienation within sections of the cricket establishment towards the 'new' cultural forms displayed during the World Cup and there are continuing deep anxieties within the white community about the threat of 'alien' ways to traditional, or 'white', English culture. More benignly, there is a concern to keep the expressive tradition of South Asian youth culture under control.

Within the context of the Cricket World Cup these fears were largely suspended by the majority white community. However, the general rejection of the relevance of the 'Tebbit test' remains largely contingent upon the specific cultural conditions of the Cricket World Cup. While a variety of national and religious identities were given legitimacy in the sporting context, those identities and the racial stereotypes that are derived from them might prove more problematic when expressed and embodied in other settings. This is not to play down the degree of cultural interchange that took place during the tournament. Rather, it is to caution against the limitations of liberal multiculturalism in the context of a sporting form that increasingly lies outside mainstream traditional notions of English national culture. There is also the concern that with a focus on international cricket, understandings of the game, of how it is played and of how it should be watched will fall into a binary, racially coded, matrix of opposition between Western nations and 'Asian' nations, through which the Asian is depicted as the deviant 'other'.

Conclusion: carnival and the World Cup, 1999

We contend that the English cricket establishment had hoped to procure a 'carnival' on their own terms, carefully circumscribed by a set of detailed prohibitions, commodified and sold to corporate sponsors. These prohibitions, in turn, emanated from a racism that dominated public discourse in Britain between the late 1960s and the early 1990s – a racism assuming the British to be a beleaguered island race of white people menaced by dark intruders whose way of life was

The Cricket World Cup, 'race' and carnival 219

different from their own. For many in the English cricket establishment of the late 1990s, drumming, chanting and standing on your seat still represent an alien culture. In this sense the officially ECB-sanctioned notion of 'carnival' was about policing and restraining the transgressive carnivalesque practices of alien cultural styles. The preferred approach was to promote an Olympian-style pageant of national differences, reaffirming an established, ethnically marked version of the world and its relationship with English cricket.

Nevertheless, supporters from ethnic minority communities at the tournament, careless both of official restrictions and of the qualms of MCC members and the partakers of corporate hospitality, effectively redefined the ECB's prescribed carnival and reasserted the essential values recognised by Bakhtin. In doing so they not only faced down the more overt versions of this racism but, at the same time, conveyed something of the complexity and contingent nature of ethnicities in contemporary Britain. Sometimes people are Bangladeshi, sometimes they're English, sometimes they cheer for the old country and sometimes, though born in Bedford, they cheer for Liverpool . . . and so on.

To the English cricket authorities the World Cup of 1999, with its cheerily hijacked carnival, may have begun to force an acceptance that the future of the game is intimately intertwined with the black and Asian communities, whose loyalty was not long ago called into question. No more telling indication that this was being recognised could be found than the reception given to England's first post-carnival test squad by the *Daily Mail*, long regarded as the voice of conservative British suburbs and the paper that employed Tebbit as a columnist. All those selected, wrote correspondent Mike Dickson, were

> English and proud of it but rarely can a collection of elite players from this country have boasted such a diverse heritage. Under the new captaincy of Anglo-Indian Nasser Hussain were Mark Butcher, Alex Tudor, Mark Ramprakash and Dean Headley (of all or part West Indian descent), Aftab Habib (Pakistani), Alan Mullally (Irish-Australian) and Andrew Caddick (New Zealand).

Afterword, 'In the interests of health and safety . . .', July 2003

Four years on from the World Cup, an opportunity arises in midsummer 2003 for the revisitation of some of these arguments. It is Sunday 6 July. The Indian A team are touring the UK and are in the East Midlands to play Leicestershire.

Leicester has a history of immigration from India that dates back to the late 1940s. Latterly, a large contingent of the Indian families expelled from Uganda in 1971 came to Leicester. By common consent, the town, half of whose population is now Asian or Asian descended, has amicable community relations, albeit that the principal areas of Asian residence are concentrated between Belgrave Gate (the Nottingham road to the east) and the London Road, to the south.

220 Tim Crabbe and Stephen Wagg

Few Leicester Asians have been drawn to the county cricket ground. But this in no way reflects the level of community integration, simply because *no* ethnic group comes to the county's Grace Road ground in significant numbers. Earlier in the season, when Leicestershire signed the exciting Indian batsman Virender Sehwag, the *Guardian* cricket writer David Hopps wrote eloquently about the possibility that Asian Leicester could now be bonded to the county team: 'But a large influx must bring with it changes. What, for example, will young Anglo Indians make of The Meet, Grace Road's mournful old tea room, where weary faces stare at the game through a fug of fried bacon fumes?'

He quotes a local Asian restaurant owner: 'It's time to bring on the samosas and the bhajis' (Hopps 2003). But the player's presence has not brought the hoped-for upsurge of Asian interest and Sehwag has gone back to India with a 'bad back' – an administrative euphemism, it's rumoured around the ground, for homesickness. Today, though, for obvious reasons, a relatively large number of Asian families have shown up. Quite a few wear the pale blue shirt of the Indian one-day side and there is a mildly boisterous air to their spectatorship; someone has a drum, for example, which he beats enthusiastically, and there is some chanting. But at the same time, little else about this unaccustomed presence of local Asians has any ethnic specificity about it. The children roam the ground, play bat-and-ball games, seek autographs (from both teams), queue with their parents for ice creams, wander in and out of the club shop . . . In principle, perhaps, they might even like to join a club that some of its members feel may be on the verge of extinction.

But the club's response to them, though apparently well-meaning, is peremptory. The man in charge of the public address system, a local accountant and sports coach, is a benevolent person, dedicated to the club. But his manner is Edwardian. In his lexicon, play doesn't start – it 'commences', and moves not to a close but to a 'cessation'. No sooner had some apparently harmless drumming and chanting begun to emanate from a cluster of young Asian men close to the pavilion than he is at the microphone instructing them to stop 'in the interests of all spectators'. They now move to the other side of the ground and resume drumming.

Later, when some young Asian boys are seen sitting on the grass behind the boundary rope, but within the white picket fence that surrounds the field, he is once again on the loudspeakers, telling them that to occupy such a position is 'contrary to health and safety regulations' and that they must move. But an anomaly is immediately apparent. A row of white, middle-aged couples are also sitting, either within the fence or in a place where the fence recesses to make space for the covers that protect the wicket. However, because, in addition to their whiteness and adulthood, they have a range of reassuring signifiers – sensible folding chairs, thermoses, *Sunday Telegraph* crosswords, picnic baskets . . . – they have been, no doubt unconsciously, exempted from the 'health and safety regulations'.

Leicester's Asian kids, like so many of the people observed in this chapter, have fallen foul of a racialised sense of order imposed by an institution veering at times perilously close to commercial oblivion.

Notes

1 The research reported here is the result of a joint effort by the authors. We each attended matches during the 1999 Cricket World Cup independently but for the sake of linguistic simplicity our accounts are reported here in the plural.
2 Wasim Akram and Showaib Akhtar were the two principal fast-paced 'strike' bowlers in the Pakistan team.
3 In a clear manipulation of the tournament rules, after 'ensuring' victory the Australians deliberately slowed their own rate of scoring, taking 13 overs to score 19 runs. This had the effect of improving the West Indies' net run rate vis-à-vis New Zealand, who also had a chance of proceeding to the next stage of the tournament. Results from the first round were to be carried over to the next 'Super Sixes' round, and since Australia had beaten the West Indies and lost to New Zealand, it served their interests to see the West Indies progress at New Zealand's expense.

References

Back, L., Crabbe, T. and Solomos, J. (1998) 'Lions, black skins and reggae gyals: race, nation and identity in football', Critical Urban Studies Occasional Papers, Centre for Urban and Community Research, Goldsmiths College, London.

Back, L., Crabbe, T. and Solomos, J. (2001) *The Changing Face of Football: Racism, Multiculture and Identity in the English Game*, Oxford: Berg.

Bains, J. and Patel, R. (1996) *Asians Can't Play Football*, Birmingham: d-zine.

Bakhtin, M. (1973) *Problems of Dostoevsky's Poetics*, trans. R. W. Rotsel, Ann Arbor, Mich.: Ardis.

Beckles, H. (1998) *A Spirit of Dominance: Cricket and Nationalism in the West Indies: Essays in Honour of Viv Richards on the 21st Anniversary of His Test Debut*, Kingston, Jamaica: Canoe Press.

Beckles, H. and Stoddart, B. (eds) (1995) *Liberation Cricket*, Manchester: Manchester University Press.

Birley, D. (1993) *Sport and the Making of Britain*, Manchester: Manchester University Press.

Bose, M. (1986) *Cricket on the Maidan*, Hemel Hempstead: George Allen & Unwin.

Bose, M. (1990) *A History of Indian Cricket*, London: André Deutsch.

Bristol, M. (1985) *Carnival and Theatre: Plebeian Culture and the Structure of Authority in Renaissance England*, London: Methuen.

Cashman, R. (1980) *Patrons, Players and the Crowd: the Phenomenon of Indian Cricket*, New Delhi: Orient Longman.

Cohen, A. (1993) *Masquerade Politics*, Oxford: Berg.

England and Wales Cricket Board (1997) ICC Cricket World Cup England 99: ticket application form – A Carnival of Cricket, London: ECB.

England and Wales Cricket Board (1999) 'ICC Cricket World Cup England 99: A Carnival of Cricket – Coming to a Cricket Ground Near You', London: ECB.

Fiske, J. (1989) *Reading the Popular*, London: Unwin Hyman.

Gardiner, M. (1991) 'Bakhtin's Carnival: Utopia as critique', in D. Shepherd (ed.) *Bakhtin, Carnival and Other Subjects*, selected papers from the International Bakhtin Conference, University of Manchester, July 1991, *Critical Studies*, 3 (2) – 4 (1/2).

Gilroy, P. (1987) *There Ain't No Black in the Union Jack*, London: Routledge.

Gilroy, P. (1993) *Small Acts: Thoughts on the Politics of Black Cultures*, London: Serpent's Tail.

222 Tim Crabbe and Stephen Wagg

Giuilanotti, R. (1991) 'Scotland's tartan army in Italy: the case for the carnivalesque', *Sociological Review*, 39 (3): 503–27.

Giuilanotti, R. (1995) 'Football and the politics of Carnival: an ethnographic study of Scottish fans in Sweden', *International Review for the Sociology of Sport*, 30 (2): 191–217.

Henderson, R. (1995) 'Is it in the blood?', *Wisden Cricket Monthly*, July.

Holt, R. (1989) *Sport and the British*, Oxford: Oxford University Press.

Hopps, David (2003) 'Indian tiger awakens foxes', *Guardian* Sport, 17 May, p. 13.

James, C. L. R. (1994) *Beyond a Boundary*, London: Serpent's Tail.

McLellan, Alastair (1994) *The Enemy Within: The Impact of Overseas Players on English Cricket*, London: Blandford.

McLellan, A. and Savidge, M. (1996) *Real Quick*, London: Two Heads.

Marqusee, M. (1994) *Anyone but England: Cricket and the National Malaise*, London: Verso.

Marqusee, M. (1998) *Anyone but England: Cricket, Race and Class*, London: Two Heads.

Morgan, J. (1998) 'Multinational sport and literary practices', in M. McNamee and S. Parry (eds) *Ethics and Sport*, London: Routledge.

O'Donnell, H. (1994) 'Mapping the mythical: a geopolitics of national sporting stereotypes', *Discourse and Society*, 5 (3): 345–80.

Oslear, D. and Bannister, J. (1996) *Tampering with Cricket*, London: Collins Willow.

Searle, C. (1990) 'Race before wicket: cricket, empire and the white rose', *Race and Class*, 31 (3) (January–March): 31–48.

Sebeok, T. (1984) *Carnival!*, New York: Mouton.

Solomos, J. (1998) 'Beyond racism *and* multiculturalism', *Patterns of Prejudice*, 32 (4): 45–62.

Thompson, G. (1983) 'Carnival and the calculable: consumption and play at Blackpool', in T. Bennett *et al.* (eds) *Formations of Pleasure*, London: Routledge & Kegan Paul.

Werbner, P. (1996) '"Our blood is green": cricket, identity and social empowerment among British Pakistanis', in J. McClancy (ed.) *Sport, Identity and Ethnicity*, Oxford: Berg.

Williams, J. (1998) 'Cricket and changing expressions of Englishness', *Scottish Centre Research Papers*, vol. 3, University of Edinburgh.

11 Sheffield Caribbean

The story of a Yorkshire cricket club

Chris Searle

How did a relatively small but determined and multi-talented arrivant Caribbean community fare when it came to live in a northern English city, dominated by heavy industry, in the closing decades of the twentieth century? There are many possible starting points to a study of this kind, and many aspects of these transplanted lives to begin to chronicle. It would not surprise anyone who knows and admires the writings of the Trinidadian C. L. R. James (James 1986) to be told that one of these roads is cricket. For the story of one particular South Yorkshire cricket club, Sheffield Caribbean, is much more than a Saturday sports story: it is the story of a new urban community and its burgeoning culture beset with a plethora of problems and difficult challenges. It is also a narrative of growth, skill, tenacity and struggle in the face of these problems and challenges.

Any local cricket club can become an institutional expression of the wider social and political life of its members – more so when it begins to represent the civic progress of a minority urban community. Here, the structural barriers met by the club and its players can seem like a metaphor for the daily bureaucratic or racist skirmishes encountered by its people and their organisations. The club's confrontations with league officials and umpires, the hostile attitudes of some rival clubs and their players, or the administrators at the higher-echelon regional institutions of their sport (in this case, Yorkshire County Cricket Club and its outmoded and exclusive rules, conventions and values) all stand as parallels with the community's daily stand-offs with mainstream institutions. In this context, dealing with cricket officialdom is simply an extension of other dealing: with the courts, with the police or with local and sometimes even national government departments and agencies. How much do the cricketers, seeking sporting success and a sense of cultural emancipation, extend their activism into the struggles of mainstream and political life?

Yorkshire is England's most celebrated (and frequently caricatured) cricketing county. Scratch a cricket ball, it may be said, and you will uncover a Yorkshire face, and unlike the cricket countenances of the southern counties, it will often be an urban face. Cricket in South Yorkshire, for example, has close associations with working-class lives and institutions, with factories and pits and with working men's clubs and works sides.

224   *Chris Searle*

According to the Channel Four cricket commentator Dermot Reeve, 20 per cent of all club cricket played in England is played in Yorkshire, which has a totality (in 2003) of 721 clubs playing in its various leagues (Channel Four, broadcast from Headingley cricket ground, 24 August 2003). It is only during the past decade that Yorkshire County Cricket Club has turned its back on over a century of parochialism and bigotry and allowed non-Yorkshire-born cricketers to play for the county. This began with the contracting of world talents such as Richie Richardson of Antigua and Sachin Tendulkar of India to boost the chances of Yorkshire CCC in the county championship. These changes prefigured new opportunities not only for Englishmen born outside Yorkshire (the present England captain, the Lancashire-born and Sheffield-bred Michael Vaughan being the most prominent recruit), but, more pertinently in the context of this essay, for young urban black cricketers with Caribbean or Pakistani roots. These cricketers came typically from migrant families who for decades had lived, worked and paid their council tax in Yorkshire cities. Yet even these developments have not significantly changed the associations that the county club has had with racism and exclusion. As recently as January 2003, Yorkshire's then captain, the Australian Test batsman Darren Lehmann, was charged by the ICC with making racist remarks about the Sri Lanka one-day international team after a World Cup preliminary match (Hoult 2003: 29). Even now (January 2004), no Yorkshire-born or -based black cricketer has ever played for Yorkshire. The past continues, savagely kicking, within the changes of the present.

Caribbean Sheffield: the making of a community

A Caribbean community grew within Sheffield from the mid-1950s onwards. An elite group of university academics and doctors developed around the influence of Professor (of law) Roy Marshall, a Barbadian who was a cousin of his namesake who played in the triumphant West Indies touring team of 1950 and later scored prolifically for Hampshire in the English County Championship. The professor became the elected chair of Sheffield's first West Indian Association, which welcomed arriving students, nurses and steelworkers to the city and on their behalf campaigned for better reception and treatment. A shortage of transport workers in Sheffield provoked a relocation of Caribbean bus drivers (mainly of Jamaican, Barbadian or Grenadian origin) from London. These black soon-to-become Sheffielders joined a longer-sojourned group, mainly of ex-servicemen who had either jumped ship in Liverpool and made their way across the Pennines to South Yorkshire or were RAF returnees who had chosen to settle in the city after demobilisation.

Very soon the community's cricketers began to filter out through the city's established clubs and found themselves playing for occupation-based teams such as Sheffield Transport or steelworks sides such as Firth Brown, Davy's, Forgemasters, Tinsley Wire or Hadfields. Although many of the cricketing newcomers found acceptance and friendship within these clubs, others experienced isolation,

Sheffield Caribbean 225

unwelcoming clubhouses, pubs and other after-match venues, and suspicious, sometimes hostile, teammates and opponents. Hence the growth of informal Sunday 'friendlies' between a nomadic, groundless team of Sheffield Caribbean cricketers and other Caribbean teams in London (to which some of the new black Sheffielders still retained strong social and sporting links), Leeds and Lancashire cities. This trend only fed the appetite for the formation of a specifically Caribbean club in Sheffield – particularly as the city's West Indian Association was becoming more confident and assured and was now based in local church premises. As family life became more consolidated with the sending for partners and children, and community growth within specific neighbourhoods such as Pitsmoor (where many Jamaicans settled) and Nether Edge in the south of the city (which became the preferred locality for Grenadians), Sheffield became, in effect, another Caribbean island, integrally linked to the wider West Indian diaspora.

In 1967, Sheffield's first youth club for young Caribbeans was formed in a glorified Nissen hut in Crookesmoor, largely the work of Sue Atkins, a recently arrived detached youth worker, who worked from the streets and other informal venues to stimulate positive activities among estranged Caribbean youth. While the West Indian Association took up the prevailing issues around the local black youth – school underachievement, the lack of resources and police hostility among them – the youth club (initially condemned by national government as a sectarian institution, while strongly supported by the local council) mobilised local black youth. This mobilisation was particularly around sports excellence and culture and, through successful activity building, it legitimised the idea of a black sports club.

A part of the new club's function was to train and empower young Sheffield black people to grapple with local bureaucracy and to develop a new and young community leadership in all aspects of essential social life, including sport. Young Caribbean cricket enthusiasts wanted to move from school cricket to club cricket, and were keen to form a team. Their approaches to Sheffield Council Recreation Department secured a ground in Firth Park in the north of the city. But this somewhat notorious site stood on an excessively steep slope and had already been refused by many other applicant clubs. Moreover, the Caribbean rejection of it coincided with a practising group of the club's young players being chased out of Millhouses Park, in the south of the city, by council officials.

Eventually, in 1967, cooperation between the Education Department and the friendly head teacher of Athelstan Junior School in south-east Sheffield secured use of both the school ground and its changing rooms. The West Indian Association provided kit, and the new team soon showed its worth, winning the Sheffield Youth Club League for the first three seasons of its existence. By 1970 the team had joined the lowest division of the senior Norton and District League and had 'poached' back several talented black players from local, predominantly white, clubs. By 1974, having won the first four divisions of this league, year by year, Sheffield Caribbean could look forward to Premier Division status, where neutral umpires were a part of the established provision.

226 Chris Searle

Certainly match officials, in the Caribbean's experience, had hitherto seemed anything but impartial. Mike Atkins, a Barbadian who arrived in Sheffield in 1962 and became an irrepressible community activist (eventually qualifying as a careers officer and becoming the first director of Sheffield City Council's Race Equality Unit), was also a fervent cricketer. He remembers two league umpires in particular, known by Sheffield cricketers far and wide as 'Trigger' and 'Fiddler'. As to the former, Atkins recalls:

> He couldn't hardly see. He could only see that you were black. I remember one match, played on a farmer's field at Mosborough [in south-east Sheffield], when he gave all ten of our wickets lbw, while as we batted the local crowd kept coming forward from behind the boundary, throwing the ball back and preventing us scoring any fours. Their wicketkeeper was constantly sledging us with racist comments and yet our players were reported as 'swearing in our own language'. We were officially told of the league's 'benefit of the doubt lbw syndrome' towards the batsman, but we never saw it'.

Such graphic reminiscences are almost cinematic in their metaphorical power. They give a snapshot of a community under siege, yet still defiant. Atkins also recalls a barrage of criticism from league officials through their match reports: 'no grass on the pitch', 'no sightscreens', 'poor changing room facilities', 'substandard teas', and all this proceeding while Sheffield Caribbean was winning the league's Premier Division and the inter-divisional cup. Sunday matches were still nomadic, with the team participating in the Clive Lloyd League and regular 'friendlies' with Caribbean teams from, among other places, Luton, Liverpool, Birmingham, Leicester and various London boroughs.

Fire versus fire

The late 1970s and early 1980s were the era of what became known in the British press and public consciousness as 'the Socialist Republic of South Yorkshire', centred around the political progress of Sheffield's left-leaning Labour city council. In 1982 the council established its Race Equality Unit, and activists within the City's black communities began to see some positive municipal responses to their long-held concerns. This was despite the gulf in commitment between some conscientious elected councillors and the many still virtually unaffected council officers. But away from the inner areas of the city, where black Sheffielders mostly lived, and towards the outskirts of Sheffield, the 'White Highlands' and the county borderlands with north Derbyshire, where many local clubs had their grounds, there had been little penetration of the ideas and remedial practices of racial justice. This partly explains the Caribbean's experiences in Mosborough, a sprawling suburb, mostly of new estates, in the south-east of Sheffield and edging Derbyshire where National Front activity was developing. A 15-year-old local schoolgirl had written the following about the experiences of a black friend and her family, who lived near Mosborough:

I live in Mosborough on the southern side of Sheffield. Recently in the local newspaper I read a report that the Ku Klux Klan are operating in and around Derbyshire. I found this very worrying as Derbyshire is next to Mosborough. A week later my friend was beaten up. Sharon lives in Eckington, near Mosborough, which is an all-white area. Her and her family have lived there for seventeen years. The family were having a driveway built at the front of the house. They had laid the concrete. While it was still wet someone had written 'NF – Get out you black bastards'.

The family were very shocked.

Then a gang Sharon knew turned on her. Sharon had known these people all her life. In one of her friend's houses she found some NF leaflets and newspapers. She confronted her friends about them. The five boys turned on her and her white friend. She was very badly beaten up and ended up in hospital with two broken ribs. Her white friend was also beaten up and called a 'Nigger Lover' (Earl Marshal School 1993: 189).

Cricket in the Sheffield area is also profoundly affected by the 'We don't play it for fun' ethic, which is paramount throughout Yorkshire cricket – the idea that the game must be played hard and any expedient must be employed in order to win. Thus, the Sheffield Caribbean played much of their cricket in the midst of a 'Mosborough world', a context where extreme gamesmanship and racist ignorance intersected, and the boundaries between the two were often too murky to discern. 'This is the way we play it Yorkshire, so you'd best get used to it' was often the riposte to protests mounted by the Caribbean, who soon learned to fight Yorkshire cricket fire with fire of their own – so much so that the team became widely respected and feared across Sheffield cricket leagues as 'the team to beat' – the strongest club side (outside the Yorkshire Council League) in the City. They brought with their cricket the powerful social and political achievement of having come both from outside and below to a position of cricketing distinction and excellence. This, in itself, carried a message that defied racism and caused many ordinary cricket-playing Sheffielders to rethink their previous attitudes and prejudices.

The summer of 1981

The inner-city resistance during the summer of 1981 of Brixton, Toxteth and Bristol found its own unique expression in Sheffield. A match with the South Yorkshire Police 'was one game we wouldn't play', remembers Mike Atkins. This was despite earnest invitations by the constabulary and the undertaking by Sheffield black churches to organise a team. 'They tried to buy us off with YOP [Youth Opportunities Programme] programmes, in return for our cooperation, particularly as tension grew, with increased recourse to "stop and search" tactics and harassment of young black men in the city centre.' A series of meetings between community activists, supportive left-Labour councillors and the South Yorkshire Police devised a peacekeeping strategy. A youth leader, Leroy Wenham,

228 *Chris Searle*

would be the link if there was a problem of increased tension. When a group of 20 to 30 black youths congregated near Castle Market, there was a serious police overreaction. Wenham was called in to defuse the situation, but soon found himself arrested, along with a number of black youngsters, and was finally convicted of obstruction. All Sheffield Caribbean players now pulled out of the appointed match between the police and the black churches, as an expression of solidarity with the arrested youths. 'It showed us very clearly how the police were prepared to use cricket, the game we loved, as a tool,' declared Atkins, as he recalled a visit soon after these events from the Home Secretary and a meeting with the police, in which black cricket activists in all quarters of the city were condemned as uncooperative and troublemakers.

Cricket and black community unity

Perhaps the Sheffield Caribbean cricketers' experience in their home city was different from that in many other English cities in one vital respect. From the outset there was little or no insularity between cricketers originating from the different islands across the Caribbean nation – hence the pride of unity behind the club's name – and, beyond this, the club fostered an authentic racial and cultural inclusiveness. From 1967 onwards the resources of the youth club were shared with youth from Sheffield's Yemeni, Bangladeshi and Pakistani communities, and Caribbean youth activists gave support to these communities in their own struggles for council-controlled resources. From its very beginnings the cricket club always welcomed Asian players, and long-time players remember 'an Asian quota' as part of team selection. When some conservative mosque leaders opposed the formation of a secular and democratic Pakistani youth club close to the Caribbean model, the youth of both communities organised at close quarters.

Sheffield Caribbean's most eminent cricketing product is the Derbyshire (and latterly Northamptonshire and Leicestershire) and England pace bowler Devon Malcolm, who played regularly for the club in the early 1980s. Devon opened the bowling with the almost-as-quick Steve Taylor, who also played for Derbyshire Seconds. Neither of these powerful bowlers of Jamaican origin had any prospect of playing for Yorkshire, although both their families were Sheffield working people. Malcolm writes movingly in his autobiography about the loyal support of his Sheffield Caribbean clubmates and about his cricketing connections with the city's Muslim communities and of the times that he was invited to play for local Asian sides:

> I remember playing for Asian sides in Sheffield, and I enjoyed getting to know about their religion, how they lived their lives. Cricket teaches you respect for others. Sheffield Caribbean club, where I first learned about cricket in any depth after coming over from Jamaica, was so important for me at a time of my life when I might have drifted, just like many other black kids. They put in so much hard work on my behalf, encouraging me to bowl fast and even

Sheffield Caribbean 229

organising transport for me and paying for my teas. I still keep in touch with them and will always be grateful to them.

(Malcolm 1998: 144; Searle 2001: 73–82)

In 1991, Earl Marshal School, a local comprehensive with a strong element of cricket-loving Pakistani students, opened the Devon Malcolm Cricket Centre with the very active leadership of members of Sheffield Caribbean. Both Steve Taylor and stalwart Owen Gittens had become teachers at the school, and Mike Atkins was appointed its chair of governors. Devon had lived near the school as a youth and became the centre's enthusiastic sponsor, making regular visits and giving talks on aspects of cricket and his own experiences at Test match level. As the school's head teacher, I was privileged to sit in on some of these sessions, and I remember well the sense of wonder and engagement on the (mostly Pakistani) students' faces as Malcolm relived through a video commentary his crushing 9 to 57 against the remnants of a white South African team at the Oval in August 1994. Later, in 1995, the paceman donated to the centre a proportion of the high court damages awarded to him after an article by Robert Henderson in *Wisden Cricket Monthly* had claimed that England cricketers born outside the United Kingdom lacked the necessary commitment to their adopted country. 'Sweet dreams are made of this!' ran the headline in the *Caribbean Times*; 'Youth to benefit from Malcolm's dismissal of cricket's racists' (Slater 1995: 1). The centre itself became a model of inner-city cricket development and the hard and talented coaching work put in by Taylor and Gittens was at its heart. Many young players – mainly from Pakistani families, but including local Caribbean, Somali and Yemeni youth too, moved on to play for the city's Asian sides, as well as for Sheffield Caribbean. A huge moment in the Centre's history was during its initial development in December 1990 when it hosted a visit from the then Pakistan captain, Imran Khan. Sheffield Caribbean administrators and activists were at the centre of what became a huge local event and celebration of international cricket.

At this point it is important to delve into the early lives of some of the club's extraordinary cricketing militants: Mike Atkins, Owen Gittens and Sam Gittens are to Sheffield Caribbean what the 'Three W's' (Frank Worrell, Everton Weekes and Clyde Walcott) were to West Indies cricket after the Second World War. Born within two years of each other in the early 1940s in villages on the tiny island of Barbados, they have done outstanding work to sustain the fortunes of the club. Moreover, each has been inspired by the cricketing glory of the Caribbean players of world renown whom they remember from their boyhood. Atkins, from Dover village, knew the West Indian fast bowler Wes Hall as his neighbour and ran errands for his cousin, West Indian Test batsman Peter Lashley. He bowled at Everton Weekes and Clyde Walcott in local nets and remembered how a back-foot drive from the all-powerful Walcott 'crashed into my hand. I couldn't move it for weeks!' Owen Gittens has been an integral part of the club as player and administrator since being demobbed from the RAF in the late 1960s. In St John, in Barbados, where he grew up, he was a contemporary of Gary Sobers and was coached at Lodge School by the great Everton Weekes. Sam Gittens, who still

230   *Chris Searle*

plays, administrates and umpires in the local Asian league, is from Bayland and grew up in the next street to Sobers and just down the hill from Sobers' cousin David Holford. He remembers early matches with Frank King and Seymour Nurse. It is these late colonial apprenticeships that provided the very fibre of a club forged in a postcolonial industrial city in Yorkshire, more than an ocean away.

The pioneering work of this extraordinary trio and other veteran club members with their provenances in other islands was directly inspired not only by the example of the boyhood heroes who lived so closely inside their lives, but also by the succeeding, all-conquering generation of Caribbean cricketers of the 'black-wash' years, who were contemporaries: Viv Richards, Andy Roberts, Clive Lloyd, Joel Garner, Michael Holding, Gordon Greenidge (a frequent visitor to Sheffield and a friend of the club) and Malcolm Marshall, whose exploits in the 1970s and 1980s made the West Indies cricket team the most powerful and successful in world cricket. Atkins, Gittens and Gittens were Barbadian exiles and new Sheffielders but, more significantly, they were West Indians abroad, a part of the diaspora, implicitly and explicitly loyal to the 'One Caribbean' Test team of their childhood memories – a team and also a metaphor for, and expression of, Caribbean integrity, which in the words of the leader of the Grenada revolution, Maurice Bishop, 'wants nothing to do with sectarianism, conspiracies or cliques but an agenda which serves our people, the Caribbean people, and confronts and seeks to resolve their multiplicity of problems' (1982: 10). For in Sheffield too these cricketers established an annexe of that same concept of a unified Caribbean nation. And as activists of their community's sporting prowess they are also agents and catalysts of an eventual Caribbean nationhood – even within the confines of a Victorian 'steel city', ironically now seeking to reinvent itself as a twenty-first-century 'city of sport', full of new, Olympic-standard complexes for swimmers and divers, athletes and skaters, but with very little to offer cricketers.

On their own ground

In 1986, Sheffield Caribbean at last secured its own ground. This was in Ecclesfield, a northern suburb of the city. This achievement followed the period of Malcolm and Taylor's bowling successes with the club, as well the prodigious run-getting of batsmen such as Buster Reynolds and the brothers Martin and Ronnie Forte. The club had won the Premier Division of the Norton and District League for three consecutive years (1982–4) and had been told by officials that they would now move directly into one of the top divisions of the Sheffield League. However, when they applied to do so, they were informed that they could only join at Division D level. (By 1989, they had moved up, on merit, to Division A, becoming League Champions in 1992.) In 1985 a previous application to join the South Riding Division of the prestigious Yorkshire Council League had eventually ended in disappointment when teams from the North, South and West Riding divisions had voted *en bloc* against them. One of the reasons given for this vote was the 'poor quality' of Sheffield Caribbean's new ground, even though a

Sheffield Caribbean 231

few years earlier the same divisions had happily accepted Knatts Sports, who at the time were using the same Ecclesfield ground. The club made indignant protest through the regional press and Yorkshire Television, but to little avail. In an article in *The Independent* in February 1987 (Foster 1987: 7) it was acknowledged that 'Caribbean had become the fastest growing sports club in Sheffield, with a formidable reputation of producing talented young players'. Yet the article also quotes the secretary of the Yorkshire Council League, William Pye, apparently claiming that Caribbean's playing standard was insufficiently high. 'We reject accusations of bias,' said Pye. 'We consider the matter closed.' The reader also learns how the Caribbean Sports Club's netball team had been expelled from the Rotherham and District Netball League for alleged 'excessive aggression and unsportsmanlike attitude'. Such backward rationales were familiar enough to the cricketers of Sheffield Caribbean.

The acquisition of the Ecclesfield ground came during the same fruitful period when the Sheffield and District African Caribbean Association (SADACCA) gained increased influence within Sheffield's education, health and social services, and took over large new premises in the city centre. SADACCA members were also strong protagonists in the setting up of the city's Black Community Forum, a campaigning organisation composed of delegates from all of Sheffield's black and minority communities. Meanwhile the cricket club continued its struggle, this time against vandals and/or racists who targeted their precious field. In 1987 the clubhouse windows were smashed and the broken glass ground into the pitch. The pavilion sustained £8,000 worth of damage in an arson attack and the club tractor was destroyed. In 1988 the scorebox was burned down. The groundsman, who had worked at the ground for thirty years, told the Sheffield *Star* he had never known such sustained violence to any sports ground (*The Star* (Sheffield), 19 May 1988).

The club made fresh applications to join the Yorkshire Council League in both 1990 and 2000. The latter instance boiled down to a contest between the Caribbean and Sheffield Works Department for one vacant place. The League could not admit the Works Department team because their ground was acknowledged to be in a poor state and their changing facilities were a Portakabin. But it remained unwilling to admit Sheffield Caribbean, citing previous reasons (widely seen as spurious), and instead played the following season one team short.

Through the late 1990s and into the new millennium, the changes within Yorkshire CCC, notably the turning away from the 'born in Yorkshire' selection policy, began to affect other old-established exclusionist practices in Yorkshire cricket culture. Pushing hard for these changes have been the diehards of Sheffield Caribbean – in particular, Mike Atkins, who gained the support of the Sports Council for an investigation into black participation within the structures of Yorkshire cricket. Atkins also presides over the county club's first ever Black and Ethnic Minority Cricket Forum, a formal subcommittee of Yorkshire County Cricket Board, on which the chief executive of the Board, the youth development officer, the marketing manager and the secretary of the board are all obliged to sit. The board is also giving five years' funding to ten Youth Development Cricket

232 Chris Searle

Centres (partly based on the inner city model of the Devon Malcolm Cricket Centre) throughout the county. Although the first young black Yorkshire cricketer is still to walk out onto the field as a member of the county first team, the grounds for optimism that he will soon do so are much stronger now.

Thus, in postcolonial Yorkshire, through a dogged and unflagging contestation, institutional racism in the county's cricket has been faced down and opportunities for black community cricketers increased as another expression of the long striving against racism in British urban life. In this context, Sheffield Caribbean continues to play and develop with all its heart and mind, mindful that cricket is an important part of the many-sided struggle of defending the Caribbean presence in postcolonial Britain, composed too, as Tim Hector wrote, of cricketers who 'make it up, and over from under' (Hector, 1998; see also Chapter 8 of this book), sustained by their own deeply flourishing roots.

References

Bishop, Maurice (1982) Speech, 7 November, reprinted in *One Caribbean*, London: Britain/Grenada Friendship Society.

Earl Marshal School (1993) *Lives of Love and Hope*, Sheffield: Earl Marshal School.

Foster, Jonathan (1987) 'A prejudice for fairness', *The Independent* (London), 6 February.

Hector, Tim (1998) 'Cricket is more than meets the eye', *Fan the Flame* website 20 February.

Hoult, Nick (2003) 'Lehmann faces ban for racial remarks', *Daily Telegraph*, 17 January.

James, C. L. R. (1986) *Beyond a Boundary*, London: Stanley Paul.

Malcolm, Devon (1998) *You Guys Are History*, London: Collins Willow.

Searle, Chris (2001) *Pitch of Life*, Manchester: Parrs Wood Press.

Slater, Ross (1995) 'Sweet dreams are made of this', *Caribbean Times*, 11 November.

12 Clean bowl racism?
Inner-city London and the politics of cricket development

Nick Miller

In November 1999 the England and Wales Cricket Board (ECB) voiced its commitment to implement an extensive campaign to tackle the problem of racism within cricket. Tim Lamb, its chief executive, stated, 'Complacency on racial equality is not acceptable' and that 'we must open our doors to everyone and ensure that all cricketers and those associated within the game are treated with respect and given every opportunity to participate in or support the game' (BBC News Online 1999). The statement was made in response to the findings of a report commissioned by the ECB to investigate racial equality in cricket. The report, entitled *Clean Bowl Racism*, revealed that 58 per cent of those consulted believed racism existed in the game (ECB Racism Study Group 1999a). In identifying and highlighting elements of racism as being 'counterproductive to the development, progress and well being of English cricket' (ibid.), the report made recommendations to combat prejudice. The ECB immediately adopted these recommendations as policy and circulated them to all cricket clubs in England and Wales in a document entitled 'Action Plans for Racial Equality in Cricket' (ECB 1999b).

In addition to stating that 'racism is unacceptable' at club, county and international levels of the game, the report went on to say that 'actively embracing and developing cricket for ethnic minorities is seen as a vital contribution to improving the standard and standing of English cricket' (ECB Racism Study Group 1999a). To achieve this, the ECB felt that the promotion of inner-city cricket would be the most 'appropriate and productive' approach to this development. In October 1999 the Sports Minster, Kate Hoey, and the England captain, Nasser Hussain, launched the ECB's Inner City Community Cricket Project at Lord's Cricket Ground. The aim of the scheme was to provide funding for facilities and coaching in the inner-city areas to encourage young people, and particularly those from ethnic minorities, to play cricket (Department of Culture, Media and Sport 2000).

The aim of this chapter is to argue that the commitment to combat racism and focus on developing cricket at grass-roots level represented a significant shift in ECB policy. This change followed a decade of widespread discussion of racism in cricket and one that particularly focused on the alienation of black and Asian players in the game. Throughout the 1990s it had become increasingly evident

234 *Nick Miller*

that, while cricket was struggling to maintain public interest, its popularity was 'thriving within Britain's black and Asian communities' (McDonald and Ugra, 1998: 1). Thousands of Asian cricketers were playing competitive cricket in Asian leagues in Yorkshire, Lancashire, Essex and east London (ibid.). However, there remained a huge discrepancy between the enthusiasm for cricket expressed by young Asians and the small number of British-born Asian players at senior level. Despite campaigns such as Hit Racism for Six (HR46), the cricket authorities refused to concede that this inequality could be attributed to discrimination within the game. Mike Marqusee (1998: 317) maintained that during this period the cricket authorities adopted a 'hear no evil, see no evil' approach to racism. Therefore, the question that must be asked is, why did this shift in ECB policy occur?

I shall argue that since 1997, a series of complex political, social and economic factors, and changes within cricket and British society, forced the ECB to review its policy towards inclusion and discrimination. I maintain that despite the recommendations in *Clean Bowl Racism*, the ECB has failed to break down the cultural barriers that continue to alienate black and Asian people from English cricket.

Central to this study is the relationship between cricket, ethnicity and national identity. I will now examine the nature of an English identity that has developed historically in the culture of cricket and the place of British-born black and Asian players within this culture. I shall argue that developments within this relationship have played a prominent role in the contestation surrounding English cricket since the 1990s.

Englishness and the village green

A brief examination of the cultural and social significance accorded to cricket in England demonstrates how sport provides a key symbolic site for the construction and reproduction of national identities (Carrington 1998: 102). Cricket has historically been presented as being quintessentially English (Williams 1999: 5). By promoting the values of civility, tradition, fair play, of the gentleman and the countryside, the notions of cricket and Englishness have become intertwined with the habitus of the male upper-class elite, which ruled the game, the country and the British Empire from the late eighteenth century. As Maguire (1999: 178) argues, cricket is seen to represent what 'England' is and as such gives meaning to the identity of being 'English'.

Despite the collapse of the Empire, cricket's status as a national relic remains and cricket continues to figure predominantly in advertisements to create immediately recognisable images of England. As McDonald and Ugra (1998: 1) maintain, 'Cricket on the village green is for many people the sunny-side-up of what England still means.'

But this represents a very narrow notion of what England's cultural identity should look like (Carrington 1998: 102) and bears little relation to the contemporary reality of multicultural, urban and modern Britain.

Inner-city London and cricket development 235

For many in the inner cities, the unemployed, the low waged, the homeless, and all those who are abused because of their race or sex, the village cricket match is a symbol of the England in which they have no part. Cricket's mythology is the product of a vision in which large sections of the population are consigned to inferior rank.

(Marqusee 1998: 46)

For Marqusee (ibid.: 46), such portrayals of 'Englishness' and cricket on the village green are neither 'accidental' nor 'incidental'. During the 1990s, cricket became fundamental in constructing a national identity that reflected a nation at ease with itself, at a time of political and economic crisis. High unemployment, a rise in violence and crime, and political pressure from Europe to join the single currency coincided with England's loss of power and lack of success in world cricket.

References to England's heritage became a feature of the discourse of the government at this time, and the most blatant example can be seen in the Prime Minister's St George's Day speech in 1993. In his address to the nation, John Major deliberately used cricket to 'invoke a mythical, nostalgic and implicitly white notion of England', an essentially rural country full of 'invincible green suburbs', with Englishmen drinking warm beer to the distant sounds of cricket being played on the village green (Carrington 1998: 102). Carrington (ibid.: 102) argues that the imagery within Major's speech represented an attempt to promote 'dreamlike constructions' of earlier 'golden ages' as a way of managing 'contemporary political, economic and social problems' by recourse to an invented past of imperial greatness when 'Britannia ruled the waves' and the English were not 'beaten at their own game' of cricket.

More importantly, while this England did not exist in multicultural Britain, the continuing refuge in nostalgic discourse of Englishmen playing village cricket had clear racial connotations. The imagined version of Major's Britain is presented as a homogeneous community undivided by race and culture, one prior to the immigration of the many black and Asian people who came to settle in Britain from the colonies (Gilroy 1993: 52). The increasing presence of this 'alien culture' is represented as the 'enemy within' and invites the conclusion that national decline and weakness coincided with the arrival of black immigrants. Gilroy (1993) argues that such analogies of modern Britain and the Empire have become increasingly common in political discourse to exclude black people from the British national identity and represent what Barker (1981: 23) has labelled 'new racism'.

English cricket and 'the enemy within'

This is illustrated during the 1990s, as the inwardly looking nationalism evident in the political climate emerged in the discourse of English cricket (Crabbe and Wagg 2000). Jack Williams in his book *Cricket and England* (1999) complained that cricket during this time was 'pervaded with snobbery, sexism and racism'

236 Nick Miller

– a view supported by Crabbe and Wagg (2000), who argue that from the 1980s English officials and commentators began to view ex-colonial teams with suspicion and hostility. Many denounced the 'viciousness' of the 'chilling' West Indian pace bowlers as 'downright thuggery' (Moorehouse 1979) and accused their Pakistani counterparts of being ball-tampering 'cheats' (Oslear and Bannister 1996; Crabbe and Wagg 2000). At the same time, Viv Richards and Imran Khan received racist abuse from members of the crowd at Headingley (Abbasi 1999).

In addition to these overt examples of racism, complaints concerning the detrimental effect that overseas players were having on the county game became commonplace within the cricket establishment. This debate took a sinister turn when an article by Robert Henderson entitled 'Is it in the blood?' was published in *Wisden Cricket Monthly* (Henderson 1995). Henderson called for 'unequivocal Englishmen' to replace 'Negroes' and other 'foreigners' in the England team because they supposedly lacked commitment to the national cause (Carrington 1998: 102). Outside the game, the Conservative politician Norman Tebbit launched a bitter attack on Britain's minority communities by suggesting that because they did not support the England cricket team, they were disloyal to the country they lived in. In what became dubbed as the 'cricket test', Tebbit demanded to know 'which side do they cheer for?' when England played against the West Indies, India or Pakistan.

The Tebbit test and Henderson's article were met with universal condemnation. However, the cricket authorities' response was far less damning. By failing to challenge Tebbit's claims, the cricket establishment appeared not only to tolerate the use of cricket as a measure of national inclusion, but to sanction it (Marqusee 1998: 160–1). Henderson's attack on the inclusion of black players in the England cricket team caused more of an outcry, but a report from the *Independent* (1994) shows he was not alone in his views:

> What made it additionally pleasing was that England's attack did not for once look like a United Nations strike force. Not since the Old Trafford Test of 1989 . . . have England fielded five bowlers with undiluted allegiance to the country that they were representing.
>
> (quoted in Marqusee 1998)

In response to allegations of discrimination within English cricket, many were keen to point out that racism was simply 'not cricket'. By portraying Henderson's article as merely an aberration against the inclusive nature of cricket, rather than recognising it as the most obvious of a number of serious racist incidents in this period, the cricket authorities not only were failing to acknowledge the existence of racism, but showed themselves unwilling to challenge and eradicate it from the game. As Marqusee argues,

> When it comes to racism, English cricket's real problem is its culture of complacency and denial, which expresses itself in a knee-jerk defensiveness

Inner-city London and cricket development 237

whenever the touchy topic rears its ugly head. The burden of the case against the cricket establishment and cricket media is not that they are racist but that they are unable or unwilling to recognise the reality of racism and the problems it poses for the game.

(1998: 314–15)

The two cultures of English cricket

The failure to acknowledge and challenge racism in cricket became more evident during 1998–9, when a number of significant events elevated to a national level the debate surrounding the place of black and Asian people in English cricket. In 1998, Roehampton Institute was commissioned to research black and Asian cricket in Essex (McDonald and Ugra 1998: 1). Previously, a programme broadcast on the BBC entitled *The Race Game* (BBC 1991) highlighted that while there was an abundance of black and Asian talent playing in local leagues in Yorkshire, no British Asian had played for Yorkshire County Cricket Club or been invited to join the county's youth development scheme. The programme argued that by following this policy the county was not only completely neglecting a major constituency of potential players, but also implementing a development system that was 'little short of apartheid' (Kew 1997: 104). The Roehampton report concluded that these concerns of exclusion were not unfounded. *Anyone for Cricket* claimed that a similar emergence of black and Asian clubs and leagues had evolved in Essex and east London (McDonald and Ugra 1998), as a result of the hostility encountered by black and Asian cricketers when they tried to join local clubs or leagues.

The authors of the report, Ian McDonald and Sharda Ugra, identified the existence of 'two distinct but related cultures of cricket, defined by ethnicity'. One is mainly African-Caribbean and Asian, urban, and confined to sub-standard council pitches with limited resources, and it exists outside the official structure. The other is white, rural and endowed with well-kept private facilities, and competes within the official ECB structure (McDonald and Ugra 1998: 41, Marqusee 1998: 316).

The report argues that despite their exclusion from the mainstream, there is an 'overwhelming desire among black and Asian teams to become integrated into the official structures of the game' (McDonald and Ugra 1998: 55). However, black and Asian teams' applications were often rejected because they failed to meet the league requirements of owning their own ground. It was also claimed that the mainstream leagues hide behind league regulations and cultural stereotypes to prevent the admission of black and Asian teams into the official leagues. White clubs did not want to play Asian teams because they viewed the 'overtly competitive' and 'highly vocal' way that Asian teams play their cricket as denigrating the importance of etiquette as a prominent value in 'English' cricket. Club secretaries also complained that few white teams would play Asian teams, because they failed to uphold the tradition of the post-match drink (McDonald and Ugra 1998: 41), and bar takings would be low.

238 *Nick Miller*

The fact that cricket leagues have developed separately over the years has occurred partly because of prejudice on both sides, but also because of different attitudes towards cricket on and off the field. For predominantly white clubs, the social aspect of cricket such as playing etiquette and post-match drinking are part and parcel of the game, while Asian players place more importance on cricket as a competitive sporting experience (McDonald and Ugra 1998: 14). There is also a belief among Asian players and supporters that the English way of playing cricket is boring. The emphasis on 'textbook' coaching tends to stifle the natural talent of players, and white teams are accused of adopting a negative approach to playing matches.

However, as McDonald and Ugra (1998) argue, this relationship is not equal, because the official structures of the cricket establishment – the affiliated clubs, the counties and ultimately the ECB – have the power to effect the integration or the continued exclusion of black and Asian teams. In comparison to the white majority, the black and Asian communities remain relatively poor and powerless (Hit Racism for Six 1999). As the dominant group within this relationship, the predominantly white cricket establishment have been able to use this power to structure cricket in their preferred ways. This has enabled them to institutionalise these practices and meanings to define what cricket is or what it should be like within social formations (Jarvie 1991: 5). Through this process, the traditional white 'English' way of staging cricket becomes the norm to which the predominantly black and Asian players need to adapt in order to become integrated (McDonald and Ugra 1998: 14).

The response of the ECB to the findings of *Anyone for Cricket* remained one of denial and defensiveness. However, in 1999, Matthew Engel's editorial in the influential *Wisden Cricketers' Almanack* took up the findings and claimed that a form of racial segregation was affecting the game in England. He wrote:

> In an informal, unspoken, very English way, cricketing apartheid has become an accepted practice in England. . . . I know of nothing that constitutes active racial discrimination in English recreational cricket. But there is a great deal of what could be called passive discrimination, a refusal to go an extra inch and welcome outsiders into a club's often clannish atmosphere. . . .
>
> It has become normal for ethnic-minority players to gravitate towards their own clubs, and there is now clear-cut evidence of segregation operating, informally, in both Yorkshire and Essex . . . the effect is that black and Asian players are operating outside the official structure. They have become second-class in all kinds of little ways.
>
> (Engel 1999: 14–15)

Therefore, while 'the culture of 'English cricket' may not be explicitly racist, the Englishness of the official game becomes a means of racial exclusion, racial stereotyping and, to a lesser extent, racial abuse of black and Asian players (McDonald and Ugra 1998: 55). As Engel insists, the removal of these barriers was not simply a moral issue, but imperative to the development of the game.

Inner-city London and cricket development 239

'English cricket should now be reaping great benefit from the generation born here of parents who came to Britain in the great wave of post-war migration from the subcontinent and the Caribbean.' By playing cricket outside the official structure of the game, they are denied the opportunities available to their white counterparts to progress in the county and international game. This inequality is borne out by Abbasi (1999), who in an article on *The Week* Internet page pointed out that in 1999 the England captain, Nasser Hussain, was one of only 24 British Asians registered as players with county clubs.

Engel's intervention represented a considerable development in the campaign against racism in cricket; furthermore, his comments took on more significant meaning during the Cricket World Cup held in Britain later that year.

The carnival of cricket

The ECB hoped that the Cricket World Cup in 1999 would provide a spectacle that would increase the profile of cricket, particularly among young people, in Britain. It was believed that this impact relied heavily on the England team performing well. However, while England's elimination in the first round seriously dented these expectations, supporters from Britain's ethnic minority communities effectively hijacked the 'carnival of cricket' (Crabbe and Wagg 2000: 86) and turned it into a hugely enjoyable and successful event. British-based Asian supporters of Pakistan, India, Sri Lanka and Bangladesh turned out in force to cheer on their teams. The fact that these fans were not supporting England and happily failed the Tebbit test (Chaudhary 1999) was irrelevant, and many commentators in the media, the government and influential figures within cricket finally identified this enthusiasm as representing a huge potential for the regeneration of cricket in Britain.

As Crabbe and Wagg (2000: 86) argue, the World Cup demonstrated how the future of the game is intimately intertwined with the black and Asian communities. Simon Barnes (2000) reflected the prevalent opinion by arguing in *The Times* that 'the future of English cricket is all tied up with the English people of subcontinental extraction'. The debate also exposed *Anyone for Cricket?*'s findings, that cricket played by ethnic groups was poorly resourced and often existed outside the official structure. In the light of this, the ECB came under increasing pressure to confront these inequalities. Simon Hughes wrote in the *Daily Telegraph* that young Asians in particular 'do not have to be led kicking and screaming to play cricket' and should be offered massive encouragement by the authorities to make up for the 'gross neglect of the past' (1999). Christopher Martin-Jenkins, also writing in *The Times*, argued:

> The challenge to the ECB is to invest as much as possible, as soon as possible in the lower reaches of the game to catch all the youngsters who have been inspired by the glamour of the World Cup. Without doubt the supporters of the subcontinental teams have contributed greatly to the fun of this World Cup.

240   *Nick Miller*

Their exuberance, occasionally a little unbridled, has underlined the need to do more, especially in the provision of facilities to encourage the abundant South Asian enthusiasm for cricket. . . . That is truly the challenge for the ECB, Local Authorities and the government.

(1999)

New Labour, social inclusion and institutionalised racism

In addition to raising the consciousness of the media, the interest generated by World Cup had a significant impact on the Labour government's perspective of cricket. The Sports Minister, Tony Banks, stated that 'one of the lessons that we must learn from the World Cup was the enormous fervour and enthusiasm for cricket among our Asian communities'. He went on to say that 'English cricket could be transformed by the greater involvement of the ethnic communities' and that he would be meeting with the ECB to discuss new initiatives to 'combat the evil of racism within the sport' (Schaefer 1999). The World Cup demonstrated to the government that, rather than being a relic of old England and Englishness, cricket was in fact the one sport all the main minority communities have a presence in (McDonald and Ugra 1999). As such, cricket represented a sport through which New Labour could focus its commitment to tackling the issues of sport and social exclusion.

During this period the government was drafting a strategy for sport that would represent a radical change in the relationship between government and national governing bodies of sport. *A Sporting Future for All* stated that 'sport can make a unique contribution to tackling social exclusion in our society' (Department of Culture, Media and Sport 2000: 39) and funding will only be devolved to governing bodies of sport that 'commit themselves to putting inclusion and fairness at the heart of everything they do' (ibid.: 20).

Therefore, the ECB was acutely aware that unless it improved opportunities for areas of deprivation, ethnic minorities, women and disabled people to lead, coach and participate in cricket activities, it would receive a reduction in funding from both the government and the National Lottery. The incentive of extra funding clearly influenced the ECB's decision to adopt more inclusive policies.

A further factor that cannot be overlooked is that the debate surrounding the marginalisation of black and Asian teams from the official structure of English cricket emerged at the same time as the Macpherson Report, published in 1999. The inquiry into the handling of the racist murder of the black teenager Stephen Lawrence accused the Metropolitan Police of 'institutionalised racism', and called for 'every institution to examine their policies and practices to guard against disadvantaging any section of their communities' (Macpherson Report 1999). The fact that the *Clean Bowl Racism* survey concluded that 58 per cent of respondents believed that racism existed in English cricket certainly generated fears that the ECB would also be perceived as being institutionally racist. Although only 12 per cent of these thought racism was ingrained (ECB Racism Study Group 1999a: 44), it was obvious that the ECB could not afford to appear complacent.

Inner-city London and cricket development   241

Therefore, the publication of the *Clean Bowl Racism* report on racial equality in cricket can be seen as a direct response to the challenges made to the ECB in the media and political sphere. The document voices a commitment to implement an anti-racist programme at all levels in the playing structure of the game. In addition to introducing codes of conduct prohibiting racist abuse in clubs, staff training on equity and cultural diversity, and an anti-racist publicity campaign, the report also required the county cricket boards to give high priority to including schemes and programmes that incorporated ethnic minority cricket into their development plans. In order 'to illustrate cricket's determination to ensure ethnic minorities have equality of opportunity' (ECB Racism Study Group 1999a), the publication of the report coincided with the launch of the ECB's Inner City Community Cricket Project in October 1999. The fact that the new Sports Minister, Kate Hoey, launched the initiative reflected the political significance of the whole process.

However, while, as David Hopps commented in the *Guardian* (1999), the report signifies a 'belated recognition that English cricket urgently needed to address racial inequality', many other commentators remained sceptical. Simon Hughes in the *Telegraph* (1999) maintained that the sum of £30,000, earmarked for each inner-city project over a three-year period, would 'not even scratch the surface' of the investment needed in areas such as London. Therefore, despite the publication of *Clean Bowl Racism*, questions remain as to whether the ECB is genuinely committed to increasing the involvement of black and Asian people in the game. Was it merely rhetoric in the face of severe criticism? The following case study of Middlesex Cricket Board's development programme and events within cricket since its publication will attempt to answer these questions.

The Middlesex Cricket Board

The Middlesex Cricket Board (MCB) is one of 38 county boards responsible for the development of cricket activities within their county boundaries. The funding for grass-roots development work is distributed by the ECB through its charitable arm, the Cricket Foundation. Each year for the four years 1999–2003, approximately £2½ million was divided between all the county boards for local development purposes (ECB 2000). The MCB is responsible for the development of cricket in the suburbs of Middlesex (on the outskirts of London) and a number of inner-city London boroughs. The development work carried out by the MCB includes a schools programme, a programme for women's and girl's cricket, club development and junior county squad training. However, recently the MCB has become involved with a number of inner-city cricket development projects that include Victoria Park Junior Cricket Club in Hackney and Stoke Newington Cricket School. These projects have been promoted in the media as an example of the ECB's commitment to 'provide more opportunities for black and Asian children from London's inner city area to play cricket' (*BBC News Online* 1999). The aim of this case study is to examine these projects and to analyse whether they represent a realistic change in the culture of cricket within the governing body.

242 Nick Miller

Victoria Park Junior Cricket Club

The most highly publicised initiative is a joint project involving the Middlesex Cricket Board and Tower Hamlets and Hackney councils, which have worked in partnership to create a new junior cricket club at Victoria Park in east London. Hackney had been identified as 'a wasteland for cricket', with no cricket pitch or club with a junior section in the borough. Despite the lack of opportunities to play, cricket was becoming increasingly popular in local schools as a result of the successful work of the London Schools Cricket Project and the Middlesex Cricket Board. Both organisations provided coaching courses that introduced cricket into the curriculum. However, the lack of facilities remained a serious barrier to the development of the game.

A working party was formed involving representatives from the MCB, Hackney Sports Development and the London Schools Cricket Project to establish a junior cricket club in Victoria Park. The project was funded by sponsorship money from Yellow Pages and enabled the MCB to run a programme of coaching sessions at the park and paid for some new cricket equipment. The high-profile cricketers Mark Ramprakash and Angus Fraser were recruited to launch the club, and the ex-England and Middlesex captain Mike Gatting was appointed as its president. The club has been a great success in its four-year existence. As one of the coaches explained,

> The sessions attracted a great number of children aged seven to thirteen years old and from a wide range of ethnic backgrounds. We had white kids, black kids and a lot of the local Bangladeshi boys came regularly. At present there are about one hundred young people registered to our club.

When asked about the future of the club, the coach was less positive. He said the initial aim of the project had been to create a successful children's cricket programme that in time would be incorporated into an established senior club as its junior section. Unfortunately, this had proved difficult because of the lack of established clubs in the area. A more significant concern for the project is that the Yellow Pages funding reduced each year, and while the club still gets some financial support from the MCB, the project has been forced to apply for a grant from the National Lottery in order to continue the coaching programme.

Stoke Newington Cricket School

The Stoke Newington Cricket School (SNCS) was founded in 1998 and provides opportunities for young people to gain cricket coaching in the local area. The project started in a school, but owing to its popularity moved to nearby Clissold Park, where the sessions took place on the tarmac tennis courts. The cricket school now boasts a regular attendance of 60 young people and plays its matches on a synthetic Flicks cricket pitch that can be laid down on any area of grass or concrete. The cricket school has generated enormous interest in Stoke

Newington, and its organiser, David Blundell, maintains that it could 'double the numbers attending each week' if it had more qualified coaches. With MCB support the school has recently run a coaching course for Hackney-based cricket leaders, which will enable the SNCS to expand its provision of cricket sessions into a number of local schools.

When asked about the support the SNCS receives from local governing body, Blundell replied that the MCB had provided

> quite a lot of money in kind. They gave us £250 to install indoor nets at the school, they supplied us some kit and the Flicks pitch. Yellow Pages paid for the places on the coaching course. They are in touch and contactable and have been good on that score. However, they invested a great amount of money into the cricket development at Victoria Park at about the same time as we were starting here, so to some extent we have missed out. Victoria Park is a top-down model, in the sense that all the money has come from the MCB, they employ the coaches and recruited the kids, whereas we are local people who want to play and develop cricket. We have been successful in gaining money from the lottery and private sponsors, which gives us a certain amount of autonomy. We are not an MCB project. We are grassroots.

As Blundell highlights, the cricket development in Stoke Newington provides an interesting contrast with the MCB in Victoria Park. It is clear that much of the success of the Hackney project can be attributed to the short-term funding provided by Yellow Pages. The injection of this money increased the cricket activities available to young people living in these targeted inner-city areas. But although it has generated a great deal of interest among young people, there was little ongoing support from the MCB to ensure that this provision of cricket was sustained when the funding had finished. However, as Blundell points out, funding alone is not enough:

> There are distinct ways in which the County Boards can and to some extent do provide, but it needs to be coupled with consultation to find out what we need – like a decent pitch, equipment and qualified coaches rather than throwing money at things that are inappropriate. By having a greater sense of what is required at grassroots level, they could use the money more productively . . . the MCB should coordinate a network and structure to support what local people are doing rather than providing top-down development.

In order to capitalise on the good work and enthusiasm created through the projects funded by Yellow Pages, the MCB needs to establish a coordinated structure for the development of cricket that includes the inner-city areas within its boundaries. Of course funding will be an issue, but, as the local governing body, it should be building on the excellent work of the London Schools Cricket Project and ensuring that a framework exists for young people to continue their

244 *Nick Miller*

cricket outside school. This does not mean the MCB should deliver the cricketing opportunities itself, but it should provide the resources and expertise to enable local people who know the area, the schools and young people and have 'a deep-rooted love for the game, to get on with the development' (interview with David Blundell, 2000). By adopting this more strategic approach, rather than what Blundell refers to as the *noblesse oblige* nature of support, the MCB will demonstrate its commitment to regenerating grass-roots cricket in the inner cities. However, a failure to do so will raise questions over whether the Yellow Pages-sponsored projects represented little more than a philanthropic public relations exercise in response to a political climate demanding a more inclusive approach.

The future

Unfortunately in this context, since September 2000 the MCB has focused its work on developing womens' and girls' cricket, competitive opportunities for schools, and county junior squads. When asked why the inner-city projects were not included, the MCB explained that the money available from the Cricket Foundation was limited and much of Middlesex's allocation had been committed to employing a women and girls' cricket development officer. Therefore, without the Yellow Pages money the MCB was seeking other sources of funding to build on the work initiated at Victoria Park. So, while the ECB stated its commitment to developing the integration of ethnic minority teams into cricket structures, no extra funding was made available to the county boards to finance this work. In fact, the money granted to the MCB in 2000 had only increased by £1,000 (MCB 2000) from the previous year.

The failure to increase the money available to county boards cast a serious doubt over the ECB's commitment to develop the game at the grass-roots level. As Marqusee (1998: 327) argues, despite the ECB's 'grandiose plans for restructuring recreational cricket', there remains a huge discrepancy between money allocated to each first-class county club and the sum available to recreational cricket through the county boards. Two and a half million pounds from the Cricket Foundation is not a lot of money to be split between 38 counties. For Marqusee (1998: 325–7), what is desperately needed to revive the game in urban areas is 'a massive, carefully planned and democratically controlled injection of resources'. However, it seems that this radical economic redistribution of ECB funds is not forthcoming despite the claims of *Clean Bowl Racism*.

The research demonstrates that individuals within the MCB are committed to developing the game in inner-city areas. However, they have to focus on ECB objectives, which view such work as an area of low priority. This makes it difficult for these individuals to effect change, and explains why 'the help comes in little bits rather than part of any framework of development' (interview with David Blundell, 2000). The injection of money from Yellow Pages enabled the MCB to provide equipment and funding in Hackney and Stoke Newington, but the failure to take a strategic approach to these developments meant that it achieved a mixed level of success. This, coupled with the lack of plans or provision to sustain the

Inner-city London and cricket development 245

projects once the funding had run out, raises the question of whether the work would have been undertaken at all without Yellow Pages backing.

The inner city and ethnic minorities

The Victoria Park project was heralded in the media as being 'designed to provide more opportunities for black and Asian children from London's inner city areas to play cricket' (BBC News Online 1999) and as such demonstrated the ECB's commitment to combat racism. However, it was evident from the research that no special considerations were made to encourage specific ethnic groups to attend the sessions. The high concentration of ethnic minorities living in Hackney meant the projects attracted young people from a diverse range of ethnic and cultural backgrounds, but this in itself does not constitute an attempt to tackle racism. What is concerning is that portraying inner-city developments as being anti-racist has become prevalent in the rhetoric surrounding the *Clean Bowl Racism* campaign. In the report (ECB Racism Study Group 1999a: 50) it is recommended that 'ethnic minority/inner city cricket will be given a higher priority than has hitherto been the case in the relevant County Board Development Plans'.

By promoting the notion of the development of cricket in urban areas as being synonymous with tackling issues of race, the ECB is simply reconstructing old myths that portray the inner cities as black, urban cricketing wastelands. As David Blundell (interview, 2000) from the Stoke Newington Cricket School argues,

> It is all too easy to point to us and say it is an inner-city project and therefore it has these characteristics and that is why we [the MCB] support it. . . . That sort of labelling bothers me. The fact that Stoke Newington is seen as an extraordinary place to develop cricket reflects quite a lot about what their ideological assumptions are about where cricket is normal, which to them is suburban.

The danger of such an approach is that by limiting its actions to delivering urban cricket projects, the MCB is doing little to remove the cultural barriers that marginalise black and Asian players from the official structures of the game. In the *Clean Bowl Racism* report the ECB stated that county boards must 'encourage ethnic minority clubs and leagues to become an integral part of the cricket family by embracing and accepting diverse cultures'. However, there is little evidence to suggest that this has been undertaken. The representative interviewed for the case study stated that the MCB encouraged Asian teams to affiliate to Middlesex Cricket Board, but 'they appear to not want to join'. When it was suggested that this viewpoint contradicted the findings of the report, the representative argued that

> *Clean Bowl Racism* did not find cricketers or officials to be overtly racist; the main issue was the lack of cricket facilities. The problem for Asian and West

246 *Nick Miller*

Indian clubs is that, being more recently formed, they were unable to find facilities; they had been snapped up by more established clubs. In fact new teams entirely of white players would face exactly the same problems.

(interview with Richard Davis)

This shows that despite the findings of the *Anyone for Cricket* report and the subsequent proposals made by the ECB's Racism Study Group, the 'culture of complacency and denial' referred to by Marqusee remains deeply ingrained in the standpoint of the English cricket establishment. Its continuing to point to the lack of facilities and a stereotypical belief that black and Asian cricketers prefer 'to keep themselves to themselves' shows that little progress has been made to unite the cultural divisions in English cricket.

In June 2002, Jonathan Rendall (*Observer Sport Monthly*) confirmed the continued segregation between Asian and white teams in Yorkshire. Mount Cricket Club successfully runs five Asian teams and has eighty-seven players on its books, but still has no ground of its own. The club plays matches on a council-owned pitch so dangerous that two players have lost eyes through injuries. Mount's secretary confirms that they play their cricket outside the official structures of the game and will continue to do so as long as 'white middle-class people' run the leagues. Despite the lack of facilities, they still manage to produce a large number of talented cricketers. Unfortunately, this has not been rewarded by Yorkshire County Cricket Club. Rendall (2002) points out that although Sachin Tendulkar was Yorkshire's overseas player during the 1990s, only one home-bred Asian player has 'made it through the gates of Headingley as a first-class player'. According to the Asian players interviewed, 'Yorkshire was a closed shop for Asians'; one says that it is 'a very, very racist club'.

These allegations were disputed by Yorkshire Cricket Board's chief executive, Chris Hassell, who stated that Yorkshire had taken positive steps to address the situation by appointing a cricket development officer with a specific responsibility for black and ethnic issues. However, as Tom Moody in the *Observer* (2003) argues, successful role models at the top will be far more effective than well-meaning initiatives devised by the ECB. Moody's county, Worcestershire, has made positive steps to 'encourage the unquenchable thirst for cricket among British Asians' (ibid.) and developed a direct route to talented cricketers by strengthening its links with the nearby Asian community. This policy is already reaping rewards as Worcester have several English Asians on their books, including Vikram Solanki and Kabir Ali, recently elevated to the England one-day squad. Moody says that 'we are not alone' in this development: Nottinghamshire has three Asian cricketers who toured Australia in 2002 with the England Under-19 squad. They included the captain, Bilal Shafayat, who originally played for West Indian Cavaliers, made his first-class debut at the age of 16 and is tipped by many to be the future star of English cricket (Mitchell 2003).

However, while the future looks more promising for British Asians, there still remains an element of distrust among sections of the Asian community, who insist it is 'only getting better because young whites are no longer interested in cricket'

Inner-city London and cricket development 247

(Rendall 2002). It is also interesting to note that the squad representing England in the World Cup in 2003 included only one black player, the captain, Nasser Hussain.

Unfortunately, few Asians see Hussain as a positive role model. During a radio interview, when asked if his appointment as England captain would inspire other Asian cricketers to play for England, he replied that all that mattered to him was 'the three lions on his chest' (Chaudhary 2001). Then, as young Asians battled with police and the National Front in Oldham and Aylesbury during the summer of 2001, Hussain asked why British Asians continued to support cricket teams from the Indian subcontinent rather than England. Referring to a recent match against Pakistan, he complained, 'It was depressing to see a sea of green Pakistani shirts at Old Trafford.' Vivek Chaudhary, writing in the *Guardian* (2001), argued that these comments demonstrated that Hussain had 'spent too long being pampered by the cricket establishment and become disconnected from the experience of ordinary Asians in Britain'. For Chaudhary, Hussain's reign as England's captain was a wasted opportunity to reach out to Asians and get them involved in the cricket establishment; rather than inspiring the cricket-mad youngsters, his comments alienated them further.

However, while it is evident that many British Asians support teams from the subcontinent as a means to express their alienation from mainstream society, the suggestion that this represents a disloyalty to Britain remains unfounded. As Chaudhary (2001) argues, in a multicultural society like Britain, people have shifting loyalties and identities. The same Asians who supported Pakistan happily cheered on the English football team in the World Cup at the same time (Aldred 2002). He goes on to maintain that supporting Pakistan or India is not only a reaffirmation of their cultural heritage; it is also fun. 'Watching and playing cricket the subcontinent way is uplifting and inspiring. The English way is pretty dull' (Chaudhary 2001).

In conclusion

The existence of two distinct cultures within English cricket, identified earlier, remains fundamental to the debate surrounding the place of black and Asian cricketers. Despite the ECB's publication of *Clean Bowl Racism* and commitment to combat racism, it is evident how the symbolic meanings attached to English cricket and Englishness continue to exclude many of Britain's ethnic communities from cricket. The promotion of the inner-city projects discussed in the MCB case study, as examples of tackling discrimination, appear to be the only concession made in this process. The assumption that because these projects were based in urban areas highly populated by Britain's ethnic communities the ECB was demonstrating its commitment to fight racism confirms how deeply ingrained within the cricket establishment the notion of cricket as a predominantly rural, white sport played out on the village green remains.

As Marqusee (1998) argues, 'cricket is not the property of any one race or culture, it belongs to everyone with an interest in the game'. Therefore, the search

248 *Nick Miller*

for a homogeneous culture or unchanging national identity in modern Britain is both futile and dangerous. For while young Asians' heroes are Sachin Tendulkar or Shoaib Ahktar rather than Michael Vaughan or Darren Gough, what better role models are there? Rather than questioning this, the ECB, the media and Hussain himself should embrace the Asians' love of cricket and take steps to integrate Britain's black and Asian communities fully into the game. This can only be achieved by a real commitment from the ECB to remove the cultural barriers and inequalities in English cricket, rather than the knee-jerk reaction to intense criticism evident in the *Clean Bowl Racism* campaign.

Bibliography

Books

Anderson, B. (1991) *Imagined Communities: Reflections on the Origins and Spread of Nationalism*, rev. edn, London: Verso.

Barker, M. (1981) *The New Racism: Conservatives and the Ideology of the Tribe*, London: Junction Books.

Birley, D. (1999) *A Social History of English Cricket*, London: Aurum Press.

Carrington, B. (1998) '"Football's coming home" but whose home? And do we want it? Nation, football, and the politics of exclusion', in A. Brown (ed.) *Fanatics: Power, Identity and Fandom in Football*, London: Routledge.

Crabbe, T. and Wagg, S. (2000) 'A carnival of cricket? The Cricket World Cup, 'race' and the politics of Carnival', *Culture, Sport, Society*, 3 (2) (Summer): 70–88.

Engel, M. (ed.) (1999) *Wisden Cricketers' Almanack*, Guildford, UK: Wisden.

Gilroy, P. (1987) *'There Ain't No Black in the Union Jack'*: *The Cultural Politics of Race and Nation*, London: Unwin Hyman.

Gilroy, P. (1992) 'The end of anti-racism', in J. Donald and A. Rattansi (eds) *Race, Culture and Difference*, London: Sage.

Gilroy, P. (1993) *Small Acts: Thoughts on the Politics of Black Culture*, London: Serpent's Tail.

Jarvie, G. (1991) 'Introduction', in G. Jarvie (ed.) *Sport, Racism and Ethnicity*, London: Falmer Press.

Jarvie, G. and Maguire, J. (1994) *Sport and Leisure in Social Thought*, London: Routledge.

Kew, F. (1997) *Sport: Social Problems and Issues*, Oxford: Butterworth-Heinemann.

McLellen, A. (1994) *The Enemy Within: The Impact of Overseas players on English Cricket*, London: Blandford.

Maguire, J. (1999) *Global Sport: Identities, Societies, Civilizations*, Cambridge: Polity Press.

Marqusee, M. (1998) *Anyone but England: Cricket, Race and Class*, London: Two Heads Publishing.

Moorehouse, G. (1979) *The Best Loved Game*, London: Michael Joseph.

Oslear, D. and Bannister, J. (1996) *Tampering with Cricket*, London: Collins, Willow.

Werbner, P. (1996) '"Our blood is green": cricket, identity and social empowerment among British Pakistanis', in J. MacClancey (ed.) *Sport, Identity and Ethnicity*, Oxford: Berg.

Williams, J. (1999) *Cricket and England: A Cultural and Social History of the Inter-war Years*, London: Frank Cass.

Reports/strategies/research papers

Department of Culture, Media and Sport (1999) *Policy Action Team 10, Research Report: Sport and Social Exclusion*, London: DMCS.

Department of Culture, Media and Sport (2000) *A Sporting Future for All*, London: DMCS.

Department of National Heritage (1995) *Sport: Raising the Game*, London: DNH.

ECB (2000) *The ECB Cricket Report 1999/2000*, London: ECB.

ECB Racism Study Group (1999a) *Clean Bowl Racism: Going Forward Together: A Report on Racial Equality in Cricket*, London: ECB.

ECB Racism Study Group (1999b) *Clean Bowl Racism: Going Forward Together: Action Plans for Racial Equality in Cricket*, London: ECB.

McDonald, I. and Ugra, S (1998) *Anyone for Cricket? Equal Opportunities and Changing Cricket Cultures in Essex and East London*, a report commissioned by Essex Cricket Association and London Community Cricket Association, London: University of East London.

Macpherson, W. (1999) *The Stephen Lawrence Inquiry: Report of an Inquiry by Sir William Macpherson of Cluny*, Cm 4262-1, London: The Stationery Office.

MCB (2000) *Middlesex Cricket Board Youth and Coaching Income and Expenditure Account 30/900*, London: MCB.

Sport England (2000) *Active Sports Development Framework for Cricket*, London: Sport England.

Newspapers/magazines

Aldred, T. (2002) 'Nationality is a thing of the past', *Guardian*, 21 June.

Barnes, S. (2000) 'The day when a national joke lost its punchline', *The Times*, 5 September.

Chaudhary, V. (1999) 'The test cricket fans are happy to fail', *Guardian*, 10 May.

Chaudhary, V. (2001) 'A question of support', *Guardian*, 29 May.

Engel, M. (2000) 'Now cricket's come home after 31 years', *Guardian*, 5 September.

Henderson, R. (1995) 'Is it in the blood?' in *Wisden Cricket Monthly*, July.

Hopps, D. (1999) 'Lord's declares war on racism', *Guardian*, 17 November.

Martin-Jenkins, C. (1999) 'England's failure tests game', *The Times*, 20 June.

Martin-Jenkins, C. (2000) 'Oval glory shapes England's future', *The Times*, 5 September.

Mitchell, K. (2003) 'Prince Billy', *Observer*, 19 January.

Moody, T. (2003) 'Potential gold mine to be tapped', *Observer*, 8 December.

Rendall, J. (2002) 'Some corner of a foreign field', *Observer Sport Monthly*, June.

Revell, P. (1999) 'Where racism just isn't cricket', *Guardian*, 25 May.

Schaefer, S. (1999) 'Hit racism for six, says Banks', *Independent*, 29 June.

Steen, R. (1999) 'Wisden editor declares racism is just not cricket', *Guardian*, 1 April.

Internet

Abbasi, K. (1999), ' The Asian flavour: English cricket seems to be ready to hit racism for six, but will it revive its fortunes', *The Week*, 19 September.

BBC News Online: Sport: Cricket (1999) 'Apartheid holding back cricket', *BBC News Online*, 1 April.

CricInfo (1999) 'Cricket's "Bible" Hits out at Racial Bias', *Cricinfo*, 1 April.

250 *Nick Miller*

DCMS (2000) 'Kate Hoey opens inner city cricket scheme to attract players of the future', *DCMS Web Site*, 18 October.

Deeley, P. (1999) 'Hussain hurt by chorus of boos', *Electronic Telegraph*, 23 August.

ECB web page (2000) 'Channel Four – investing in the future', *ECB Web Page*, 4 July.

Hit Racism for Six (1999) 'submission to ECB Racism study group', *HR46 website*, 29 August.

Hughes, S. (1999) 'Ethnic minorities in search of a level playing field', *Electronic Telegraph*, 28 August.

Marqusee, M. (1998) 'Two cultures of English cricket', *HR46 website*, June/July.

Television

BBC 1 (1991) *The Race Game*, quoted in F. Kew (1997) *Sport: Social Problems and Issues*, Oxford: Butterworth-Heinemann. 1991

Interviews

David Blundell   –   (SNCS)
Richard Davis   –   (ECB)
David Holland   –   (MCB)

13 The ambush clause

Globalisation, corporate power and the governance of world cricket

Mike Marqusee

Long before it was a global game, cricket was an imperial game. At least, that was how it was seen by the rulers of the British Empire, in Whitehall and at Lord's. Their subjects sometimes saw it differently, playing cricket often in spite rather than because of its imperial origins, as a means of claiming space within the Empire or challenging it from without. When the anti-colonial movements ended British rule, they also initiated the slow collapse of the structures and assumptions on which world cricket was based (this process was completed only in the early 1990s, with the downfall of the apartheid regime in South Africa). Cricket itself remained, however, and in some regions, notably South Asia, acquired ever-greater popularity. After an exceedingly slow start, the governors of world cricket raced to catch up with the new postcolonial reality. But by the time they did so (again, only in the mid-1990s), they found themselves plunged into a neo-liberal world flux characterised by corporate power, extreme inequality among nations and the dominant sway of the United States. Among the latter's many cultural peculiarities was a reluctance to worship at the shrine of cricket. Cricket's institutions and traditions, inherited from the imperial era, have nearly buckled under the strain.

A spectre haunting cricket: Rupert Murdoch and the Cricket World Cup of 2003

Most cricket fans will not have heard of it, but there is indeed an entity called the Global Cricket Corporation (GCC). It's a name that says so little and yet so much. Bland and nondescript, yet bristling with hubris. Corporate self-aggrandisement at its most egregious. It is nonetheless an apt description.

GCC is a small slice of News Corporation, Rupert Murdoch's global media–entertainment conglomerate. In 2003, News Corporation boasted total assets of $43 billion and annual revenue of $17 billion (Jamaica's GDP, by comparison, is $10 billion). Among its liabilities is a guarantee to pay the International Cricket Council (ICC) a minimum of $550 million over five years in return for global broadcasting and marketing rights for the World Cups of 2003 and 2007 (and other ICC events).[1]

252   Mike Marqusee

This is hardly an onerous guarantee for News Corp, and not only because of Murdoch's vast and diverse assets. Already most of it has been recouped through the sale of South Asian television rights to Sony. What's more, built into the contract are clauses that protect the Murdoch empire from many of the vicissitudes that afflict the game.

'Apparently two factors went in favour' of the Murdoch bid, reported cricket commentator Harsha Bhogle. 'One of them was a fascinating qualitative factor – the commitment to build the ICC as a brand . . . to nurture it, to look after it and protect it like you would a child.' The second factor arose from what Bhogle called 'a brown–white split' in world cricket. The rival bid from Indian-based Zee was rejected, despite being almost $100 million higher than Murdoch's, in what Bhogle described as 'an obvious move by a power bloc to counter the Asian administrative offensive'.[2]

Though Murdoch will eye the fortunes of 20th Century Fox, Fox News, the *Sun* and other major News Corp holdings with greater interest than the ups and downs of the ICC, cricket is nonetheless an integral part of his corporate strategy. Sport, he has famously declared, is a 'battering ram' with which to secure entry into new markets. And cricket has already given Murdoch a valuable foothold in millions of Indian homes. It is also a contributor to the corporate 'synergy' through which Murdoch's various assets enhance each other. The ICC deal gives any Murdoch subsidiary or affiliate 'first right of refusal and the last right to match' any bid for the broadcast rights in any particular territory. So even where Murdoch's broadcasting arms – in South Asia, Australia, New Zealand, the United Kingdom or North America – lose the bidding war, their very presence ensures that there will be a battle for the rights – to GCC's advantage. In the World Cup of 2003 the exception was the United Kingdom – where the rights were left to Murdoch's Sky because neither the BBC nor Channel Four was interested in making a bid.

Nonetheless, for Murdoch, cricket is an auxiliary investment, one among many; for the ICC, in contrast, the Murdoch deal is make or break. All the Test-playing countries are reliant on the income stream it guarantees – and that has given Murdoch tremendous clout within the world game.

This became apparent in the wake of the 2003 World Cup, when GCC withheld some $15 million in payments owed the ICC. Murdoch's team were claiming compensation for revenues lost as a result of England's refusal to play in Zimbabwe, New Zealand's refusal to play in Kenya, and alleged violations by Indian players of the 'ambush clause'. The latter was designed to protect GCC's exclusive right to sell sponsorships, and, as will become clear, embodied claims and carried implications likely to shape world cricket in the coming years.

Initially, the ICC decided to dock New Zealand $2.5 million, England $3.5 million and India $6.5 million. Though these amounts were later scaled down, the GCC compensation claim was still an onerous one for all concerned. 'Approximately 30 per cent to 35 per cent of our forecast income for the next five years would be lost [if GCC pulled out of the deal] and that would have a huge impact on all aspects of cricket in New Zealand including player payments,' warned New Zealand's cricket manager, Martin Snedden. So although the GCC

Globalisation, corporate power and cricket   253

deal was supposed to free national boards of financial anxieties – and enable them to focus on development – it has introduced a new and over-riding anxiety, one characteristic of an economy globalised from the top down.

Zimbabwe: human rights and double standards

The dependence on Murdoch money weighed heavily in the run-up to England's World Cup boycott of Zimbabwe. 'Sport is a business,' Tim Lamb, the chief executive of the England and Wales Cricket Board (ECB), kept saying. 'We are a company and we have signed contracts for a multi-million pound event. This is not a game of beach cricket.' But under pressure from the media, the government and the players, Lamb and the ECB shifted their position. Now it was 'security' and not finance that was to be the deciding issue. Despite the entreaties of the ECB, the ICC ruled that the venue was safe and the match should proceed. At the insistence of the players, England then unilaterally forfeited the match – along with a possible berth in the Super Six (the World Cup's intermediate round) and several million dollars.

As the debate unfolded, the hypocrisies on all sides defied enumeration. In Britain there were strident demands for a boycott from people who had been equally strident, not so long ago, in denouncing the boycott of apartheid South Africa. The plight of white farmers in Zimbabwe seemed to reawaken old racial alliances: sections of the British media peddled a not very well-disguised appeal to back our white 'kith and kin'. On the other side, there was the surreal spectacle of African National Congress (ANC) politicians solemnly declaring that politics has no place in sport – the same people who once recited the mantra 'no normal sport in an abnormal society'. The Indian government would not allow its team to play in Pakistan – but had no problems with Zimbabwe. The British government railed against Mugabe, but was delighted with General Musharraf's military dictatorship. In the midst of the World Cup, Britain and the United States launched their attack on Iraq. As Imran Khan pointed out, there was a powerful case for a boycott of Britain as an international aggressor and violator of the UN Charter.[3] Because of fear of an al-Qaeda attack, New Zealand refused to play in Kenya – but would they have refused to play in New York?

For the United Kingdom and Australia, Mugabe was a handy Third World bully against whom they could afford to take a moral stand – while continuing to promote the policies and forces that had brought independent Africa to its knees. For the South Asian nations, backing Mugabe carried a hint of anti-imperialist fervour – but one that did not require them to actually challenge the imperial power or the multinational corporations they were trying meanwhile to seduce. Both sides shouted 'hypocrite' at the other and both were right.

Zimbabwe's crisis is rooted in the legacy of empire. The negotiations that led to majority rule left disproportionate economic power – not least land ownership – in the hands of the white minority (as did the later transition in South Africa). In the early years of his reign, Mugabe extolled cricket as a tool with which to build 'a nation of gentlemen'. But cricket never became a mass sport in Zimbabwe

254 Mike Marqusee

and remained associated with the white farmers, who in time became the targets of Mugabe's desperate bid to camouflage his failures with anti-colonial rhetoric.

The fog of double standards and expedient rationales should not obscure some salient facts about Zimbabwe. Mugabe has ruled the country as a corrupt and petty autocrat, and it was his servile compliance with the 'structural adjustment' demands of the IMF that first fuelled mass opposition to his regime. The democratic opposition forces in Zimbabwe – not the white farmers but the Zimbabwe Trade Union Congress, the popularly elected opposition politicians of the Movement for Democratic Change (MDC) and the human rights organisations – called for a boycott of the cricket as part of their call for wider sanctions against the regime. That call should have been respected – by cricketers, corporations and ordinary citizens.

As in the past, the same cricket authorities who speak freely of the spirit of fair play and the virtues of cricket as a nation and character builder hotly denied any ethical or political responsibility. While ready to crack down on a glare of dissent, they permit the game to be used by dictators, demagogues and corporate raiders. In contrast, the England players – and even more, the Zimbabwean dissidents Henry Olonga and Andy Flower – decided in the end to draw a moral demarcation.

The motives and politics of the England players may have been muddled, but they showed greater wariness about how history will judge them than did the ECB or ICC. Like other international cricketers, they struggle with the multiple roles they are expected to play in the modern game. On the one hand, they are 'just cricketers' and their sole mission is 'to win'; on the other, they are 'ambassadors for their country', 'ambassadors for their sport' and, of course, ambassadors for the sponsors. They perform for the population of the host country and at the same time for the folks at home. In a world of warfare, repression and gross economic inequalities, Zimbabwe is likely to pose cricket only one of many dilemmas.

A cancelled sports event always costs money, but it is hard to see why GCC should not bear at least some of the burden. The crisis in Zimbabwe was clearly not of the ICC's making. And the pressure not to play in Zimbabwe came from governments that Murdoch supports – Tony Blair's in the United Kingdom and John Howard's in Australia – and from some of Murdoch's own newspapers. Synergy, it seems, maximises profits and minimises responsibility. And what of GCC's vaunted concern for the ICC 'brand name'? The dispute did nothing to enhance the reputation of world cricket.

'Relationships of ownership, they whisper in the wings'[4]

In contrast to their muddle over human rights, the cricket authorities and the GCC showed sterner mettle in protecting the rights of sponsors and advertisers.

The contracts signed by GCC (on behalf of the ICC) and the sponsors ('partners' in corporate-speak) contained an 'ambush clause' guaranteeing the sponsors exclusivity and prohibiting attempts by competitors to cash in on the World Cup. The clause was binding not only on the ICC and the World Cup

Globalisation, corporate power and cricket 255

organisers, but also on the participating governing bodies and the individual players. Effectively, it barred players from endorsing any rivals to official sponsors for the duration of the Cup. It also made the ICC the disciplinary agent for GCC – thus reversing the chain of accountability that binds the ICC to the national boards and through them the players.

The players cried foul. Their rights had been sold without consultation or compensation. A long, intricate and (at the time of writing) still unresolved controversy ensued. Indian players, who stood to lose most because of their extensive personal endorsements, refused to sign the original contracts. They agreed to participate in the tournament only on amended terms that diluted the original clauses. As a result, in the wake of the tournament, GCC withheld a substantial part of its payment to the ICC, which passed that penalty – $6.5 million – to the Indian Board. The Indian Board protested, and eventually counter-charged the GCC with 'inadequate marketing'.

The champions of globalisation are militant in their assertion of 'intellectual property rights' – private and exclusive ownership of brand names or scientific formulae or indeed sporting events. In an effort to placate the World Trade Organisation and the multinational corporations, South Africa had already passed a tough new statute against ambush marketing; violators could be sentenced to jail. GCC and others had made clear to the ICC that if it wished to maximise the value of the World Cup, and of world cricket in general, it had to ensure that the rights it sold were exclusive. No one else was to enjoy the opportunity to exploit the game.

During the World Cup itself the cricket authorities were vigilant in enforcing the ambush clause. At the match between Australia and India at Pretoria, a spectator was ejected for the offence of opening a can of Coca-Cola – official sponsor Pepsi's arch rival. The renegade Coke guzzler was Arthur Williamson, a Johannesburg businessman, who claimed that security personnel 'manhandled' him out of the stadium. World Cup communications head Rodney Hartman argued that the restrictions were clearly printed on the back of all match tickets and were necessary 'to protect the interests of sponsors'.

This neo-liberal effort to protect corporate property rights stripped players and national boards of rights and property they had long considered their own. Moreover, the ambush clause rested on an assertion of exclusive ownership by the ICC – a body whose legal basis is a Monaco-based corporation. At what stage and on what basis were the assets of world cricket in their entirety appropriated by the ICC – to be sold to Murdoch? By what right does the ICC make its claim on the players' faces and bodies and names? It is a claim that certainly cannot rest on the ICC's performance as a world governing body or its track record in managing cricket's assets effectively or accountably.

What the ambush clause imbroglio demonstrated is that there is an ongoing and unresolved struggle within the game over the division of the spoils. And it is not just about how the pie is sliced, but also about who gets to wield the knife. In other games, the increased market value of sport in a media-saturated society has bred player power as the stars have learned how to exploit their growing celebrity.

256   *Mike Marqusee*

In this, as in so much else, cricket has lagged behind. But having found themselves ambushed by the ambush clause, the cricketers are increasingly considering their options. At a meeting in autumn 2002 of more than 100 Test players from nine nations, Tim May, the Australian off-spinner who leads the nascent Federation of International Cricketers, attacked the employers' presumptions. 'The ICC has sold your images to the sponsors without permission. You don't want a situation where a player is standing next to Pepsi and endorsing it for free. He needs to be paid for the personal endorsement.'[5]

May also warned the players of the dangers inherent in a dispute with GCC. Given the decline in the rights market, he speculated that the $550 million deal might be worth only half what it had been when it was signed in 2001. He speculated that GCC would welcome an excuse to withdraw – a prospect that frightens both the ICC and the national boards.

Cricket was a creation of the world's first market society – eighteenth-century England – and the cash nexus has always played a role in shaping the game. But for more than a century, cricket was shielded from the market by aristocratic and imperial privileges. No longer (Marqusee 1994). As the aftermath of the 2003 World Cup vividly demonstrated, the game is now subject to all the vicissitudes of capitalist globalisation. It is a fate for which cricket's history has left it ill-prepared.

The inherited terrain: the ICC in an unequal world

The ICC was a late bloom of the British Empire. Its history has been shaped by imperial hierarchies – and its transition to a post-imperial order has been belated and incomplete.

The Marylebone Cricket Club (MCC) was founded in London in 1789 – and rapidly became the recognised arbiter of the game, in England and overseas. It was, and remains, a private members' club, and for generations its leadership was drawn from Britain's ruling elite. Over the years, the game followed English soldiers, sailors, colonists and merchants around the world, but international competition remained informal and *ad hoc* until 1877, when England and Australia played the inaugural official Test. Here two teams widely recognised as representative of the best cricketers from each of the two countries met for the first time. But the Test series and cricketing relations between the two countries were at this stage and for many years to come governed through negotiations between the MCC in London and its counterpart in Melbourne.

The family of Test-playing nations was expanded to include South Africa in 1888. At this time, South African cricket was less developed than cricket in North America, but the compulsions of empire were always uppermost in the minds of the MCC elite, and at that moment the empire was deeply engaged in staking a claim to South Africa, where vast gold deposits had been discovered. Cricket was used to bolster that claim, and specifically to support the English-speaking colonists against their Boer rivals. After the Boer War, imperial priorities shifted. The aim now was to incorporate white South Africa as a whole, and

Globalisation, corporate power and cricket 257

cricket tours were seen as a means of fostering friendship between 'Briton and Boer'. It was largely in order to consolidate the empire in South Africa that the ICC was founded – as the Imperial Cricket Conference – in 1909, with three member nations, England, Australia and South Africa (at a stroke severing the United States from world cricket).

As part of its imperial burden, the MCC took responsibility for administering the ICC, and the MCC chairman and secretary became, *ex officio*, president and secretary of the ICC. This amateur arrangement continued for the next eight decades. Unlike that of football, cricket's spread remained confined to societies under the direct rule of the British Empire. As a result, the MCC's imperial prerogatives were rarely challenged. And when they were, as in the bodyline controversy during England's tour of Australia in 1932–3, it was very much a confrontation between two senior members of the world cricketing club; the other nations, and the ICC itself, stood aside.

Just as the MCC widened its circle of members as and when it suited the convenience of the dominant elite, so the ICC welcomed new Test-playing countries. After South Africa, the next to join the club were the West Indies in 1928, New Zealand in 1929 and India in 1932 – all of which reflected in different ways the impact of nationalist politics and the ongoing effort by the empire's masters to incorporate and manage the new forces emerging within it (Guha 2002; Bowen 1970; Beckles 1999). After partition, India sponsored Pakistan's admission to the Test club, despite English scepticism. Sri Lanka's application was in turn backed by both India and Pakistan, but resisted by the English for many years. Even after they won Test status in 1981, the Sri Lankans found themselves treated as a second-class Test nation by the English authorities for nearly 20 years. Within the ICC it has always been the case that some Test-playing nations are more equal than others.

Until recently the ICC's role in organising international cricket competition was minimal; tours and Tests were arranged bilaterally, according to the traditions or whims or political designs of the separate national boards. The ICC never required recognised Test nations to play against each other. The old South Africa refused to play against the West Indies, India or Pakistan. Australia shunned New Zealand (playing an initial Test only in 1946 and not again until the 1970s) in an attempt to assert regional supremacy and in keeping with the Australian view that New Zealand were unworthy opponents. Neutral umpires – a device that would seem a *sine qua non* for any international sporting competition – were not even contemplated in cricket until the late 1980s, when they were unilaterally introduced by Pakistan.

Cricket's transition from colonialism was remarkably retarded. In 1993 the paternalistic, Anglocentric system was replaced by an elected president and the beginnings of an independent full-time administration. The patricians of the MCC gave way to hard-headed businessmen and politicians from South Asia, South Africa and Australia. Members of elites from various countries with various priorities, they have all been united in a desire to exploit the emergent global marketplace.

258   *Mike Marqusee*

However, the ICC is still governed by the exclusive club of Test-playing nations – and the Test-playing nations retain the right to decide who shall be admitted to their ranks. Apart from apartheid South Africa between 1971 and 1992, the ICC has never stripped a country of Test-playing status. No matter how poor your cricket is, no matter how routinely you are beaten by others, if you're a Test-playing nation you will retain your vote on the ICC's top table – cricket's equivalent of a permanent seat on the UN Security Council. It is sometimes assumed therefore that long-term cricket development is a one-way process, that it may stall but cannot recede. The recent evolution of Zimbabwe's cricket – to cite only the most salient example – suggests otherwise. Yet it is hard to imagine any country ever losing Test status. Political and commercial imperatives will continue to make it virtually impossible to assemble a consensus within the ICC to relegate anyone.

Test cricket still lacks the kind of transparent and internally consistent global competitive structure that football boasts. The national boards continue to prefer the contests they know they can sell – England versus Australia, for example – to those demanded by a more equitable and open system. But it is not only the parochialism of the boards that presents problems to ICC modernisers here. There are problems in the scale and logistics of such a competition that derive ultimately from cricket's origins in an earlier, pre-industrial age. Five- and six-test series evolved not only because they were supreme and sustained challenges for mastery that made for rich entertainment, but also because the exigencies of global travel demanded longer visits. It is hard to see how global cricket, with its numerous seasonal and geographical peculiarities, can ever be rationalised in accordance with the norms of an age of a deracinated virtual reality.

In comparison with soccer's world governing body, FIFA, the ICC is top-heavy, dominated by the big cricket nations, and at the same time less centralised, with far more powers remaining in the hands of the national boards. The new president of the ICC, Ehsan Mani, a Pakistani accountant long resident in the United Kingdom and with many years of service in the corporate sector, is the latest in a series of would-be modernisers hoping to push the ICC towards the FIFA model. He is seeking greater control (not least commercial control) over all international cricket. Like his predecessors, Mani will find his efforts inhibited by the sheer unevenness of the global cricket market. You can hear him struggling with this dilemma in an interview he gave shortly after his appointment:

> If cricket is to survive it has to compete with other sports. In the subcontinent, cricket has no competition. So, the development priorities are different. In these countries, what we lack are top infrastructure facilities – high-performance coaching centres, academies. . . . But in England, and in some other countries, cricket is competing with other sports such as football and rugby. . . . What the England and Wales Cricket Board has to do is to go out and attract the young kids who go into other sport. . . . In the long run, I am very clear that members will have to yield more power on a variety of issues to the central body. It has to happen. Only then can the ICC go

Globalisation, corporate power and cricket 259

forward . . . at the ICC, we are constantly looking at the way Test and one-day cricket is structured in terms of where the ownership should lie and whether it should be programmed centrally. On whether or not ICC should own all Test and one-day cricket, we are of the opinion that the ICC ought to leave behind money to countries to run their own cricket. Imagine India without any money at the board level! It may change in the future. Every country has its own rights and we don't want to step on those.

The ICC has inherited a lopsided game in a lopsided world. The South Asian Test-playing countries boast a total population of 1.5 billion, and within these countries cricket is unrivalled as a spectator sport. In contrast, Britain, Australia and New Zealand – a bloc of predominantly white, advanced capitalist economies – boast a total of 84 million, and cricket competes in these societies with a much wider array of sport and leisure activities. However, it is in the nature of the globalised economic order that some people are more equal than others. Average GDP per capita in the Anglo-Australasian bloc is ten times greater than in the South Asian bloc. The 'Old Commonwealth' countries' combined GDP is some two-thirds that of the South Asian countries, whose population outnumbers theirs by 17 to 1. The 84 million in Australia–Britain–New Zealand consume the same volume of electricity each year as the 1.5 billion in South Asia. There are more people connected to the Internet in Australia (pop. 19 million) than in India (pop. 1.1 billion). Britain's military expenditure is three times India's – and equivalent to the entire GDP of the West Indies or Zimbabwe.

South Africa's role as a swing power within the ICC reflects its peculiar position in the global hierarchy. Its average GDP per capita is about midway between South Asian and Western levels – but this 'average' disguises the unspeakable gulf between the wealthy, mostly white minority and the impoverished black majority. There may be nearly as many cell phones in South Africa as in India, but life expectancy – at 46 – is by far the lowest of any cricket-playing country.[6]

Making a killing: national identity in a globalised economy

As Ehsan Mani is only too aware, the ICC has been riven by conflict between the South Asian and Anglo-Australians blocs. The South Asian bloc's economic and political clout is formidable, and the Anglo-Australians have found that reality hard to swallow. Jagmohan Dalmiya, former ICC president and for some years the dominant figure on the Indian board, has frequently characterised this attitude as an 'imperial hangover'. That element is certainly present. But the South Asian bloc's case has been weakened by its inability to tackle its own problems – as it tacitly admitted when a former commissioner of the London's Metropolitan Police was drafted in to deal with the match-fixing crisis. But even more than the allegations of corruption and incompetence, the South Asian bloc is compromised by the continuing disruption of the India–Pakistan cricket rivalry – world sport's fiercest derby and, apart from the soccer World Cup final, perhaps its biggest single spectator attraction. The absence of competition between India and Pakistan has been the hole in the heart of world cricket.

Its future depends, of course, on the evolution of relations between the two countries. Here too, cricket finds itself dogged by the legacies of imperialism. But while cricket cannot bring an enduring peace between India and Pakistan, it can be used to advance or obstruct the processes that might lead to this peace.

The principal culprits in the disruption of India–Pakistan cricket relations have been the forces of right-wing Hindu nationalism in India. They have used cricket (usually ignoring other sports) in their attempts to rally public opinion against the designated enemies without (Pakistan) and within (Indian Muslims). The questions raised by cricket between India and Pakistan become, in times of international tension, tests of patriotism. A frustrated Pakistani board routinely denounces the Indians for 'playing politics' with cricket – which is a bit rich coming from men appointed by a military dictatorship.

Meanwhile, the India–Pakistan cricket rivalry is sublimated offshore – in Sharjah, Singapore, Bangladesh, Australia, England and South Africa. This displacement seems to have made it an attraction of even greater intensity for television spectators at home. A report in the Indian press by Anand Vasu described reactions on both sides of the border to India's victory over Pakistan in the 2003 World Cup, thanks to a masterful innings by Sachin Tendulkar.

> There was a spontaneous eruption of firecrackers, cheers, chanting and joy across the length and breadth of a large country as India pulled off a stunning win against the old enemy Pakistan for the fourth time in as many World Cup clashes. . . . It was always going to be a day of heated arguments, passionate following and a tense battle out in the middle. Several cities in India had declared a public holiday to watch their team take on Pakistan in a one-dayer for the first time in three years. Cities that did not were paralysed as children stayed away from schools, offices emptied out by the start of the game and the streets wore a deserted look. Time stood still, life was put on hold as India delivered the game that a billion people wanted. . . . There will be mourning in the streets of Lahore and Karachi. There will be heartburn in Pakistan's provinces. There will be calls for a change of captain and coach. There will be anger, there will be disappointment and there will be a sense of shock.[7]

One of the paradoxes of globalisation is that it has fostered the attractive power of parochial identities. In a world dominated by the likes of the GCC, national identity, in particular, is a prized commodity – malleable, manipulable, profitable. When India played Pakistan in Australia in early 2000, the series was promoted by its South Asian broadcasters, Star-ESPN, under the slogan 'Qayamat!' – apocalypse – accompanied by thunderous rumblings and flashes of light. For Murdoch (owner of Star) and the Disney Corporation (owner of ESPN), the clash between the two nuclear-armed neighbours, replete with religious connotations, was merely handy matter with which to attract an audience and enhance the value of their investment in cricket.

Globalisation, corporate power and cricket 261

The American delusion: the World Cup, 2007

With a mere six million people and a combined GDP of only \$28 billion (New Zealand has about two-thirds as many people, but its GDP is three times larger), the West Indies are today, as they have always been, a marginal outpost in the global cricket marketplace. Nonetheless, in 2007 they will host the World Cup. In other circumstances it might have been the fulfilment of C. L. R. James's vision of West Indians 'making their way with bat and ball into the comity of nations'. But much has changed since 1963, when James's classic *Beyond a Boundary* was published.

As elsewhere in the British Empire, cricket in the West Indies reflected social and racial hierarchies. It was the genius of James to see that the game did not belong exclusively to the colonial power or the local elite and that it could be an instrument for national unity and liberation. As if in fulfilment of his prophecies, during the 1960s and 1970s the West Indian cricketers became the game's first real global champions, winning hearts and minds in Australia, India, Pakistan and Britain.

It was always remarkable that a sequence of world-beaters should have sprung from the Caribbean: an impoverished society with a relatively small middle class, economically and strategically marginal, an entity embracing numerous nation-states and diverse cultures. Buoyed up by the anti-colonial movements of the era, their peripatetic cricketing representatives forged a new unity and played with unrivalled purpose. Thanks to their Caribbean and worldwide prestige, the cricketers exercised both a political and a financial independence rarely seen before in the game. Kerry Packer's star-studded breakaway series of the late 1970s rattled world cricket from top to bottom and led to the banishment of some of the game's biggest names, but the West Indian cricketers played for Packer unpenalised. They also used their clout to block the Packer series from being used as a Trojan horse by apartheid South Africa.

Just as no one – except C. L. R. James – had foreseen the West Indies' rise to dominance, no one foresaw their precipitate decline. Various reasons have been advanced for this manifest downturn in the standard of West Indian cricket since the mid-1990s: the impact of US sports via television, the difficult economic conditions of the past twenty years, insularity and disunity, the waning of post-independence élan. Whatever the diagnosis, cricket authorities, politicians and cricket fans across the region are joined in a hope that the 2007 World Cup will usher in a West Indies cricket revival.

What is being dubbed 'Windies World Cup 2007' will be the largest single sporting or cultural event ever undertaken by the region. Tourism, sponsorship and the sale of intellectual property rights are expected to generate over half a billion US dollars, with other World Cup-related activity bringing in several times that mount.

Across the West Indies there has been much emphasis on the fact that 'the world will be watching' – and much anxiety about the region's capacity to perform. At a press conference in Guyana in March 2003 the ground rules were

262   Mike Marqusee

spelled out by the managing director of Windies World Cup 2007 Inc., Chris Dehring, an investment banker:

> What we're talking about is the International Cricket Council Cricket World Cup. That is extremely important for people in the Caribbean to understand. This is not the West Indies' World Cup, to do what we want with and to any standards we choose. There are standards to be met, even while maintaining a distinct Caribbean flavour . . . Windies World Cup 2007 has to be seen and appreciated as a global event that the West Indies have been given the privilege of hosting.

Dehring emphasised that 'right alongside us' will be the Global Cricket Corporation.

> This international event will come with its international sponsors and there will be little room for domestic sponsors. In fact, it is anticipated that 'sunset' legislation will have to be put in place to guard against ambush marketing, such is the seriousness with which we have to protect the rights of international sponsors who have paid all that money. Understand clearly what we are saying because there will be grave consequences for Guyana if you do not. As an example, Bourda [one of the West Indies' long-established Test venues, in Georgetown, Guyana] and its environs will have to be absolutely clean of all signage in order for it to be usable as an official stadium in 2007.

As if to rub home the point to the Guyanese, Dehring stressed that Bourda could not assume it had a right to stage a World Cup match just because of its traditional status as a Test ground.

> No venue in the Caribbean has ever hosted an ICC World Cup match, so there can be no 'traditional' World Cup venue. To compare the traditional hosting of a Test match to that of hosting a World Cup match is like using the qualification of being a teller in a commercial bank in Guyana to apply for the job as head of the World Bank.[8]

In response to Dehring's warnings, an editorial in the *Stabroek News* commented:[9]

> For Guyana's part, it is inconceivable that the World Cup could be brought to the West Indies without matches being staged in the land of Kanhai, Lloyd, Kallicharran, Gibbs, Fredericks, Croft, Hooper, Chanderpaul, Sarwan et al. Guyanese here and abroad would simply not be able to comprehend this possibility. But there should be no mistake about it. There is a risk that matches might not be staged here unless we – all of us, not only the government and the Guyana Cricket Board – spring out of the inertia that cocoons us until it is usually too late to act.

Globalisation, corporate power and cricket 263

The newspaper went on to argue that unless the local authorities moved quickly, Guyana could find itself squeezed out of a World Cup match. Since the ICC and GCC called the shots,

> Guyana is unlikely to benefit from any sentimental considerations of its cricketing legend, the immaculate beauty of the Bourda sward or the near fanatical attachment of its citizens to cricket. Purely hard-nosed determinations will be made by the venue analysers who will scour the region in the upcoming months.

In the absence of traditional prerogatives, Bourda would find itself in open competition with newer but better-appointed venues in Grenada, Antigua and St Vincent. And as if that were not threat enough, the newspaper noted that 'the ICC and GCC are clearly of the mind to expand the reach of cricket in the region, if only to make the tournament more lucrative'. Florida, New York, Bermuda, the Cayman Islands were all mentioned as possible Windies World Cup venues. 'This means even tougher competition for Guyana.'

The ICC has always been reluctant to grant the West Indies a World Cup, not only because of doubts about facilities but also because it is bound to be a less lucrative proposition when it comes to advertising and media rights than South Asia, England or Australia. But in compensation there is the lure of the United States. Indeed, for the ICC and the GCC, the main attraction of the Caribbean seems to be its proximity to the United States.

Expanding cricket's domain into the United States has been a long-standing dream of the big players in the ICC. Since the mid-1990s there has been talk of staging a one-day series in Disneyworld. In 2002 a board meeting of the ICC in Monaco was treated to a commercial presentation by Major League Baseball. Ehsan Mani explained the strategic thinking to Rediff.net:

> We have to take cricket to new areas and new markets like the United States. We are working very hard to stage World Cup matches there in 2007. If we don't do it, cricket will get blocked out in the United States. Just the sports revenue market of the US is $100 billion a year. The ICC is talking about raising $550 million over seven years. That puts into perspective the gap we have in this area. The game needs money to move forward, for development, to set up proper structures for the ICC and its members. We are not in a position to just play cricket and say that we are not interested about the money.

It seems as if the lords of cricket are worried that in the absence of a toehold on the American mainland, they will always be second-class citizens in the global empire of sport. In the end, however, the ICC decided not to stage any 2007 World Cup matches in the United States. The factionalism that has hobbled US cricket for 20 years made the whole proposition too fraught with peril, political, financial and legal. Instead, in an attempt to go over the heads of the competing

264 *Mike Marqusee*

factions, the ICC employed a British businessman as director of something called 'Project USA', whose main aim is to find ways of staging one-day internationals in the United States. But factionalism in cricket is by no means confined to the United States. The deeper problem is that cricket's American dream is both a vainglorious delusion and a colossal failure of the imagination. The US sports market is indeed the world's richest but it is also its most competitive. While the South Asian communities now resident in North America are sizeable enough to provide big audiences for occasional matches, there is little likelihood that cricket will ever break out of the immigrant niche and grab a piece of the action from baseball, basketball or American football. Even soccer has prospered in the United States only after decades of intensive grass-roots development and with the help of an immigrant and immigrant-descended base many times larger than cricket enjoys.

Overall, globalisation as currently designed and managed is more likely to foster the export of US sports (and culture in general) than the import of alien games such as cricket. But for the cricket bosses the US market offers a short cut to prestige and wealth. So much easier than the long-term grass-roots investment needed to develop cricket in its existing markets – where the game is inhibited by either mass poverty or the strength of its competitors.

In the run-up to Windies 2007, as elsewhere, globalisation promises to eradicate local traditions in favour of the priorities of multinational corporations. The preparations for the tournament also confirm the gravitational pull of US wealth and power within the neo-liberal world order – of which, after all, Rupert Murdoch is the great champion. The local boards and even more the local fans feel themselves helpless playthings in the grand schemes of the ICC, but the ICC feels itself a plaything in the hands of the GCC and global market forces.

Yet one can never be completely pessimistic about cricket, even about the fate of a commercial pawn such as the World Cup. As Eduardo Galeano, the Uruguyan novelist, said of football in South America, 'The more the technocrats programme it down to the smallest detail, the more the powerful manipulate it, the more it continues to be the art of the unforeseeable.'

Notes

1 News Corporation Annual Report, 2003, http://www.newscorp.com/investor/annual_reports.html.
2 http://www.rediff.com/sports/2000/jul/01harsha.htm.
3 'Who's the real villain?', Imran Khan, *Guardian* (London), 24 January 2003.
4 'Gates of Eden', Bob Dylan.
5 'Players unite to take on ICC: more sponsorship rows loom before World Cup', David Hopps, *Guardian*, (London), 21 September 2002.
6 Statistics from the *CIA World Fact Book*.
7 Anand Vasu, Cricinfo (www.cricinfo.org), 1 March 2003.
8 Frederick Halley, *Guyana Chronicle*, 5 January 2003.
9 *Stabroek News*, Georgetown, Guyana, 31 March 2003.

References

Beckles, Hilary McD. (1999) *The Development of West Indies Cricket*, 2 vols, London: Pluto Press; Kingston, Jamaica: University of the West Indies Press.

Bowen, Rowland (1970) *Cricket: A History of its Growth and Development throughout the World*, London: Eyre & Spottiswoode.

Guha, Ramachandra (2002) *A Corner of a Foreign Field: The Indian History of a British Sport*, London: Picador.

Marqusee, Mike (1994) *Anyone but England*, London: Verso.

Index

A *Sporting Future for All* (government strategy document) 240
Abbas, Zaheer 123
Abbasi, Arif Ali Khan 124
Abbott, Tony 17
Abeysekera, Karunaratne 143
Abeysekera, Sam 145
Abeywardene, Lassie 147
Aboriginal and Torres Strait Islander Commission (ATSIC) 20
Aboriginal Cricket Working Party 20
Adams, Paul 61
Advani, L.K. 77
African National Congress (ANC) 49, 51, 253
Afrikaner Nationalist Party 49, 52–6, 60, 63, 64–8
Agnew, Jonathan 198
Ahktar, Shoaib 248
Ahmed, Niaz 121
Akram, Wasim 125
Ali, Kabir 246
Aligarh College 111
All Blacks, (of 1905) 28; 35–6, 42
Alley, Bill 195
Allison, Lincoln 52
Altaf, Dr Zafar 209
Amarasuriya, Hemaka 133, 153
Ambrose, Curtley 56, 161
Ames, Leslie 121
Anandarajah, C.E. 134
Anderson, Benedict 12, 94
Annetts, Denise 19
Antigua Cricket Club 162
Anyone for Cricket report 238–9, 246
apartheid 21–2, 48–9, 54, 173, 261
Appadurai, Arjun 95, 111
Arnold, Russe 154

Ashcroft, Bill 3
Atkins, Mike 226–31
Atkins, Sue 225
Attlee, Clement 182
Austin, H.B.G. 163
Australian Broadcasting Corporation (ABC) 17–18
Australian Cricket Board (ACB) 10, 16, 20, 22–3, 136, 148, 151
Azad, Kirti 90
Azharuddin, Mohammed 87–90

Bacher, Dr Ali 48, 50, 55, 57, 62–3, 67
Badcock, Capt. F.C. 147
Badenhorst, Alan 62
Baig, Abbas Ali 80, 147
Bailey, Jack 195
Bailey, Reverend Brooke 137
Bailey, Trevor 187
Bakhtin, Mikhail 213
Balakrishnan, C. 135
Bale, John 3
Balfour, Ngconde 62
Ball of Fire 194
Bandaranaike, S.W.R.D. 134
Bangladesh war (1971) 100
Banks, Tony 240
Bannister, Alex 184, 187–8
Barbados Cricket League (BCL) 163
Bari, Wasim 123
Barlow, Eddie 64
Barmy Army 104, 214
Barnes, Simon 239
Barrington, Ken 197
Bateman, Colin 198
Baucom, Ian 106
Beazley, Kim 14
Beckham, David 89

Index 267

Beckles, Hilary 3, 160, 167–8, 170,173–4
Bedi, Bishen Singh 81, 169, 193
Bedi, Mandira 105–6
Benaud, Richie 189
Bennett, Fred 148
Berlins, Marcel 194
Berry, Scyld 82,166
Betting scandals ('Cronjegate') 87–8
Beyond a Boundary 106, 261
Bharat Army 104–5
Bharatiya Janata (Hindu Nationalist) Party (BJP) 5, 87
Bharti, Uma 87
Bhimani, Kishore 101
Bhogle, Harsha 252
Bhutto, Zulfiqar Ali 113, 117, 120–3
Binny, Roger 89
Bird dynasty (of Antigua) 159
Bird, Harold 'Dickie' 198
Black Caps 39
Black, Peter 192
Blainey, Geoffrey 12
Blair, Tony 254
Bloomfield Cricket Club 133
Blundell, David 244–5
Board of Control (later Australian Cricket Board) 16
Board of Control for Ceylon Cricket (BCCC) 142
Board of Control for Cricket in India (BCCI) 79, 82–3, 84, 88, 91,112
Board of Control for Cricket in Pakistan (BCCP) 112–14, 121–5
Board of Control for Cricket in Sri Lanka (BCCSL) 133, 145–6, 148–9, 152
Bodyline controversy 191, 257
Bogra, Mohammed Ali 120
Boon, David 13
Border, Allan 14, 84
Bosch, Tertius 51
Bose, Mihir 79, 83, 95, 100
Bourda cricket ground, Georgetown 186–7, 262
Boycott, Geoffrey 200–1
Bradman, Sir Donald 3, 10–11, 14, 18–19, 21, 23–4, 143
Bramble, William 175
Bray, Charles 185
British Nationality Act (1981) 5, 196, 201
Broad, Chris 199
Buchanan, John 136
Bukhatir, Sheikh Abdul Rahman 84
Buller, Sid 194

Burki, Shahid Javed 122
Butcher, Mark 219

Caddick, Andrew 219
Campaign Against Racism in the Media 201
Carrington, Ben 235
Cashman, Richard 10, 80,118
CENTO (Central Treaty Organisation) 122
Central Province Cricket Association (CPCA) 147
Cesaire, Aime 168
Ceylon Broadcasting Corporation (CBC) 142
Ceylon Cricket Association (CCA) 139, 142
Challenor, George 183
Chanderpaul, Shivnarine 161, 262
Chandrashekhar, Bhagwat 81, 169
Chanmugan, Neil 147
Channel Nine TV 17
Chappell, Greg 20, 37, 150
Chappell, Ian 20
Charter of Freedom for Colonial Peoples (1942) 182
Chatterjee, Partha 95
Chaudhary, Vivek 247
Chauhan, Chetan 90
Chrisman, Laura 3
Churchill, Sir Winston 15, 186
Clark, Belinda 19
Clean Bowl Racism campaign 233–4, 240–1, 244–5, 247–8
Clinton, President Bill 77
Clive Lloyd League 226
Close, Brian 190, 193–4
Cohen, Leonard 2
Collis, John 200
Colombo Academy 137
Colombo Cricket Club (CCC) 133, 136, 149
Colts Cricket Club 133, 138, 140
Commonwealth Immigration Act (1962) 192
Compton, Denis 195
Concerned Group of Cricketers 68
Confederation of South African Trade Unions (COSATU) 60, 66
Congress Party (of India) 110
Constantine Learie 147, 163, 166, 168, 183
Constantine, Mr Carlton 191

268   *Index*

Cornelius, Justice R.A. 114
Cowdrey, Colin 189–90
Crabbe, Tim 236, 239
Cranwell RAF College 145
Creech Jones, Arthur 182
Cricket and England 235
Cricket and Race 19
Cricket Foundation 244
Cricket Max 39–40
Cricket Wallah 82
Cricket World Cup 1999 204–20, 239
Cricket World Cup 2003 251–6, 260
Cricket World Cup 2007 261–4
Croft, Colin 198, 262
Cronin, Mike 3
Cronje, Hansie 51, 56, 64
Crossroads township 60
Crowe, Martin 39

D'Oliveira affair 49
D'Oliveira, Basil 197
Dakin, Geoff 51
Dalmiya, Jagmohan 85, 88, 99, 259
Daniell, Thomas 136
Das, S.S. 88
Dassanayake, S.B. 152
Davidson, Jim 208
Davies, Charles 65
Dawn (Pakistani newspaper) 115
de Caires, Cecil 165
de Fransz, W. 138
de Klerk F.W. 51
de Kretser, R.L. 140
de Saram, D.L. 140
de Saram, F.C. 140, 143–4, 146, 154
de Silva D.S. 143
de Silva, A.E. 146
de Silva, Ajit 149
de Silva, Aravinda 151–2
de Silva, D.H. 143, 146
de Silva, D.P. 143
de Zoysa, L.E. 140
Deane, William (Governor General of
   Australia) 11
Dehring, Chris 262
Denness, Mike 85, 92
Desailly, Marcel 90
Dev, Kapil 81, 83, 87, 89, 99
Devon Malcolm Cricket Centre 229, 232
Dexter, Ted 189
Dias, Roy 149
Die Stem (South African national anthem)
   52

Digby, William 137
Disney Corporation 260
Dissanayake, Gamini 142–3, 148
Donald, Alan 51, 64
Doordarshan (Indian broadcasting service)
   102
Dos Santos, Sir Errol 186
Dravid, Rahul 89, 105
Duleepsinhji, Kumar Shri 140
Durkheim, Emile 213
Dyson, John 147
Dyson, Michael Eric 164

Eden Gardens, Kolkata (Calcutta) 84–5,
   99, 100
Eden Park, Auckland 28, 32, 35, 38
Edrich, John 188
Edwards, T.C.T. 146, 147
Empire CC (Barbados) 163, 172
Engel, Matthew 238
England and Wales Cricket Board (ECB)
   204–7, 210, 213, 219, 233–4, 237,
   239–48, 253–4, 258
ESPN (satellite TV channel) 102, 260
Evatt, Herbert 16
Examiner (Sir Lankan newspaper) 138

Faulkner, John 16
Federation of International Cricketers
   256
Fernando, H.I.K. 145–6
Fernando, Tyronne 142
Fleming, Scott 85
Flintoff, Andrew 89
Flower, Andy 22, 254
Foenander, S.P. 139
Folley, Malcolm 193
Foot, Sir Hugh 16
Forbes, O.B. 139
Forte, Martin 230
Forte, Ronnie 230
Fraser, Angus 242
Fredericks, Roy 262
Friendship Cup 86
Fuard, Abu 142–3, 145–6

Gaelic Athletic Association 15
Gairy, Eric 176
Galeano, Eduardo 264
Gandhi, Indira 81
Gandhi, Leela 2
Ganguly, Sourav 77, 88–9, 103
Gardiner, Michael 213

Index   269

Garner, Joel 199, 230
Garvey, Marcus 160
Gatting, Mike 242
Gavaskar, Sunil 81, 83, 99–100, 125
Gemmell, Jon 3
Georgetown Cricket Club 172
Gibbs, Herschelle 63
Gibbs, Lance 167, 262
Gibson, Pat 193–6, 197, 198–200
Gilbert, Eddie 19–20
Gilchrist, Roy 200
Gillespie, Jason 19
Gillete Cup 34
Gilroy, Paul 208, 210, 235
Gittens, Owen 229–30
Gittens, Sam 229–30
Giulianotti, Richard 210, 215
Global Cricket Corporation (GCC)
    251–2, 255–6, 262–4
Goddard, John 165, 183–4
Gooch, Graham 197
Goonesena, Gamini 144–5
Gough, Darren 209, 248
Gover, Alf 193
Government College 111
Gower, David 96, 200, 218
Grace Road, Leicester 220
Grace, Dr W.G. 96, 196
Greatbatch, Mark 39
Greenfeld, Liah 97
Greenidge, Gordon 175, 230
Greig, Tony 196
Griffith, Charlie 188, 194
Griffith, S.C 145
Growth, Employment and Redistribution
    strategy (GEAR) 60, 66
Guha, Ramachandra 78, 89, 103
Gul, Aftab 121
Gunasekara, Dr C.H. 140
Gurusinghe, Nihal 146
Guyana Cricket Board 262

Habib, Aftab 219
Hadlee, Richard 35–36, 38, 150
Hadlee, Walter 35
Haigh, Gideon 10
Hair, Darrel 150
Hall, Stuart 2, 9
Hall, Wes 188–90, 200, 229
Hammond, Wally 96
Harms, John 10
Harper, Roger 175–6
Hartman, Rodney 255

Hassan, Syed Fida 121
Hawke, Bob 16
Hazare, Vijay 96, 107
Headingley cricket ground, Leeds 207,
    211–13, 223
Headley, Dean 219
Headley, George 168, 183
Hector, Leonard 'Tim' 159–76, 232
Henderson, Claud 62
Henderson, Robert 205, 229, 236
Hero Honda (Indian company) 88
Heyn, Charles 138
Hignell, Andrew 31
Hillary, Sir Edmund 28, 35–6, 42
Hilton College 59
Hindutva (renewal of Hindu pride) 90
History of the Pan African Revolt (1934)
    160
History of West Indies Cricket 164
Hit Racism for Six campaign 234
Hobbs, Sir Jack 96, 140
Hoberman, John 126
Hoey, Kate 233, 241
Holding, Michael 192–5, 230
Holford, David 230
Holkar Cricket Association 144
Hooper, Carl 174–5, 262
Hopps, David 220
Howa, Hassan 52
Howard, John 10, 14, 17, 20, 254
Hughes, Kim 148
Hughes, Simon 239, 241
Hulme, Peter 201
Humayun, Shahzad 116
Hussain, Munir 116
Hussain, Nasser 219, 233, 239, 247
Hutton, Len 145, 186–7
Hutton, Will 60

Iftikar Nawab of Pataudi 140, 189
Imperial Cricket Conference 257
Imperial Cricket Council 49
Inman, Clive 144, 145
Inner City Community Cricket Project
    233, 241
Insole, Doug 190
International Cricket Council (ICC)
    21–2, 85, 89, 112, 126, 149, 224, 253,
    255–9, 262–4
International Monetary Fund (IMF) 66,
    172, 176
Iqbal, Asif 123
Islamia College 112

270 *Index*

Jackman, Robin 197, 201
Jadeja, Ajay 87–8
Jaffna Central CC 141
Jagan, Dr Cheddi 176, 186
Jalil, Hassan 116
James, C.L.R. 3, 90, 95, 106, 159–60, 162–3, 165–6, 223, 261
Janata Vimukti Peramuna (JVP, People's Liberation Front) 135
Jardine, Douglas 15, 191
Jatika Chintanaya (Nationalist Thought) 154
Jayasinghe, Stanley 144–5
Jayasuriya, Sanath 143, 151
Jayaweera, Neville 142–3
Jayawickrema, S.S. 140
Jayewardene, J. R. 142
Jinnah, Muhammad Ali 113
Jones, Deborah 18
Jones, W.S. 186
Jordan, Michael 170
Joseph, E.H. 138

Kaif, Mohammed 88, 90–1
Kallicharan, Alvin 175, 262
Kaluperuma. Lalith 149
Kaluwitharana, Romesh 136
Kanhai, Rohan 166, 175, 188, 191, 262
Kapoor, Raj 80
Kardar, Abdul Hafeez 114
Kardar, Shahid Hafeez 122–3
Karunaratne, E.M. 139
Kehelgamuwa, T.B. 133
Kelaart, 'Banda' 138
Kelaart, Collin 138
Kelaart, Edward 140
Kelaart, Tommy 140
Kellaart, Dr Edgar 138
Kemp, Gerald 191
Kernot, Cheryl 16
Khan, Air Marshal Nur 124
Khan, Bashir 116
Khan, General Muhammed Ayub 120–1
Khan, General Nur 114
Khan, Imran 101, 114, 123, 125, 169, 236, 253
Khan, Majid 119, 123
Khan, Mansur Ali 80
Khan, Muawar Ali 123
Khan, Zaheer 88, 90
Khayelitsha township 60
kilikiti (Pacific version of cricket) 41
Kiwi Cricket 38

Klein, Naomi 60
Klusener, Lance 57
Knatts Sports Cricket Club 231
Kontouri, Alex 152
Kriket Kriket (Hindi cricket journal) 103
Ku Klux Klan 176, 227
Kumar, Dilip 80
Kureishi, Omar 116
Kuruppu, Brendon 133

Lagaan (Indian film) 91–2
Laker, Jim 195
Lamb, Allan 196
Lamb, Tim 207, 233, 253
Lara, Brian 56, 171, 174–5
Lashley, Peter 229
Lawrence, Ken 200
Lawton, James 193
Le Pen, Jean Marie 90
Lehmann, Darren 224
Letlhake, Donald 63
Liberation Tigers of Tamil Eelam (LTTE) 134, 151, 153
Lieversz, Darrel 146
Lillee, Dennis 14, 169
Lister, Joe 146
Littlemore, Stuart 18
Lloyd, Clive 81, 173, 175, 193, 195, 199, 230, 262
London Schools Cricket Project 242–3
Lord Beginner 184
Lord Kitchener, 164
Lords cricket ground 233
Lords, West Indies first test victory against England at (1950) 182–5
Lucas, Slade 160

Mackerdhuj, Krish 51
MacLean, R.A. 59
Macmillan, Brian 61–2
Macpherson Report (1999) 240
Magiet, Rushdi 52
Maguire, Joseph 234
Mahanama, Roshan 151
Maharaj Kumar of Vizanagram 140
Mahaweli Development Board 148
Mahinda College (Galle) 141,143
Mahmood, Fazal 123
Major, John 235
Makopanele, David 63
Malay Cricket Club 140
Malcolm, Devon 228–9
Mandela, Nelson 48, 51,53, 55, 173

Index 271

Mandle, W.F. 10, 11
Mangeshkar, Lata 77
Mani, Ehsan 258–9, 263
Mankad, Vinoo 107
Manley, Michael 164
Manley, Norman 175
Mann, George 1
Mann, Simon 1
Manning, J.L. 191
Mantanzima, George 58
Mantanzima, Kaiser 58
Maple Cricket Club (Trinidad) 162
Marasinghe, T.B. 147–8
Marker, Jamshed 116
Marqusee, Mike 3, 150, 234–5, 244, 247
Marshall, Malcolm 167, 198
Marshall, Pat 184
Marshall, Prof. Roy 224
Martin-Jenkins, Christopher 239
Marylebone Cricket Club (MCC) 31,
    139–40, 162, 172, 219, 256
Mascarenhas, Mark 85
Mashile, Elias 59
Masood, Asif 121
May, Peter 200
May, Tim 256
Mbeki, Thabo 52, 55–6, 59, 68
McCarthy, Pat 140
McDonald, Ian 234, 237–8
McGlew, Jackie 63, 189
McGrath, Glenn 19
McKay, Jim 9
McWatt, Clifford 186
Medellin Cartel 176
Melbourne Cricket Club (Jamaica) 172
Mendis, Duleep 149, 152
Menzies, Badge 186
Menzies, Sir Robert Gordon 15–17,
    20–1
Merchant, Vijay 83, 95, 96, 140, 141
Miandad, Javed 84–5, 91, 107
Middlesex Cricket Board (MCB) 241–5
Midnight's Children (novel) 3
Miller, Keith 14, 189–90
Miller, Toby 9
Mirza, Iskander 120
Montego Bay conference (1947) 182
Moody, Tom 246
Morgan, William J. 210
Morrell, Randy 147–8
Morris Isaacson School 59
Mottau, Owen 148
Mount Cricket Club 246

Movement for Democratic Change
    (MDC) 254
Mpephu, Patrick 58
Mugabe, Robert 253–4
Muhamed, Sadiq 123
Muhammed, Mushtaq 123
Mujahid, Chisty 115
Muldoon, Robert 37
Mullally, Alan 219
Muralitharan, Muttiah 134–6, 150
Murdoch, Rupert 5, 85, 251–5, 260, 264
Murray, Deryck 197
Musharraf, Gen. Pervez 253
Muslim League (of India) 110
Muthiah, A.C. 88

Nandy, Ashis 78, 89, 95
National University of Singapore (NUS)
    136
Nawab of Mamdot 123
Nayudu, C.K. 96, 140
Nehru, Jawarharlal 91, 107
Nepia, George 28
New Zealand Cricket Almanack 32, 34–5
New Zealand Cricket Council (NZCC)
    30–1, 34–5
New Zealand Cricket Inc. (NZC) 39–40
New Zealand Herald 3
New Zealand Listener 33
News Corporation 5, 251–2
Ngam, Mfuneko 59
Nielsen, Tim 136
Nimmo, Derek 208
Nkosi Sikeleli' Afrika (South African
    national anthem) 52
Noman, Omar 125
Nondescripts Cricket Club (NCC) 133,
    140
Norgay, Tenzing 28
Norton and District League 225
NRIs (Non Resident Indians) 104–5
Ntini, Makaya 59, 61
Nunes, Karl 186–7

Old Trafford, Manchester 208, 216
Old, Chris 169
Olonga, Henry 22, 254
Ontong, Justin 57
Opatha, Tony 149
Outschoorn, Laddie 144

Packer, Kerry 36–7, 82, 87, 100, 101, 124,
    171, 261,

272   Index

Pakistan Cricket Board (PCB) 114, 124
Pakistan Times 115
Palmer, V. 12
pan Africanism 160
Parish, Bob 148
Parker, Robert 194
Pascoe, Len 20, 169
Patel, Brijesh 80, 147
Patel, Imtiaz 64
Patriotic Front 154
Patron's Trophy 113
People's Progressive Party (PPP) 186–7
Pereira, George 140
Perera, Palitha 142–3
Perera, Ruchira 136
Perera, S.S. 136, 139
Phillipson, Eddie 189, 194
Philpott, Peter 147
Piachaud, Dan 145
Pickwick Cricket Club (Barbados) 162
Pierce, N. 165
Pieris, P.I. 145, 147
Pires, B.C. 208–9
Pirzada, Abdul Hafeez 122–3
Pokhran nuclear test (1974) 100
Pollock, Shaun 55–6, 68
Ponnambalam, G.G. 144
Ponniah, Mano 145, 147
Ponting, Ricky 22
postcolonial studies 2
postmodernism 2
Powell, Enoch 192
Prahran Cricket Club 148
Prasanna, Erapalli 81
Proctor, M.J. (Mike) 59
Putnam, Robert D. 40
Pye, William 231

Qaddafi Stadium 123
Qadir, Abdul 169
Quaid-i-Azan Trophy 112–13, 115
Queens Park CC (Trinidad) 162

Ramadhin, Sonny 164–5, 184, 200
Ramprakash, Mark 219, 242
Ranatunga, Arjuna 146, 148, 151, 152,
    154
Ranatunga, Dhammika 152
Ranatunga, Prasanna 154
Ranji Trophy 79, 97–8, 140, 144
Ranjitsinhji, K.S., Jamsaheb of Nawanagar
    91, 96, 140
Rao, Narasimha 102

Rastafarians 168
Ray, Robert 16
Reconstruction and Development Programme
    (RDP) 55, 60, 67
Reeve, Dermot 224
Reid, Buddy 146, 147
Reliance (Indian conglomerate) 84
Rendall, Jonathan 246
ressentiment 97–8, 100
Reynolds, Buster 230
Rice, Clive 57
Rice, Jonathan 59
Richards, Donald 'Donnymitch' 169
Richards, Vivian 167, 169, 170, 173, 175,
    196, 199, 230, 236
Richardson, Richie 161, 171, 224
Richmond Cricket Club 141
Rising Sun Cricket Club (Antigua) 163,
    172
Rivals Cricket Club (Antigua) 163
Roberts, Anderson ('Andy') 167, 173, 230
Robins, Walter 190, 194
Rockwood, Dr John 139
Roebuck, Peter 20
Rohinton Baria Trophy 112
Rosselli, John 97
Rostron, Frank 185–6
Rotherham and District Netball League
    231
Rudolph, Jacques 57
Rushdie, Salman 3

Sabina Park, Jamaica 171
Salahuddin, Brigadier 114
Salve, N.K.P. 84
Sandiford, Keith 4
Sara Trophy 147
Saravanamuttu, P. 139
Sarkar, Tanika 97
Sarwan, Ramnaresh 262
Sathasivam, M. 140, 143
Schaffter, Chandra 136, 145–6
Scindia, Madhav Rao 79
SEATO (South Atlantic Treaty
    Organisation) 122
Sebe, Lennox 58
Sehway, Virender 220
Senanayake, Robert 142
Shafayat, Bilal 246
Shannon Cricket Club (Trinidad) 163,
    172
Sharjah cricket tournament 83–4, 95,103,
    150

Sharma, Ajay 87
Sharma, Chetan 107
Shastri, Ravi 83
Sheffield and District African Caribbean Association (SADACCA) 231
Sheffield Caribbean Cricket Club 223–232
Sheffield City Council 225–6
Sheffield Shield 32
Sheffield Wednesday Football Club 217
Sheffield Youth Club League 225
Shiv Sena movement 86, 126
Silva, Amal 133
Sinclair, Abraham 63
Singh, Harbhajan 88
Singh, Maninder 89
Singh, Raj 79
Singh, Tavleen 101
Singh, Yuvraj 90
Sinhalese Sports Club (SSC) 133, 140, 143
Smit, Mark 67
Smith, Alan 197
Smith, Chris 196
Smith, Don 147
Snedden, Martin 252
Snell, Peter 28
Snell, Peter 35–6
Sobers, Garfield ('Gary') 147, 148, 166, 175, 190, 229–30, 246
Sonn, Percy 53, 57
South African Communist Party (SACP) 49, 66
South African Council on Sport (SACOS) 58
South African Cricket Board (SACB) 51, 64
South African Cricket Union (SACU) 149
Soweto uprising 59
Spartan Cricket Club 172
Spivak, Gayatri 2
Sportsworld magazine 101
Sri Lanka Freedom Party (SLFP) 134, 143, 154
St Anthony's College, Kandy 135
St John's Cricket Club (Antigua) 141, 162
St Johns College, Jaffna 134
Star Sports (satellite TV channel) 85, 102, 260
Stewart, Mickey 188
Stingo Cricket Club (Trinidad) 163
Stoddart, Brian 4

Stoke Newington Cricket School (SNCS) 242, 245
Sumathipala, Thilanga 152–3
Sunday magazine 101
Sutcliffe, Herbert 140
Swanton, E.W. 183
Sweeney Sports Research Consultants 13
Symcox, Pat 62

Tamil Union Cricket Club 133, 135, 138, 144
Taylor, Steve 228–9
Tebbit, Norman ('Tebbit test') 105, 181, 204–5, 236, 239
Tendulkar, Sachin 85, 103–5, 224, 246, 248, 260
Tennekoon, Anura 147–8
Test and County Cricket Board (TCCB) 195
Test Match Special 80
Thackeray, Bal 86, 126
Thatcher, Margaret 200–1
The Case for West Indian Self Government (1932) 160
The Race Game (BBC programme) 237
Thomasz, Patrick 138
Thomson, Jeff 169
Tillakaratne, Hashan 150
Tissera, Michael 145–7
Trans World International (TWI) 85
Transformation Charter 56
Transvaal Cricket Board 52
Trent Bridge, Nottingham 207
Trinidad Cricket Club 162
Trueman, Fred 187, 190, 193–4
Trumper, Victor 14
Tshwete, Steve 53, 63–4
Tudor, Alex 219
Turner, Glenn 35–6
Turner, Ross 20

Ugra, Sharda 234, 237–8
Umrigar, Polly 192
Underwood, Derek 169
United Cricket Board of South Africa (UCB) 49, 51, 55–7, 63–4, 68
United National Party (UNP) (Sri Lanka) 135, 142
urban riots in UK, early 1980s 197, 227

Vaas, Chaminda 134
Vajpayee, A.B. 86

274 Index

Valentine, Alfred 164–5, 184, 200
Van Gennep, Arnold 213
Van Hoff, Oswald 138
Vanderspar, George 139
Vaughan, Michael 224, 248
Venkataraghavan, Srinivas 81, 169
Vereenidge Oost-Indische Compagnie
  (Dutch East India Company) 137
Verwoerd, H.F. 58
Victoria Park Junior Cricket Club 242
Vij, Gen. N.C. 77
Vitharana, Dr Vinnie 143
Vorster, Balthazar Johannes ('John') 21,
  197
Vryburg High School 59, 61

Waddy, Rev E.F. 139
Wagg, Stephen 236, 239
Wakefield, Edward Gibbon 29
Walcott, Clyde 96,168, 185, 193, 229
Walker, Ashley 139
Walling, 'Sir' Sidney 162
Walsh, Courtney 173
Ward, Russel 12
Warnapura, Bandula 148–9
Warne, Shane 19, 212
Warner, Sir Pelham ('Plum') 11
Washbrook, Cyril 183
Waugh, Mark 19
Waugh, Steve 13, 14, 19
Weaver, Paul 208
Weekes, Everton 168, 229
Weerasinghe, Dhanasiri 145–6
Weinman, 'Jillah' 138
Weinman, Edward 138
Wenham, Leroy 227
Werapitiya, T.B. 142
Werbner, Pnina 212, 215
Wessels, Kepler 51, 62, 64
West Indian Cavaliers 246
West Indies Cricket Board of Control
  (WICBC) 151,165, 172, 186, 199
West Indies Federation 167

Wettimuny, Sidath 148, 153
Whatmore, Dav 147, 148, 152
White Australia Policy 19, 24
White, Crawford 188, 190
White, Jim 216
White, Raymond 52, 57, 63
Whitelaw, William 201
Wijetilleke, Rienzie 153
Wilkins, C. 138
Williams, Jack 19, 182, 235
Williams, Patrick 3
Williams, Stuart 161
Williamson, Arthur 255
Willis, R.G.D. ('Bob') 169
Wisden Australia 19
Wisden Cricket Asia 89
Wisden Cricketers' Almanack 15, 238
Woodcock, John 193–4, 197–201
Wooldridge, Ian 188, 190–1
World Bank 66
World Series Cricket (WSC) 82, 101,
  104, 124
World Tel 85
World Trade Organisation (WTO) 255
Worrell, Frank 165–8, 188, 189, 191, 194,
  229

Xingwana, Lulu 54

Yardley, Bruce 147
Yardley, Norman 185
Yorkshire Council League 227, 230–1
Yorkshire County Cricket Club 223–4,
  231, 239, 246
Young Ceylon journal 138
Young Guns 39
Young, Robert 1
Yuvraj of Patiala 140

Zee (Indian media corporation) 252
Zia-ul-haq, General Muhammed 117, 122,
  124–6
Zimbabwe Trade Union Congress 254

Printed in Great Britain
by Amazon